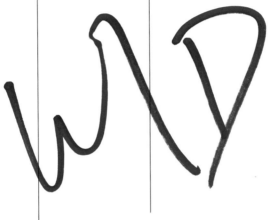

Bethune's legacy to youth is depicted in this seventeen-foot bronze sculpture by Robert Berk, which was dedicated in Lincoln Park, Washington, D.C., on July 10, 1974. Sponsored by the National Council of Negro Women, it was the first statue on federal land in Washington, D.C., to honor either an African American or a woman. *Daytona Beach News-Journal.*

Mary McLeod Bethune

Building a Better World

ESSAYS AND SELECTED DOCUMENTS

EDITED BY

Audrey Thomas McCluskey

AND

Elaine M. Smith

Indiana University Press

BLOOMINGTON AND INDIANAPOLIS

This book is a publication of

Indiana University Press
601 North Morton Street
Bloomington, IN 47404-3797 USA

http://iupress.indiana.edu

Telephone orders   800-842-6796
Fax orders   812-855-7931
Orders by e-mail   iuporder@indiana.edu

First paperback edition 2001
© 1999 by Indiana University Press
All rights reserved

Manufactured in the
United States of America

Library of Congress Cataloging-in-Publication Data

Bethune, Mary McLeod, 1875–1955.
    [Selections. 1999]
    Mary McLeod Bethune : building a better world : essays and selected documents / Audrey Thomas McCluskey and Elaine M. Smith, editors.
    p.   cm.
    Includes bibliographical references (p.   ) and index.
    ISBN 0-253-33626-0 (cloth : alk. paper)
    1. Bethune, Mary McLeod, 1875–1955. 2. Afro-American women educators Biography. 3. Afro-American educators Biography. 4. Bethune, Mary McLeod, 1875–1955 Archives. 5. Afro-Americans—Education—History—20th century Sources. 6. Afro-Americans—Civil rights—History—20th century Sources. 7. Afro-American women—Education—Florida—History—20th century Sources. 8. United States—Race relations Sources.   I. McCluskey, Audrey T.   II. Smith, Elaine M., date.   III. Title.
E185.97.B34A25   1999
370'.92—dc21
[B]   99-43292

ISBN 0-253-21503-X (pbk.)

3 4 5 6 7 11 10 09 08 07 06

To Our Children

Malik Douglass, Jerome Patrice,
and John Touré McCluskey

&

Alfred Redie
and Jonathan Thearthur Smith

Our children must never lose their zeal for building a better world.

—Mary McLeod Bethune,
"My Last Will and Testament"

Contents

V. POLITICS AND PUBLIC ISSUES:
STATESWOMAN IN WASHINGTON (1936–1945)
Introduction by Elaine M. Smith / 199

Preface

WHEN Mary McLeod Bethune died on May 18, 1955, she had lived most of her nearly eighty years as an advocate and spokeswoman for the oppressed and disenfranchised. Since then, her reputation has been sustained by the institutions she founded, the lingering memories of those who knew her, and the periodic release of some of her writings. The best-known of those works is "My Last Will and Testament," her reflective last published essay, which originally appeared in the August 1955 edition of *Ebony*. "My Secret Talks with FDR," appearing first in *Ebony*, was reprinted in Bernard Sternsher's *The Negro in Depression and War* in 1969. Gerda Lerner's groundbreaking *Black Women in White America: A Documentary History*, published in 1972, contained "Faith That Moved a Dump Heap" and three other pieces by Bethune. In 1975, Florence Johnson Hicks collected sixteen speeches and essays in *Mary McLeod Bethune: Her Own Words of Inspiration*. It includes "Seventy-four Years Young," Bethune's insightful reflections on the occasion of her birthday. "Certain Unalienable Rights," her important essay in Rayford Logan's *What the Negro Wants* (1944), has also attracted notice. Yet in relation to Bethune's pivotal leadership during the "Jim Crow" era of legal racial segregation, her published writings are scant.

Despite the scarcity of published sources and the belated attention of scholars, few women have matched Bethune's influence in such varied venues as education, service organizations, and government. In 1930, noted journalist Ida Tarbell included Bethune on her list of America's greatest women. Demonstrating her continuing relevance to racial advancement, *Ebony's* 1989 survey of black scholars listed Bethune among its "50 Most Important Figures in U.S. Black History," alongside Frederick Douglass, W. E. B. Du Bois, and Martin Luther King, Jr.

Bethune ascended to such heights from the most humble of beginnings. This African American woman from rural South Carolina developed into a leader who brought race and gender issues to the national agenda. Through her tireless activism, she challenged the popular assumptions of most white Americans, who maligned and stigmatized black women as "immoral scourges."[1] Her visibility, and her confident and dignified demeanor, contradicted notions of black inferiority. An important symbolic presence in national and international affairs, Bethune was one of the few members of her race and sex among the higher echelons of power and influence in the United States during the last decades of de jure segregation. She played a pivotal role in promoting and representing African American interests at the federal level and in establishing and enhancing black institutions. One national black women's organization expanded under her leadership, while another launched an international agenda, promoting dialogue among women of African descent, and seeking to maximize black women's political and economic clout.

One of the few women college founder-presidents in the world, Bethune remained at the helm of Bethune-Cookman College for twenty years. Her leadership of the National Association of Colored Women (1924–1928) and the National Council of Negro Women, which she founded in 1935, solidified her imprint. From 1935 to 1943, as head of the Negro Division of the National Youth Administration, she channeled crucial "New Deal" funds into black education—secondary, collegiate, and vocational. With the ear of First Lady Eleanor Roosevelt and President Franklin Roosevelt, Bethune was the foremost advocate within the administration for the inclusion of blacks at all levels of government. In 1936, she organized the Federal Council on Negro Affairs, popularly called "the Black Cabinet."

While her role in significant events of her time resulted in a rich abundance of documentary materials, many of the published sources emphasize a single aspect of her multifaceted personality—Bethune as exalted mother figure and inspirational leader. Columnist Louis E. Martin wrote in a 1955 eulogizing editorial, "It is difficult to understand how much Negroes needed inspiration in the early years of this century and how much of a contribution a person who knew how to inspire others like Mrs. Bethune really made to the general welfare. She gave out faith and hope as if they were pills and she some sort of doctor."[2] While true, such an emphasis has created an imbalance in historical perceptions of Bethune, neglecting other facets of her personality and leadership such as her fierce and opportunistic partisanship, her unflinching faith in American ideals, and her political expediency. This volume of original documents and essays is intended to present a fuller, more comprehensive reading of Bethune and the sociopolitical milieu she inhabited as she rose to the peak of her powers. Guiding her actions was a zeal for building a better world—a world in which women and black Americans would enjoy an uncompromised citizenship. She viewed herself as their voice and their representative to white America. "When they see me, they know that the Negro is present," Bethune remarked about the fact that she was often the only member of her race at high-ranking public policy meetings. This work presents an opportunity for a focused re-evaluation of her role during her years in the national spotlight, and of the scope of her multifaceted legacy.

Presented herein are seventy-five documents that Bethune created or contributed to. They have been culled from many sources, including newspapers, magazines, books, specialized library holdings, and manuscript collections, both private and institutional. Unlike any previously published work on Bethune, the papers in this volume cover more than half a century, from 1902 to 1955. The fact that only one document is included from her pre-Daytona period is due primarily to a fire in 1904 that consumed her papers and home in Palatka, Florida. The documents are varied: an interview, an excerpt from an early school catalogue, the transcript of a telephone conversation, collaborative policy statements, minutes of meetings, excerpts from conference transcripts, as well as articles, speeches, and letters. The letters are to such notables as Booker T. Washington, Margaret Murray Washington, Charlotte Hawkins Brown, Julius Rosenwald, Henry Stimson, Eleanor and Franklin Roosevelt, and Ada Lee, a staunch Bethune supporter who is representative of her most steadfast support group—black women. Her presidential addresses to organizations she led are included, as are speeches that reveal her educational ideas, among them her acceptance speech at the NAACP's Spingarn Medal ceremony and, in the twilight of her life, a farewell address to a World Assembly for Moral Re-Armament. Articles range from socially prescriptive essays such as "Unalienable Rights" to her *Chicago Defender* newspaper columns.[3]

The six parts and extensive chronology reflect major thematic divisions in Bethune's life and work. A summative essay provides context and interpretation for each set of documents that follow. The introduction to Part I, "In Pursuit of Unalienable Rights," offers a biographical and historical assessment of Bethune and her legacy. It locates Bethune within the context of the race, gender, and sociopolitical issues that framed her leadership. Part II, "Self-Revelations," focuses on the personal traits and beliefs that endowed Bethune with the qualities of a leader. Part III, "Educational Leadership," provides a discussion of the girls' school she founded in 1904 and nurtured into a college, tracing its evolution through key documents that detail her arduous struggle and untiring efforts to keep the college afloat and dictate its future. Part IV, "Womanist Activism," discusses Bethune's pivotal role as an organizer and activist on behalf of women. Part V, "Politics and Public Issues," presents documentary evidence of her role at or near the center of power in Washington, D.C. The final part, "The Last Years: 'Building A Better World,'" covers her active "retirement" in Daytona Beach during the last five years of her life. Bethune's concern with preserving her legacy and disseminating her ideals was the focus of this final stage of her life. Yet the phrase "building a better world," from "My Last Will and Testament," captures the essence and intent of her entire public life. "Milestones: A Selected Chronology" provides important details and dates in Bethune's life.

Given the plethora of documents generated by Bethune in more than fifty years of public service, our selections were based on the following criteria: documents that were written or spoken in Bethune's own voice, or that resulted from a collaboration with others; documents relevant to her personality and style of leadership, or that shed light on significant, little-known facts about her involvement in important issues of her day; documents that can be authenticated and placed within an historical or thematic context; and documents that are representative of the diversity and range of available primary sources on Bethune. We have preserved the authenticity of the original sources; thus some sentences and phrases may appear awkward. Because Bethune normally dictated what appeared under her name in written form, much of her writing reflects an oral style. Following standard practice, we corrected typing, spelling, and grammatical errors. We changed underlining to italics and used brackets to indicate insertions.

As we approach a new millennium, the outlook for scholarship on black women's history grows ever brighter. This is due, in part, to access to rich, newly available sources of information. We tapped two such sources—the microfilm publications of the National Association of Colored Women's Clubs' Archive and the Mary McLeod Bethune Foundation Archive—along with numerous other collections and archives, for this documentary history. *Mary McLeod Bethune: Building A Better World* confirms Bethune's pivotal role as an arbiter of the gender and racial divide and demonstrates important continuities with African Americans' present struggle for justice and respect as human beings. We offer this volume as a contribution to the recent scholarship that is enriching and enlivening discourses within African American, women's, and American studies.

Audrey Thomas McCluskey
Elaine M. Smith

NOTES

1. Paula Giddings, *When and Where We Enter: The Impact of Black Women on Race and Sex in America* (New York: William Morrow, 1984), p. 82.
2. Louis E. Martin, "Dope 'n' Data," Memphis *Tri-State Defender,* June 4, 1955, p. 5.
3. We were unable to include representative columns from the *Pittsburgh Courier* newspaper, to which Bethune contributed from January 1937 through June 1938, because the terms of permission imposed by the grantor were exorbitant.

Acknowledgments

THIS BOOK has been a labor of love and friendship. Combining several years of work and our mutual passion for uncovering and interpreting the life of an extraordinary woman—Mary McLeod Bethune—has been a joyous but arduous task. When events were not unfolding as planned, we lifted each other up and continued. Resolve, however, was not enough. We depended upon and received the support and assistance of many people, without whom this book could not have been completed.

I, Elaine M. Smith, gratefully acknowledge a National Endowment for the Humanities Fellowship for College Teachers and an Alabama State University research grant, which gave me the opportunity to examine sources in various repositories prior to the conception of this volume. Additionally, I acknowledge individuals who, from the 1970s to the 1990s, introduced me to pertinent Bethune papers and/or facilitated their use. Among them were archivists Robert L. Clarke and Harold T. Pinkett at the National Archives and Daniel Williams at Tuskegee University. Historians included Distinguished Professor Gerda Lerner; De Witt S. Dykes, Jr., Rochester University; Oscar Williams, Virginia State University; John H. Bracey, University of Massachusetts; Joseph E. Taylor (who also assisted Audrey); and Sheila Flemming of Bethune-Cookman College. Other Bethune-Cookman personnel who facilitated my use of sources were former president Richard V. Moore; former director of the Learning Resource Center, Harvey Lee; and former director of the Mary McLeod Bethune Foundation, B. J. Moore.

Once the project was under way, Helen W. Bronson, the present director of the Mary McLeod Bethune Foundation, and Randolph H. Boehm, senior editor at University Publications of America, provided gracious assistance, as did the library staff at Alabama State University. James Cowan, Olivia F. Reid, Gregory B. Gray, and Yolanda Kendrick contributed typing and computer services, the latter two through the Alabama State University Testing Center. Virginia Jones, my department chairperson, and Alfred S. Smith, my husband, made critical comments on the essays. B. J. Moore, my mother, encouraged me throughout the work.

Long before I, Audrey Thomas McCluskey, began working on this project, the late Wilmer Baatz, resource librarian at Indiana University, supplied me with Bethune materials and sources that were crucial to a beginning researcher. Elaine has noted the help we received from people at Bethune-Cookman College, and I add to that list Marion Speight, the Reverend Rogers Fair, and the late Mr. Edward Rodriguez, who consented to a long interview and shared insights and information that increased my understanding of Mary Bethune. As I progressed with my research, the Ford Foundation's Post-Doctoral Minority Fellowship Program made it possible for me to devote time and resources to this project. During my fellowship year, 1994–95, I was aided by the courteous and knowledgeable staff of the Moorland-Spingarn Research Center at Howard University, especially Drs. Thomas Battle and Janet Sims. I also acknowledge the assistance and reliability of Susan McElrath of the Mary McLeod Bethune Council House National Historic Site, and the helpful proofreading and commentary of Karen House of Howard University, who used her genealogical research skills to locate census data at the National Archives. Additionally, Darlene Clark Hine and Christie Farnham gave very encouraging advice at an early stage. At Indiana University, the computer skills of graduate assistants Crystal Keels, a whiz at transferring ravaged old documents to disk, and Darxavia Stephens were indispensable. Colleagues Phyllis Klotman and Jean Robinson were very supportive, as were sister-friends Georgia Alexis and Maxine Legall.

We thank the following archives, repositories, and persons for their permission to publish certain documents: Daniel Williams of the Tuskegee University Archives; Joan Morris, Florida State Archives; Wayne Furman, New York Public Library; Dick Dunkel, *Daytona Beach News-Journal;* Eugene F. Scott, *Chicago Defender;* Portia A. Scott, *Atlanta Daily World;* and Donna Wells, Moorland-Spingarn Research Center; and Joseph E. Taylor of Bethune-Cookman College. Special thanks are also extended to the University of North Carolina Press; Darwin H. Stapleton of the Rockefeller Archive Center; Alton Hornsby, Jr., of the *Journal of Negro History;* L. Dale Peterson of the General Commission on Archives and History of the United Methodist Church; Daniel Meyer at the University of Chicago Library; Patricia L. Fletcher, National Association of Colored Women's Clubs; Minnie H. Clayton, the Atlanta University Library Center; and Susan McElrath of the Mary McLeod Bethune Council House National Historic Site. We extend a special thanks to Helen W. Bronson of the Mary McLeod Bethune Foundation for providing most of the documents in this volume. We also thank the anonymous reviewers and Joan Catapano and the staff of Indiana University Press for useful advice and editorial comment.

Together, we thank our friends, and especially our families and children, for their unwavering belief and support.

Abbreviations

ARC   Mary McLeod Bethune Papers, Amistad Research Center, Tulane University

AUC   Division of Archives and Special Collections of the Atlanta University Center

B-CCA   Bethune-Cookman College Archives, Daytona Beach, Florida

BF   Mary McLeod Bethune Foundation, Bethune-Cookman College, Daytona Beach, Florida

CH   Mary McLeod Bethune Council House National Historic Site, National Park Service, Washington, D.C.

FAMUA   Florida A & M University Archives, Tallahassee

FDRL   Franklin D. Roosevelt Library, Hyde Park, New York

FSA   Florida State Archives, Tallahassee

FUA   Fisk University Archives, Nashville, Tennessee

GEBA   General Education Board Archives, Rockefeller Archive Center, Sleepy Hollow, New York

HUSC   Hampton University Special Collections, Hampton, Virginia

JRL   Joseph Regenstein Library, University of Chicago

LC   Library of Congress, Washington, D.C.

M-SRC   Moorland-Spingarn Research Center, Howard University, Washington, D.C.

NA   National Archives, Washington, D.C.

NACWP   National Association of Colored Women's Club Papers, Washington, D.C.

SL   Schlesinger Library, Radcliffe, Cambridge, Mass.

TUA   Tuskegee University Special Collections and Archives, Tuskegee, Alabama

UCL   Department of Special Collections, University of Chicago Library

UMCA   General Commission on Archives and History, The United Methodist Church, Drew University, Madison, N.J.

YLUF   P. K. Yonge Library of Florida History, University of Florida, Tallahassee

PART I

In Pursuit of Unalienable Rights

Mary McLeod Bethune
in Historical Perspective (1875–1955)

Introduction

Audrey Thomas McCluskey

MARY McLEOD BETHUNE was a commanding and revered figure in American history. Yet to a great extent, her unprecedented role in education and public affairs has remained shrouded in anecdote and hagiography. Thus her accomplishments are often celebrated without proper context and are inadequately understood.

Dubbed the female Booker T. Washington, his "worthy . . . successor,"[1] by the black press after the Tuskegee leader's death in 1915, Bethune projected a strong presence of achievement and pride that resonated among African Americans along a spectrum of class and political differences. The young poet Langston Hughes vividly recalled being invited by Bethune to give a reading at Bethune-Cookman College in 1929. Afterwards, Bethune hitched a ride with Hughes and his friend to New York City for one of her many Northern fundraising treks. Hughes noted that although they were crowded together in his small coupe, Bethune made them feel at ease. They were able to avoid much of the indignity of segregated service facilities along the way because, reported Hughes, "Colored people all along the eastern seaboard spread a feast whenever Mrs. Bethune passed their way."[2] According to a popular saying, continued Hughes, "Before Mrs. Bethune reached the wayside home of any friend anywhere, the chickens, sensing that she was coming, went flying off frantically seeking a safe hiding place. They knew some necks would be wrung in her honor to make a heaping platter of southern fried chicken."[3]

Such popularity, however, does not necessarily inspire scholarly engagement. While published works on Bethune are voluminous, historical assessments of her role as a racial mediator and leader have been scant at best. Even the emergence of black studies in the academy in the 1960s and of women's studies in the 1970s and 1980s failed to generate much enthusiasm for scholarship on Bethune. While her pragmatism and deceptive conventionality, and even her gender, may have limited her appeal to historians, Bethune's populism and her wide-ranging interests and involvements in a half-century of public service may have contributed to her scholarly neglect. Situated historically and ideologically between Booker T. Washington and W. E. B. Du Bois, Bethune, in her multiple roles as educator, organizer, and public policy activist, sought common ground in relentless pursuit of what she called the unalienable rights of citizenship for black Americans.

This examination of Bethune's legacy comes at a propitious time for black women's studies. Recent scholarship in the field is reclaiming the neglected history of individual black women and their organizations, theorizing about the effects of the obstacles of race, gender, and class that they have faced and the manifestations of their "multiple consciousness"[4] in confronting those obstacles. This essay presents the outlines of Bethune's biography and a reading of her multiple consciousness. It also offers a selective review of scholarly and popular literature on Bethune, and examines recurring themes in her public life. A theme that loomed large among her concerns was the attainment of full citizenship for black Americans. In her pursuit thereof, she argued forcefully that because blacks shared the burdens of citizenship— serving valiantly during war, paying taxes, and honoring the Constitution— they deserved all the privileges of citizenship taken for granted by other Americans. In "Certain Unalienable Rights," one of her strongest political statements, Bethune deftly iterated the importance of challenging the status quo of white supremacy, even as she sought interracial alliances: "We must challenge, skillfully but resolutely, every sign of restriction or limit on our full American citizenship . . . we must seek every opportunity to place the burden of responsibility upon him who denies it. We should therefore, protest openly everything in the newspapers, on the radio, in the movies that smacks of discrimination or slander."

Bethune was born in 1875 near Mayesville, South Carolina, in the waning years of Reconstruction. In its wake, virulent anti-black violence spread throughout the South. Under conditions of growing displacement and disen-franchisement, many black people maintained their faith in God and in the power of education to transform their lives. As the fifteenth of seventeen children of former slaves Patsy and Samuel McLeod, young Mary Jane benefited from her birth order and the improving fortunes of the thrifty farm-owning McLeods. They encouraged their "different acting and differ-ent looking" daughter to attend the mission school run by Emma J. Wilson. Bolstered by her family's attentions, she felt destined for great work in spite of the obstacles of race, gender, poverty, and a very dark complexion. Bethune believed that divine intervention had created the fateful circum-stances that led her to earn a scholarship to Miss Wilson's alma mater, Scotia Seminary for Negro Girls in Concord, North Carolina. (Renamed Barber-Scotia College in 1932, it became coed in 1955.) The school was founded in 1867 by Luke Dorland, a white official of the Presbyterian church, and was governed during Bethune's tenure by the stern taskmaster, Dr. David J. Satterfield. After six years (1888–94) of Scotia's highly regimented, Chris-tian-centered learning environment, the basics of Bethune's educational philosophy were in place. Following her Scotia training and a year in Chicago (1894–95) at the institute founded by evangelist Dwight L. Moody that became the Moody Bible Institute, Bethune strengthened her inclination toward missionary work. After being rejected for a post in Africa, however, she turned her zeal to education.

There were several influences that led Bethune toward education. The example of Miss Wilson, her experiences at Scotia with its mixed curriculum of academic and vocational training in "head, heart, and hand," and its philosophy of "female uplift," geared toward educating girls for leadership in their communities, were significant. Also of great importance was the example of service set by Lucy Craft Laney, the founder of Haines Institute in Augusta, Georgia, with whom Bethune apprenticed in 1896–97. Bethune shared Laney's notion that educated black women should assume the "burden" to uplift their families by providing moral, Christian leadership at home and in their communities, but she added to it a more politically tinged female-centered activism. A lifelong commitment to improving the economic and political clout of black women exemplified this belief.

In 1898 Mary McLeod married Albertus Bethune, a clothing salesman and former student at the famed Avery Institute for Negroes in Charleston, South Carolina. Although she revealed very little about her nine years of married life—which produced one son, Albert McLeod, in 1899—she described Albertus as handsome and possessing a strong singing voice.[5] Soon after the birth of Albert, the family moved from Savannah, Georgia, where Mary Bethune had worked briefly as an insurance agent, to Palatka, Florida, where she opened a mission school. In the U.S. census of 1900, their residence was noted as being in the twenty-fifth precinct of Palatka, and her profession was listed as "teacher" and Albertus's as "day laborer."[6] Better economic prospects for a school inspired the move to nearby Daytona in 1904. There she founded the Daytona Educational and Industrial School for Negro Girls. Albertus helped with the school initially and was listed as a member of the board of trustees in 1906, but he clearly played a minor role in his wife's expanding orbit. Albertus Bethune left the family in 1907 and returned to South Carolina. Although they never divorced, Mary Bethune's apparent uneasiness about how the social ramifications of marital failure reflected on her image led to her being listed in the 1910 U.S. census as a widow even before Albertus died in 1918.[7]

The growth of the renamed Daytona Normal and Industrial School led to a merger in 1923 with Cookman Institute of Jacksonville, Florida, under the aegis of the Methodist Episcopal church. The new institution, which changed names several times, developed into the four-year, coeducational Bethune-Cookman College. Bethune served as president until 1942, and again in 1946–47. At the time of the merger, she was a highly visible leader in black education and the black women's club movement. Through her activities as president of the Florida Federation of Colored Women's Clubs (1917–25), Bethune founded a home for delinquent black girls in Ocala, Florida. She served as president of both the twelve-state Southeastern Federation of

Colored Women's Clubs (1920–25) and the National Association of Teachers in Colored Schools (NATCS) in 1923–24, a professional organization of black teachers from mostly Southern states. At the national level, her consensus-building skills helped her win the presidency of the faction-prone National Association of Colored Women; she handily defeated the more established but "disputatious" Ida B. Wells-Barnett.[8] This office ensured that Bethune, as the national spokeswoman, would be heard on major national issues concerning black Americans. After leading the organization for two ambitious terms (1924–28), during which she emphasized efficient management and developing a presence in national and international affairs, Bethune decided that a new, more activist organization was needed. In 1935 she founded the more politically attuned National Council of Negro Women.

Her success in guiding her school from its meager beginnings to collegiate status, plus her involvement in Republican politics, led to an invitation from President Herbert Hoover to attend a White House conference in 1930. Allied with the Republicans while they were in power, the politically pragmatic Bethune became a partisan Democrat after being tapped by Franklin Delano Roosevelt, along with Howard University president Mordecai Johnson, for the advisory board of the National Youth Administration. She joined the NYA's Division of Negro Affairs in 1936, and as director became the highest-paid black in government.[9]

Bethune remained in the administration until 1944, helping to convene the unofficial "Black Cabinet." During World War II, she was active in mobilizing support for the war effort among African Americans. She led the NCNW's "Buy War Bonds" drive and served as special assistant to the secretary of war for the Women's Army Auxiliary Corps, with a five-day mission to recruit black women for army officer training.[10]

By this time Bethune had become one of the most active national leaders in America. On the heels of her presidential appointment, she organized the hugely successful 1937 National Conference on the Problems of the Negro and invited a gathering of influential government leaders, including First Lady Eleanor Roosevelt, to address the delegates. The event received wide media coverage and praise in black newspapers, which further confirmed Bethune's role as the premier national black leader. In 1945 Bethune served as associate consultant to the U.S. delegation—the only black woman in an official role—at the conference to draft the United Nations charter in San Francisco. She received many awards and held several honorary offices in national organizations associated with progressive causes, including the National Urban League, the NAACP, and Planned Parenthood. From 1936 to 1952 she held the largely ceremonial office of president of the Association for the Study of Negro Life and History— the organization founded by her friend Carter G. Woodson, considered the father of black history. Bethune published several important public addresses in the organization's periodical, the *Journal of Negro History*. She also published her speeches and a regular column in the *Aframerican Women's Journal,* and later in the renamed *Women United,* the official voice of the National Council of Negro Women.

Pure charisma, accentuated by a melodious and authoritative speaking voice, endeared Bethune to national audiences and to the black press. While she lived in Washington, D.C., between 1936 and 1944, her activities were consistently covered by black newspapers across the nation. Through her weekly columns in the *Pittsburgh Courier* and later the *Chicago Defender,* her frequent speaking engagements, and her general ability to woo the media, she created a public persona of a life idealized by work, sacrifice, and overcoming poverty and ignorance. By today's standards, Bethune would be considered a media star; she drew praise and some criticism from journalists, who referred to her as "the most glorious woman of the race."[11] She responded to such accolades by harking back to her humble beginnings as the daughter of former slaves—situating herself on the mantle of racial possibility.

In her many inspirational speeches and topical articles that reached audiences via leading black journals such as *Opportunity, Crisis,* and *Ebony,* Bethune cited black achievers of the past such as Sojourner Truth, Harriet Tubman, Lucy Craft Laney, and Booker T. Washington. She considered herself a voice of black aspirations among the political and cultural elite of America. She insisted that her primary interest was the plight of the masses, not the "uppercrust,"[12] although most of her organizing activities were among the latter group. Yet she maintained an identification with rural folks such as her own family and developed a following, as noted by Langston Hughes, among everyday blacks, who saw her as a mother figure and their advocate. Bethune lobbied the political establishment on a range of issues affecting working-class blacks, including farm tenancy, fair housing, and education. She developed associations with black businesswomen and philanthropists such as banker Maggie Lena Walker and hair-care magnate Madame C. J. Walker, and she forged a lifelong affiliation with cosmetologists, led by Marjorie Joyner, whom she helped to form an influential professional organization for black beauticians. Through such alliances, Bethune built a constituency that transcended class lines as well as gender and race.

Her inclusive approach served her well among both black and white audiences. She appealed to blacks as a role model and leader, and to white progressives as a voice of reason and conciliation on racial matters. That duality and her embodiment of race uplift and self-help were valuable assets in fundraising for her college, especially among wealthy whites.

Arguably Bethune's Southern roots and agrarian upbringing help explain much of her pragmatic politics and her resemblance to fellow Southerner Booker T. Washington.[13] Yet her stance was not simply a politics of accommodation. It was based on her firm belief that ultimately only a racially integrated America could safeguard black rights, as well as on her intuitive sense of how to navigate the treacherous currents of the reluctant white power establishment. Initially avoiding buzzwords such as "integration" and "social equality," Bethune stressed themes such as democracy, patriotism, and equal opportunity.

However, Bethune did not turn away from direct action when she deemed it necessary. In the early years of her school, she faced down the Ku Klux Klan at least once when they staged a late-night march on her campus because of her leadership role in registering black voters. She also led a group of black women to the polls in 1920 after the ratification of the Nineteenth Amendment.[14] Although Bethune preferred the conference table to the picket line, she joined the protest against Peoples' Drugstore in Washington, D.C., in 1939 for its failure to hire black clerks in black neighborhoods. In the 1930s, she was also photographed at a rally against lynching sponsored by the Southern Conference on Human Welfare. Yet she was most comfortable using a quieter approach, including her newspaper columns, to trumpet interracial cooperation and to attack racial injustice.

Although outspoken in her opposition to lynching, Bethune served a mediating role in the debate over strategies between blacks and white anti-lynching activists. When disagreement flared between the Association of Southern Women for the Prevention of Lynching, a white women's organization headed by Jessie Daniel Ames that favored an educational approach to ending lynching, and black leaders who were lobbying Congress for legislative initiatives that would signal a toughened stance against lynching, Bethune tried to calm white anxieties by assuring Ames that she had her support.[15] Yet in 1939, in an act that appeared to be the opposite of political caution, Bethune wrote a heated letter to Governor Cone of Florida demanding an investigation after two white men who had murdered a black taxi driver were acquitted by an all-white jury. This occurred during a period when lynching was a common form of violence and intimidation against the whole black community. Bethune boldly chided the governor for his inaction: "What do you have to say about this cold-blooded murder? We appeal for your intervention and investigation. Is there no safety for any colored citizens in this state?"[16] In a newspaper interview, she continued to press for a response from white Floridians: "How long will you kick us and shoot us and burn us without your conscience speaking to you?"[17]

Bethune made her mark on the public discourse by utilizing lessons from her own family and schooling—self-help, pride, and religious faith. She was reportedly fond of saying, "I have faith in God, and in Mary Bethune." Upon returning to her campus home in Daytona in 1949, purportedly to "retire," she continued her activities with international travel to Haiti and Liberia, and economic development projects for blacks in Daytona. The most ambitious was the Bethune-Volusia Project, in which she joined African American businessmen to develop beachfront properties for blacks, who were denied access to the beaches because of their race. In the remaining years of her life, she enlisted friends such as Eleanor Roosevelt to help create the Mary McLeod Bethune Foundation, whose purpose, Bethune asserted, was to house her papers and to promote her ideals of black educational advancement, interracial cooperation, and service to young people. Late in her life she embraced Moral Re-Armament, a socially conservative, anti-Communist movement led by a Lutheran minister, Frank Buchman, an apostle of universal brotherhood and "spiritual rebirth." Bethune had publicly professed her faith throughout her life and was a lifelong church member. Yet in her waning years, it was Moral Re-Armament, a marginal social movement, that ignited one of her most reflective and self-critical statements, about being neglectful of her son during his formative years. Mary McLeod Bethune died of a heart attack at her home in Daytona Beach on May 18, 1955.

A firm sense of history and of her own role in it inclined Bethune toward preserving and documenting her public activity and leadership during an important period in American history. In the process she invented a life story which, in some instances, is not verified by the facts. For example, she liked to dramatize her family's poverty, but as land-owning farmers, the McLeods were better off than many of their black neighbors. Bethune also had lots of help in starting her school with the legendary $1.50. From the beginning she depended upon the black community, particularly the church community, which helped her in every way possible. She also received early assistance from whites, especially segments of the local white establishment. Prominent Daytona resident Dora Maley introduced her to the wealthy women of the Palmetto Club, many of whom became fundraisers for the school and served on the women's advisory board that Bethune established.[18] Her by-the-bootstraps story, embellished in fundraising appeals, fit in well with the American mythology of the underdog. Her self-invented life served her well, feeding her image as a selfless public servant and race woman. It also showed her keen understanding and negotiation of gender, race, and socio-economic divisions in America.

"Mary McLeod Bethune treated racism like a puddle—she stepped around it." Novelist Charles Johnson's astute assessment of Bethune recognizes her important role as a bridge builder and conciliator. However, given the racial politics of her era, "stepping around it" was not always possible, especially for a public-spirited black woman such as Bethune. She endured her share of racial slights and criticism from whites, and even from other blacks. Her sense of personal righteousness and political timing allowed her to deflect some of it, and to adapt to different social circumstances. For example, in 1931, Bethune gave a speech to a Southern interracial group that prompted comparisons to Booker T. Washington's famous "Atlanta Compromise" speech of 1895, in which he seemed to endorse racial segregation. In that speech Bethune emphasized her desire for "racial integrity" and for "no intimate social contact between the races."[19] In 1949, in a speech in Washington, D.C., about fair housing, Bethune condemned those whom she called "false prophets" who would exploit the black struggle by giving in to the "subversive" call for "discrimination and segregation."[20] The difference in her message did not reflect merely the passage of time, since segregation still reigned supreme in most of America. The earlier speech had occurred away from major media markets in tiny Lakeland, Florida, where the simple fact of blacks and whites' meeting to discuss race was considered progress to some, but sacrilege to most of the town's leaders. The second meeting took place in the nation's capital, where the headquarters of Bethune's National Council of Negro Women was located, and where she had served as an adviser to the president of the United States.

In his appraisal of Bethune, Aubrey Williams, the white Southerner under whom Bethune worked in the NYA, attributed such tactics to her keen political skills: "[She was] a damn good politician. [She] knew how to use other people to get what she wanted to achieve. She never played the losers. She played winners. She made the Republicans her friends when they were in power; she made the Democrats her friends when they were in power. She had good goals. There was nothing small about them, and she used any means at hand to achieve them."[21]

Convinced that her role was charted by destiny, Bethune often provided assessments of her own historical importance and that of other race leaders. In 1927, she wrote to her friend, fellow school founder and perennial club woman Charlotte Hawkins Brown,[22] "I think of you and Nannie Burroughs and Lucy Laney and myself as being in the most sacrificing class in our group of women. The work that we have produced will warrant love or consideration or appreciation or confidence that the general public may see fit to bestow upon us."[23] Bethune embodied a vision of black empowerment made possible by seizing opportunities in education and public life. That vision reflected—despite the imbroglio of racism—an unwavering, determinedly optimistic belief that America's founding principles of democracy and equality would ultimately triumph over its history of discriminatory practices based on color, caste, and gender.

The published literature on Mary McLeod Bethune falls into three categories—anecdotal, popular, and scholarly. Like Langston Hughes's recollection of one of his encounters with her, many of the stories about Bethune are preserved in personal remembrances that have become part of black popular culture or oral tradition. Those who knew and worked with her shared many versions of events such as this one: Bethune, on one of her frequent visits to the White House, was referred to as "auntie" by the white elevator operator (another version names a railroad conductor). Bethune's reported response was, "Now tell me, which of my sister's children are you, Jack or Joe?" A student recalled Bethune's being introduced at an interracial gathering as "Mary McLeod Bethune." Feeling the affront to black womanhood and to her own stature, Bethune calmly took the podium and corrected the introduction by asserting that her name was *"Mrs.* Mary McLeod Bethune."[24]

Another example of Bethune's insistence on being respected is related by Miamian Bernice Sawyer: "She would walk into a room where men were sitting and would stop and say: 'Gentlemen! Stand up! Don't you see a black lady in your presence?'"[25] The vast majority of the published works on Bethune are in the popular genre. Newspaper and magazine articles span the gamut in style, content, and source, including articles in church journals, daily and weekly newspapers, and widely circulated news magazines. The earliest full-length biographies of Bethune were written by white women journalists. The first, *Mary McLeod Bethune* (1951) by Catherine Owens Peare, created a minor controversy. Bethune consented to several interviews with the author and wrote the foreword, but she later sued Peare and Vanguard Press for $150,000, alleging that the author had misrepresented the project as a series of magazine articles for children.[26] The suit was unsuccessful. Emma Gelders Sterne's *Mary McLeod Bethune,* published in 1957, relies heavily upon secondary sources such as magazine articles and previously published interviews. Dates are often incorrect because of the author's lack of independent research. The book, primarily anecdotal, contains few attributed sources. Journalist Rackham Holt's *Mary McLeod Bethune: A Biography* appeared in 1964. Bethune named Holt her official biographer, granting her access to institutional and personal records as well as providing her with accommodations at Bethune-Cookman College. The result, however, was a curiously uneven, even distorted, effort. Holt stressed Bethune's alliances with white leaders and the role that interracialism played in her life, but only skimmed her work in black women's organizations. She relied on Bethune's own flawed memory as the source of information about her early life. Nevertheless, Holt's work remained the principal source on Bethune until 1975. These early biographies all suffer from a lack of focus, omission of significant people and Bethune's work with them, and, most seriously, the absence of primary sources. Yet they remained virtually unchallenged until more specialized and scholarly assessments of Bethune began to emerge in the mid-1970s.

A second set of popular Bethune biographies, aimed at juveniles, emphasize her role as an educator. These books present her reverentially as someone who overcame tremendous odds to attain the American dream. Among the most prominent are Ella Kaiser Curruth, *She Wanted to Read:*

The Story of Mary McLeod Bethune (1966); Eloise Greenfield, *Mary McLeod Bethune* (1977); Milton Metzer, *Mary McLeod Bethune: Voice of Black Hope* (1979); Patricia and Fred McKissack, *Mary McLeod Bethune: A Great American Educator* (1985); Malu Halasa, *Mary McLeod Bethune: Educator* (1989); and Richard Kelso's *Building a Dream: Mary McLeod Bethune's School* (1993).

Most of the early scholarly literature sought to remove the stigma of the slave experience in America by recovering a lost history of black achievement and pride. Significant in this genre is Sadie Daniel's collection of in-depth portraits of African American women, *Women Builders* (1923), which prominently featured Bethune. An updated history of black women, *Beautiful, Also Are the Souls of My Sisters* (1978), by educator Jeanne Noble, also invoked an uplift theme, describing Bethune gloriously as "First with the mighty bow."

In 1975, the first sustained scholarly examinations began with B. Joyce Ross's critical study of Bethune's role in President Franklin Roosevelt's New Deal administration. Ross chipped away at Bethune's saintly veneer, arguing that she accepted segregation as the price of her limited success in funneling resources to black constituents.[27] Ross also hints that Bethune was not the intellectual equal of some of her co-workers and peers associated with the Black Cabinet. Moreover, Ross dubs Bethune "Janus-faced" in maneuvering between her black and white constituents and concludes that Bethune was more a symbol than a powerful presence in the federal bureaucracy. While Ross acknowledges the strict scrutiny that pioneering blacks received in the federal government, she seems to separate this fact from her assessment of Bethune's compromises with white power.

In an essay published in 1980 that covered the same period, historian Elaine M. Smith offers a more charitable view. She portrays Bethune as an untiring and often successful advocate for black people in an administration that was all too comfortable with the racial status quo. As the highest-ranking black in the Roosevelt administration, Bethune used her access to the First Family to win concessions for blacks in an otherwise discriminatory federal environment. Her advocacy helped blacks win NYA jobs in states that had consistently refused to hire them. Although unsuccessful in changing racially biased policies, Bethune, Smith argues, sought exclusions and exemptions to existing practices that resulted in monetary allotments for black students and their institutions. Smith and Ross agree that being uniquely sandwiched between the white power elite and growing black aspirations caused Bethune to veer "toward the white establishment,"[28] but Smith is more willing to credit Bethune with being single-minded in her crusade to increase black participation and leadership within NYA programs.

Historian Jack B. Kirby (1980) concurs with Smith. He concludes that while head of the Federal Council of Negro Affairs (the Black Cabinet), Bethune promoted a black presence throughout the federal government but was forced to accept "separate but equal" because President Roosevelt would not challenge Southern segregation. Another noted historian, Booker T. Washington biographer Louis R. Harlan (1977), calls Bethune the "gadfly" of the New Deal administration because of her persistence in trying to equalize funding for black programs.

Scholarly literature focusing on Bethune as an educator began to appear in the 1980s, although a few earlier dissertation studies were conducted in the 1950s and 1970s. Historian Carol O. Perkins (1988) charts Bethune's evolution from imitating Booker T. Washington's brand of industrialism to exhibiting her own brand of "pragmatic idealism," which called for more academically oriented education associated with black empowerment in a curriculum that reflected the competing philosophies of Washington along with Du Bois's "talented tenth" approach. Historian Bettye Collier-Thomas (1993) credits Bethune with disseminating the study of black history through her speeches and writings and her ongoing work in organizations such as the Association for the Study of Negro Life and History.

Encyclopedia articles on Bethune, like those on a number of notable black women, are a source of important, sometimes pioneering scholarship. Entries on Bethune have appeared in several specialized volumes, including Jessie Carney Smith's *Notable Black Women* (1992) and Darlene Clark Hine's *Black Women in America: An Historical Encyclopedia* (1993).

My own work on Bethune (McCluskey 1989; 1994a; 1994b; 1997) has concentrated on her educational leadership within the paradigm of race uplift ideology as practiced by black women of the early twentieth century. It also posits Bethune as a model of black female leadership defined by her multiple agendas and her strategies for achieving them. Linsin (1997) applies the useful phrase "integrated autonomy"[29] to those multiple efforts and strategies. Bethune never relinquished the idea of achieving total integration of black Americans into the fabric of American life, but she also recognized and fought for black stewardship of black institutions.

Bethune's involvement with religion and the Methodist establishment is another notable area of scholarly research. An openly religious person who began each day with meditation and scripture reading, Bethune proclaimed a personal relationship with God that emanated from her devout family and rural Christian community. She liked to stress that she was on a mission dictated by God, and that her faith and her work justified each other. Theologian Clarence G. Newsome (1992), using limited documentary evidence, concludes that Bethune's relationship with the Methodist Episcopal hierarchy (which began with the church's agreement to assume financial responsibility for the school in 1923) was dictated more by politics than by religion. Despite Bethune's activism within the lay leadership and the stature that she brought to the governing body, Newsome asserts that the entrenched male hierarchy viewed her with suspicion, questioning her judgment about school matters and turning away many of her requests. Meanwhile Bethune worked behind the scenes to install her favorites as church appointees and board members. According to Newsome, her attempts to persuade the trustees to return Bethune-Cookman to all-female status—by arguing, as she had years before, that the responsibilities of black women require special skills[30]—were ignored as the sentimental and meddlesome musings of an aging woman. Even after she resigned the presidency of the college in 1942, the new president confided that he felt that Bethune was trying to subject him to "petticoat rule."[31] Newsome's assertions warrant substantiation by a closer examination of more church documents, particularly related correspondence and minutes of board meetings. His own evidence suggests that despite the infighting, Bethune was able to exert considerable influence on the board in advancing her agenda.

While it is difficult to assess the degree and ultimate effect of sexism in the Methodist Episcopal hierarchy, Bethune recognized gender discrimination. Contrary to white feminist historian Sara Evans's (1989) contention that Bethune was more interested in race issues than in gender, her work to increase the prospects for black women is not easily separated from her work to increase opportunity and justice for all black people.

Conclusion:
Bethune in Historical Perspective

While detailed research on Bethune has been slow to emerge, proclamations of her greatness have not. Popular lore and scholarly assessment converge on at least this point: Mary McLeod Bethune was a living contradiction to conventional notions of black and female achievement. Poet Margaret Walker, in her poem "For Mary McLeod Bethune," pays homage to Bethune in awe-inspiring language, writing, "Great Amazon of God behold your bread / washed home again from many distant seas."[32] Eleanor Roosevelt said of Bethune, "I have real admiration for Mrs. Bethune and her devotion to her race; as well as [for] her tact and wisdom."[33] Theologian Channing Tobias, another of her contemporaries, considered Bethune to be "cautious but courageous," a view reflecting her persistence and her penchant for calculating outcomes before making her move.

Bethune's contemporaries, including Howard University sociologist E. Franklin Frazier, expressed amazement that she could accomplish so much with so little education and social privilege. Frazier also suggested that her meteoric rise created in her an "ego problem" that prevented self-reflection and self-criticism: "She became more domineering and arrogant as she acquired power and prestige."[34] Although generally positive about Bethune, Congressman Adam Clayton Powell, responding to an unsubstantiated rumor that she might move to New York and run for his congressional seat, charged that she was sentimental and naive (referring to her view that people should be able to overcome race and get along).[35] There was also disagreement among some of the black literati about whether her occasionally supplicating demeanor was an artful manipulation to accomplish her goals in a racially segregated, male-dominated society, or just too much bowing and scraping.

One of the difficulties historians face in rendering assessments of a complex person such as Bethune is that she defies sociological categories and stereotypes. She lived almost eighty years, a lifetime that reached from the post-Reconstruction era to the dawn of the civil rights era. She remained socially and politically engaged throughout her adult life, participating in major social and political events that changed her, and America. For that reason, an ideological framework that overlooks her skills in the politics of pragmatism will not be fruitful. Bethune adapted to the times by, as Aubrey Williams noted, "playing winners." Although she held fast to her core beliefs—including religious faith, racial pride, and equal opportunity for black women and men in America—she adjusted her approach, if not her values, to the existing climate as needed. Despite her limited education, she possessed an orator's command of the language. She also showed an ability to adapt quickly to new situations rather than to be marginalized by the winds of political change, as when she changed her party affiliation from Republican to Democrat when the "New Dealers" came to power.

Scholarly treatment of black women in history demands expansive paradigms to accommodate their multi-layered identities and complexity. Bethune's complexities included her sophisticated political instincts, which came more from observation and practice than from reading and self-reflection; her staunch and unwavering patriotism; and her strong sense of self in a society that demeaned and devalued people who looked like her. Despite the numerous instances of racism shown toward her, and even unsubstantiated charges that she was a Communist sympathizer, Bethune maintained her belief in America. She delighted in wearing a paramilitary uniform and accepting the honorary title of general in the Women's Army for National Defense (WAND). She preached race pride and the study and teaching of black history, but according to Ross, she was not above making racially disparaging remarks. Bethune herself had to overcome many such remarks. Her race, her gender, her very dark skin, and her limited formal education would be considered barriers to success for most people. Yet Bethune turned them into assets by ignoring slights from both the black intelligentsia and white racists, and trumpeting her pride in being of "royal African heritage." If such proclamations concealed inner torment or self-doubt, she hid it well. She walked with stately grace and carried a cane that had once belonged to Franklin D. Roosevelt for added nobility. Meanwhile, by fighting for her core beliefs, she earned the admiration not only of luminaries such as Eleanor Roosevelt, but of millions of everyday Americans. She concluded the essay "Certain Unalienable Rights" with an exhortation to blacks to claim their rights of citizenship by taking "full part in the political life of our community, state, and nation."

As an historical subject, Bethune's life provides a window into the racial politics of her day. Of particular note is her use of multiple strategies for advancing racial progress, judged by non-ideological parameters such as access to power and capital. Although she greatly enjoyed the attention of being dubbed black America's "first lady" and the "most glorious woman of the race," her sense of personal power was used for a group-oriented agenda. Today, her name continues to be invoked as a symbol of black pride and purposefulness. She was the first black woman to have a national monument dedicated to her in the nation's capital. Several schools in states as diverse and non-Southern as New York and California have been named in her honor,[36] as have the Bethune Museum and Archive (Bethune Council House) in Washington, D.C., a college dormitory at Howard University, and streets and other public places.

The continued examination of the complexities of African American leaders such as Bethune will give scholars much to research and argue, as evidenced by the varying approaches and perspectives that even the present limited scholarship on Bethune has produced. Undoubtedly, Bethune had an ego as large as her frame, and this was a problem for some of her contemporaries, especially males. Interestingly, critiques of giants such as Booker T. Washington, W. E. B. Du Bois, and other male leaders seldom mention this aspect of their character. The gender dimensions of her leadership and comparisons with other African American leaders invite further study. Additionally, future research into her role in cross-racial organizations, her focus on international affairs, and her importance as an institution builder and a womanist organizer, and the production of overdue scholarly biographies should keep researchers engaged for years to come.

DOCUMENTARY SOURCES

The themes noted above are conveyed in documents throughout this volume. One essay in particular, "Certain Unalienable Rights," is a cumulative statement of Bethune's moral, philosophical, and political moorings. Adopting the Declaration of Independence as her model, she changed "inalienable" rights to "unalienable" rights in bringing together her poignant mix of ideas and aspirations that were a rallying cry for social change. Bethune used her skills as a platform speaker trained in sustaining rhetorical constructions to imbue this written piece with a sense of immediacy and urgency, addressing it to both white and black audiences. By invoking the patriotism of black Americans as symbolized by courageous actions of black soldiers past and present and comparing the black struggle to the struggle for American independence, she voiced the anger of the black masses, who were continually frustrated by the "wall" of white racism that kept them from enjoying their full rights as Americans. Although Bethune had once embraced the views of Booker T. Washington, here she pointedly rejected his "separate fingers" endorsement of segregation in favor of the "clasped hand" of an open and integrated society. Bethune offers a nine-point outline of "What the Negro Wants." It calls for an end to lynching and to the poll tax that kept blacks in the South from voting. Her outline also includes issues that still demand space on the nation's agenda, such as equal job opportunity and federal intervention to help the poor. This essay also depicts her staunch internationalism and her willingness to be an agent of reconciliation. These concerns are the blueprint of her legacy—one made evident by the path she and others helped to lay, a path that the civil rights movement, still a decade away, would follow.

Notes

1. *Literary Digest,* March 1937, p. 8.

2. Langston Hughes, *I Wander As I Wonder* (New York: Hill and Wang, 1956), p. 40.

3. Ibid.

4. Multiple consciousness is a theoretical construct that posits the interconnectivity of systems of oppression that confront black women on the basis of their race, gender, economic class, and sexuality. This work is being done by scholars such as Deborah K. King, "Multiple Jeopardy, Multiple Consciousness: The Context of a Black Feminist Ideology," in Micheline R. Malson et al., eds., *Black Women in America: Social Science Perspectives* (Chicago: University of Chicago Press, 1988), pp. 265–296.

5. Charles S. Johnson, interview with Mary McLeod Bethune, 1939, BF (included in this volume).

6. *Twelfth Census of the United States, Schedule of Population, 1900* (Washington, D.C.: National Archives).

7. In the 1910 census, Bethune is listed as a head of household, a school principal, and a widow. *Thirteenth Census of the U.S., 1910* (Daytona, Fla.: Precinct No. 8).

8. Paula Giddings, *When and Where I Enter: The Impact of Black Women on Race and Sex in America* (New York: Morrow and Co., 1984), p. 180.

9. Bethune began her job in the NYA as an administrative assistant in charge of Negro affairs. In 1939 she became director of Negro affairs for the agency. Her annual government salary was reported to be $5,000 in 1938. "Mary McLeod Bethune High On Pay List," *Amsterdam News,* November 2, 1938.

10. The author interviewed Dovey Johnson Roundtree, one of the young women whom Bethune convinced to apply for the officers corps. She remembers that Bethune insisted that she accept the commission and overlook—in a move that foreshadowed Jackie Robinson's heroism in another venue—the racism and hostility that the pioneering officer-trainees would face. Bethune reminded them that this was an opportunity to advance racial progress while serving the country. "Mrs. Bethune did not accept no for an answer," said Roundtree. Interview with attorney Dovey Johnson Roundtree, who, in the spirit of Bethune, serves as legal counsel to the NCNW for $1 a year—November 4, 1994, Washington, D.C.

11. Dan Williams, "The Cotton-Picker Still Sings," newspaper clipping, Mary McLeod Bethune Vertical File, M-SRC [1942].

12. Clipping from the New Jersey *Herald News,* October 14, 1939, Mary McLeod Bethune Vertical File, M-SRC.

13. Audrey Thomas McCluskey, "Ringing Up a School: Mary McLeod Bethune's Impact on Daytona," *Florida Historical Quarterly* 73, no. 3 (October 1994): 211.

14. "Personal Remembrances of a Great Woman by One of Her Students," unpublished manuscript, n.d., p. 3, BF. Elaine M. Smith, "Black Female Icon: Mary McLeod Bethune, 1875–1955, Introduction to the Mary McLeod Bethune Papers: The College Collection" (Bethesda, Md.: University Publications of America, 1995) documents Bethune's defiant stand against the Klan by leading a campaign to get out the black vote.

15. Bethune wrote Ames to assure her that she had the continued support of black women even though she was working against passage of an anti-lynching bill, favoring an emphasis on changing white public opinion. Some more radical black women leaders such as Atlanta's Lugenia Burns Hope felt that Ames's emphasis on education was misguided and deserved censure. See Jacquelyn Dowd Hall, *Revolt against Chivalry: Jessie Daniel Ames and the Women's Campaign against Lynching* (New York: Columbia University Press, 1979).

16. "Bethune Sends Protest in Florida Killing," *Washington Afro-American,* June 17, 1939.

17. *Daytona Beach Evening News,* June 1, 1939, in Mary McLeod Bethune Vertical File, M-SRC.

18. Letter from Dora Maley on the occasion of Bethune-Cookman College's 50th anniversary (1955), Mary Bethune vertical file, Volusia County (Halifax), Fla. Historical Society.

19. William N. Jones, "Day by Day," Mary McLeod Bethune Papers, box 3, folder 8, ARC.

20. Mary McLeod Bethune, "Step Up the Pace," May 29, 1949, BF.

21. Earl Devine Martin, "Mary McLeod Bethune: A Prototype of the Rising Consciousness of the American Negro" (M.A. Thesis, Northwestern University, 1956), p. 84.

22. Charlotte Hawkins Brown founded Palmer Memorial Institute in Sedalia, North Carolina, in 1901, transforming the rural one-room vocationally oriented school into a mecca of academic education for the daughters and sons of the black elite. Linked by their interests in educating young people and the elevation of black women, she and Bethune were friends and colleagues through most of their adult lives. Brown served as vice president of Bethune's organization, the National Council of Negro Women.

23. Bethune, letter to Charlotte Hawkins Brown, October 29, 1927, BF.

24. Edward Rodriguez, "Bethune-Cookman College Anniversary Address," copy given to the author by Mr. Rodriguez.

25. Marvin Dunn, *Black Miami in the Twentieth Century* (Gainesville: University Press of Florida, 1997), p. 155.

26. "Mary McLeod Bethune Files Suit in Florida," *Pittsburgh Courier,* April 1955, p. 1.

27. B. Joyce Ross, "Mary McLeod Bethune and the Administration of the National Youth Administration," *Journal of Negro History* 40, no. 1 (January 1975): 1–28.

28. Elaine M. Smith, "Mary McLeod Bethune and the National Youth Administration," in Mabel Deutrich and Virginia Purdy, eds., *Clio Was a Woman* (Washington, D.C.: Howard University Press, 1980), pp. 149–177.

29. Christopher E. Linsin, "Something More Than a Creed: Mary McLeod

Bethune's Aim of Integrated Autonomy as Director of Negro Affairs," *Florida Historical Quarterly* 76 (Summer 1997): 20–41.

30. Mary McLeod Bethune, "Bethune-Cookman's Next Urgent Step," memorandum, Archives Division of the United Methodist Church, Commission on Archives and History, November 28, 1938.

31. Clarence G. Newsome, "Mary McLeod Bethune and the Methodist Episcopal Church North: In but Out," *Journal of Religious Thought* 49, no. 1 (1992): 7–20.

32. Margaret Walker, *This Is My Century: New and Collected Poems* (Athens: University of Georgia Press, 1989), p. 116.

33. Eleanor Roosevelt, "My Day," New York *World Telegraph,* August 9, 1940.

34. Martin, "Mary McLeod Bethune," p. 84.

35. "That Sweetheart Again," *Amsterdam News,* January 15, 1938.

36. Using Mary McLeod Bethune as a keyword, one can find her name at hundreds of sites on the Internet.

Certain Unalienable Rights
(1944)

I T IS A QUIET NIGHT IN December, 1773. A British merchant ship rides easily at anchor in Boston Harbor. Suddenly, some row boats move out from the shore. Dark stealthy figures in the boats appear to be Indians in buckskin jackets with feathers in their hair; but as they reach the ship, clamber aboard, climb down into the hold and carry out boxes of the cargo, the muffled voices speak English words. Their voices grow more excited and determined as they open the boxes and dump the King's tea into the ocean. The Boston Tea Party is in full swing. Resentment has reached flood tide. "Taxation without representation is tyranny!" The spark of the American Revolution has caught flame and the principle of the "consent of the governed" has been established by a gang disguised as Indians who take the law into their own hands. In this action a small and independent people struck out against restrictions and tyranny and oppression and gave initial expression to the ideal of a nation "that all men are created equal, that they are endowed by their Creator with certain unalienable rights."

It is a Sunday night in Harlem in the year of our Lord 1943. Along the quiet streets dimmed out against the possibility of an Axis air attack, colored Americans move to and fro or sit and talk and laugh. Suddenly electric rumor travels from mouth to ear: "A black soldier has been shot by a white policeman and has died in the arms of his mother." No one stops to ask how or why or if it be true. Crowds begin to gather. There is a rumbling of anger and resentment impelled by all the anger and all the resentment of all colored Americans in all the black ghettos in all the cities in America—the resentment against the mistreatment of Negroes in uniform, against restriction and oppression and discrimination breaks loose. Crowds of young people in blind fury strike out against the only symbols of this oppression which are near at hand. Rocks hurtle, windows crash, stores are broken open. Merchants' goods are tumbled into the streets, destroyed or stolen. Police are openly challenged and attacked. There are killings and bodily injury. For hours a veritable reign of terror runs through the streets. All efforts at restraint are of no avail. Finally the blind rage blows itself out.

Some are saying that a band of hoodlums have challenged law and order to burn to pillage and rob. Others look about them to remember riots in Detroit and Los Angeles and Beaumont. They will look further and recall cities laid in ruins by a global war in which the forces of tyranny and oppression and race supremacy attempt to subdue and restrain all the freedom of the world. They are thinking deeply to realize that there is a ferment aloose among the oppressed little people everywhere, a "groping of the long inert masses." They will see depressed and repressed masses all over the world swelling to the breaking point against the walls of ghettos, against economic, social and political restrictions; they will find them breaking open the King's boxes and throwing the tea into the ocean and storming the Bastille stirred by the clarion call of the Four Freedoms. They are striking back against all that the Axis stands for. They are rising to achieve the ideals "that all men are created equal, that they are endowed by their Creator with certain unalienable Rights, that among these are Life, Liberty and the pursuit of Happiness." With the crash of the guns and the whir of the planes in their ears, led by the fighting voices of a Churchill and a Franklin Roosevelt, a Chiang Kai-shek and a Stalin, they are realizing that "Governments are instituted among men" to achieve these aims and that these governments derive "their just power from the consent of the governed." They are a part of a people's war. The little people want "out." Just as the Colonists at the Boston Tea Party wanted "out" from under tyranny and oppression and taxation without representation, the Chinese want "out," the Indians want "out," and colored Americans want "out."

Throughout America today many people are alarmed and bewildered by the manifestation of this world ferment among the Negro masses. We say we are living in a period of "racial tension." They seem surprised that the Negro should be a part of this world movement. Really, all true Americans should not be surprised by this logical climax of American education. For several generations colored Americans have been brought up on the Boston Tea Party and the Declaration of Independence; on the principle of equality of opportunity, the possession of inalienable rights, the integrity and sanctity of the human personality. Along with other good Americans the Negro has been prepared to take his part in the fight against an enemy that threatens all these basic American principles. He is fighting now on land and sea and in the air to beat back these forces of oppression and tyranny and discrimination. Why, then, should we be surprised when at home as well as abroad he fights back against these same forces?

One who would really understand this racial tension which has broken out into actual conflict in riots as in Harlem, Detroit, and Los Angeles, must look to the roots and not be confused by the branches and the leaves. The tension rises out of the growing internal pressure of Negro masses to break through the wall of restriction which restrains them from full American citizenship. This mounting power is met by the unwillingness of white America to allow any appreciable breach in this wall.

The hard core of internal pressure among the Negro masses in the United States today is undoubtedly their resentment over the mistreatment of colored men in the armed forces. The Negro faces restrictions in entering certain branches of the service, resistance to being assigned posts according to his ability; and above all there is the failure of the Army and his government to protect him in the uniform of his country from actual assault by civilians.

Letters from the men in Army camps have streamed into the homes of their parents and friends everywhere, telling of this mistreatment by officers, military police and civilians, of their difficulties in getting accommodations on trains and buses, of numerous incidents of long, tiresome journeys without meals and other concrete evidences of the failure of their government to protect and provide for its men, even when they are preparing to fight in defense of the principles of that government.

They need no agitation by newspaper accounts or the stimulation of so-called leaders. These things are the intimate experiences of the masses themselves. They know them and feel them intensely and resent them bitterly.

You must add to these deep-seated feelings a whole series of repercussions of the frustrated efforts of Negroes to find a place in war production: the absolute denial of employment in many cases, or employment far below the level of their skills, numerous restrictions in their efforts to get training, resistance of labor unions to the improving and utilization of their skills on the job. Pile on to these their inability to get adequate housing even for those employed in war work, and often, where houses are available, restrictions to segregated units in temporary war housing. At the same time they see around them unlimited opportunities offered to other groups to serve their country in the armed forces, to be employed at well-paying jobs, to get good housing financed by private concerns and FHA funds.

Even those observers who have some understanding of the Negro's desire to break through all these restrictions will charge it to superficial causes, such as the agitation of the Negro press and leaders; or they counsel the Negro to "go slow." It is as though they admit that the patient is sick with fever and diagnosis reveals that he needs twelve grains of quinine, but they decide that because he is a Negro they had better give him only six. They admit that he is hungry and needs to be fed, but because he is a Negro they suggest that a half meal will suffice. This approach, of course, is a historical hang-over. It is a product of the half-hearted and timorous manner in which we have traditionally faced the Negro problem in America.

In order to maintain slavery, it was necessary to isolate black men from every possible manifestation of our culture. It was necessary to teach that they were inferior beings who could not profit from that culture. After the slave was freed, every effort has persisted to maintain "white supremacy" and wall the Negro in from every opportunity to challenge this concocted "supremacy." Many Americans said the Negro could not learn and they "proved" it by restricting his educational opportunities. When he surmounted these obstacles and achieved a measure of training, they said he did not know how to use it and proved it by restricting his employment opportunities. When it was necessary to employ him, they saw to it that he was confined to laborious and poorly-paid jobs. After they had made every effort to guarantee that his economic, social and cultural levels were low, they attributed his status to his race. Therefore, as he moved North and West after Reconstruction and during the Industrial Revolution, they saw to it that he was confined to living in veritable ghettos with covenants that were as hard and resistant as the walls of the ghettos of Warsaw.

They met every effort on his part to break through these barriers with stern resistance that would brook no challenge to our concept of white supremacy. Although they guaranteed him full citizenship under the Constitution and its Amendments, they saw to it that he was largely disfranchised and had little part in our hard won ideal of "the consent of the governed." In the midst of this anachronism, they increasingly educated his children in the American way of life—in its ideals of equality of all men before the law, and opportunities for the fullest possible development of the individual.

As this concept took hold among the Negro masses, it has evidenced itself through the years in a slow, growing, relentless pressure against every restriction which denied them their full citizenship. This pressure, intensified by those of other races who really believed in democracy, began to make a break through the walls here and there. It was given wide-spread impetus by the objectives of the New Deal with its emphasis on the rise of the forgotten man. With the coming of the Second World War, all the Negro's desires were given voice and support by the world leaders who fought back against Hitler and all he symbolizes. His efforts to break through have responded to Gandhi and Chiang Kai-shek, to Churchill and Franklin Roosevelt.

The radios and the press of the world have drummed into his ears the Four Freedoms, which would lead him to think that the world accepts as legitimate his claims as well as those of oppressed peoples all over the world. His drive for status has now swept past even most of his leaders, and has become imbedded in mass-consciousness which is pushing out of the way all the false prophets, be they white or black—or, be they at home or abroad.

The Negro wants to break out into the free realm of democratic citizenship. We can have only one of two responses. Either we must let him out wholly and completely in keeping with our ideals, or we must mimic Hitler and shove him back.

What, then, does the Negro want? His answer is very simple. He wants only what all other Americans want. He wants opportunity to make real what the Declaration of Independence and the Constitution and Bill of Rights say; what the Four Freedoms establish. While he knows these ideals are open to no man completely he wants only his equal chance to attain them. The Negro today wants specifically:

1. *Government leadership in building favorable public opinion.* Led by the President himself, the federal government should initiate a sound program carried out through appropriate federal agencies designed to indicate

the importance of race in the war and post-war period. The cost of discrimination and segregation to a nation at war and the implications of American racial attitudes for our relationships with the other United Nations and their people should be delineated. Racial myths and superstitions should be exploded. The cooperation of the newspapers, the radio and the screen should be sought to replace caricature and slander with realistic interpretations of sound racial relationships.

2. *The victory of democracy over dictatorship.* Under democracy the Negro has the opportunity to work for an improvement in his status through the intelligent use of his vote, the creation of a more favorable public opinion, and the development of his native abilities. The ideals of democracy and Christianity work for equality. These ideals the dictatorships disavow. Experience has taught only too well the implications for him and all Americans of a Nazi victory.

3. *Democracy in the armed forces.* He wants a chance to serve his country in all branches of the armed forces to his full capacity. He sees clearly the fallacy of fostering discrimination and segregation in the very forces that are fighting against discrimination and segregation all over the world. He believes that the government should fully protect the persons and the rights of all who wear the uniform of its armed forces.

4. *The protection of his civil rights and an end to lynching.* He wants full protection of the rights guaranteed all Americans by the Constitution; equality before the law, the right to jury trial and service, the eradication of lynching. Demanding these rights for himself, he will not be misled into any anti-foreign, Red-baiting, or anti-Semitic crusade to deny these rights to others. Appalled by the conditions prevailing in Washington, he joins in demanding the ballot for the District of Columbia and the protection of his rights now denied him within the shadow of the Capitol.

5. *The free ballot.* He wants the abolition of the poll tax and of the "white primary"; he wants universal adult suffrage. He means to use it to vote out all the advocates of racism and vote in those whose records show that they actually practice democracy.

6. *Equal access to employment opportunities.* He wants the chance to work and advance in any job for which he has the training and capacity. To this end he wants equal access to training opportunities. In all public programs, federal, state and local, he wants policy-making and administrative posts as well as rank and file jobs without racial discrimination. He wants a fair share of jobs under Civil Service.

7. *Extension of federal programs in public housing, health, social security, education and relief under federal control.* Low income and local prejudice often deprive him of these basic social services. Private enterprise or local government units cannot or will not provide them. For efficiency and equity in administration of these programs, the Negro looks to the federal govern-

ment until such time as he has gained the full and free use of the ballot in all states.

8. *Elimination of racial barriers in labor unions.* He demands the right of admission on equal terms to the unions having jurisdiction over the crafts or industries in which he is employed. He urges that job control on public works be denied to any union practicing discrimination.

9. *Realistic interracial co-operation.* He realizes the complete interdependence of underprivileged white people and Negroes, North and South—laborers and sharecroppers alike. He knows that they stay in the gutter together or rise to security together; that the hope of democracy lies in their co-operative effort to make their government responsive to their needs; that national unity demands their sharing together more fully in the benefits of freedom—not "one as the hand and separate as the fingers," but one as the clasped hands of friendly cooperation.

Here, then, is a program for racial advancement and national unity. It adds up to the sum of the rights, privileges and responsibilities of full American citizenship. This is all that the Negro asks. He will not willingly accept less. As long as America offers less, she will be that much less a democracy. The whole way is the American way.

What can the Negro do himself to help get what he wants?

1. In the first place, he should accept his responsibility for a full part of the job of seeing to it that whites and Negroes alike understand the current intensity of the Negro's fight for status as a part of a world people's movement. As individuals and as members of organizations, we must continue to use every channel open to affect public opinion, to get over to all Americans the real nature of this struggle. Those of us who accept some measure of responsibility for leadership, must realize that in such people's movements, the real leadership comes up out of the people themselves. All others who would give direction to such a movement must identify themselves with it, become a part of it, and interpret it to others. We must make plain to America that we have reached a critical stage in the assimilation of colored people.

We have large and growing numbers of young and older Negroes who have achieved by discipline and training a measure of culture which qualifies them for advanced status in our American life. To deny this opportunity creates on the one hand frustration with its attendant disintegration, and, on the other, deprives American civilization of the potential fruits of some thirteen millions of its sons and daughters.

Through our personal and group contacts with other racial groups, we must increasingly win their understanding and support. Only in this way can the swelling force among minority racial groups be channeled into creative progress rather than exploded into riots and conflicts, or dissipated in hoodlumism. While we seek on the one side to "educate" white America, we must continue relentlessly to make plain to ourselves and our associates the increased responsibility that goes with increased rights and privileges. Our fight for Fair Employment Practices legislation must go hand and hand with "Hold Your Job" campaigns; our fight for anti–poll tax legislation must be supported equally by efforts of Negroes themselves to exercise fully and intelligently the right of franchise where they have it.

2. We must challenge, skillfully but resolutely, every sign of restriction or limitation on our full American citizenship. When I say challenge, I mean we must seek every opportunity to place the burden of responsibility upon him who denies it. If we simply accept and acquiesce in the face of discrimination, we accept the responsibility ourselves and allow those responsible to salve their conscience by believing that they have our acceptance and concurrence. We should, therefore, protest openly everything in the newspapers, on the radio, in the movies that smacks of discrimination or slander. We must take the seat that our ticket calls for and place upon the proprietor the responsibility of denying it to us.

We must challenge everywhere the principle and practice of enforced racial segregation. We must make it clear that where groups and individuals are striving for social and economic status, group isolation one from the other allows the rise of misunderstanding and suspicion, providing rich soil for the seeds of antagonism and conflict. Recently in the city of Detroit [during a racial upheaval], there was no rioting in the neighborhoods where whites and Negroes lived as neighbors, and there was no conflict in the plants where they worked side by side on the assembly-lines. Whenever one has the price or can fill the requirements for any privilege which is open to the entire public, that privilege must not be restricted on account of race.

Our appeal must be made to the attributes of which the Anglo-Saxon is so proud—his respect for law and justice, his love of fair-play and true sportsmanship.

3. We must understand that the great masses of our people are farmers and workers, and that their hopes for improvement in a large measure lie in association with organizations whose purpose is to improve their condition. This means membership in and support of labor and farmer unions. Within these organizations it means continuous efforts with our allies of all racial groups to remove all barriers which operate in the end to divide workers and defeat all of their purposes. The voice of organized labor has become one of the most powerful in the land and unless we have a part in that voice our people will not be heard.

4. We must take a full part in the political life of our community, state and nation. We must learn increasingly about political organization and techniques. We must prepare for and fight for places on the local, state, and national committees of our political parties. This is a representative government and the only way that our representatives can reflect our desires is for us to register and vote. In a large measure the whole of our national life is directed by the legislation and other activities of our governmental units. The

only way to affect their action and to guarantee their democratic nature is to have a full hand in electing individuals who represent us. The national election of 1944 represents one of the most crucial in the life of this nation and of the world. The Congressional representatives that are elected to office will have a large hand in the type of peace treaty to be adopted and the entire nature of our post-war domestic economy. All of our organizations and individuals who supply leadership must fully acquaint our people with the requirements of registering and voting, see to it that they are cognizant of the issues involved and get out to register and vote.

Negro women and their organizations have a tremendous responsibility and opportunity to offer leadership and support to this struggle of the racial group to attain improved cultural status in America. We have always done a full part of this job. Now, with large numbers of our men in the armed forces and with considerable numbers of new people who have migrated into our communities to take their part in war production, we have a bigger job and a greater opportunity than ever. Our women know too well the disintegrating effect upon our family life of our low economic status. Discrimination and restriction have too often meant to us broken homes and the delinquency of our children. We have seen our dreams frustrated and our hopes broken. We have risen, however, out of our despair to help our men climb up the next rung of the ladder. We see now more than a glimmer of light on the horizon of a new hope. We feel behind us the surge of all women of China and India and of Africa who see the same light and look to us to march with them. We will reach out our hands to all women who struggle forward—white, black, brown, yellow—all. If we have the courage and tenacity of our forebears, who stood firmly like a rock against the lashings of slavery and the disruption of Reconstruction, we shall find a way to do for our day what they did for theirs. Above all we Negro women of all levels and classes must realize that this forward movement is a march of the masses and that all of us must go forward with it or be pushed aside by it. We will do our part. In order for us to have peace and justice and democracy for all, may I urge that we follow the example of the great humanitarian—Jesus Christ—in exemplifying in our lives both by word and action the fatherhood of God and the brotherhood of man?

From *What the Negro Wants,* edited by Rayford W. Logan. Copyright © 1944 by the University of North Carolina Press; renewed 1972. Used by permission of the publisher.

General Mary McLeod Bethune, National Commander of the Women's Army for National Defense (WAND), organized in 1942 to facilitate black women's patriotic service. During World War II, Bethune also served on the National Board of Directors of the American Women's Voluntary Services (AWVS), a similar interracial organization founded in 1940. *Tuskegee University Archives, 1944.*

PART II

Self-Revelations

"Like Bruises on an Oyster" (1940–1955)

Introduction

Audrey Thomas McCluskey

AFRICAN AMERICAN WOMEN'S HISTORY is imbued with what historian Darlene Clark Hine calls "multiple dichotomies": different, seemingly contradictory responses to the oppression black women have faced.[1] This is only partly true of the life of Mary McLeod Bethune, who was able to merge dichotomous issues into an unchanging agenda for black progress. She promoted interracial cooperation while working tirelessly to create and sustain black-controlled institutions and organizations. To her mind, there was no contradiction between these two activities; her strategy for tackling the interlocking obstacles of racism, poverty, and sex discrimination required both.

At her peak, Bethune harnessed a considerable amount of moral authority as black America's "First Lady."[2] She used her skills as a consensus builder to push an agenda for racial and gender inclusion. Having forsaken conventional family life—although she espoused it for race uplift—Bethune contented herself with being the symbolic "Mother Bethune" to a whole race. Except for her son, Albert (and even he felt neglected by his mother's frequent travels and preoccupation with work), her own family life was mostly nonexistent. She was, however, quite supportive of a large, extended family, some of whom she helped to educate at her school.[3] She said that Albert was her first child and Bethune-Cookman College her second.[4]

Bethune viewed her primary role as that of racial representative, speaking and acting on behalf of her race and sex. "When they [whites] see me [at their meetings] they know the Negro is present," she often remarked. As the architect of her own self-invention who zealously courted the media, she created a public persona as robust as her short, stout frame. Writing a supporter during one of the frequent financial crises at her college, Bethune declared, "My own life story should be gotten together and sent out. I think this is the psychological time for it."[5] She understood the value of confirming America's sense of itself as a society fostered by hard work and fair play, especially when that confirmation came from the daughter of former slaves.

The focus of "Self-Revelations" is on documents in which Bethune explicates the beliefs and values that were central to how she functioned as a leader. Although she established politically motivated allegiances that other black leaders sometimes questioned,[6] she was seldom self-critical or reflective, viewing her own motives as pure and directed by a higher authority. She added to that persona by portraying herself as a "dreamer" who didn't take time to plan. In reality, however, she was a careful planner, guided by faith in God and in herself. She inscribed her values with scriptural authority and symbolic meaning. Spiritual strength, race pride, interracial harmony, and faith in America's possibilities were at the core of Bethune's beliefs and advocacies. These beliefs show her to be a relentless optimist who dissolved dichotomies by holding fast to her values even when tested by confounding events.

DOCUMENTARY SOURCES

Although Bethune peppered her speeches with phrases such as "in all humility" and "I humbly accept," her exalted sense of self and of her place in history comes through in these documents. They also come as close as any of her public statements to revealing glimpses of her inner life. Included are recollections about her childhood in rural South Carolina that give insight into the formation of her character.

In an interview conducted by noted Fisk University president Charles S. Johnson, which took place between 1939 and 1940, Bethune shares some of the life-shaping forces of her early years, as well as rare details about her family and her marriage to Albertus Bethune, a topic that she tended to avoid in public statements after he left the family in 1907. Johnson, a skilled social scientist, was interested in discerning characteristics of leadership among African Americans. His interview with Bethune is one of a series of interviews that he conducted with black leaders of the period. Bethune, more un-guarded that usual, comes across as a self-willed individual who, rather than succumb to adversity, responded with the type of willful fortitude associated with heroism. By conquering the villain and growing stronger, Bethune placed herself within the beloved American tradition of the underdog. In her case, the villain was the cumulative effects of discrimination caused by race, poverty, gender, and dark skin color. Turning a perceived negative into a positive, she spoke of her dark skin as a source of race pride and family legitimacy, despite the fact that her uplift work placed her among a circle of fair-skinned black women and men who were identified with an intraracial caste based on skin color.[7] In assessing Bethune's personal triumph over such adversities, Johnson used a metaphorical description. Her life, he said, was "like the bruises on an oyster that produces a pearl."

In "Spiritual Autobiography," one of a collection of essays written by well-known Americans about their faith,[8] Bethune expands the motivational themes raised in the Johnson interview and reveals her deeply religious nature. She declared, "There is in me always that deep awe and reverence for God, and His way of working in me. I feel Him working in and through me, and I have learned to give myself freely—unreservedly to the guidance of the inner voice in me." Such resoluteness couched in non-denominationalism suggests why some critics called her stubborn and high-handed. Yet these characteristics cannot be separated from Bethune's iconic stature and the beliefs that propelled her toward leadership.

Bethune's faith in America was another deeply held belief, although it was not a simplistic one. While she emphasized the importance of black patriotism, she also criticized the gap between the rhetoric of democracy and the lack of civil rights for black Americans. It was this combination of religious and patriotic impulses that attracted her to the cult-like Christianity and political conservatism of the Moral Re-Armament Movement. The year before she died, Bethune was an invited guest at the World Assembly for Moral Re-Armament in Caux, Switzerland. The virulently anti-Communist international organization was founded by Frank Buchman in 1938 to bring forth a new world order based upon ethical principles and committed to peace.[9] Converts vowed to uphold four absolutes: "Absolute Honesty, Absolute Purity, Absolute Unselfishness, and Absolute Love." MRA offered Bethune the spotlight that had gradually faded in the last decade of her life. It also invoked the themes of her lifelong advocacies: God, interracialism, and democracy. The speech at Caux shows Bethune in an atypically reflective and self-disclosing light. The confessional nature of Moral Re-Armament meetings prompted her to publicly admit to "my imperfections," which included putting her school before the needs of her son. This unusual self-accounting came near the end of her life. Back in the United States, several months later, feeling free (perhaps for the first time in her life) of her weighty burdens and responsibilities, she told an interviewer what the trip had meant to her: "For four weeks I sat in those meetings and didn't think about my college or my country or my children or myself. I used the time to turn the searchlight on Mary McLeod Bethune."[10]

This was followed a few months later by a final public declaration that sought to articulate her core beliefs and principles while reaffirming her own legacy. "My Last Will and Testament" (1955), published in *Ebony* just months after she died, is the document that most Americans associate with Mary McLeod Bethune. Like her lesser-known speech in Caux, it is reflective and contemplative. It was meant to bequeath her accumulated wisdom and insight to future generations of black Americans, whom she fully expected to continue the struggle for equality. She wanted for each of them what she lived herself—a purposeful, principled life. She shares her hopes and aspirations for black America in an exhortation that resonates with the causes she espoused. In "My Last Will and Testament," Bethune combined the stellar optimism and cautious pragmatism that epitomized her life. She predicted a future for African Americans that would be "unhindered by race taboos and shackles." Yet she also reminded them that "We live in a world which respects power above all things," and warned that her people must learn to respect the uses of power. Her "soul shines through" in these nine axiomatic principles, states historian Elaine M. Smith.[11] They embody the life she invented for herself and wanted for others of her race.

These representative documents reveal core themes and beliefs that framed Bethune's life and work. Oblivious to the notion of divided loyalties, she merged several agendas in her advocacy of the rights and duties of black Americans. Even these self-disclosing utterances had a decidedly public purpose: They were her prescription for healing a racially divided America.

NOTES

1. Darlene Clark Hine, "Lifting the Veil, Shattering the Silence: Black Women's History in Slavery and Freedom," in *The State of Afro-American History: Past, Present, and Future*, ed. Darlene Clark Hine (Baton Rouge: Louisiana State University Press, 1986), p. 223.

2. "Florida's First Negro Resort," *Ebony*, February 1948, pp. 23–26.

3. Her niece, Jerona Miller, attended Bethune-Cookman College. Bethune provided support—financial and otherwise—to several other members of her extended family.

4. She expressed these motherly sentiments toward Bethune-Cookman several times, most notably in her retirement memo to the board of trustees of the college, in which she stated that she had "two children, Albert and Bethune-Cookman College." (See Minutes, Special Call Meeting, Board of Trustees [excerpt] (1942), in Part III of this volume.)

5. Gerda Lerner, *Black Women in White America: A Documentary History* (New York: Pantheon Books, 1972), p. 145.

6. In one of several instances in which Bethune played both sides of the racial divide, she supported black government workers' push for inclusion of black women in the new Women's Army Auxiliary Corps. She also went against black leadership in her support for Mrs. Oveta Culp, a Texan who, in 1942, was named director of the WAAC by Secretary of War Henry Stimson. Instead of joining the black protest against the Southerner, Bethune, under the aegis of NCNW, asked to be appointed assistant director of the Auxiliary (*New York Times,* May 16, 1942, p. 15). She later had a short-lived consulting role with the WAAC, helping to ensure that black women were among the officers selected.

7. Bethune spoke of her descent from "royal African blood," but gained grudging acceptance from many upper-class black women despite her agrarian origins and dark complexion. See "Faith That Moved a Dump Heap," reprinted in Lerner (1972); also Stephen Birmingham, *Certain People: America's Black Elite* (Boston: Little, Brown and Co., 1977), pp. 287–288. While it can be argued that the mentioning of skin color may have been an unconscious attempt to thwart the effects of light skin privilege (colorism), Bethune did so convincingly.

8. Louis Finkelstein, ed., *American Spiritual Autobiographies: Fifteen Self-Portraits* (New York: Harper, 1948).

9. Tom Driberg, *The Mystery of Moral Re-Armament* (New York: Alfred A. Knopf, 1965), p. 12.

10. Robert L. Sloan, "The Miracle Years of Mrs. Bethune," *Christian Century,* February 1, 1956, p. 140.

11. Elaine M. Smith, "Mary McLeod Bethune's 'My Last Will and Testament': A Legacy for Race Vindication," *Journal of Negro History* 81, nos. 1–4 (1996): 105–122.

Charles S. Johnson, Interview with Bethune

[abridged] (1940)

DR. JOHNSON: I have been trying to analyze those qualities that seem to me to constitute stature. We have concluded that they are at least among these: most persons who attain to greatness can boast at least family status, as a beginning, or a tradition of education which permits an even start with the world; or the advantage of economic position, or of class, or a race favored by circumstances inherent in that status. The important factor to me seems to rest in the fact that you had none of these at the beginning . . . but, instead you had every conspicuous disadvantage upon which our modern society has placed a valuation.

In the first place, sex is a disadvantage, although not entirely so. There has been historically an advantage in mixed blood, and you represented an unmixed ancestry, like a large majority of the submerged Negro population. You came from a part of the country steeped in general and mass backwardness from which emergence is especially difficult. There was no advantage of wealth; there was no tradition of education nor of any important degree of participation in what we are pleased to call our American civilization.

In overcoming these on your own initiative and drive, and lighting your own path from some inner fire, it was inevitable that this spiritual quality would take possession of the personality itself . . . until at a point of full maturity it becomes difficult to distinguish between Mary Bethune as a person and Mary Bethune as a social and spiritual institution. The thing that I am interested in now is some of the scars, some of the bruises that, like the bruises on an oyster, produce a pearl. Every life is full of them—that is, every life that has eventually grown around them into major stature. Some of the early injuries to the personality; incidents—any one will do to start with . . . in thinking of an early hurt, whether racial, personal, or class.

MRS. BETHUNE: I think that possibly the first and real wound that I could feel in my soul and my mind was the realization of the dense darkness and ignorance that I found in myself—when I did find myself—with the seeming absence of a remedy. What I mean by that was the recognition of the lack of opportunity. I could see little white boys and girls going to school every day, learning to read and write; living in comfortable homes with all types of opportunities for growth and service and to be surrounded as I was with no opportunity for school life, no chance to grow—I found myself very often yearning all along for the things that were being provided for the white children with whom I had to chop cotton every day, or pick corn, or whatever my task happened to be. I think that, actually, the first hurt that came to me in my childhood was the contrast of what was being done for the white children and the lack of what we got.

JOHNSON: At what age did this occur?

BETHUNE: Around nine or ten years.

JOHNSON: Sometimes we may be feeling that thing under the surface for a long time and a little instance touches it off. Do you remember any such?

BETHUNE: My mother kept in rather close contact with the people she served as a slave. She continued to cook for her master until she [saved enough to purchase] five acres of land. [Her former master] deeded her five acres. The cabin, my father and brothers built. It was the cabin in which I was born. She kept up these relations. Very often I was taken along [to my mother's job] after I was old enough, and on one of these occasions I remember my mother went over to do some special work for this family of Wilsons, and I was with her.

I went out into what they called their play house in the yard where they did their studying. They had pencils, slates, magazines and books. I picked up one of the books and one of the girls said to me—"You can't read that—put that down. I will show you some pictures over here," and when she said to me, "You can't read that—put that down," it just did something to my pride and to my heart that made me feel that some day I would read just as she was reading. I did put it down, and followed her lead and looked at the picture book that she had. But I went away from there determined to learn how to read and that some day I would master for myself just what they were getting and it was that aim that I followed.

One day we were out in the field picking cotton and the mission teacher came from Maysville, five miles away, and told mother and father that the Presbyterian church had established a mission where the Negro children could go and that the children would be allowed to go. I was among the first of the young ones to enroll, and . . . so it seemed to me.

That first morning on my way to school I kept the thought uppermost, "Put that down—you can't read," and I felt that I was on my way to read and it was one of the incentives that fired me in my determination to read. And I think that because of that I grasped my lessons and my words better than the average child and it was not long before I was able to read and write.

JOHNSON: What was the attitude of your mother? Or, did you tell her about it?

BETHUNE: Yes, I told her. You know, my mother was one of those grand educated persons that did not have letters. She had a great vision, a great understanding of human nature. When I told her, that instant, you know, she said to me—"Oh, never mind, my child, your time will come. You will learn some day." My mother had a great philosophy of life. She came down from one of the great royalties of Africa. She could not be discouraged. No matter what kind of plight we found ourselves in, she always believed there was, through prayer and work, a way out. And it was one of the greatest things she stimulated life with . . . that determination that there was a way out if we put forth effort ourselves.

JOHNSON: Did you ever hear her call the name of the African race or tribe she belonged to?

BETHUNE: If so, it has passed out of my memory.

JOHNSON: Do you remember any words that suggested continuity of any African traditions?

BETHUNE: No. My mother was very, very dark with soft, keen features: small of stature. She wasn't large. I took my robustness from my father. My father wasn't as strong willed as my mother. He was very kindly disposed, very sympathetic. My mother's will power and drive gave the impetus that held our household together. The majority of our family married off early.

There were seventeen of us, you know. I had nieces and nephews far older than myself. There were seventeen full sisters and brothers and it took my mother's spirit to build a home. Father and my brothers got the logs that built the cabin, the cabin where I was born—I was born in our own home cabin, and on our own soil.

JOHNSON: Were any older brothers born during slavery?

BETHUNE: Oh, yes. Some of my older sisters and brothers belonged to slave masters. . . . some were scattered. . . . My father was a McLeod—my mother was a McIntosh; they handed her down to Ben Wilson, who was one of the family—I think the husband of one of the girls, one of the daughters, and it was this Ben Wilson for whom she continued to cook.

JOHNSON: How did the family reassemble after slavery, or do you remember?

BETHUNE: Oh yes. They were not sold very far apart and after slavery they all reassembled on the old McLeod place where my father was and took their stations in life.

JOHNSON: Do you remember anything, their telling any stories about how they first got together after freedom?

BETHUNE: My oldest brother, Samuel, and my oldest sister, Satira—odd names, eh!—heard tell when freedom came. They did not know they were actually free until called together a few days after, and they eventually found their way back to where my father was and father brought mother home on the McLeod plantation and they all assembled for a family reunion. They brought the grand children that mother and father had not seen. When my son Albert was born, he was my mother's ninetieth grand child—my family was very productive. My sisters had ten, twelve and thirteen children—a very productive family. The[y] found their way into motherhood and fatherhood early in life, because there was no opportunity opened up to them. They settled largely in . . . and some of them, of course, developed. . . . None of them had much opportunity, none of the older ones had the opportunity for any kind of academic training that could give them a clear vision of the full life they were capable of living. My two sisters over me, Julia and Rebecca, did learn after they were grown, how to read, and were able to get hold of some ideas. And my brother, immediately over me, William Thomas, got some opportunities after he was grown, to learn how to read some.

JOHNSON: It might be well here to have you name your sisters and brothers, possibly chronologically.

BETHUNE: Let's see, now if I can. There was Sally, she was the oldest, then Satira, Samuel, Julia, Kissie, Kelly, Carrie, (all old-fashioned and odd names) Beauregard (named in honor of General Beauregard), Cecelia, Rebecca, Magdalena (we called her Margie), Mary Jane (myself, of course), Hattie Bell, William Thomas, Monday (a common South Carolina name). . . .

JOHNSON: What do you suppose it was—you had no one to suggest this to you originally, that you desired something better than you were getting. Most children born in situations like this accept this as their lot in life and never feel any different about it.

BETHUNE: My mother said when I was born I was entirely different from the rest—I was the most homely child, I was just different. In the ordinary things that the children engaged in I wouldn't. I had the type of leadership like mother. She said I was just different from the others. My taste for food was different. I would just look at it and not eat it. I had my own ideas about even that. I had just a different setting in my acceptance of things from the rest of the children, and she very early detected that I was just a little different.

My older sisters wanted to get married early. I had no inclinations that way. I had more of a missionary spirit—the spirit of doing things for others. Any one sick in the community, I would tantalize my mother to make them some soup. If any child had no shoes, I always wanted to share my shoes. She had to watch me to keep me from giving away things that were mine.

Mother used to make grape wine. . . . the other children drank it. I did not care for it. I did not have the same tastes as they. My ideas were somewhat different. My mother was quite proud of it. She felt, "Here comes one of the children who is going to do something in life." My father felt the same way. The children themselves were very proud of me. They were not mean to me about it. My family all conceded to me in my ideas. I was particular about things, but they accepted my leadership from those days to this moment and looked to me as the one in the family that might go places and they were willing to concede to my ideas because I was always striving to set up something that was going in the opposite direction from the general mass of things and doing. . . . And, of course, after I got just a little mental training I had a very definite creative mind that I would put into operation such things as would inspire and help them.

JOHNSON: Were there any other colored children around your age? What was their outlook?

BETHUNE: There was nothing for them to aspire to; it was an incentive to me, and of course, many followers after that, many boys and girls of the community. A new life came into the district. Sunday afternoon I would take the farm children for miles around—I would give them whatever I had learned during the week. Poetry, reading, songs, etc. . . . I would give to them as often as I got. As I got I gave. They gave me a broader capacity for taking in and I feel that up to today, I feel it in all things, and I feel that as I give I get.

Of course, I became a very definite favorite in the family—my mother, father, sisters and brothers, people in the community all loved me. I never had difficulty getting people to follow me. Never, from the start. They seemed to realize the seriousness and unselfishness of my motives. When I got so I could do the counting, all the papers—of both the whites and colored people—were put into my lap—the papers showing the weights of the cotton, and how much . . . from the weighing of the cotton. When we went to pick cotton for white people they said, "Let Mary Jane put down the number of pounds." I became useful . . . I won the[ir] respect and admiration. I made my learning, what little it was, [help others. I did nothing] that would put me above the people about me. When I went off to school and came back I was accepted and [they] looked forward to my coming back. They knew that whatever I had, they knew I would adapt [it] to use of the people there.

Those were great days when the masses needed the few who could read or write so badly. As I look now, you are opening deep channels where I can look down through the channel of years. There were people looking to someone who would come and lead them, to teach them, to organize them into . . . singing, schools, etc.

JOHNSON: Was there not some individual who gave you a special thrill because you were able to see your knowledge transferred to his life or life in such a way that they could recognize it? Some older person who had sought new life, some young person who had been with you and could recognize it?

BETHUNE: I think the very first thrill I got from being able to transfer a desire for learning and the buckling down to getting something was from my own brother who was older than I was. When he saw what it was doing for me and that I was able to help him master his letters, and words so that he could open his eyes, and he could see and he began to realize what it meant to get some learning and to . . . be awakened to such extent as to go ten miles at night to the Maysville village and attend night school until all could read, write and apply himself. Things got and remembered was what he got, what my immediate family got and the awakening came to mother and father when [they were] able to sit down and read the newspapers and magazines and the Bible to them—that they had in their own home somebody who could do that—that was the greatest thrill. Of course, that was just the beginning of the thousands and thousands of lives that have been touched and awakened all along the way.

JOHNSON: I am very much interested in seeing just how a kind of family setting, however impoverished it may be, may have something that would set a person off. . . . How did this radiate in the community?

BETHUNE: In this way, that a new standard for living was set up in many of the homes and different little school centers were set up and workers who did not have much money, but more than they had before; and the little Sunday School, and the little chorus, and things of that kind. It brought about a growth—a desire for learning. It gave to the masses there an understanding that they just did not have to continue in darkness—that there was a chance.

JOHNSON: What did the white people around Sumter community feel about Negroes getting an education at that time?

BETHUNE: They thought it was folly; that we did not need an education and that our part was to do chores on the farm. But I thought it was remarkable the way [people] accepted me when I came back—how they used me to put down their figures for them. . . . [It] seemed then that every Negro boy and girl who could read and write could be of great service on the farm. You see I became a help. We kept on growing. The majority of schools kept on growing. I thank God for the Presbyterian church, from whom so many little country schools were begun.

JOHNSON: Who was the person who came in and told you about that school?

BETHUNE: The Presbyterian church sent a woman, Miss Emma Wilson, a very fa[i]r Negro—couldn't tell her from white. [S]he was the first [black] person [white people in the county] we knew to call "Miss." She was employed to start school in Sumter County near Maysville. She had gone to Scotia and had gotten some education. [She] came from Manning, South Carolina.

JOHNSON: Describe the mission as you remember first going into it.

BETHUNE: It was a small church. There were some home-made benches, a little table, and desks, a little pulpit, a little wood stove in the corner . . . had a blackboard on the wall. . . . The first morning I went in, Miss Wilson was standing at the door and received me. There was a crowd of boys and girls. [M]ost of them [were] very crudely dressed, just as you find in any rural school today. We had our little singing that morning, prayer, Bible lesson. We were started on our way to learning!

The things that affected me most about Miss Wilson were her patience, and her tenderness and kindly way in which she handled us. The beautiful smile which was always kept on her face. We were not afraid of her. We could approach her at any time.

JOHNSON: What was the length of time for which she contacted your life?

BETHUNE: She remained there continuously after that.

JOHNSON: Tell me about your own life as a student.

BETHUNE: I was always considered a very earnest, cooperative student, with the teachers and with my class-mates. I was not always the best in the class, but I was never the worst. [I] was always proclaimed as the leader. I don't know why, but [I] always was the captain of this or the chairman of that. If it was a little base-ball team, I was the captain, or if it was a committee, I was the chairman. My word was always accepted for their decisions—I don't know why. I think it was because I loved them all and would always try to conduct myself so they would always love and respect me. I always felt that if we give out love and respect, we would get it. I feel that [way] today.

JOHNSON: Early childhood associations in school which you felt influence your life, or vice-versa?

BETHUNE: I have always been a pretty good mixer. I could be influenced by some of the things that were good and some of things that were not so good. I was normal in this respect. I have by no means been a perfect child in school, but could so soon find my mistake and always had will power enough to retrace my steps toward the safe side of life. Some of the girls, of course, who had so much better homes and clothing and what they called influential family ties that I so very much desired. But I never permitted myself to become antagonistic and dislike them because of that, but bided my time and felt that someday I, like they, would have them. I used to pass the girls' houses sometimes and wish I lived in a house like that. It might be just a weather-board house . . . I realized that I lived in a log-cabin, a log-house, but I felt that someday [that all] would come, if I studied and worked; and so, the first thing I did when I was able to earn my own money, was to tear down the log cabin and build a comfortable home for my mother and father [with] weather-boards and glass windows. . . . I never permitted myself to become discouraged. I know from some spirit within me that a better day was coming by and by. I have always found that to become discouraged was failure. And today I feel that [neither] God nor man can use to advantage a discouraged person.

JOHNSON: How long did you remain in this school?

BETHUNE: Until I completed possibly the sixth or seventh grade. That was about as high as they went.

JOHNSON: What were some of the outstanding incidents of that period?

BETHUNE: My work in the communities and in the churches, setting up little clubs on the plantations around, working in the Sunday School conventions, speaking contests (you know, I used to be a great debater) and debating contests.

JOHNSON: [Did you have a d]riving urge at this period and things that influenced or fired it?

BETHUNE: I wanted very much, before I learned to read well, I craved some education so I could go out and help people. There was such a need for somebody to go and do something. Instinctively, I felt that leadership was needed, someone to inspire and build a program to tell the people something else aside from this very scanty life we were called upon to live. I wanted to train that I, myself, could [be] better prepared and above all, be able to help others. And queer enough, the light came to me and during these years I have been trying to extend it to others. I just wanted to help folks.

I heard Dr. Bowen's address on Africa's need of people . . . need of missionaries to carry them the light. It was a rainy, cold night, we had driven from Maysville, ten miles, with father, who was going to sell cotton the next day. We found that Dr. Bowen was to speak at the Methodist church. I got with Sister and went over to hear him. As I heard him tell about African people and the need of missionaries, there grew in my soul the determination to go some day and it has never ceased, and I sent up a prayer to God to give me the light, to show me the way that I, in turn, might show others. And for years I just had a yearning to go to Africa and thought that when I was through with my education I could be sent, but instead, I found my way into the deep South.

JOHNSON: What incident diverted your attention from Africa to your own country?

BETHUNE: When I completed my work at Scotia, I was sent to the Moody School in Chicago, Illinois. I studied there for two years, applying myself. I applied to the Mission Board in New York for a chance to go to Africa. They informed me that no openings were available where they could place Negro missionaries, so they sent me to Augusta, Georgia to work with Lucy Laney.

JOHNSON: May we go back to Scotia and have an accounting of your stay there?

BETHUNE: At about fifteen or sixteen years of age, after completing my work in Maysville, I returned to the cotton fields. I had gotten what I could at the Mission school and did all I could in the community to keep alive the interest in education, keeping up intercession for opportunity to train myself that I might be of service to others. On one October day, our same teacher who had been joined by Mr. Simmons, a Negro man who had done so much for the Negro people, came to the farm field and said to mother and father that they had been sending out literature about the work done at Maysville mission and a piece of the literature had gotten into the hands of a white woman in Denver, Colorado, Miss Mary Chrisman—a rural school teacher who would often do dress-making after school hours—who became inter-ested in what had been done for the Negro children in South Carolina and wrote to the teachers asking if they could find a little girl who would make good if given a chance, and that out of the money she was earning, she would give for that little girl's education. They [came] to the farm field to tell mother and father I was the little girl they had selected to go to Scotia. It was a thrilling day for me, when I was called from the field by my father and teacher said, "Mary Jane, would you like to go to Scotia?" I asked, "What is Scotia?" and they told me it was a school in Concord, North Carolina, and that a good woman was going to send me. I pulled my cotton sack off, got down on my knees, clasped my hands, and turned my eyes upward and thanked God for the chance that had come. So mother and father started getting me ready to go. I did not have a trunk. We used to have little cracker boxes. We kept our clothing in them, so my father went down and got me a little trunk. Some neighbors knitted a pair of stockings, some gave me a little linsey dress, little aprons, this that and the other, and when that October day came I can see myself now, going down to Maysville to take the train for the first time in my life.

All of the neighbors stopped work that afternoon, got out the wagons, mules, ox-carts; some riding, some walking. They were going to Maysville to put me on the train to go to school. I had never before been on a train. It was all so strange. My teacher wired on to Columbia to Dr. Johnson to meet me and put me on the right train since I had to change. My little heart was going pit-a-pat. I can see my mother as she clasped me in her arms and she said, "God bless my child." Tears and hand-shakes; all bidding little Mary good-bye. As the train move[d] on, I had so strange a feeling and wondered what it was all about. It seemed that as the train was puffing its steam it was saying, "Scotia, Scotia, Scotia." I got to Concord, was met at the station [and] taken to this beautiful brick building. I had never been in a brick building before. I was taken upstairs. I had never been upstairs before. I was taken into a beautiful little room, with two beds; [there was a] pretty spread on my bed. Oh, it was different, so different. I was received by the matron, and my roommate who was named Janie Shankle. Oh, she was so patient and kind to me. I got down on my little knees and thanked God.

The next morning the big bell rang. I bounced up, was gotten ready and was taken down to the beautiful dining room, with [a] white table cloth, knives and forks; girls from cities, town and country. It was all so strange. I made so many blunders not knowing whether to use my knife or fork. But all the rough edges soon fell off and an integration into the school life of that beautiful Christian institution was mine and I began finding my way into [a] broader atmosphere.

I was soon known and beloved, by the students and teachers. They were so interesting and there were so many interesting things at school. I don't know why, but I entered in the school life there just as I did in the little mission, finding things to do and people to serve. I was called peace maker there. Homesick girls would always find me. Girls with their problems, difficulties, and disappointments always would come to me, for advice. The girls always called me "Dick" McLeod in school. I never knew why, but that was the pet name for me. I did all types of work at Scotia. I used to do special laundry for Dr. and Mrs. Satterfield on their special clothing. I was considered an exceptional laundress. I was the prize winner in making breads and cakes; and a fine scrubber. I worked in the big kitchen in the morning, getting in the coal and starting the fires. Nothing was too menial or too hard for me to find joy in doing, for the appreciation of having a chance. Oh, I was a member of the chorus class, the quartet, on the debating team. There was a great opportunity for me to prepare myself for the great task that was awaiting me. It was the first time I had had a chance to study and know white people. They had a mixed faculty at Scotia. I can never doubt the sincerity and interest of

some white people when I think of my experience with my beloved, consecrated teachers who took so much time and patience with me at a time when
patience and tolerance were needed.

JOHNSON: What were some of the highlights of your school experience?

BETHUNE: My contact with the fine young Negro teachers—Hattie Bomar,
Rebecca Cantey, and others who gave to me the confidence in the ability of
Negro women to be cultured, gave me my very first vision of the culture and
ability of Negro women and gave me the incentive and made me feel that if
they could do it I could do it, too. My contact with white teachers, such as
Miss Barnes, Miss Cathcart, and others, clinched my confidence in the
interest, and the wholeheartedness of white people in Negroes.

JOHNSON: [Was there] any special attachment between you and certain
instructors?

BETHUNE: I was a general favorite, but I think that possibly Miss Cathcart
was closer to me than any. She was so interested in my personal affairs, in my
clothing. She would help supply me. Called me to her room and asked how
my shoes were. In the spring she would get materials for my spring clothes.
When I graduated from Scotia she had her Sunday School Class of La
Grange, Indiana, send me material for my dress and underwear. She taught
me mathematics and music. She and Mrs. Barnes were spared to visit my
work in Daytona Beach two years ago. They wept with appreciation when
they saw what God had wrought through the efforts they themselves had
contributed to me years ago. They now live in Concord, North Carolina.

JOHNSON: When you decided to go to Europe you were going to some
Central conference, or were you just going abroad?

BETHUNE: I was just going over to see Europe and study it. I had had the
desire for a long time to know just a little more about the setting of foreign
people in their own homes and in their own surroundings and get a clear idea
of what was happening across the waters. I made up my mind to go see for
myself. About that time Dr. Wilberforce Williams of Chicago was getting up
a party of people to go over and not having been to Europe before, I thought
it a fine thing to get with experienced men like Dr. Williams, who had been
over several times. I joined the party. It was an interesting group including
Mr. and Mrs. E. A. Webb of Little Rock, Arkansas; Dr. and Mrs. M. D. Miller
and others. I was to join them in New York to go over and it came [at] just
about my commencement time and I had a very narrow escape in making
connections. I left Daytona Beach—there were many people deeply interested in my going. [A]mong them was Anna Malone of Poro College who was
very gracious to me and made a contribution of about $1,200 because she felt
I had given so unreservedly for others.° She would do that to help me get this

---

°Annie Turnbo Malone (1869–1957) was reportedly the first black woman millionaire in
America. A noted philanthropist and supporter of black causes, especially education, she made
millions developing and marketing black-hair care products and beauty culture.

experience so I was well prepared to go. Other friends gave me gifts and baggage and money, so I was in good shape for my trip. My earning capacity did not maintain such a thing on my part.

I took the train for New York. The train was delayed for half an hour. I wired on to the steamship line stating that I would be late and asking them to wait for me. It was a daring thing to do . . . but they held the boat for thirty minutes for me. It was the most interesting thing. [W]hen I got down there, one of the m[ale] passengers said, "For God's sake, let me see the woman who is holding up the whole ship!" We moved off. It was a most delightful trip. It was a great and new experience for me. I met many interesting people.

JOHNSON: You met Lady Astor, didn't you?

BETHUNE: Yes. When we landed we were located in an American hotel in London. We took many days there and went to Westminster Abb[e]y—it gave me a thrill I can't put in words. We went to the House of Commons and were received there and we met the Lord Mayor . . . of London. He had us to tea. Lady Astor saw through one of the London papers that I was there. She was thirty-five miles away. She came into London and opened her very beautiful home and had a very beautiful party for me while I was there. . . . We went from there to Scotland and met Lady McLeod—same name as mine. She had a beautiful party for me. I went to the International House of Women. . . . My card of membership in the Council of [Women] gave me entree into those places. My entire visit was very interesting. When in Italy, I went to Genoa, into the house where Columbus was born.

JOHNSON: You also went to Vatican City, did you not?

BETHUNE: Yes—I went up and was received. We assembled in a large room and the Pope gave his blessing to the body as he always does. Everybody kissed his ring. When he came to me he stopped and held his hands over my head and said sentences in Latin. I do not know what he said. It was done too rapidly for my translation. I looked up into his face and said, "Pope Pius, I thank you." Webb and those men wept. And strangely, the attendant who was with the Pope put his arms about my shoulders and said, "Oh, blessed art thou amon[g] women."

JOHNSON: I wonder why he said that? Do you know?

BETHUNE: It was all so strange. We never knew. It must have been something very special. He might have been calling all the darker people of the world and he probably was paying a tribute to the rest of them. But there were . . . other dark people there. [It] did something to me. I don't know, but it did something to me.

I think when I was in Rome we visited St. Peter's; down to the Appian Way, and out on the Seven Hills there where Caesar and Brutus had their quarrel; the many interesting cathedrals, especially St. Peters where hangs the painting of the Last Supper.

JOHNSON: I was especially interested in Lady Astor. How did she happen to know you? Had you met her before?

BETHUNE: No. She knew who I was. She had gone to an entertainment for [Charles] Lindbergh and saw in the paper that I was an educator and she wanted to come over and do something for me. She was beautiful to me. She said, "I am particularly proud because you are real, a real Negro, a real American. The things you are doing are so real and I want you to know I appreciate them." She is wonderful herself. . . . I had great experience[s] in going around the Mediterranean. I was impressed with the cliff dwellers and the poverty of the people over there and the ignorance of the people in Lower Italy.

JOHNSON: Were you impressed at any point with the great poverty of Europe over that of the Americas?

BETHUNE: I felt that the poorest peasants, the poorest share-croppers in Mississippi and Georgia were much better off than many of the poor white, or rather, waifs, I saw. One gets many very different ideas. [W]e are not the only sufferers and burden bearers in the world. I stiffened my back and got new courage to come back to America with greater appreciation for the blessings we did have.

JOHNSON: Mr. [Booker T.] Washington had the same sort of shock when he was there and came back and wrote his book, *The Man Farthest Down.*

BETHUNE: It was the greatest thrill to go into the Blue Grotto. I thought Switzerland beautiful but after all, I did not seem to see more real beauty in Europe than I see in sections of my own country. And I think of Lower Florida, Oregon and Washington State, sections of the West and California—San Diego. I did not see any beauty in Europe that I thought out-classed our own country. I was happy when I went to Europe that I had seen America first.

We were wonderfully received over there. The foreigners liked me very much. My dark skin did not hamper me at all. They were very fond of me. I liked them. I like folks. I had a birthday in Venice and all Italians were very gracious. [T]hey made a cake for me. I had received a cablegram from America. They thought I was wonderful. All were fond of me. I was never lonesome. Someone was always with me. They came to keep me company. I had no lonely hours.

JOHNSON: I want to give you the privilege of [five] things from which to select the situation you feel like talking against. (1) One of them is some of the things in the development of women's clubs in America. No one has written their story yet. How they came into being and then how you became crystallized in these organizations and became head of these clubs and their leader, and established the Council of Women. (2) To see [if you] were conscious of any of the educational principles current about the time of the development of Bethune-Cookman. (3) Your association with Lucy Laney and also with Booker T. Washington. (4) Some of the New Deal personal stuff. Of course I know how Roosevelt turned with great feeling of ease and how you knew him well enough to shake your finger in his face and give him some friendly advice; and about your acquaintance with Mrs. James Roosevelt, and your contacts with Mrs. Eleanor Roosevelt. Your associations with that group has certain ramifications. (5) A picture of Mr. Bethune.

BETHUNE: I think the educational situation of Florida and possibly of the lower East coast is very vague. I went there because I was looking for a hard place to work.

JOHNSON: How did you know Florida was hard?

BETHUNE: I knew of Florida. . . . [There] . . . was building . . . down there and Negroes were flocking there and I went by to see what was being done.

JOHNSON: Did you know anyone there?

BETHUNE: No. [M]y first married year was in Savannah, Georgia. That was when I was quiet from active work. That year I took off. My boy was born that year and I was engaged in civic things, church clubs, community work with women and children. On Roberts Street where I lived I had a group working with and for them, and while I was there my friend Irene Smallwood, who later became Mrs. J.W.E. Bowen, was with me when I taught at Lucy Laney's school. While visiting me in Savannah, a man named Reverend, I met him— he was the pastor of the Presbyterian church in Palatka, Florida. I told him of going into a new district and how I wanted to build an institution of my own and [how I] wanted to go into some congested district where little was being done for my people and he suggested that I start a parochial school in connection with his church. I got to Palatka and started . . . this community school and worked in the jails two and three times a week. [I went] out to the sawmills there and, in general, among the young people in clubs there, and built up a very interesting setting. I stayed there for five years. Then I made up my mind to go down on the East coast and study the situation there and see what was being done, and found very little being done. . . . The new minister, Reverend S.P. Pratt, . . . told me he thought I would be interested to see what was happening in that section.

I had no money. I was doing a little insurance work in connection with my other work—I sold insurance for the Afro-American [insurance company] and saved up a little money and went to the coast to study what was being done there. As I studied the situation I saw the importance of someone going down there doing something. So I selected Daytona Beach, a town where very conservative people lived and where James M. Gamble (of the Procter and Gamble Company of Cincinnati); Thomas White (of the White Sewing Machine Company of Cleveland); and other fine people [owned homes]. A fine club of white women in that section formed a philanthropic group, [the] Palmetto Club, through whom I thought approaches could be made.

The colored people had little to offer. A splendid man of the Baptist Church, Rev. A.L. James; another fine man of the little Methodist Episcopal Church, had conferences with these people and a little woman named Mrs.

Warn, had some daughters who felt the importance of some one doing something in that section and gave their cooperation with my idea of starting a school. I made up my mind that I would do it and started out.

I used the money I had earned with the Afro-American to make this exploration down the coast, and when I got to Daytona I had only one dollar and a half left in cash. I got a little rented house. . . . I couldn't pay the rent. The house belonged to a Negro man named John Williams; he rented the house to me for eleven dollars a month. I told him I had no money but he said he would trust me. I had no furniture. I begged dry good boxes and made benches and stools; begged a basin and other things I needed and in 1904, five little girls there started school.

Before starting school I had three significant dreams. You see, I still believe in dreams. The first was: I was standing on the bank of the St. Johns River and had to cross that river but seemingly there was no way for me to get over. And as I stood pondering that stream, and that I must go over, I looked [to the] back of me and there was a great army of young people, all coming toward me. And then someone came up to me and said, "You are planning to cross this river, but before you cross it you must take this book," and handed me a book "and register the names of all those young people that you see there in the distance." I was ill and when I had that dream and a friend came in to see me and I told him the dream he said to me, "I'll be the Joseph and interpreter of your dream. That means that you are to build a great work for young people and that many years will be spared you yet to lead them on."

My second dream was: I was again on the bank of the St. Johns River and was making another attempt to cross that river. My mother and father were both alive then and the president of dear old Scotia, Dr. Satterfield, who was president during my stay there. They locked arms with me, Dr. Satterfield on one side and my mother and father on the other. They started out with me, wading out into the deep currents. My mother and father held on and went as far as they could go and mother turned and said to me, "My child, we have brought you as far as we can go, but now we must leave you and you must make it for yourself." Dr. Satterfield still plodded on and as the water came up and up, he stopped and said, "Mary, I have brought you to the distance, I can go—now you will have to make the balance of the way yourself."

I wondered what it meant. Just seemed to me they meant, my mother and father, that they had prepared me for a life of service; they gave all they could give in my education and my training, and then they left me to dear old Scotia to carry me to heights they could not reach; and then dear old Scotia carried me and gave me what she could give and sent me out into the world now to carry on.

My third dream: I thought I was standing on the bank of the Halifax River (all of the time by the waters), praying for help and for the way to build my school. I thought as I looked up that I saw a man galloping down the street on a beautiful horse. He was dressed in a uniform suit, and when he got near me he jumped off his horse and approached me and said, "What are you sitting here for?" I said to him, "I am just trying to see my way clear to build my school." He said, "I am Booker T. Washington," and he placed his hand back in his hip pocket and pulled out a parcel in a seemingly soiled handkerchief—a soiled handkerchief that had evidently been used for mopping off the perspiration—and out of this handkerchief he gave me a large diamond and said, "Here, take this and build your school." And again he remounted his horse and galloped away. That was my first contact with Booker T. Washington. But oh, I had been a worshipper at his shrine when I read of what he was doing in the building of Tuskegee. I felt that this diamond represented confidence, will power, stick-to-it-iveness, work, suffering, friends, doubt, wisdom, common sense—everything necessary for the building of a beautiful Bethune-Cookman.

I had such an interesting demonstration of faith in my life, [and] work. When I first started I did not have dishes. A friend was kind enough to me to lend me dishes. It was in October when she loaned them to me. About Christmas time, one Saturday I was cleaning my little girls and my little baby boy who was then about five years old, getting ready for our Christmas. This woman had taken private work at Ormand and said I might use her dishes. This day she came in and said, "Mrs. Bethune, I am awfully sorry, but my husband is going to have dinner for the Masons and must have the dishes." And my little boy said, "Mother, what will we do?" Just at that time there was a knock at the door. I said, "Wait a minute, Mrs. Jamison, you were kind enough to let us have them this long." When I got to the door, a man was standing there with a note in his hand and a basket. He handed me the note and said that Mrs. Thompson had asked [him] to bring them to [me]. We lifted it to the inside, and believe me or not, friends, but when I took the paper off, there was a basket chuck full of dishes and I opened the note from my dear friend, Mrs. . . . [which read] "My son, Burt, has given me a new set of dishes for Christmas and I thought I would send these over to you and your little school." I looked up into the face of my Father and I realized that even before we call, sometimes he answers.

One Saturday I did not have food. I went then to one of the stores and asked the Negro man there if he would let us have groceries for my children for the week. He said, "Why, Mrs. Bethune, I would like to, but I am not able." But when I got back to the little house four men were seated on the porch. They were men who had been attending my night school, coming in to be taught how to read and write. (You see I was doing adult education way back there.) One of them said, "Mrs. Bethune, you have been so kind. We got paid today and we brought you some money." Each owed me two dollars—so I had eight dollars and how I thanked God and went hastily to the store and paid the cash to the man who could not afford to advance me food for my little children, the food necessary for them.

One day we needed food—that morning in our little assembly as I prayed and asked God to supply us. He knew what we needed, and you know, before we got through singing our last hymn, a man drove up in his wagon with a load of vegetables and potatoes and food stuff that a friend had sent over. And one of my little girls said, "Mrs. Bethune prayed for food and here is a man with a wagon full." That faith has sustained us.

We needed a roof on the house. It was leaking. We did not have any money to buy a roof, and I felt that it had to be fixed. I had sent out letters of appeal and no returns had come and finally one morning I said to my helpers, "Build scaffolding around the house. We have enough lumber for scaffolding." The men said, "Where are the materials?" I said, "Build the scaffolds and get ready," and friends, will you believe me, when the mail came in the late afternoon, just about the time the scaffold was finished—I was sitting on the ground directing the men on the scaffolding and opened the mail bag right where I was sitting and will you believe me—I opened the letter from a darling friend who had sent me one thousand dollars to be used as I needed it. And I called my men then from the scaffold and we bowed in prayer there together, thanking God for the supply. I could not help but remember the story of the building of the altar—how Abraham was commanded to build that altar and give an offering and when he looked around for a ram it was there. That is the kind of faith that has built Bethune-Cookman.

When I was sent to Lucy Laney, I was just out of school. It was such a pleasure to have the opportunity to teach with a woman like Lucy Laney. Haines Institute was the creation of her own soul and mind. She started in the basement of her church years ago for her people. She had Mamie McCrory Jackson, Irene Smallwood Bowen. I found them working with her. All were a great inspiration to me. How Mrs. Jackson stood side-by-side with Lucy Laney, gave twenty-five years of her life helping build Haines Institute, and Irene Smallwood who gave years and years. I was so happy for the chance to blend my life with the lives of those women—Lucy Laney with her spirit of service, quick steps, determination, will, alert mind, again demonstrated to me that it could be done. I studied her, watched her every move and gave myself full to the cause she represented. They knew no hour when service was needed. Around Haines Institute there was the very thickly settled community—settled with colored people. On Sunday afternoons the streets were crowded with children, and having had such a fine opportunity for training at the Moody Institute, I felt that here was a chance to help children and asked permission of Lucy Laney to start a mission Sunday School. [S]he granted it. I took the girls of the science class and my own class and went out and combed the alleys and streets and brought in hundreds of children until we had a Sunday School of almost a thousand young people and people in the community came in. Among whom was Judson Lyons and others. This mission school lasted for years, and became one of the great assets of Haines Institute. Lucy Laney, the great inspirer, the great educator, the great leader among our group, fired me with greater ambition for service. I remained with her for one year, after which I went to Sumter, South Carolina, to work in another mission school where I met my friend Estelle Roberts, now Estelle Harrison, and we together had our experience in helping develop the work of the Kindle Institute, headed by Rev. C.J. Watkins, another field for real service, never tiring. I gave my best: meeting friends and working up interest—working with people in jails, with the underprivileged, building Sunday schools, with people in the community, young people's meetings. [I]n the choir of our church, [is where] I met a young man, Albertus Bethune. He had a beautiful tenor voice. He was interested in the activities of the church, and a student at Avery Institute, Charleston, South Carolina. He lacked one year of completing his work there. He had to withdraw in order for his brother Jesse to enter school. Bethune and I met, became well acquainted and loved. The following year we were quietly married. This married life was not intended to impede things I had in mind to do. He found business employment in Savannah, Georgia, where we moved and lived simply and quietly and remained there for sixteen months. Then my only boy, Albertus, Junior, was born. The birth of my boy had no tendency whatever to dim my ardor and determination for my dream work, the building of an institution.

Mr. Bethune was not interested in educational work, but put no barriers in my way to carry on my work. It was mine to struggle on alone. He died in the early days of my beginning, without realizing the possibility of my ambitions.

JOHNSON: Something personal about Mr. Bethune? His background, etc.?

BETHUNE: I met him after he was grown. He was reared in South Carolina and educated there. He was a very fine young man, with fine parentage and family, average in educational background and interested in business.

[*Note:* The text has been edited slightly for clarity, and bracketed words have been inserted to complete missing text.]

Mary McLeod Bethune Papers, Mary McLeod Bethune Foundation, Bethune-Cookman College, Daytona Beach, Fla.

Spiritual Autobiography

[abridged] (1946)

I have lived seventy-one years. I do not recall my birth by incident, but I do believe that providential blessing was bestowed upon me when I came to be the fifteenth child of my devoted parents. Before I came into the world I was given an unusual advantage. My mother was a consecrated, clear-thinking, careful woman, and my father was a principled man with more than average devotion to his family and to the best that he knew. I was loved before I came into being, and I have treasured this heritage of love and have made it the foundation of my life. It seems to me that from the very beginning, I have practiced the affirmation of devotion to love of humanity, and I have precious contentment in my realization of God as my spiritual Father.

My birth into wisdom and spiritual acceptance is a very real fact to me. Out of the womb of salvation and truth my new life was born, and it is in that life that I live and move and have my being. Continually, I commune with the God who gave me that birth. He is the Guide of all that I do. I seek him earnestly for each need. My thanksgiving to Him has been unconsciously spontaneous. I believe that the thanksgiving which is continually in my heart and upon my lips is the source of my power and growth in personality development. Any time, any place, I can hear myself saying "Father, I thank Thee," or "Thank Thee, Father."

Through the discipline that my "self" has received, my spiritual vigor has been quickened and energized. Before I fully knew myself, my mother disciplined my life in order that I might know humility, stamina, faith and goodness. I was shown goodness by precept and example. And because my parents believe[d] so implicitly in me and my understanding I learned to believe in other people.

Early in my childhood my mother taught me to hold the little New Testament which the minister brought around, and to sit quietly in communion with it and God, even before I could read. My tongue was ready to recite the 23rd Psalm and other precious passages from the written page, when once my intellect was prepared to meet the yearnings of my heart—to read the Scriptures. The Word has been hidden in my heart by that knowing which is not literacy, but which is so basic to literacy. As we sing the beautiful spirituals and remember that they flowed from unlettered hearts, we can appreciate more deeply how their social significance is interwoven with their spiritual understandings. Our forefathers had been freed from the yoke of bondage about twelve years when I was born. My early heritage was the spirit of fight and determination which had helped my parents and others to fight for freedom, and which was during my childhood helping them to build security for their children. My dear old grandmother told me the stories because she thought I would understand, hold the idea until I was mature enough to do something about it. When our fathers sang: "Nobody knows the trouble I see," they did not stop on a note of complaint. They burst forth immediately with "Glory Hallelujah." This is definitely a part of my spirit. To be sure I have seen trouble, I have had difficulty; the way has not been easy, but I have thanked God and said "Glory Hallelujah!"

Often I thank God for my rugged ways. Have not my people come over a way that with tears has been watered? But we are stronger today through the struggles with overcoming. I am stronger today because as I have taken the steep, hard way, I have taken time to be faithful, persevering and hopeful.

I believe today that spiritual growth comes with meditation and commun-ion when alone I sit with God. Through the years my meditative moments have grown into habitual continuation. They are not too habitual, however, to keep away the fervor which comes with each experience. There is in me always that deep awe and reverence for God and His way of working in me. I feel Him working in and through me, and I have learned to give myself—freely, unreservedly to the guidance of the inner voice in me.

I can remember when I longed to know the inner voice and searched my mind for an answer to its meaning. It came about in the late hours of those nights when I listened to my mother. She took her lonely vigils when she thought everyone in the house was asleep. There she was, in the dark, on her knees. I knew the form kneeling in the moonlight which poured in upon her, sometimes beside her bed, sometimes beside a chair. She would ask God for faith, for strength, for love, for forgiveness, for knowledge, for food and clothing—not for herself but for her children and for all the poor people. I gained faith in her way when I saw these things she prayed for coming to pass. Many a poor man left our home happy because mother and father had given some simple thing that met his need. Many were the times that our little family was happy when a gift of something we needed came almost miracu-lously. And my mother's "Thank You, Father," made me realize early in life that all things must come from God. I began to see that the full life must be mine only as I learned to live close to God and to trust Him always. I thank my mother and heavenly Father for imparting to me this strength and vitality which has led me from that picture in the closed hours of those nights to the light of this full new day, when I am enjoying the fruits of that first seed-sowing. The desire for spiritual start in living grew on me, and I know today that effectual, fervent desire does not go unrewarded.

As I grew I knew what it meant to absorb my will into the will of God whom I claimed as my Father. Where He reigned at first I do not know. I am sure my child mind personalized Him; but when I knew Him to be a great Spirit, His fatherhood increased because His spirit could dwell in me and go with me and never leave me to my own devices. Part of that learning His will was in the secret of knowing how to hold the faith with the desire, and how to work continually to bring things to pass. When I had my first experiences with people who could read when I could not, and with seeing fine churches, when my people worshipped in shacks, I asked God to open to me the opportunity to do something about that. The idea that I needed gripped me. I found myself endowed with creative power within. I put all negative thoughts away from me, as I do now, and then and there I affirmed my needs, my hopes, and my aspirations. That affirmation with God took me from the cotton fields to the little mission school to Scotia College to Moody Bible Institute, and, finally, to the planting of the Bethune-Cookman College—the real child of my desire. That is how I could say to my good friend, Mr. James N. Gamble, when he visited my little cabin school and saw nothing but a few drygoods boxes and five little girls, and asked "What do you want me to be trustee of ?" "I want you, Mr. Gamble," I said, "to be trustee of the thing that I have in my mind to do." He trusted me and was the Chairman of our Trustee Board for twenty years.

I am blessed with the power to visualize and to see a mental picture of what I would desire. I am always building spiritual air castles. Only those with a spiritual understanding can appreciate my feeling when I say that I saw in my mind's eye the Bethune-Cookman College of today—even in that first week in 1904, when I was surrounded by little children sitting on drygoods boxes with questioning faces turned to me. That is how I could say to our good friend, Mr. Gamble, when he visited my school, that I wanted him to be a trustee of what I had in my mind. He trusted me and was one of our staunchest friends through the years.

Love, not hate, has been the fountain of my fullness. In the streams of love that spring up within me, I have built my relationships with all mankind. When hate has been projected toward me, I have known that the persons who extended it lacked spiritual understanding. I have had great pity and compassion for them. Our Heavenly Father pitieth each one of us when we fail to understand. Jesus said of those who crucified him:

> "Father forgive them,
> For they know not what they do."

Because I have not given hate in return for hate, and because [of] my fellow-feeling for those who do not understand, I have been able to overcome hatred and gain the confidence and affection of people. Faith and love have been the most glorious and victorious defense in this "warfare" of life, and it has been my privilege to use them, and make them substantial advocates of my cause, as I press toward my goals whether they be spiritual or material ones.

In this atomic age, when one small materialistic possession has wrought fear among peoples of the world, I am convinced that leadership must strive hard to show the value of these spiritual tools which are as real as anything we touch or feel, and far more powerful. Being possessed of these qualities has added to my courage. I think our Master, Jesus Christ, showed how the use of them in His life brought courage and determination and even the quality of righteous indignation, when it was necessary to call people to a sense of their duty. I have cringed; I have been a fighter for the things that are just and fair for myself and for my people, and my people are all mankind.

My love is a universal factor in my experience, transcending pettiness, discrimination, segregation, narrowness and unfair dealings with regard to my opportunities to grow and to serve. Through love and faith and determination I have been persistently facing obstacles, small and large, and I have made them stepping stones upon which to rise.

The principle of the Golden Rule is inherent in this wisdom. In my spiritual life, the ideal of the Golden Rule charges me to contend for the products of what is fair and just, and for the equality of opportunities to become my best self—not Peter, not John, not Ruth, not Esther, but Mary McLeod Bethune. As I received those things that are true, honest, lovely and beautiful, I pray that others shall have them, too. Oh, how I love to open the doors to let people in to a fuller experience. I liked to hear one of my women in the Council express her appreciation for the "open door" which, in their opinion, I have made. She said that if Mrs. Bethune can but get into the doorway, she will stand there and hold the door open so that other women may pass through. The glory of this action from me impresses me that I am building the tomorrow. I must open the doors to fuller life—I must open many of them—as I pass this way, so that there may be greater realities and varieties for the people who come after me. With this type of spiritual interpretation, I am strongly *inter*-denominational, *inter*-racial and *inter*-national.

From this kind of prompting came my desire to unite all of the Negro organizations of women. The National Council of Negro Women purports to blend the energies, the faiths, the aspirations, the abilities and powers of all the Negro women in order that those who have leadership gifts may use them for the good of the whole. Through this organization we hope to make and further relationships with other groups of women throughout the world. We extend the collective hand and add beauty and force to our voices as we plan together and work together with courage, self-reliance and heroism.

My spiritual philosophy provides a full life for me. I give my best at all times and accept without complaint the results. I expect the best. Life is full and joyous and after three score and ten years, I know the secret of peaceful living. I am not waiting for peace and happiness to come to me in another world. I am enjoying it here day by day. Because of this growing, giving, learning experience, I believe that I shall have greater capacity for receiving when I shall see Him who is the foundation for my life. We hear much about "readiness" today in the field of education; readiness to read, readiness to act; readiness to learn. I am in a state of spiritual readiness at all times. I am ready to read the signs of the times and interpret them for my people, for the world. I am ready to act with faith and love and wisdom for justice and progress and peace. I am ready to keep an open mind—to follow the guides toward upward trends and forward progress which will make our world the ONE GREAT WORLD—A world where all men are brothers.

Original manuscript in Mary McLeod Bethune Papers, Mary McLeod Bethune Foundation, Bethune-Cookman College, Daytona Beach, Fla.

Address to a World Assembly for
Moral Re-Armament

in Caux, Switzerland, July 27, 1954

This is a more glorious moment now than it was two weeks ago when I entered. I have longed for a moment like this. I want first of all to bring again my gratitude to God for having given to the world a man like Dr. Frank Buchman (founder of Moral Re-Armament) who has so fully surrendered his own life and so definitely permitted God to guide him that he has given to the world this ideology, the something that we all feel will bring mankind together everywhere, if they will only believe and act.

When you see me, you see a representative of 16 million black people in America, and I think of the darker peoples of the world who have been hungering, thirsting, to join hands with mankind everywhere. To join hands with mankind everywhere to bring about a world of peace and brotherhood and understanding.

When I look back 79 years ago, I see myself coming from the home life of slaves. My mother and my father were slaves in America. We were hungry and thirsting for help, for light, for that thing that would help us to grow and become what we believed our God and your God wanted us to be. We wanted light, intelligence; we wanted that spiritual guidance that would guide us into that full manhood and womanhood that could help bless the world. As I look back and realize where I am standing today, I cannot help but ask myself, "What hath God wrought?"

I want here and now to express my gratitude for the opportunities that have been mine, for the doors that have been opened for me that I may be prepared in head, in hand and in heart to lead mankind from darkness and sin and point him to the light. How I thank God for this ideology that has come to us. So simple, so all-inclusive that it places us, as I said to some of my friends, on the lower shelf where all of us regardless of our creed, our class, our color, can reach and become enriched thereof.

The day has come. The hour is here. The clock strikes twelve now in all of our lives to reach out and partake of this great fountain, this stream that offers and flows so freely that we might be of service together. During my years I have been an educator. I have been trying to reach out to help prepare men and women to serve. Just fifty years ago with one dollar and fifty cents, faith in God and a desire to serve, we planted Bethune-Cookman College. There were no schools comparable for the training of my people in that particular section of the country. There was no leadership that would guide them in the paths in which they should go. Because of what God has done for me, because of the spiritual guidance I sought to the extent of my ability, I felt called of Him, as Dr. Buchman and others have felt, to go out and open a way, make a path, that they could follow.

I think now of my imperfections. I think of the four standards that we have as our guide here. I cannot help but express from my heart the feeling in saying how short I have been of the perfection of these standards in my humble life. I think first of my son, my only son, my only child, how I had to leave him in the care of others as I tramped all over America looking for nickels, dimes, dollars and quarters, that I might build an institution that not only my son, but thousands of others might come. I had to neglect him. I could not give to him the care, the guidance, that a tender mother needed to give to a child. He often looked into my face and said, "Mother, the School comes first and I come last." Now when I recognize all the defects in his life and as I have studied myself, I have analyzed these four standards we measure our lives by and I feel that my first apology is to my son Albert, who is waiting for my return.

Now in my 80th year, as I look back and see the thousands and thousands that my life has touched, I am wanting, desiring to unfold to them in whatever medium, or through whatever change I can, the real thoughts that I have found here in Caux. I feel that Caux is providing us the principles to unite the minds and hearts of the peoples of the world, the nations of the world. I feel that this is the cure that we must carry with us, every single one of us, until we can pass it on and on and on, until the entire world shall know.

I have felt this week that this is a great center for the meeting. The uniting of minds and how we team together and the power that we are enabled to send out because of the force of our unity. I have longed to know the peoples of the world. I have longed to feel that I am just a human being, just one among the great creation of mankind. Here I have found no sign of segregation, discrimination. "You have to go through the back door while I go through the front door. You can't have a cup of tea, hear this music, go into this park here," these are words of a segregated nation. Under God we have the peoples of the world who have united their hearts and their minds in such a way that we feel as one.

I am asking Dr. Buchman. I am asking all of you gathered from the several areas of our world to know with me, that even at 80, life just begins in a more perfect way, to carry out the desires, dictations and directions of the God we love and serve.

I know you cannot all remember my name, but you will remember this face, remember this crown of white hair, remember the yearnings of a heart that is pleading for the unity of the world, that all of us may brothers be.

God bless you. God inspire you. God give to Dr. Buchman and to all of the teams that are here years of great service, great meditation, great power and great influence that the place we live in may be a better world.

Today the whole of mankind is faced with the threat of slavery, my experience here has freed me from that threat. The millions of the world have been dreaming, praying, sacrificing and waiting for this idea. I implore you, in this hour of great urgency, to accept this ideology and cure the sickness of this nation.

Either we choose to be governed by God, or we condemn ourselves to be ruled by tyrants. It is God's way or tyranny. The fateful decision of our day is whether or not we will change. I have always worked for the betterment of my people. . . . Today we must upturn the world. I listened to God this morning and the thought came to me, "any idea that keeps anybody out is too small for this age—open your heart and let everybody in—every class, every race, every nation."

> We must remake the world. The task is
> nothing less than that. To be part of
> this great uniting force of our age is
> THE CROWNING EXPERIENCE OF OUR LIFE.

Good-bye, I leave you tomorrow. Pray that my influence might be felt by everyone with whom I come into contact.

The four standards of the Moral Re-Armament are:

- honesty
- purity
- unselfishness
- love

Mary McLeod Bethune Foundation, Bethune-Cookman College, Daytona Beach, Fla.

My Last Will and Testament

(1955)

Sometimes as I sit communing in my study I feel that death is not far off. I am aware that it will overtake me before the greatest of my dreams—full equality for the Negro in our time—is realized. Yet I face that reality without tears or regrets. I am resigned to death as all humans must be at the proper time. Death neither alarms nor frightens one who has had a long career of fruitful toil. The knowledge that my work has been helpful to many fills me with joy and great satisfaction.

Since my retirement from an active role in educational work and from the affairs of the National Council of Negro Women, I have been living quietly and working at my desk at my home here in Florida. The years have directed a change of pace for me. I am now 78 years old and my activities are no longer so strenuous as they once were. I feel that I must conserve my strength to finish the work at hand.

Already I have begun working on my autobiography which will record my life-journey in detail, together with the innumerable side trips which have carried me abroad, into every corner of our country, into homes both lowly and luxurious, and even into the White House to confer with Presidents. I have also deeded my home and its contents to the Mary McLeod Bethune Foundation, organized in March, 1953, for research, interracial activity and the sponsorship of wider educational opportunities. . . .

Sometimes I ask myself if I have any other legacy to leave. Truly, my worldly possessions are few. Yet, my experiences have been rich. From them, I have distilled principles and policies in which I believe firmly, for they represent the meaning of my life's work. They are the product of much sweat and sorrow. Perhaps in them there is something of value. So, as my life draws to a close, I will pass them on to Negroes everywhere in the hope that an old woman's philosophy may give them inspiration. Here, then, is my legacy.

I leave you love. Love builds. It is positive and helpful. It is more beneficial that hate. Injuries quickly forgotten quickly pass away. Personally and racially, our enemies must be forgiven. Our aim must be to create a world of fellowship and justice where no man's skin, color or religion, is held against him. "Love thy neighbor" is a precept which could transform the world if it were universally practiced. It connotes brotherhood and, to me, brotherhood of man is the noblest concept in all human relations. Loving your neighbor means being interracial, interreligious and international.

I leave you hope. The Negro's growth will be great in the years to come. Yesterday, our ancestors endured the degradation of slavery, yet they retained their dignity. Today, we direct our economic and political strength toward winning a more abundant and secure life. Tomorrow, a new Negro, unhindered by race taboos and shackles, will benefit from more than 330 years of ceaseless striving and struggle. Theirs will be a better world. This I believe with all my heart.

I leave you the challenge of developing confidence in one another. As long as Negroes are hemmed into racial blocs by prejudice and pressure, it will be necessary for them to band together for economic betterment. Negro banks, insurance companies and other businesses are examples of successful, racial economic enterprises. These institutions were made possible by vision and mutual aid. Confidence was vital in getting them started and keeping them going. Negroes have got to demonstrate still more confidence in each other in business. This kind of confidence will aid the economic rise of the race by bringing together the pennies and dollars of our people and ploughing them into useful channels. Economic separatism cannot be tolerated in this enlightened age, and it is not practicable. We must spread out as far and as fast as we can, but we must also help each other as we go.

I leave you a thirst for education. Knowledge is the prime need of the hour. More and more, Negroes are taking full advantage of hard-won opportunities for learning, and the educational level of the Negro population is at its highest point in history. We are making greater use of the privileges inherent in living in a democracy. If we continue in this trend, we will be able to rear increasing numbers of strong, purposeful men and women, equipped with vision, mental clarity, health and education.

I leave you a respect for the uses of power. We live in a world which respects power above all things. Power, intelligently directed, can lead to more freedom. Unwisely directed, it can be a dreadful, destructive force. During my lifetime I have seen the power of the Negro grow enormously: it has always been my first concern that this power should be placed on the side of human justice.

Now that the barriers are crumbling everywhere, the Negro in America must be ever vigilant lest his forces be marshaled behind wrong causes and undemocratic movements. He must not lend his support to any group that seeks to subvert democracy. That is why we must select leaders who are wise, courageous, and of great moral stature and ability. We have great leaders among us today: Ralph Bunche, Chaining Tobias, Mordecai Johnson, Walter White, and Mary Church Terrell. (The latter two are now deceased.) We have had other great men and women in the past: Frederick Douglass, Booker T. Washington, Harriet Tubman, Sojourner Truth. We must produce more qualified people like them, who will work not for themselves, but for others.

I leave you faith. Faith is the first factor in a life devoted to service. Without faith, nothing is possible. With it, nothing is impossible. Faith in God is the greatest power, but great, too, is faith in oneself. In 50 years the faith of the American Negro in himself has grown immensely and is still increasing. The measure of our progress as a race is in precise relation to the depth of the faith in our people held by our leaders. Frederick Douglass, genius though he was, was spurred by a deep conviction that his people would heed his counsel and follow him to freedom. Our greatest Negro figures have been imbued with faith. Our forefathers struggled for liberty in conditions far more onerous than those we now face, but they never lost the faith. Their persever-ance paid rich dividends. We must never forget their sufferings and their sacrifices, for they were the foundations of the progress of our people.

I leave you racial dignity. I want Negroes to maintain their human dignity at all costs. We, as Negroes, must recognize that we are the custodians as well as the heirs of a great civilization. We have given something to the world as a race and for this we are proud and fully conscious of our place in the total picture of mankind's development. We must learn also to share and mix with all men. We must make an effort to be less race conscious and more conscious of individual and human values. I have never been sensitive about my complexion. My color has never destroyed my self respect nor has it ever caused me to conduct myself in such a manner as to merit the disrespect of any person. I have not let my color handicap me. Despite many crushing burdens and handicaps, I have risen from the cotton fields of South Carolina to found a college, administer it during its years of growth, become a public servant in the government of our country and a leader of women. I would not exchange my color for all the wealth in the world, for had I been born white I might not have been able to do all that I have done or yet hope to do.

I leave you a desire to live harmoniously with your fellow men. The problem of color is world-wide. It is found in Africa and Asia, Europe and South America. I appeal to American Negroes—North, South, East and West—to recognize their common problems and unite to solve them.

I pray that we will learn to live harmoniously with the white race. So often, our difficulties have made us hyper-sensitive and truculent. I want to see my people conduct themselves naturally in all relationships—fully conscious of their manly responsibilities and deeply aware of their heritage. I want them to learn to understand whites and influence them for good, for it is advisable and sensible for us to do so. We are a minority of 15 million living side by side with a white majority. We must learn to deal with these people positively and on an individual basis.

I leave you finally a responsibility to our young people. The world around us really belongs to youth for youth will take over its future management. Our children must never lose their zeal for building a better world. They must not be discouraged from aspiring toward greatness, for they are to be the leaders of tomorrow. Nor must they forget that the masses of our people are still underprivileged, ill-housed, impoverished and victimized by discrimination. We have a powerful potential in our youth, and we must have the courage to change old ideas and practices so that we may direct their power toward good ends.

Faith, courage, brotherhood, dignity, ambition, responsibility—these are needed today as never before. We must cultivate them and use them as tools for our task of completing the establishment of equality for the Negro. We must sharpen these tools in the struggle that faces us and find new ways of using them. The Freedom Gates are half ajar. We must pry them fully open.

If I have a legacy to leave my people, it is my philosophy of living and serving. As I face tomorrow, I am content, for I think I have spent my life well. I pray now that my philosophy may be helpful to those who share my vision of a world of Peace, Progress, Brotherhood and Love.

Originally published in *Ebony,* August 1955. Copyright 1955 by National Council of Negro Women. Reprinted by permission of the Mary McLeod Bethune Council House National Historic Site, National Park Service, Washington, D.C.

Bethune in a family photograph. *From left to right:* son, Albert M. Bethune, Sr.; grandson, Albert, Jr.; Mary McLeod Bethune; niece, Georgia McLeod (who lived with Bethune for many years); and foster son, Edward Rodriguez.   *Florida State Archives, 1948.*

A young and stylish Mary McLeod Bethune in front of Faith Hall, the first building erected (1907) at the Daytona Educational and Industrial Training School.   *Florida State Archives, circa 1910.*

Bethune crosses a side lawn of her residence (shown in the background), en route to the customary Sunday afternoon "Community Meeting" at Bethune-Cookman College. She designated her home as the site of the Mary McLeod Bethune Foundation in 1953. *Library of Congress, 1943.*

PART III

Educational Leadership

"The Unfolding of My Soul" (1902–1942)

Introduction

Audrey Thomas McCluskey

E VEN AS President Franklin Delano Roosevelt's appointed director of the Negro Division of the National Youth Administration, Mary McLeod Bethune was quick to remind people that she was "not a politician but an educator."[1] This comment served her public relations agenda while she juggled the difficult task of being both a college president and a government bureaucrat, but it also reveals her commitment to what she considered her true calling. Bethune believed that education was the key to advancement and the fulfillment of American democracy for black Americans. Using herself as an example of a life transformed by education—in her case, by the opportunity to attend Scotia Seminary for Negro Girls from 1888 to 1894— she wanted a similar outcome for other blacks, who, at the dawn of freedom, had an illiteracy rate of nearly 95 percent.[2] The establishment and uninterrupted operation of her college altered the public perception of black women's limited prospects in higher education.

Bethune's emphasis on educating black girls reflected her years at Scotia and the popular notion of a "female burden" for racial uplift espoused by her role models such as Scotia graduate Emma J. Wilson and Atlanta University graduate Lucy Craft Laney.[3] Wilson was Bethune's first teacher at Trinity Mission School near Mayesville, South Carolina, and Laney founded Haines Institute in Augusta, Georgia, where Bethune apprenticed in 1896–97. In the early years of her career as an educator, Bethune also taught in South Carolina and rural Palatka, Florida. In 1904, with $1.50 in capital and no guarantee of a salary, she founded her own school, the Daytona Literary and Industrial Training School for Negro Girls, to help black girls "earn a living."[4] The first students—five girls aged six through twelve and her five-year-old son, Albert—attended classes in a rented house in the black section of Daytona. They studied at makeshift desks, using ink made of elderberry juice. The curriculum reflected Bethune's indoctrination into the industrial education movement as championed by Booker T. Washington and the white political-industrial elite who supported him. The tenuous existence of most black schools in the South necessitated a curriculum that accommodated Southern racism, the circumscribed job market, and the paternalism of Northern philanthropy. Bethune's negotiation of these boundaries showed the pragmatism that became the imprimatur of her public life.

Bethune chose the resort mecca of Daytona Beach, winter home to Northern millionaires, in part because it offered better financial prospects. Located on the route of the Florida East Coast Railroad and home to black settlers from the Reconstruction era as well as newly arriving black laborers, Daytona was an ideal location for Bethune.[5] She received support from the local black churches and volunteers who offered gifts of food, money, equipment, and service. She also courted the wealthy elite—particularly white women's groups such as the elite Palmetto Club—and named powerful white men to her board of trustees, including James Gamble, founder of Procter and Gamble. Thomas White, president of White Sewing Machine Company, was also an early benefactor. The uniqueness of the Bethune school, however, was not in its grassroots origin, its curriculum, or the zealous recruitment of wealthy donors; rather, it was in the charismatic leadership of its founder.

The school grew, adding grades and courses, and enrollment swelled. By 1915, high school courses were listed in the catalogue, an indication of the founder's aspirations for her girls. The value of the physical plant had increased to more than $100,000 by 1920.[6] Although her enthusiasm for vocationalism did not diminish, the need for teachers who could teach higher-level courses pushed Bethune to concentrate on teacher education and to rename the school the Daytona Normal and Industrial Institute. She served as principal of the girls' school until 1923, when, seeking long-term financial stability, she accepted the proposal of the Negro Education Board of the Methodist Episcopal Church to merge with the co-educational Cookman Institute of Jacksonville, Florida.[7] At that time her school had a debt-free physical plant valued at more than $250,000, and a reputation for excellence among educators.[8] The school underwent a series of expansions and name changes, finally becoming the coeducational Bethune-Cookman College.

Bethune hoped that the new financial oversight of the Methodists would provide a reliable annual appropriation and financial stability. However, the actual appropriations, although helpful, often fell short of expectations, failing to alleviate the financial burden that Bethune continually faced. Her biggest financial coup occurred in 1935, when, after years of futile requests, the General Education Board, the philanthropic foundation founded by John D. Rockefeller in 1905, granted Bethune-Cookman College its largest gift ever—$62,000.[9] The need for funding was constant. Meeting operating expenses became a ritualistic experience of groveling for money from all possible sources, and the strain affected her health.[10] Bethune served as president until 1942, then reluctantly relinquished the position because of health problems and advancing age.

The best-known early sources on Bethune's educational initiatives, including Rackham Holt's *Mary McLeod Bethune* (1964) and Sadie Daniel's *Women Builders* (1970), focus on her friendship with wealthy white donors, her skill at institution building, and her outreach to the larger community. Gerda Lerner's *Black Women in White America* (1973) presents Bethune's view of her work as noble and self-sacrificing. While these versions have truth and merit, they ignore important aspects of the story, such as her unrelenting struggle to keep this growing enterprise afloat, and the gender dimensions of her educational vision. There was friction between her and the post-merger Methodist overseers, often over money. During her constant travels, she was ever in search of "new friends" for her school. Her friendship with President Franklin Roosevelt's family helped this cause. The network of black women who founded Bethune clubs, held bazaars and recitals, and launched other fundraising campaigns on behalf of the school has also been a neglected subject.[11]

Black women supported the school at every stage of its development. The first cadre of teachers included Portia Smiley and Frances Keyser, who were among those responsible for developing the two-pronged curriculum of vocational and academic subjects.[12] Bethune never relinquished the sense that she had a special mission to educate black females.

The institution that became Bethune-Cookman College was, in every way, molded upon the beliefs and values of its founder. One of Bethune's characteristics as an educational leader was her ability to absorb the ideas of others and to incorporate them into her programs. Thus her school bore the imprint of important mentors such as Wilson and Laney—black women who inspired Bethune's sense of mission as a teacher and its value in race uplift. From Scotia, where she spent most of her teenage years, she developed a passion for industrial education, and its particular relevance to improving the condition of black women. Booker T. Washington, who made a side trip to her school in 1912, showed her the value of public relations and appealing to white beneficence. Bethune was also blessed with the ability to inspire confidence and loyalty in those who worked with her. For this reason, she was able to attract talented people, especially women, who devoted much of their lives to implementing her dream. These women included Smiley and Keyser in the early years, and later Bertha Mitchell Loving, her devoted secretary, who managed much of the business of the college while Bethune took on weighty national responsibilities in the federal government and in the National Council of Negro Women. Bethune was also aided by a growing national network of supporters who organized fundraisers for the always fiscally challenged college. Her triumphs as an educator, acknowledged in the black press and celebrated with the bestowal of the prestigious Spingarn Award from the NAACP, belied the shaky foundation of the unendowed school. Yet her acclaim was as much a recognition of the pluck and mettle it took to grow and sustain an institution of higher learning under such conditions as it was for the accomplishment itself.

DOCUMENTARY SOURCES

The documents in Part III represent two distinct phases of Bethune's work as an educational leader and institution-builder. The works in the section "School Founder" span the years from 1902 to 1923, when she struggled to develop and maintain her girls' school, and include Bethune's eulogy to the woman most instrumental in that process, Frances Reynolds Keyser. The second section, "College President," extends from the 1923 merger with Cookman Institute to her retirement in 1942, forced by illness and the pull of her NYA job in Washington, D.C. The early documents show a confident young school founder-teacher, passionate in her sense of mission, bold and strategic in her cultivation of support from others. Bethune mailed the solicitation letter to Booker T. Washington (1902) from Palatka, where she operated a small mission school prior to moving to the "greener pastures" of Daytona in 1904. She wrote many letters to powerful people, including notable representatives of white Northern philanthropy such as Robert Ogden, chairman of the Hampton Institute board of trustees and founding member of the General Education Board. The GEB coordinated grants to Southern schools, and Ogden was, according to James D. Anderson, responsible for bringing together Northern philanthropy and white Southern educational reformers.[13] These efforts showed Bethune's dogged persistence, but produced few immediate results.

An excerpt from the earliest complete extant catalogue of the Bethune girls' school (1910–11) shows the rapid expansion of the school's faculty and a 500 percent increase in enrollment in just six years. At that time Bethune employed six teachers, all females. The catalogue, which begins with a brief overview of the work accomplished to date, shows the strong industrial focus of the curriculum. The school's stated aim was "to send forth women who will be rounded homemakers and Christian leaders." The grammar and model school curriculum lists "English," "Biblical," and "Industrial" as areas of study. Like all catalogues, it served as an effective public relations instrument to advertise and to garner donations. It was also one of the earliest documents produced by the fledgling school to show the range of course development and school organization.

Bethune's pleading letter to Sears, Roebuck founder Julius Rosenwald (1915) was sent two years before he established the Rosenwald Fund for rural school construction in 1917. Bethune was probably motivated by the philanthropist's $25,000 donation to Booker T. Washington in 1912, to be dispersed to black schools that followed Hampton-Tuskegee's industrial education model. There is no known record of Bethune's having received any of this money. Gradually, Bethune refined her technique and began to use a more personal tone in her courtship of the white establishment. Her letter to the local newspaper, the *Daytona Morning Journal* (1915), emphasized that her school should be seen not as a threat to whites but as in their best interests, and therefore it deserved their support. The short open letter to the *New York Times* (1920) is one of several that Bethune sent to the newspaper in which she promoted her school as providing a benefit for white people. Cognizant of the volatile racial climate of the early 1900s, she stressed themes such as vocationalism and Christian morality in her efforts to attract contributors beyond black churches and community groups. Her approach was to build a two-tiered group of local and national supporters.

While Bethune's emphasis on vocationalism is the best-known of her educational ideas, "A Philosophy of Education for Negro Girls" [1920] provides a fuller explanation of the educational views she absorbed at Scotia Seminary. This speech reflects the influence of "the cult of true womanhood," a set of beliefs widely disseminated among middle-class white women, especially those educated in seminaries during the middle and late nineteenth century. It advocated women's special but restricted role as torchbearers of piety and domesticity.[14] Yet unlike "true women," Bethune sought a life for black girls beyond the quiet domestic sphere. She espoused a curriculum that would teach girls to express the "inner urges that [made] them distinctive" as they pursued responsible work. Her letter to "big sister" Margaret Murray Washington, widow of Booker T. Washington, expressed her delight at the prospect of the school's expansion and merger. It also shows the connections and shared motives among the network of black club women, whose leadership consisted primarily of educators engaged in the weighty work of "race uplift."

The death of her longtime associate Frances Reynolds Keyser was a personal blow to the usually composed Bethune. In her eulogy (1932), Bethune expressed deep appreciation for her friend, acknowledging her less publicized but pivotal contribution to the school. In 1912 Bethune had convinced Keyser, an established and respected educator and graduate of Hunter College, to leave her supervisory position at New York's White Rose Mission settlement and join her in Daytona. This marked a crucial turning point for the as yet undistinguished school. Keyser, working as a virtual "academic dean,"[15] revamped the curriculum and helped the school become a respected academic institution. Her capable presence and the addition of other dedicated female faculty allowed Bethune to concentrate on fundraising and the administrative tasks associated with becoming the first black woman college president.

The "College President" phase of Bethune's educational leadership coincided with her increasing visibility within the black women's club movement. Her board of trustees accepted the proposal for merging with Cookman Institute of Jacksonville, Florida, offered by the Board of Education for Negroes of the Methodist Episcopal Church on April 17, 1923.

Overlapping Bethune's ascendancy to the college presidency was her election as the first woman president of the National Association of Teachers in Colored Schools, the forerunner of the all-black American Teachers Association, which was meant to parallel the then all-white National Education Association. The NATCS membership consisted of a diverse group of college presidents, public school teachers, principals, and others involved in education. The goal of the organization was to improve the professional skills of black teachers and to raise educational standards in black schools. In her annual presidential address (1924), Bethune vigorously promoted the organization as "the voice" of black people on educational matters. She exhorted the membership to become politically involved and to take direct action on behalf of schools in their home communities. In an effort to professionalize the organization, she supported the hiring of an executive director to manage its affairs.

Bethune's letter to P. J. Maveety (1926), secretary of the Methodist Episcopal Board of Education for Negroes, who made the initial contact with Bethune about Methodist affiliation, is another indication that the new relationship did not provide the financial security that Bethune had envisioned. It also reveals Bethune's behind-the-scenes attempt to get the board to assume more of the financial burden. That same year the advisory board voted to rename the school in honor of Bethune and Cookman Institute founder Alfred Cookman. In a detailed letter to fellow club woman and school founder Charlotte Hawkins Brown (1927), Bethune wrote about both personal and professional issues, including her candid thoughts and frustrations about running a school with no money. She considered Brown, principal of the prestigious Palmer Memorial Institute in Sedalia, North Carolina, a kindred spirit throughout their lifelong friendship.

In 1929, Bethune issued the Twenty-fifth Annual Report to the board of trustees, which highlighted the continuing evolution of the curriculum and the inclusion of more liberal arts courses in her quest for collegiate standing and accreditation. (The Association of Colleges and Secondary Schools granted accreditation in 1931.) The report reveals the constraints and pressure of functioning largely without an endowment. It details the precarious state of the school's finances and reveals that the centerpiece of Bethune's self-help philosophy, the labor-intensive school-operated farm, was barely breaking even. Bethune referred to that Depression year as one of "insurmountable financial difficulties." Nevertheless, she celebrated the school's silver anniversary by announcing that the college was on its way to reaching perfection in its expanding academic curriculum, as well as in the more established vocational courses.

Bethune continued an upbeat campaign for a united front among black educators. In the essay "A Common Cause" (1932), she implored the members of the Florida State Teachers Association to work together and to speak with a united voice, rather than as competitors. Bethune's strong ties with the black community are exemplified in organizational structures such as the FSTA, which were built upon personal relationships. One of the most steadfast of those relationships was with a lifelong friend and supporter of Bethune-Cookman College, Mrs. Ada M. Lee of Jacksonville. Lee organized and presided over the first Bethune Circle, whose constitution listed as its stated purpose "the uplift of humanity generally and the fostering of Bethune-Cookman College."[16] Bethune's network of black women supporters, exemplified by Lee's friendship and devotion, was crucial to her success in both her school and women's organizations.

While "A Philosophy of Education for Negro Girls" iterates Bethune's views regarding girls, "The Educational Values of the College-Bred" (1934) was a more comprehensive statement about the role and function of higher education. Addressing the graduating class of Hampton Institute, the alma mater of Booker T. Washington, Bethune called education "the great American adventure" that makes real the promise of democracy for all its citizens. In some ways it was the conventional commencement speech, exhorting the graduates to live committed lives of service to humanity. Bethune also took advantage of Hampton's emphasis on teacher training to impart her views on the transformative role of teachers in society.

The letter to Jackson Davis of the General Education Board (1935) seeking assistance for the school is one example of many requests that she sent out. But her persistence paid off in 1934, when the John D. Rockefeller–backed General Education Board finally made a $62,000 grant to Bethune-Cookman, the largest the school had ever received. That acknowledgment of Bethune's educational leadership was followed by her being awarded the National Association for the Advancement of Colored People's revered Spingarn Medal for promoting black progress and racial harmony. Bethune accepted the award (1935) in the "name of women" and urged others to work to make educational opportunity available to the masses.

Female support continued to be an important dimension of Bethune's educational initiative throughout her presidency and beyond. She relied on a national network of women friends and supporters, both black and white. Her correspondence with these women reveals numerous instances of their generosity toward the school and Bethune. The letter to Mrs. Ferris Meigs (1935) of Bronxville, New York—the daughter of educator Sarah Lawrence—is an example. Mrs. Meigs financed a vacation for Bethune. Bethune ingratiated herself with these women by mixing flattering personal remarks with her appeal for funds. Of this group, Eleanor Roosevelt was her most flaunted friend. Bethune's ingratiating tone in her letter to the First Lady (1941) partially obscures her more serious objective, which was to inform and educate Mrs. Roosevelt about the conditions and aspirations of black Americans. Bethune-Cookman College deserved support, she told Mrs. Roosevelt, because it was not "just another school," but a symbol of black self-help and achievement. Bethune later wrote directly to President Roosevelt (1941) to ask for his help. In this letter, she gently reminded him that she had answered his call to service when he asked her to leave her college to become deputy director of the National Youth Administration.

While she was still serving in Washington, Bethune wrote to Bethune-Cookman College trustee Harry Wright McPherson, arguing that "Bethune-Cookman's Next Urgent Step" (1938) should be to return the school to its previous all-female status. This shows her lasting focus on female uplift and leadership, and perhaps a look over her shoulder at the ascendancy of the all-female Spelman and Bennett colleges. At the time, Bethune was hardly in her strongest negotiating position. She was spending most of her time in her NYA job in Washington, and serving as only a "part-time" president of Bethune-Cookman. The following year the board published a public response to her memo, affirming that "the boys will stay."[17]

Bethune maintained her part-time presidency until 1942, when increasing health problems and divided responsibilities—if not loyalties—prompted her memorandum to the board of trustees asking to be relieved of her duties as president. She expressed a deep disappointment in not finding a woman to carry on her work. (Bethune resumed an interim presidency for the 1946–47 school year after engineering the ouster of president James Colston.)

Through it all, Bethune referred to the pursuit and realization of her dreams, prayers, and vigilance on behalf of Bethune-Cookman as "the unfolding of my soul." This dedicated but sometimes controversial work was also an affirmation of a half-century of leadership by a woman answering her true calling.

NOTES

1. "Politics Out, Says Bethune," Washington *Afro-American,* February 23, 1939, p. 1.
2. James D. Anderson, *The Education of Blacks in the South, 1860–1935* (Chapel Hill: University of North Carolina Press, 1988), p. 16.
3. Throughout her life, Bethune continued to emphasize the importance of educating women, whom she considered to have a civilizing effect on the world.
4. Walter Bowie, *Women of Light* (New York: Harper and Row, 1963), p. 123.
5. T. E. Fitzgerald, *Volusia County: Past and Present* (Daytona Beach, 1937), p. 197.
6. Benjamin P. Brawley, *Two Centuries of Methodist Concerns: Bondage, Freedom, and Education of Black People* (New York: Vantage Press, 1974), p. 185.
7. Sheila Y. Flemming, *The Answered Prayer to a Dream: Bethune-Cookman College, 1904–1994* (Daytona Beach: Doninger Publishers, 1995), p. 32.
8. Elaine M. Smith, "Black Female Icon: Mary McLeod Bethune, 1875–1955" (manuscript version), Introduction to *The Mary McLeod Bethune Papers: The Bethune-Cookman College Collection, 1922–1955* (Bethesda, Md.: University Publications of America, 1995).
9. *The Mary McLeod Bethune Papers: The Bethune-Cookman College Collection, 1922–1955,* reel 6 (Bethesda, Md.: University Publications of America, 1995).
10. Bethune suffered from severe asthma, which was aggravated by stress.
11. The first Bethune Circle was incorporated in 1934 in Jacksonville, Florida. The by-laws stated that its mission was "for the uplift of humanity generally and the fostering of Bethune-Cookman College." Ada M. Lee, its founder, was a stalwart among a phalanx of black women supporters. Similar efforts, formal and informal, were led by black women in other cities. *The Mary McLeod Bethune Papers: The Bethune-Cookman College Collection, 1922–1955,* reel 9.
12. Audrey Thomas McCluskey, "Mary McLeod Bethune and the Education of Black Girls, 1904–1923" (Ph.D. diss., Indiana University, 1991), chap. 4.
13. Anderson, p. 86.
14. Barbara Welter, *Dimity Convictions: The American Woman in the Nineteenth Century* (Athens: Ohio University Press, 1976), chap. 1.
15. Flemming, p. 28.
16. *Mary McLeod Bethune Papers: The Bethune-Cookman College Collection, 1922–1955,* reel 9: 0551, "The Bethune Clubs" (Bethesda, Md.: University Publications of America, 1996).
17. Flemming, p. 62.

School Founder

Letter to Booker T. Washington

(1902)

Palatka, Fla.,
Nov. 3rd 1902

Honored Sir:

I hope a note of this kind may not greatly surprise you, as a man in your sphere must expect such.

I am engaged in a Mission work in this town and I greatly desire your interest in it. It is an Interdenominational work therefore [it] has no support. It is a work that is most sadly needed to be done, and it takes great sacrifices to get it in shape. I have a rented room where I gather the poor an[d] neglected children and teach them daily. Aside from this I do general city mission work, the jail work included. I have no support what ever save some few of the children who are able to pay a little tuition. Now I would like to ask you, would you recommend this humble work to some friend asking their assistance? Would you yourself make a donation toward helping us secure an organ for the Mission room? Do you know any friend who would even send a few [articles of] clothing to be used for the poor? God has wonderfully blessed you and used you and I know He will be pleased to have you lend your influence towards the sustenance of this work.

I trust you may consider well before answering.

Very respectfully,
Mary McLeod Bethune

Booker T. Washington Papers, Library of Congress, Washington, D.C.

Letter to Robert Ogden

(1905)

SEPT. 11, 1905
Mr. Robert Ogden
New York

Dear Sir:

Learning of your interest in the uplifting of fallen humanity and your deep sympathy for the less fortunate, I venture to acquaint you with our effort here and to ask your cooperation and assistance in the work we are endeavoring to carry on.

We have planted the above named institution here for the training of Negro girls. They are in sore need of some wholesome training to prepare them for usefulness in this life.

I shall enclose one of the announcements and beg that you read it carefully,—and then if in your mind you deem it a worthy work, please aid us to the extent of your judgment. Our Father will repay you.

> Gratefully,
> Mary McLeod Bethune

Folder 303, box 33, RG 1.1, General Education Board Archives, Rockefeller Archive Center, Sleepy Hollow, N.Y.

Sixth Annual Catalogue of the Daytona Educational and Industrial Training School for Negro Girls

[abridged] (1910–11)

THE WORK ACCOMPLISHED TO DATE

The Daytona Educational and Industrial Training School was founded in October 1904 to meet the pressing needs of our people for systematic training and education, domestic and industrial. From a five-room cottage with five pupils and one teacher, the institution has grown to a commodious four-story building with thirty-five rooms, including dormitory, kitchen and laundry, and all modern conveniences when fully completed. There is ample space on the campus for larger additions when required. The support of the public and those interested in our work has been generous, but it will require continuous assistance to enable us to carry on the work for some years to come and until the institution is placed in position where it becomes self-supporting.

The Board of Trustees is planning to enlist the active financial assistance of the several institutions throughout the nation who have control of endowment funds, set aside for such purposes as our school has in view, by philanthropic founders. We hope to receive ample support from this source before long.

Our present enrollment is one hundred and two students, seventy-six in the boarding department, with six teachers. Already there is pressing demand for additional land to extend the buildings and to provide for the raising of garden truck, dairy produce and poultry to supply the school with fresh food and supplies direct from the soil. Negotiations are under way to secure an adjoining tract to cover these needs and $4000 are required to consummate this deal.

The funds to carry on the work of the school so far have been raised by subscription, volunteer contributions and the proceeds from public entertainments. But it has been hard and continuous work to keep an even balance and has mainly fallen upon the shoulders of the founder who makes the success of the undertaking her life problem.

A revision of the present charter is under consideration by the Board of Trustees looking for an extensive membership enrollment and regular contributions from this source. May we urge upon all in sympathy with our work to enlist further active support in our behalf and the bringing about of still greater results for the good of our race.

COURSE OF STUDY

The course of study at the present shall be English, Biblical and Industrial.

English Department
The special aim of this department is to supply the mental training our young women so sadly need, and to enable those who are especially adapted to training the minds of others to take up that specific work.

Industrial Department
It is the sole object of this department to teach girls, theoretically and practically, the performance of the duties of the household and to assist in the training of skillful, economical and self-supporting young women. There is no work more noble or needful than the real care of the home.

Biblical Department
This work is strictly non-sectarian. We seek guidance rather than creed. Daily instruction is given in the study of the Bible. Two quiet periods are observed each day for quiet Bible reading. Regular attendance at church and Sunday school is required. Sunday afternoon practical mission work for street children is conducted by advanced pupils and teachers.

AIM

The aim of this institution is to uplift Negro girls spiritually, morally, intellectually and industrially. The school stands for a broad, thorough practical training. To develop Christian character, to send forth women who will be rounded home-makers and Christian leaders is the aim of its founder and supporters, a trained mind, heart and hand being their idea of a complete education.

Location

This institution is located in the Negro settlement of Daytona known as Midway. Daytona is 110 miles south of Jacksonville, on the East Coast Railway, on the Halifax River. It is the most naturally beautiful town in Florida. Huge oak trees, from which hang graceful festoons of the old Spanish gray moss, form an archway through the principal streets. Orange trees abound. The climate is mild and healthy. Tourists from every section of the country gather here during the winter season. There is no other school of this type south of Jacksonville. All of these conditions tend to make this one of the most desirable places for such an institution in the whole Southland. Send us your girls. Invest your money in such a thriving, hopeful Negro enterprise.

Expenses, Board and Tuition

Entrance fee $2.00 for each student. Day pupils $1.50 per month. Boarding pupils above 12 years, $9.00 per month; below 12 years $10.00 per month.

Vocal music taught free to all students.

Instrumental music to boarding students, $2.00 per month; to outside students $3.00 per month.

All payments are required in advance.

Government and Discipline

We try in governing our school to work by fundamental principles. We think education is as much for the sake of character as for knowledge. The purpose of order is to secure mental application and systemic development. We assume that our students want to know what is proper and right and we expect them to do it as fast as they know it, not because they have to, but because they want to. We teach them the moral law, the rules of propriety and good manners, and to give what is due in respect and obedience. No student is considered a model who either disobeys rules or has to be made to obey them. We are trying to get our students prepared for real life. We cannot and will not keep students who will not, at least, show a willingness to obey the rules and regulations.

OUR RELIGIOUS WORK

It is our object to give a thorough religious training. The supreme need of our people beyond doubt is Christian leadership. There is a crying need among us for women qualified as moral and Christian leaders. We are endeavoring to teach an every-day practical religion. The Bible is prominent in every department of our work. It is the guide of our lives. We feel more keenly than we can express the necessity of preparing the girls entrusted to our care for the great religious duties of life. We believe this to be the foundation of a successful career. They are needed as home makers, wives, teachers and missionaries in destitute places. Our effort here is to meet, if only in part, the great need of prepared women among our people. The very atmosphere of our school has a tendency to draw them nearer the path of right. Two periods a day, morning and evening, are given to each student to tarry alone in the great school of prayer. They must give some public thought each day as a result of private study.

THE READING ROOM

Very few of our students have had access to good books and periodicals before coming here, hence it is an unexpected pleasure to many of them to have placed in their reach these helpful companions. Those who have not a real taste for reading are gradually cultivating it. Good books for girls will be a most appreciat[ed] gift.

GENERAL INFORMATION

This school is open to all worthy young women of all denominations and is strictly nonsectarian. It is desired that all applicants to the boarding department should be at least twelve years of age. By making special arrangements, a very limited number of younger students may be taken. Girls who enter this institution are required to bring recommendation from some trusted person in their community, and a doctor's statement as to health.

Text books cost extra and must be paid for in cash. All payments should be made in advance. Ten days after bills are presented settlement must be made. If they remain unpaid students must return home. When students are sent home on account of unpaid bills, their property will be retained until settlement.

There is an entrance fee of $2.00 for each student. This should accompany application. Each student is required to furnish the following articles: two sheets, two pairs of pillow cases, one blanket, four table napkins, towels, comb, brush and tooth-brush, for their personal use, one white bed spread. Students must have adequate under-clothes, colored petticoats, three ging-ham aprons, work dress, and four white aprons. They will only be allowed white dresses by special permission.

They must bring their own needles, thimbles and scissors. All girls must wear blue dresses, and bring with them a dark blue serge coat suit for church and street uniform and black sailor hats. Positively no jewelry is allowed. Warm flat-heeled shoes with rubber heels must be bought by each student, if not supplied with these they will be placed by the school at the expense of parent or guardian. In addition to these bring rubbers, wrap and umbrella. All articles must be marked with owner's name in indelible ink. Students must bring medium size trunks.

Student's correspondence is subject to inspection and regulations. Stu-dents must be vaccinated before entering school. Students and teachers are required to attend religious services in a body. Students are required to bring Bibles.

School opens for 1910–11, September 14th. School closes on May 14th.

Mary McLeod Bethune Papers, Florida State Archives, Tallahassee.

Letter to Julius Rosenwald

(1915)

Dec. 1, 1915
Mr. Julius Rosenwald
Chicago, Ill.

My dear Mr. Rosenwald:

My work is very much in need of help. We have lost two crops this year from heavy rains. We have been forced to buy every thing for our boarding department. We are six hundred dollars behind with our November ex-penses, this is very unusual. We have one hundred seventy seven dollars in treasure, which will not carry us a week. Will you give us two thousand dollars toward our running expenses? Will you help me now? I am doing my best. My mind is anxious. Let me hear from you.

Thanking you in advance for any consideration.

I am gratefully yours,
Mary McLeod Bethune

P. S. I met you at Mrs. Lathrop's last spring.

Julius Rosenwald Papers, Department of Special Collections, The Joseph Regenstein Library, University of Chicago.

Letter to the Editor, *Daytona Morning Journal*

(1915)

For eleven years we have conscientiously done our best to develop a much-needed institution of Negro girls, in head, hand, and heart, and fitting them for the duties of life. Later were added a hospital for the care of the old and sick among our people, and the training of Negro nurses, and community work among adults and boys. This work has been done without any official recognition from the city in whose interest we were working, as well as our own. Feeling that the work of these years had passed the experimental stage and that the influence of our institution is evident in higher aims, better homes, better conduct among our people in Daytona, in fact that our efforts had made for better citizenship, we solicited a visit of investigation from the Mayor and the City Council. The request was courteously granted and Thursday, Nov. 11, was set for the official visit of this honorable body.

The President and several other members of the Advisory Board were present as the large body of students filed into the chapel to greet the distinguished visitors. The Principal told the council the story of the work, paid a tribute to the city of Daytona, claiming that it offered excellent opportunities and a fair measure of justice to the Negro, pleaded with them to know the race better that their needs might be fully considered and invited them to make a thorough investigation of the entire plant.

The students then sang the Negro folk song "O Freedom" with great enthusiasm, and the Flag Song, composed by two Florida Negroes. A few pointed remarks were made by Mrs. J. D. Maley, the vice-president of the Advisory Board, and then students were dismissed to their classes. In five minutes, every department of the institution was in working order, and guided by the Principal, the city officials made a complete tour of the buildings and grounds. In the class rooms, in the rug and broom rooms, in the basketry class, the plain rowing and dressmaking departments, the model laundry, the domestic science department, the farm, the model home, the business department, the hospital—everywhere the guests found students at work, demonstrating the methods used here, in theory and in actual work. The gentlemen were generous in their praise of all that they saw and heard, saying repeatedly, "We had no idea that this sort of work was being done." They were particularly interested in the special work being done by the vocational classes. The paper modeling in the dressmaking department, the expert work in the model laundry and the advanced work in domestic science, model home, rug room as well as the hospital, elicited strong words of commendation from the distinguished visitors. Resolutions, expressing their impressions will be adopted at their next meeting. We know that our friends will rejoice with us at this latest manifestation of interest and approval.

We desire to express our full appreciation of the broad spirit that was manifested both by the visit of this distinguished body of men and by their friendly attitude and evident interest in all that they found here. Truly we are laboring for the best interests of our beautiful city, in our effort to make a desirable citizenry of our people. We cordially invite the inspection of all of the citizens of Daytona and shall fully appreciate any endorsement of the work or any contribution towards its maintenance.

Yours for service,
Mary McLeod Bethune

"City Officials Visit the Training School: Daytona Educational and Industrial Training School Honored with a Visit from Mayor Titus and the City Council." *Daytona Morning Journal*, November 13, 1915, p. 1.

Letter to the Editor, *New York Times*

(1920)

April 18, 1920
To Help Negro Girls

To the Editor of The *New York Times:*

The Daytona (Florida) Normal and Industrial Institute for Negro Girls is in urgent need of $50,000 for a dormitory. It is essential to the welfare of the institution that this money be provided at once. The institution was founded in 1904 to train Negro girls to be good Christian women and it has well fulfilled its mission. Hundreds of girls have received good educations, forty-seven having completed the full high-school course, and ten being teachers in the State and county schools. Trained nurses from our hospital are rendering service in both white and colored homes.

Here is a home charity capable of exercising a direct influence on the colored race and performing a duty for the white people. It is worthy of the sympathy of the benevolent and deserves their generosity. Subscriptions may be sent to me at the Institute, Daytona, Florida, and will be gratefully acknowledged.

Mary McLeod Bethune
Principal

Hampton University Special Collections, Peabody Newspaper Clippings Collection, Hampton, Va.

Letter to Mrs. Booker T. Washington

(1923)

March 20, 1923
Mrs. Booker T. Washington
Tuskegee Institute
Tuskegee, Alabama

My dear Big Sister:

You don't know how happy I am over the thought of having you visit me. It was so beautiful of you to come. You made a wonderful impression on all the people you met. I want you to look upon this as your winter home. A place where you can come and stay as long as you like.

I have been so busy I feel like I am coming out of a trance, but things are going wonderfully well. The more I think of the proposition that has been made to us by the Board of Education for Negroes, the more pleased I become because to my mind it does insure the future of the school, and after all it is the school that we are most concerned about.

Our Bazaar brought us in $2100.00. I know you are happy to know this. It was a wonderful Bazaar, wasn't it? The ladies are very happy over the results.

Mrs. [Mary Church] Terrell spoke to a very appreciative audience here Sunday afternoon. I think she was very much pleased with all she saw here. They came back elated over their auto drive. I hope you enjoyed it.

I am glad you got a chance to go out to Collier's school. I sent the fruit as you directed. The bill was $3.17. The girls in the cottage miss you very much. They enjoyed serving you.

Mrs. Dickerson went down as far as Miami. She passed through Sunday but did not stop. Dr. Coleman is still with me, she is improving very much. The Dr. seems to think her trouble comes from her teeth.

With every good wish. I am

Sincerely yours,
Mary McLeod Bethune

A Philosophy of Education for Negro Girls

(1926)

For the past seventy years the Negro has experienced various degrees of freedom. That which was given him in the early years of emancipation was more genuine and perhaps more benign than that which, today, he must take. For today he must free himself by reason of his ability and by merit, and by whatever trust and confidence may be found in himself.

A great deal of this new freedom rests upon the type of education which the Negro woman will receive. Early emancipation did not concern itself with giving advantages to Negro girls. The domestic realm was her field and no one sought to remove her. Even here, she was not given special training for her tasks. Only those with extraordinary talents were able to break the shackles of bondage. Phyllis Wheatley is to be remembered as an outstanding example of this ability—for through her talents she was able to free herself from house hold cares that devolved upon Negro women and make a contribution in literary art which is never to be forgotten. The years still re-echo her words.

"Remember, Christians, Negroes, black as Cain
May be refined, and join the Angelic train"

Very early in my life, I saw the vision of what our women might contribute to the growth and development of the race—if they were given a certain type of intellectual training. I longed to see women, Negro women, hold in their hands diplomas which bespoke achievement; I longed to see them trained to be inspirational wives and mothers; I longed to see their accomplishments recognized side by side with any woman, anywhere. With this vision before me, my life has been spent.

Has the Negro girl proved herself worthy of the intellectual advantages which have been given her? What is your answer when I tell you that Negro women stand at the helm of outstanding enterprises; such are Nannie Burroughs, Charlotte Hawkins Brown; they are proprietors of business. We recall Madame Walker and Annie Malone; they are doing excellent work in the field of Medicine, Literary Art, Painting and Music. Of that large group let us mention Mary Church Terrell and Jessie Fauset; Hazel Harrison, Caterina Jarboro and Marian Anderson as beacon lights. One very outstanding woman is a banker. Others are leaders in Politics.

In the rank of average training we witness strivings of Negro women in the school rooms of counties and cities pouring out their own ambitions to see them achieved in the lives of the next generation. The educated Negro girl has lifted the standard of the Negro home so that the present generation is better born and therefore has the promise of a better future.

If there is to be any distinctive difference between the education of the Negro girl and the Negro boy, it should be that of consideration for the unique responsibility of this girl in the world today. The challenge to the Negro home is one which dares the Negro to develop initiative to solve his own problems, to work out his own problems, to work out his difficulties in a superior fashion, and to finally come into his right as an American Citizen, because he is tolerated. This is the moral responsibility of the education of the Negro girl; It must become a part of her thinking; her activities must lead her into such endeavors early in her educational life; this training must be inculcated into the school curricula so that the result may be a natural expression born into her children. Such is the natural endowment which her education must make it possible for her to bequeath to the future of the Negro race.

The education of the Negro girl must embrace a larger appreciation for good citizenship in the home. Our girls must be taught cleanliness, beauty and thoughtfulness and their application in making home life possible. For proper home life provides the proper atmosphere for life everywhere else. The ideals of home must not forever be talked about; they must be living factors built into the everyday educational experiences of our girls.

Negro girls must receive also a peculiar appreciation for the expression of the creative self. They must be taught to realize their responsibility and find ways whereby the home and the schoolroom may encourage our youth to be creative; to develop to the fullest extent the inner urges that make them distinctive and that will lead them to be worthy contributors to the life of the little worlds in which they will live. This in itself will do more to remove the walls of inter-racial prejudice and build up intra-racial confidence and pride than many of our educational tools and devices. This is the Gibraltar that we need. Lest it be sunken in the sea of carelessness and improper emphasis, let us, quickly, set it upon the table and let us stress this standard of conduct and individual creative nurture in the education of our girls. The spiritual reactions are sure to harmonize when we safeguard this phase of our education.

Negro women have always known struggle. This heritage is just as much to be desired as any other. Our girls should be taught to appreciate it and welcome it.

> "Let mine be a hearty soul that wins
> By mettle and fairness and pluck
> A heart with the freedom of soaring winds
> That never depends on luck!"

This characteristic should be sought in that ardent way. Every Negro girl should pray for that pioneering spirit. Let her Arithmetic, History, Economics and what not, be taught with the zeal of struggle; the determination to win by mettle and fairness and pluck. For such she needs after she leaves the school life and enters the Life's school.

> "God give us girls—the time demands
> Strong girls, good girls, true girls with willing hands;
> Girls whom the world's gold cannot buy,
> Girls who possess opinions and a will;
> Girls who honor and will not lie
> Girls who can stand before the motley crowd
> And down its treacherous flatteries without winking
> Tall girls, sun-crowned Girls whose voices cry aloud
> And give us a challenge to the whole world's thinking."

Mary McLeod Bethune Papers, Amistad Research Center, Tulane University, New Orleans, La., Box 2, Folder 13.

A Tribute to My Friend and Co-Worker, Frances Reynolds Keyser

(1932)

Frances Reynolds Keyser was a rare gift of Providence. Her high intelligence bordered on genius, and was so matured through erudition that she radiated culture and refinement to any environment of which she found herself a part. Her gentle virtues, her sweet benevolence, her womanly intuition and broad wisdom were such as people in past ages were wont to ascribe to saints,— personal attributes of those who were canonized after death. In grateful memory of my past associations with her in a mutual labor of love, I would offer this simple tribute to the memory of her gracious personality and benevolent influence.

It was twenty years ago when we first met. I had gone to New York City in search of friends for my work in Florida. I had heard and read of Mrs. Keyser, but I did not know her. I had been informed that she was supervising the work of the White Rose Mission in New York, and I found my way to that center, and made myself known to her. The next morning she came down to the barren room which was my lodging, and I opened my heart to her regarding my vision and the task to which I had set myself in the far South. As she listened to my story, great tears welled up in her eyes.

"I love Florida," she said. "I have given the best of my life to it, teaching and directing the youths who have come to the Florida A. & M. College in Tallahassee. My dear, if you will take me with you, I will give the balance of my life to the development of the work which is so close to your heart." And there, in that dingy little room on West 53rd Street, on bended knees and with clasped hands, we bowed together and sealed our compact, pledging our allegiance to God and to each other in the building up of the institution now known as Bethune-Cookman College. From that moment, Frances Keyser became very near and dear to me, and during the years, our personal and professional friendship grew and grew until it formed a spiritual union and communion that can never be described.

At the close of that first memorable interview, she took me, in her gentle, beautiful manner, from that small, dark room to the White Rose Mission where she installed me in brighter, more comfortable quarters.

She came to work here when we had little of material compensation to offer; but she gave untiringly of her service in every phase of the work. Oh, how she stood by me in my efforts to build up the system! How earnestly she labored to bring in that academic and cultural atmosphere which she, only, could insure! She was tireless in her efforts to promote higher stands for the school. Very often Mrs. Keyser and I would work all day, and then all night. She never grew weary of her task. She believed in me and in the ideals I sought to instill into the young girls who came to our institution.

For ten years she served—not only the school itself, but the community and state. She entered the club work of Florida—so much in need of inspiration—and served as president of the State Federation of Colored Women's Clubs for many years. She had served, formerly, as president of the Empire State Federation of New York; and her experience and outstanding academic ability made her invaluable to our women here. She exerted great influence for progress in the educational program of the state. And how well she was able to do this! for she was an honor graduate of Hunter College of New York. It is impossible to estimate the full value of her contribution in the laying of the foundation for genuine training in this school and throughout Florida.

Mrs. Keyser was never inactive in her service to our institution. During the past ten years she has endured acute physical suffering in her home in New York City. But through it all, she has been miraculously patient, and her physical illness has seemed to strengthen her ardent love for humanity and her splendid faith. As long as her fingers could hold a pen, she made use of her admirable ability as a writer in our behalf. After the use of her hands was gone, through her friends and relatives in New York she dictated messages of cheer to us when the hours were dark here—messages of love and encouragement. The weight of her prayers was felt in every crisis.

We are thankful that the school was able, in a small way, to administer to her material needs during those last days of confining illness. Her contribution to the building of this institution serving, annually, hundreds of young men and women, was an investment from which the most significant dividends were the Master's "Well done!", the appreciation of those who worked with her and the development of those young people who came under her influence.

Students, teachers and friends of Bethune-Cookman College, and the Women of Florida and the Nation offer a tribute of love and gratitude to the memory of Frances Reynolds Keyser. She has gone on to her reward of peace and freedom from pain but her outstanding character will serve as a star to all who have known and loved her. We offer this tribute to her spiritual firmness, to her dauntless vision of service, to her peerless literary qualifications, to her all-embracing love for mankind.

The Advocate 28 (September 1932), pp. 3–4. P. K. Yonge Library of Florida History, University of Florida, Tallahassee.

College President

President's Annual Address to the National Association of Teachers in Colored Schools

[abridged] *(1924)*

Mr. Chairman, Fellow Teachers, Ladies and Gentlemen:

It is with a mingled sense of pride and humility that I stand before you tonight. Pride in the honor that you have bestowed upon me by placing me, a woman, for the first time in the history of this organization, in the presidency! Pride in my profession, with its long unbroken record of service that stretches as far back as the first longing of men to know! Pride in the glory which is the crown that adorns the sacrifice and travail of spirit that we alone who labor in this field know. Pride in the achievement of the teachers of my group who in the face of handicaps, greater than have ever been placed in the path of the world's workers have led a race from darkness to light; from ignorance to the blessed promise of knowledge. And I stand in unfeigned humility before the large trust that has been placed in me and in you, my fellow-workers, when we are called to have a part in the task of converting the children and youth of today into the citizenry of a reconstructed world tomorrow.

I want to take this opportunity, too, to thank our capable executive secretary, and all who have cooperated so loyally with him to bring to pass what we see here tonight. This meeting more than justifies the wisdom shown in creating and making permanent the office of executive secretary of this Association, in order that it may become for the race and for the Nation a powerful and efficiently managed educational organization.

To say that organization is the watchword of the age—the driving force behind this generation, is to utter a platitude. Men have accepted long ago as the fact which lies at the basis of all social achievement, that men were not created to live to themselves alone. Only as they labor together under trusted leaders whose ideals and methods they can trust, can they hope to possess the boundless heritage handed down them from the ages that are past. So thoroughly has the spirit of organization taken possession of our age, that it is seen in the play of children, in the budding social activities of adolescence, and in the manifold interests of early youth and manhood. Every ideal, every cherished dream, every radical program, has its coterie of ardent believers banded together by oaths and bylaws; by pledges and by grips and passwords, for the purpose of perpetuating them and handing them on for the amelioration of the world and the uplifting of mankind.

And it is no accident that this spirit of organization is the most compelling fact in modern life. Our institutions are so complex and far reaching; our problems are so bound up with the destiny of all men everywhere; the tasks we have set ourselves to so herculean; the responsibility we have accepted for the general welfare of the sons of men so boundless that only as hearts and hands and brains are harnessed and directed could results, creditable to our day and generation, be obtained.

I need not in this presence cite examples in support of my assertion. We have only to turn our heads, or to stretch forth our hands to be fully conscious of the complete bending of our generation to its prevailing spirit. In art and letters; in science and invention; in commerce and trade; in the professions and callings, and in politics, religion and philanthropy, individual effort and contributions are made more possible and more effectual through the strength and power of organization. The most outstanding and convincing evidence of the larger human service that can be rendered through organization, is the increase in the number of chain retail stores handling the staple commodities of daily consumption. One famous retail grocery concern has ten thousand stores scattered all over the country from coast to coast. Over three hundred million dollars represents the annual receipts of these stores. Better goods, more efficient service, lower prices, standardized quality and more scientific and sanitary methods of handling food products are some of the beneficent social results accruing from organization on a big scale in this basic human service. The cigar and tobacco business, the drug business, the five and ten cent notion and department stores, restaurants and news service, are other notable examples of what can be accomplished through organization as the way of raising the standard of production and service in the retail trade. The great industrial combinations which for almost two generations have been the marvels of the world and the greatest empire builders in the history of mankind bear eloquent testimony to the irresistible sweep of the dreams, the constructive thought, and material resources of men when they are merged and masterfully directed. The American people today bid fair to be the masters of the world because they are masters of the science and art of co-operative effort in nearly every field and phase of their social, family and political life.

It is a lesson that has been learned all too tardily by our group. Every close student of our social life; every critic, friendly or otherwise, of the magnificent effort we have made to fully take on the civilization in the world in which we have been placed, makes the same entry on the debit side of our account. The achievements of individuals and of small groups in selected fields have in many instances been worthy of the highest praise. In his religious and fraternal institutions, the Negro has shown his greatest accomplishment through organized effort. His extensive and valuable church property holdings; his lodge buildings and rapidly increasing numbers of magnificent fraternal temples; the large sums of money raised annually for the support of churches and their allied social and philanthropic activities; the vast sums paid in and disbursed for the beneficial and protective aspects of his fraternal orders would prove beyond the shadow of a doubt that the Negro is not incapable of being directed by the spirit of the age in which he lives. Of recent years encouraging signs of an increasing ability and willingness to organize have shown themselves among our group.

The National Medical Association is proving an effectual means of raising the standard of the medical profession throughout the entire country and of bringing to the laity a knowledge of preventive medicine and the importance of the establishment and use of properly conducted hospitals that could not be gained through any other channels. The National Negro Business League, founded by the late Booker T. Washington and carried forward by his distinguished successor, has done more to encourage and foster the growth and expansion of Negro business than anything else in the history of the race. Its leadership has been progressive and far-visioned; its program has been constructive; its ideals sound. It has been the means of helpful and productive organization among some of the special businesses composing its membership, and the last child of its creation—the National Negro Finance Corporation—to safeguard the establishment and sound development of Negro business and industry—should [become a] powerful addition to the agenc[y's] function. . . . In the more advanced social services . . . we have the Urban League and the N.A.A.C.P. These bodies are convincing the most skeptical that collective action obtain more recognition in industry, . . . and at the bar of public sentiment than all the individual or isolated endeavor, however able it may be, that can be exercised. Mention should also be made of the National Association of Colored Women, and the magnificent program of racial and civic service which in the past ten years they have promulgated. If nothing else has been accomplished, the securing of the home of Frederick Douglass as a shrine for Negroes of all generations to serve as a concrete embodiment of their struggles, their aspirations and their triumphs would more than glorify the organized efforts of our Negro women.

Fellow teachers, the facts that I have brought to your attention present a powerful challenge to us. Those of us gathered here at this convention are a pitiful representation, large though the number of delegates may be, of the thousands who are engaged in the most vitally important work of humanity—the training of men and women to carry on in the next generation. Forty or more thousand of us are scattered all over the length and breadth of the land. Our problems are more vexing, our difficulties more real and trying, our objectives loftier and more difficult to reach, and our obligations more sacred than in any other field of the world's work. The National Educational Association, which recently closed a notable session in Washington, D.C., represents an organization of nearly one hundred and fifty thousand white teachers so profoundly conscious of the magnitude of their job that they have called to it the collective strength and inspiration of their organized profession. No agency in the country is doing more to raise the quality and standard of education than the N.E.A. Its word, representing the collective opinion of thousands of teachers, is rapidly becoming the last word in educational action, whether it be by legislatures or boards of trustees. Do I need remind you of the pressing demand for such organization among the teachers of our group? The National Association of Teachers in Colored Schools is an effort to meet this demand. But up until the present it can only be rated as a very feeble effort. Three hundred members of this Association cannot speak for thirty-seven hundred others. The time has come to plan a program that will appeal to the teachers of Negro youth throughout the entire country. It is our plain duty to search out the cause of their indifference and if possible to remove it. There are other organizations of a local character which are attempting to perform for their communities a service which should find its origin and direction in our National Association. . . . [unrecovered text] [To pledge that every] child's . . . right to an education [should be] limited only by his capabilities, is our plain duty. To pledge ourselves to the defeat of the Sterling Read Bill which would lend Federal sanction and support to the unjust discrimination against the Negro child in education in all the Southern states is our sacred obligation. To lend our moral support and, if possible, financial assistance through scholarships to the students of our group who are furthering their special training for the work of teaching in our colleges and universities should be our privilege. My fellow teachers, this great big God-given task of ours of training a restless, eager generation for the arduous duties of the coming day is too overwhelming for us to undertake alone. It needs our combined strength and learning and prayers and faith! Let those of us who have dreamed the dreams and seen the visions, never cease to carry on nor grow faint or weary in the task of bringing into a strong, mighty organization for leadership in the work of Negro education the forty thousand or more black men and women who have heard and obeyed the divine call to teach.

That our association may more fully perform the service which was in the minds of those who were responsible for its organization, I desire, in conclusion, to make the following definite recommendations:

First: That the National Association of Teachers in Colored Schools go on record as being the channel through which the voice of the people shall be heard in all matters touching the education of our group, whether they be national or local.

Second: That as soon as possible a full-time executive secretary be secured. . . .

Fellow teachers, this is no time to parley or hesitate. The gauntlet is down, the challenge is out. It is ours to meet it in the might of our organized strength, and through this organization make known our educational needs and rights, and contend for every educational privilege, vouchsafed to our children as the coming citizens of a free democracy.

The Bulletin [periodical of the National Association of Teachers in Colored Schools]. Tuskegee University Special Collections and Archives, Tuskegee, Ala.

Letter to P. J. Maveety

(1926)

December 15, 1926
Dr. P. J. Maveety
Chicago, Illinois

My dear Dr. Maveety:

I have just arrived in my office, and I have found things in splendid condition. I had a conference with Mr. Gamble and Mr. Brown [members of the B-CC Board of Trustees]—with the latter, in fact, for Mr. Gamble simply sat and listened without a word, and Mr. [Brown] did all of the talking. I asked for some assistance on this deficit of $22,000.00, but Mr. Brown refused to allow Mr. Gamble to give a dollar until something is done by some of the other trustees. He stated that, if the other trustees will give something, Mr. Gamble will give further contributions. I feel that it is very unlikely that we shall get any more money from Mr. Gamble, for Mr. Brown's attitude, in the whole affair, is very discouraging.

I found the school in wonderful condition, with the exception of there being no money. We have none with which to pay our bills—now what can we do? Would your Board be willing to borrow a sufficient amount of money to tide us over? You have our properties, and we have plenty to stand back of us on a loan. Our creditors are piling in now, and they are pushing us unmercifully. Times are so hard here with everybody. We would like to know, therefore, if it will not be possible for you to borrow ten or fifteen thousand dollars for us in order that we may settle up some of the most pressing bills.

Will you be kind enough to send me a copy of Dr. Seaton's report as quickly as possible? I want it for the early part of next week. I want to thank you for your attendance upon the meeting in Cincinnati.

Mary McLeod Bethune

Mary McLeod Bethune Papers, Mary McLeod Bethune Foundation, Bethune-Cookman College, Daytona Beach, Fla.

Letter to Charlotte Hawkins Brown

(1927)

October 27, 1927

My dear Charlotte:

It delights my heart to know that you are in Wellesl[e]y, studying to make more permanent the excellent foundation that you have for your educational work.

I am so happy that you had a Tour abroad this summer and regretted exceedingly that I did not get to see you in Europe. It was such a joy to see you and Miss Glover at Lucerne. I was so sorry that I did not see you in Paris. I gave you the name of my hotel, and expected that some word would have come for me. However, I had a wonderful time, and I am sure you did. We have many things in common to talk about when we meet.

I am going to be in the East for several weeks. I shall possibly come to Boston and Cambridge and shall be very happy to see you and talk over with you any suggestions that you may have to give. Our Institution is desperately in need of money and I am trying hard now to make some new contacts and so strengthen the confidence of my old friends that they will help us to pull through. This has been a most trying year for Florida, from an economic standpoint. Our students have been terribly handicapped because of a lack of funds with which to enter school, and with which to maintain them during the year. I am sure that the tide will turn, however, at the appointed time. We have cut off all of the lower grades from our school, too, and the cutting off has taken about one hundred thirty-five or forty children from the enrollment. Our work now deals with the High School and Junior College work. It is necessary for us to concentrate upon higher standards and a finer calibre of student. We have one hundred seventy-three outstanding, well-balanced, fine young men and young women. The air of our campus is very different. My desire it to have a school that will carry about two hundred or two hundred twenty-five students—not more. I want the institution to be very efficient, rather than very large. We are working hard toward getting the work standardized, and when we accomplish this, we hope to put on the other two years of college work, which will give to us the full four years' college. Florida needs this so much. It is very hard to pull up the Junior College work in this State because the educational system is so poor. We are hoping to get a new Library and a new Science Hall some day.

I am very happy that your needed buildings have been supplied, and that your burden is lighter from a financial standpoint. I think of you and Nannie Burroughs and Lucy Laney and myself as being in the most sacrificing class in our group of women. I think the work that we have produced will warrant love or consideration or appreciation or confidence that the general public may see fit to bestow upon us. I have, unselfishly, given my best, and I thank God that I have lived long enough to see the fruits from it.

The picture has not yet reached me. I shall greatly appreciate it and value it. I am sending you one of my own, from which you may have a larger one made for your chapel. It is lovely of you to want one of me.

I received a telegram from Mary McDowell, asking that I come to Chicago to speak at the Women Voters' League Forum, on the twelfth of November. I am accepting the invitation, because I think it is a wonderful opportunity to get over the program, the desires and aspirations of our National Association, Bethune-Cookman College and our people in general, in the various sections. The meeting will be held on November twelfth, and I am asked to speak on "Race Relations." I wonder if you have a few suggestions or thoughts that you might send to me, relative to this subject? I like to include the thoughts of my outstanding women, with my own, on these occasions. I shall be very glad for any suggestions or outlines concerning this that you may have. We have studied this so closely together during the past eight years.

I am sure that the opportunities that you are having in speaking frequently in that section will mean much for your school work, and for the welfare of our people with whom you come in contact. Now, when I come there, [there is] one thing I want to have you do and that is to make it possible for me to make some contacts with friends who might be interested in what we are doing here. I am sure that whatever can be done in this particular, will be done.

I am not losing faith in you as regards our National work, because I know you are going to measure up one hundred per cent. I am on the last lap, and I thank God that a real job has been done. I think those who doubted me most can say now, without reflection upon their own consciences, that a good job has been put over. I am hoping that as much of the twenty-five thousand dollars as possible may be raised, for our building. Some time when you are in Washington, go out to see our National Headquarters. We will go up about the first of June and open them up and see that they are ready for our work in July. I shall appoint an executive secretary, who will take charge of the work until the next president shall come; then she may make any other changes that she desires to make. My idea is to have the executive secretary to be also the editor of National Notes, and have our publication come out from National Headquarters. I am very sure that the editor of the Notes must be on salary. We can, no longer, have this work done free of charge. We were able to do as well as we did with it because my office force assisted with it and my institution stood behind it, generally.

The Durham conference is a very important one and I am so sorry that it is coming at the same time as the Biennial Convention of the National Council of Women, which convenes from December 5th through 10th, in New York City. I have had a notice of this Council meeting sent to you. I am hoping that as many women of our group, as possible, may attend. For fear the notice has not reached you, I am sending you one of the calls. We can have only five delegates there, but as many of our women may attend as desire to do so. You will note, that on December sixth, at eight-fifteen, p.m. that they will have what is known as "Presidents' Night." We have thirty-seven National organizations as members of this Council, and out of the thirty-seven, they are using twelve as speakers for that night. The President of the National Association of Colored Women has been selected as one of this number. I think this means so much to our organization. As I said, however, the conference at Durham is a very important one. I was in Durham some weeks ago, as one of the executive committee to help make the program and formulate the plans for the meeting. I think, however, that this Council meeting is the vitally important thing for us just now and I am hoping that quite a number of us will be there.

Now, I have written you a very full letter. It is seldom that I do this, but I felt that I wanted to write you at length.

Very sincerely yours,
Mary McLeod Bethune

Charlotte Hawkins Brown Papers, Schlesinger Library, Radcliffe College, Cambridge, Mass.

Twenty-fifth Annual Report of the President

[abridged] (1929)

To the Trustee and Advisory Boards, and Friends at Large, of Bethune-Cookman College: I have the honor to submit to you my report on the work of Bethune-Cookman College for the year 1928–29, the twenty-fifth year of its activities.

Our school has had a marvelous growth during the quarter of a century it has been established. From its meager beginnings a great plant has been developed, which commands the admiration of all who visit it. From the status of one teacher and an enrollment of five, it has grown to a place when twenty-five well-trained, consecrated men and women are employed on the teaching staff, and two hundred thirty-five boys and girls are enrolled in the departments ranging from the eighth grade through the Junior College. The twenty-five years of seed-sowing has brought forth an abundant harvest.

The year opened with a prospect of almost insurmountable financial difficulties, but we did not permit discouragement to creep into our hearts. The successful termination of the year's work is the result of the faith and prayer which have made possible the maintenance of the school during these twenty-five years. Our friends, old and new, have given of their means, their influence and their time, that we might continue the work. The deficit in operation is less than one-half of the figure of the deficit at this time last year. We are sincerely grateful to our friends and patrons for this continued confidence in us, during these days when we have been confronted with distressing problems.

Again, I wish to express my earnest appreciation to the Board of Education of the Methodist Episcopal Church for their valuable assistance, both in sane and constructive advice with regard to the forward program of the school and in material aid toward maintenance. At this stage of our institution's history, when the program is being expanded to more fully meet the needs of our people, we need and solicit the sympathetic cooperation of the Board of Education and of our Advisory and Trustee Boards, in order that the foundation of the splendid institution toward which we are working daily, may be secure. Times have been very hard during the past few years and we have been forced to practice most severe economy wherever it was possible to do so without jeopardizing the efficient running of the school. However, we have kept the work constantly before the public, to the end that friends might know of our progress and students might be secured. We hope to have our enrollment increase year by year that our service may reach a maximum number of communities. It is gratifying to note the improvement in the organization, the academic program and bearing of our teachers and students as we expand in the direction of higher and more efficient training.

Without the full cooperation of our instructors and students in the various phases of the institution's program, no success could be assured. I am sincerely grateful to them for their loyalty to our plans, and for their enthusiastic help in the academic, industrial, music and extra-curricular activities.

Our Twenty-fifth Annual Commencement was the most outstanding in the history of our school. . . . Thirty young people were given diplomas from the high school, thirteen from the junior college, three from the department of music, and twenty certificates from the departments of Business and Home Economics.

The confidence of our community is being very appreciably strengthened. Through the Sunday afternoon community meetings a bond is established that definitely cements the friendship and interest of tourists and residents. The attendance at these meeting[s] all during the year attests to the appreciation and interest of the entertainment of this unique, colorful gathering. The cooperation of the community has been secured through the College Musical organizations, the services of the teaching staff, the help of students, evening opportunity classes, and through the Annual Community Conference, which stresses the work and progress of farming, industrial work and home-making in this section.

The school is becoming more closely affiliated with activities, educational, civic and social, in the State. The State Department of Education has been most gracious in their consideration of our work, and through their representatives have given valuable instruction and advice to insure its continued progress.

ACADEMIC DEPARTMENT

The Academic Department, under its organization of Junior College, Normal Training, College preparatory, and Eighth grade, has grown very efficiently during the past year. More strenuous efforts are being put forth to secure upper-class students, and to make improvements to the organization. We still retain the eighth grade, because it serves to feed the high school with more certainty of proper classification. We are giving more serious thought each year to the selection and placing of instructors and are trying to secure the best-prepared men and women in the country—with the spirit of service and possessing the personalities of real teachers. We have realized that it is largely through our teaching force that our academic work may reach the highest stage of perfection. The past year closed with a minimum of conditioned students, and the scholarship record, generally, was very good. A new note of interest and enthusiasm is pervading our student body. They are rapidly assuming the bearing of young men and women of concentration and purpose. We report encouragement in the work of our Academic Department. We need more instructors and in some departments increased salaries, that our boys and girls may receive the very best literary training.

INDUSTRIAL DEPARTMENTS

The Industrial Departments have, during all of these years, proven their worth to the Institution through the practical training of our boys and girls and through their contribution to the cooperative publicity work fostered during the school term. Much of the success of this work is due to the assistance given the instructors by special committees of the Advisory Board, organized for this purpose.

The Domestic Science and Art Departments, attractive both in the nature of the courses and the beauty of the finished work, have been efficiently maintained during the year. Both departments are important factors in the Annual Bazaar and in other public functions given by clubs or boards for assistance to this particular work. The classes in Domestic Science and Domestic Art were furnished with much-needed materials and equipment through cooperation with the Advisory Board in teas, luncheons, sales, etc.

The Commercial Department is making distinct progress. The annual demonstration each year, which is one of the interesting features of pre-commencement week, proved that the students are applying themselves diligently to these courses. Excellence both in typewriting and shorthand as well as consistent general work are rewarded with prizes and medals from the Isaac Pitman Company.

Industries for boys include instruction and laboratory work in practical agriculture and general training in repairs and manual training. It is needless to state that our agriculture department is of inestimable value to the Boarding Department. Not only are vegetables of all kinds supplied the dining room and campus families, but also meats, canned goods, dairy products, flowers and ice cream.

The work in Manual Training has, because of the shortage of funds, been placed on a part-time basis, but is has proven no less helpful in preparing the boys for general service along the line of repairs and carpentry.

We have been unable to foster the full Industrial program for boys, because of the lack of an adequate building. There is an imperative need for a Trades building, with full equipment, for the teaching of Boys' industries. Our boys need this practical training if they are to fill places in their communities with credit.

A new course has been added to the Industrial Department, and has been opened to both boys and girls. This course, Fine Arts, has been under the direction of one of the best instructors in this field in America. Oil painting, water coloring, stenciling, basketry, handicraft, china and glass painting and novelty-making, have been given. So popular has been the work, and so great the need for it, that students have, in many instances, resorted to readjustments in their program, that the course in Fine Arts might be included. Through this department another bond has been cemented with the community. Teachers of the public schools, housewives and mothers, are enthusiastic in their desire for this work after school hours. This course was added as an experiment, and we feel justified in continuing it for its worth to the students enrolled for it, and for its attractiveness to the institution.

THE SUMMER SCHOOL

The summer school for teachers, the first session of which was held last summer, is now an established item in the program of Bethune-Cookman College. It is our aim to place review work and training within the reach of those teachers whose small salaries and humble circumstances will not permit them to enroll in larger, more distant institutions. Their academic foundation must be strengthened, and they must have inspiration and help. The State Department of Education has recognized the standard courses offered by our Institution and has agreed to give extension of certificates and credit to teachers who satisfactorily complete the courses. The small appropriation from the General Education Board, has been directed by State Education officials, to our school this year. The summer school is perhaps our largest piece of extension work. We are meeting with gratifying success in it, and we feel happy for the opportunity to further serve the youth of this state, through these teachers.

For a second time also, we have opened the ten days' School of Social and Religious Training, which is established, through the cooperation of officials of the Methodist Episcopal Church, to give review work to ministers, and religious and social workers. This work is offered during the summer school period and is maintained in conjunction with the session for teachers.

MCLEOD HOSPITAL

Although our institution does not now have the responsibility of the financial maintenance of McLeod Hospital, the same influence, supervision and cooperation is given the work as previously. The Halifax Hospital Commission, together with three active governors, join forces to carry on, with the school, the work that has been so well established in this hospital. McLeod Hospital has more than justified its existence. It has rendered yeoman service and continues to prove a blessing to the sick of our Community.

RELIGIOUS LIFE

Bethune-Cookman, founded on faith and prayer, has always been permeated with the spirit of religious fervor. This spirit is carried on through the years by the Young Men's and Young Women's Christian Association, by instructors and students in the Daily Chapel hour, Sunday morning Church Services, and the mid-week gathering for prayer and song. Courses in Religious Education and Biblical History are taught on the par with academic and industrial courses. Development of the "heart" for Christian service and moral uplift, is one of Bethune-Cookman's three main factors.

MUSIC

Our Music has always been our pride and joy. This department of our work has made thousands of friends for the institution. We are steadily creating constructive and scientific courses in all musical branches, and for the first time this year, three young women received diplomas for the completion of prescribed courses. The Music organizations—the Chorus, Band, Orchestra,

Glee Clubs, Male Quintette, Mixed Concert Group and individual soloists—have done much toward the rapid march of the school toward an enviable place along this line of work.

Self-Help

The work of the Institution is done largely through student labor, under the direction of head workmen in the several departments. Scores of boys and girls, unable to find money with which to educate themselves, are applicants for work to take care of their expenses. Jobs are given to as many of these boys and girls as possible, and credit given them on their expense accounts. We do not have enough work to distribute among them all, and in view of the economic conditions of the state, it is violating the purpose for which our institution was established to turn them away without any encouragement. For this purpose, we are earnestly soliciting part scholarships of one hundred fifty dollars and full scholarships of three hundred dollars, to assist in the training of these students. Alumni Clubs and Clubs including in their membership patrons and interested friends of the School are being organized to help swell the scholarship fund. A recently inaugurated idea of a "Birthday Club" in which friends may join by contributing in small or large sums on their birthdays to a scholarship fund, gives a prospect of material help to these needy students.

Health

The health of students and teachers continues good. Wholesome environment guarantees good health and happiness among our school group.

Needs

We solicit again the interest, the cooperation and suggestion of members of our Boards. Ours is a great task, and can only be performed through consecrated, whole-hearted, united effort. At the end of twenty-five years, we feel greatly encouraged. Not one phase of our program has made a backward step. Our boys and girls are realizing their opportunities. Our people are realizing their responsibilities and are joining hands with us in fostering a program of Christian education. Our friends continue to stand by us and to invest in these human lives entrusted to our care. We submit the following financial report for your information, and hope that you may join us in fervently thanking our Father for His care during these difficult months.

A quarter of a century has proven to us that we are on the right track. We are re-dedicating our lives for larger tasks during the coming years.

Yours for continued service,

Mary McLeod Bethune

FINANCIAL REPORT

CASH BOOK STATEMENT

Cash Balance, June 1, 1928 .... $441.01
Receipts, June 1928 to June 1, 1929 .... 98,345.48
    Total $98,786.49
Disbursements, June 1928 to June 1, 1929 .... 96,483.26
    Balance $2,303.23

BANK STATEMENT

Treasurer's Balance, May 30, 1929 .... $2,285.61
Operating Account Balance, May 30, 1929 .... 358.85
    Total $2,644.46
Less Outstanding Checks 341.23
    Cash Balance, June 1, 1929 .... $2,303.23

RECEIPTS

JUNE 1, 1928–JUNE 1, 1929
Educational

Board of Education—Regular Appropriation $19,983.33			
Any Other 357.00			
For Ministers' Institute 75.00		$20,415.33	

Interest on Invested Funds 507.67

Donations (Undesignated) $21,289.16

(Designated):
Scholarships $2,833.75
For Greenhouse 500.00
For Summer School 2,040.84
For Truck 175.00
For Bus 1,057.30
Thomas H. White Estate 2,700.00
Flora D. Curtis Estate 3,152.50
Funds from Conferences .... 1,133.38 .... $13,592.77 $34,881.93
                                                                  $55,804.93

Student Fees

Entrance .... $ 320.00
Tuition 2,934.74
Commercial 144.50
Laboratory 176.00
Breakage 133.00
Industrial and Domestic Arts 292.52   4,003.76

Student Activities

Athletics $1,690.23

Y.M.C.A. 39.00
Y.W.C.A. 133.85
Literary 43.00
Sunday School .... <u>44.44</u>   <u>1,960.52</u>

Accounts for Business Enterprises
School Books $276.93
Dormitory Room Rent 1,129.49
Laundry 904.02
Music 759.00
Boarding Department .... <u>$13,555.88</u>
Carried Forward .... <u>$16,625.32</u>   <u>$61,759.21</u>

Farm:
Cash Sales $238.08
Supplies to Boarding Dept. .... 3,801.25 .... 4,084.33
McLeod Hospital, for
Light and Power 74.16
Teachers' Houses 320.00
Notes Payable—Loan on Insurance Policy 11,877.20
Refund on Negro College Survey Expense 41.69
Miscellaneous .... <u>522.80</u>   <u>33,545.50</u>
Annual Bazaar 2,203.81
Annual Students and Teachers Rally ....   <u>836.96</u>
             Total Receipts **$98,345.48**

DISBURSEMENTS
JUNE 1, 1928–JUNE 1, 1929
Administration
Salaries $10,227.41
Office Supplies, Expense 916.09
Publications, Publicity, Postage
    (including 25th Anniv. Publicity) 6,240.90
Telephone, Telegraph 718.98
Premium on New Insurance 1,017.00
Replacement (Chevrolet Car) 649.00
Travel and Auto Expense .... <u>2,377.09</u>   <u>$22,146.47</u>

Operation and Maintenance of Plant
Repairs to Buildings $4,485.01
Wages 3,175.38
Fuel, Water and Light 3,747.32
Repairs, Replacements, Equipment 1,676.61
Supplies 1,357.82
New Equipment:
Truck $175.00
Bus .... <u>1,485.71</u>   <u>1,660.71</u>   <u>$15,102.85</u>

Dormitories
Salaries and Wages $2,300.82
Equipment, Repairs and Replacements 666.04   2,966.86

Educational Expense
Salaries $13,536.72
Laboratory Supplies 1,132.15
Commencement Expenses 137.87
School Supplies and Equipment 1,080.99
Industrial Supplies and Equipment 1,222.75
Student Aid 110.00   17,220.48

Boarding Department
Salaries and Wages $5,066.97
Food Supplies:
Cash 11,646.31
Farm Produce 3,801.25
Equipment, Repairs, Replacements 360.13   20,874.66

Music Department
Salaries $2,616.75
Supplies 519.20   3,207.95

Laundry
Wages $887.50
Equipment, Repairs, Replacements 144.07
Supplies 70.77   1,072.34

Farm
Salaries $1,505.00
Wages 1,754.32
Feed, Seed, Fertilizer, Repairs, Equipment (including
     new Barn and Dairy) 4,101.25   7,360.37

Student Activities
Athletics .... $ 2,085.71
Y.W.C.A. 132.14
Y.M.C.A. 35.00
Library.. 288.74
Sunday School 33.49   2,575.08

Store and Cafeteria 28.03
School Books 300.74
Summer School 2,782.09
Green House 500.00
Annual Bazaar Expense 172.82
Miscellaneous 172.32

Total Disbursements **$96,483.26**

ENDOWMENT

Receipts

Cash in Savings Account, June 1, 1928	$655.64
From Florida Conference	18.00
From South Florida Conference	71.02
Donations—June, 1927–June, 1929	3,087.50
P.E. Meyers Mortgage Paid	2,900.00
From Board of Education Office	1,342.00
Sale of 100 Shares Florida Power and Light Company Stock	1,057.50
Interest	40.94

$ 9,161.60

Investments

Adah B. Smith Mortgage	3,087.50
Roscoe C. Raub Mortgage	3,600.00
Undesignated Conference Funds, transferred to Operating Account	736.66
For purchase of Bus, designated by Donor, authorized by Executive Committee	1,057.60
Total Investments	$8,481.66
Balance on Hand, on Deposit in Savings Account, Merchants Bank & Trust Co.	679.94
	$9,161.60

$9,161.60

FARM REPORT

JUNE 1, 1928–JUNE 1, 1929

Furnished to Boarding Department

Vegetables	$1,542.00
Beef—1300 lbs. at 15c.	195.00
Beef—700 lbs. at 20c.	140.00
Pork—3255 lbs. at 15c.	488.25
Sweet Milk—240 Gals. at 60c.	144.00
Sweet Milk—2055 Gals. at 50c.	1,027.50
Butter Milk—325 Gals. at 20c.	65.00
Butter Milk—30 Gals. at 40c.	12.00
Butter—56 lbs. at 50c.	28.00
Ice Cream—110 Gals. at $1.00	110.00
Chickens—120 lbs. at 40c.	28.00
Lard—110 lbs. at 15c.	16.50
Eggs—10 Dozen at 50c.	5.00
Total to Boarding Department	$3,801.25
Cash Sales	283.08
Total Farm Receipts	**$4,084.33**

Published as an issue of *The Advocate* [periodical of Bethune-Cookman College], vol. 25, no. 9. P. K. Yonge Library of Florida History, University of Florida, Tallahassee.

A Common Cause

(1932)

The problems presented by the status of education in Florida to engage the deepest consideration of every man and woman with one ounce of interest in the future welfare of its Negro boys and girl constitute a challenge that stiffens the spine and squares the jaw and puts a new gleam of determination into the eye of every student who views the facts in the case and fully comprehends their import.

Somewhere, wandering about the streets and alleys of our cities, loafing about the railway stations and vacant lots of various villages, drudging out a dreary existence in rural places, approximately fifty thousand Negro children between the ages of six and twenty-one, over one third the Negro school population of the state, are out of school, losing their inherent right to training and development, sacrificing the opportunity for future competence, worthy citizenship and notable achievement. Of those who are in school, a fine array of promising tots, approaching a hundred thousand in the primer classes, dwindles year by year through the upper grades, until only a pitiful handful of a few hundred emerge as high school graduates.

Who is the fault remains to be determined. The facts constitute a blotch on the record of the commonwealth—and a challenge to every red-blooded man and woman to unite with head and heart in one common cause with every man and woman to save the situation for the rising generation. There is demand for union of endeavors and perfect co-operation all along the line in the grim combat against ignorance, prejudice, indifference and vice—the inevitable oppressors of the youth of tomorrow unless the fight is waged relentlessly by every warrior who is able to wield a weapon.

People equipped for the job, teachers trained and willing, are far too few for the task in hand. Importations from other states are being made every year, and someone has suggested that the number of importations be materially increased. Never was the demand stronger than now that every teacher-training [a]gency in the state be gauged at its highest efficiency and afforded every encouragement to produce re-enforcements with all possible speed for the struggle against the common enemy.

There is splendid opportunity for the various advanced institutions to render service separate and distinct each in its individual field. One school, by virtue of its background, equipment, location and supporting agencies, may be peculiarly fitted to make a particular contribution impossible to other schools. Nevertheless, its aim is one with that of other institutions—to elevate the intellectual, economic, and moral status of the Negro in Florida. And the most direct method is fairly to saturate the neglected portions of the state, every obscure nook and corner, with qualified, consecrated instructors who will grasp the hands of those eager boys and girls groping helplessly in the dark and lead them to the light.

How exceedingly unfortunate it would be, how cruelly destructive to the highest interest of all, if any of the agencies that ought to be cooperating in the desperate struggle should, in a spirit of mistaken jealousy, turn against a struggling companion the weapons that ought to be aimed at the common foe. Unfriendly rivalry was never more needless, never more inexpedient among the schools of Florida than just now. There is no need for strife over undeveloped student material—no fear of a shortage. There is vastly more than any one or two colleges can accommodate. Every year enough high school and college students of Florida seek educational facilities outside the state to populate one or two institutions. In a system where scholarship doles and service in lieu of cash are overworked in balancing school expense accounts, these migrating students constitute some of the best cash-paying school attendants of the state, of the South. Annually the deposit in the treasuries of outside schools [amounts to] thousands of dollars that, invested at home, would go far to strengthen and improve the colleges of their home state. If all of these registered within their native state, the advanced institutions of Florida with their present equipment would be inadequate to accommodate the host. There is no need for academic proselytizing, no grounds for a policy of destructive competition in the belief that the welfare of one college depends upon the retardation of another.

Ill-advised competition among institutions in a bid for student preference will inevitably lead to jealous flaw-picking which, rammed home to the attention of youths, will inspire them to seek beyond the state schools and colleges free from the faults and weaknesses of home schools that have been so magnified before their eyes. Thus will be encouraged the abnormal exodus of students that has been draining Florida colleges of much needed cash support.

If those five thousand Negro children now deprived of their rights to school training are to be saved, if that fearful mortality between the primary grades and high school is to be checked, every teacher-producing factory in the state should be equipped and keyed to its highest efficiency and encouraged to its fullest capacity with all haste, that more instructors, adequately prepared, may be rushed into the field.

There are many grounds for encouragement. Every year the number and efficiency of teachers increase, by fresh outputs of graduates, by importations and by specialized studies in Summer Schools and post-graduate courses. New school houses are springing into existence; high schools are enlarging their courses; more and more are being added to the accredited list, terms are lengthening; salaries are increasing. These the resultants not merely of multiplied zeal on the part of Negroes but of changing attitudes, a developing sense of fair play and a most commendable show of interest on the part of state and county officials.

Florida faces a new day in education. Grim as the picture appears today, it is not nearly so bad as it was just a few years hence, and the aspect is rapidly changing for the better; a veritable miracle is transpiring before the eye. The day for which many warriors now aging in the service have longed, the day for which they have prayed and sweat drops of blood—that new day of the hoped-for better things is approaching. With the scent of victory in the nostril, may every agency redouble its zeal; with jealousies forgotten, with the spirit of competition thrust aside, may every organization and individual unite under the banner of One Common Cause, the grim battle against ignorance and vice, and carry the issue to a glorious victory.

Florida State Teachers' Association Bulletin, March 31–April 2, 1932, pp. 3–4. Florida A&M University Archives, Tallahassee.

Letter to Ada Lee

(1932)

June 29, 1932

My dear, dear Ada,

I have been thinking of you almost daily —thinking that it would be lovely to have you come down and spend a few days with me. I am busy, of course, but it would be very pleasant to have you and I am sure it would be restful for you.

I just want you to know how grateful we are for your efforts in behalf of Bethune-Cookman College. No other Negro woman in Florida has been more diligent in her interest. You have given of yourself, in order that our work might go forward. I am grateful for your friendship and for the interest you have manifested in my personal welfare. I don't have the time to give to affectionate, appreciative expression to my friends but I am sure they know that I have sincere regard for them.

I passed through Jacksonville on my way to and from the tour I made of schools in Georgia, the Carolinas and Tennessee, but I was so rushed when I went up and when I returned it was so late I would not disturb you. I am glad to know that you are planning to come down for the Tournament. You know that you are always welcome in my home. I shall be very glad to have you and if Mrs. Myers is to be with you I shall be glad to have her also. We are going to try to make everyone comfortable at that time.

Continue to do the best in the way of securing students. We must have a large enrollment next year. We want particularly, to increase the enrollment of our college department. We will do everything we can to help students, but we must stay within our budget. We cannot make any definite promises to take students for only eight dollars a month cash. The enclosed letter will give you an idea of the rules we must follow in the way of student labor. We have made the rates very reasonable, as you will note from the circular of information I am sending you under separate cover and we will have to take in more students who can pay their expenses. We are charging only $16.00 for board and room this year, and if we give girls jobs to take care of $7.00 of this it will mean that only $11.00 will have to be paid in cash; that is, after the first month. The fees and tuition come in the first month, which raises the amount due to fifty-odd dollars. The labor credit will be deducted from this amount, however, making it smaller by five or seven dollars, according to the particular job which may be assigned to the student.

Lovingly yours,
Mary McLeod Bethune

Mary McLeod Bethune Papers, Mary McLeod Bethune Foundation, Bethune-Cookman College, Daytona Beach, Fla.

The Educational Values of the College-Bred

(1934)

Mr. Chairman:

May I express my gratitude to your committee for your gracious invitation to be present with you on this historic day and to participate in the parting greetings to this remarkable class that must soon find its way out into the world of service.

One's heart is moved with emotions as we look backward and think of the seed-sowers of this grand old Institution, and of thousands who have arisen from the lowly fields of ignorance and poverty to the great fields of knowledge ripened with opportunities to serve. We think today in terms of deep appreciation and affection of those who have been faithfully carrying on during all of the long, long years, enduring hardness, very often, like good soldiers. We congratulate you upon the standard of this Institution, for what it means to a race and to a Nation. Its influences are seeping through to all races and classes with its fine, new-day program of Education.

Education is the great American Adventure, the world's most colossal democratic experiment. Education is the largest public enterprise in the United States; in my opinion, the country's most important business. This is emphasized when I remind you that, according to Edgar Knight of the University of North Carolina, the public school property of this country amounts to seven billion dollars; that three billion dollars are spent annually for school support; that one million two hundred thousand teachers are employed; and that there are thirty million students enrolled in our various types of institutions; that two persons out of every seven in the United States are giving full time to this education.

Why this large investment in education? Why do we educate people, anyhow? Why do we spend these huge sums? Obviously, it is just this: Nature has stored up in individuals native powers, possibilities, potentialities, and it is the problem, the work of education to release these powers—to make actual and real these possibilities and potentialities in order that the individual himself may live life to the fullest and make a contribution to the sum total of human happiness.

In my mind there are three factors that have contributed to make Education the great enterprise it is today:

The first is Science with its powers of production, distribution, transportation and communication. The second is the Ideal of Democracy. In former years education was a luxury to be enjoyed by the members of higher castes; now it is within the reach of the masses. The third is Religion. All science points toward God—God the Maker, the Preserver, the Director of all of our lives. As you grow in the knowledge of Science, young people, strive to grow more like God. Amid the collapse and crumbling of economic and social structures, religion is the vitalizing element in all education.

I believe, as does Glenn Frank, President of the University of Wisconsin, that our colleges are charged with tremendous responsibilities, chief among them being, in my opinion, the underprivileged masses who are impatiently awaiting that sane, sympathetic, patient, Christian leadership that must come year after year from the colleges of our country. Further, colleges have three other responsibilities: 1) to produce the Investigator, 2) to produce the Interpreter, 3) to produce the Inspirer.

Schools have two giant responsibilities: THE RESPONSIBILITY OF INVESTIGATION and THE RESPONSIBILITY OF INTERPRETATION. The man in the laboratory may investigate; the man in the lecture room may interpret. But the teacher has a still diviner commission than either the investigator or the interpreter. These men deal with the matter of their subjects. The teacher must deal with the minds of his students—minds that are plastic and can be shaped into whatever the teacher's own character may design. Schools have many functions, but their chief function is to furnish society with three sorts of servants: investigators, interpreters, inspirers. Speaking loosely for a moment, the teacher is of the third sort. The teacher's primary business is that of a stirrer-up. He is not, save secondarily, a salesman of knowledge. He is primarily, a stimulator of knowledge and curiosity. But the good teacher manages to combine all three functions to the ministry of his pupils. The good teacher is an investigator. He is not content to squat behind the breast-works of accumulated knowledge; he flirts with the unknown out on the frontiers of knowledge; only so can he bring the spirit of intellectual adventure and conquest into his classroom; an incurious teacher cannot stimulate curiosity.

The good teacher is also an INTERPRETER. He not only knows more about his own subject than any other subjects but he knows enough about other subjects to keep his own subject in perspective. The good teacher is an INSPIRER. He knows that the art of teaching lies in starting something in the student's mind. He is not content with merely putting something into the student's mind as a butcher stuffs a sausage-skin. In short, therefore, the good teacher is an INVESTIGATOR, an INTERPRETER, an INSPIRER.

The future of America, young men, young women, is in the hands of two men—the investigator and the interpreter. We shall never lack for the administrator, the third man needed to complete this trinity of social servants. And we have an ample supply of investigators, but there is a shortage of readable and responsible interpreters, men who can effectively play mediator between specialist and layman. The practical value of every social invention or material discovery depends upon its being adequately interpreted to the masses. Are we willing to blaze the way to that shut-in mass that we may interpret to them the way up, out, and over to the real realm of American Citizenship? They are calling for the interpreter, who will answer—"Here I am, send me."

Our fathers and mothers prayed for the leadership and the interpretation, young men and women, that you are able to give today. Will you give it? Science owes its effective ministry as much to the interpretative mind as to the creative mind. The knowledge of mankind is advanced by the investigator, but the investigator is not always the best interpreter of his discoveries. Rarely, in fact, do the genius for exploration and the genius for exposition meet in the same mind. The interpreter stands between the layman and the investigator, whose knowledge of one thing is authoritative. The investigator advances knowledge. The interpreter advances progress. History affords abundant evidence that civilization has advanced in direct ratio to the efficiency with which the thought of the thinkers has been translated into the language of the workers. A dozen fields of thought are today congested with knowledge that the physical and social sciences have unearthed, and the whole tone and temper of American life can be lifted by putting this knowledge into general circulation.

But where are the interpreters with the training and the willingness to think their way through this knowledge and translate it into the language of the street? Young men, young women, I raise the recruiting trumpet for the Interpreters.

Now, in order to do properly the work of the college-bred, there are certain very essential qualities. In the days of King Arthur, it was customary for the knights, if they would go on their pilgrimages, to take certain vows in the prosecution of their work. I am going to do a similar thing here today and ask you—as Crusaders of Knowledge—to take with me certain pledges or vows for the performance of your task. I would have you take with me, first, the vow of definite and specific preparation—for, to recognize the major needs of our fellowmen is often a difficult task. To face the sacrifice necessary for training, even though hearts are consecrated, is more difficult. Only the spiritually determined will triumph.

Second—the vow of a sympathetic attitude. To fortify you with supreme tolerance of the groping, ofttimes slow and pain-filled efforts of those we are dedicated to serve—for how often are these efforts interspersed with frequent disillusionment for both teacher and student.

Third—the vow of industry. The bud of determination cannot reach fruition until it has blossomed forth into labor—consistent, steady, untiring labor, the force of which, whether manual or mental, may carve alike beauty from rugged native stone or keen thinking from untried minds.

Fourth—the vow of idealism. Seek your ideals from Nature's plan of perfection, for in it is reflected Deity. Strive for the heights of the mountains, the turbulent strength of the sea, the fine and delicate loveliness of the primrose, the shining glory of the stars.

Fifth—the vow of courage. When the inevitable obstacles, pitfalls, frustrations, misunderstandings, even failures confront you, this vow will stand in good stead, for your spirit will be permeated with a veritable armor of Courage, which is the heritage only of those who are sure of their way—and being sure, scorn the undergrowth or the bypath.

Sixth—the vow of Faith. Has it ever occurred to you that Faith—simple Faith—so often made complex by our own clumsy efforts to force it into our consciousness—is merely the serene confidence, the inward smiling assurance of rightness begetting rightness? Faith is the substance of things hoped for, the evidence of things not seen.

In the rural section of the South, farmers on an occasion viewed with alarm the parching of their crops from drought. Days of piercing sun cracked the earth, and the plants, upon which the very subsistence of the group depended, withered in agony. One devout woman suggested a concentrated prayer for rain at the little meeting house. At the time indicated every soul blended in supplication for material salvation. And the rain came in torrents even as they prayed. Following the glorious thanksgiving the farmer folk made ready to go home but, alas, the blessed rain prevented their venturing out—all but one little girl. "I brought my umbrella," she said, "for I KNEW if we prayed for rain, it would come." Hers was the Vow of Faith!

May I earnestly exhort YOU to have Faith—in God, in yourselves, your possibilities—faith in Mankind.

Mary McLeod Bethune Papers, Mary McLeod Bethune Foundation, Bethune-Cookman College, Daytona Beach, Fla. Amistad Box 2, Folder 15. (Also published in *The Southern Workman* 63 [July 1934]: 200–204.)

Response, Twenty-first Spingarn Medalist

(1935)

St. Louis, Missouri

Mr. Chairman, My Fellow Citizens, Members and Officers of the National Association for the Advancement of Colored People: There is a great happiness in my heart tonight—not a selfish, personal happiness, but a happiness and satisfaction that come to one who has labored in the heat of the day for the common good, and now as the shadows of life begin to lengthen comes to receive a "Well Done," a signal recognition of one's life work. And with this happiness comes a humble gratitude for the distinguished approval of this organization dedicated to the cause of social justice and human welfare. To be worthy of being included in the illustrious group of Spingarn medalists, who by their intelligence, courage, devotion, faith and work have helped to shape and build a better world, one must respond to the stimulus of this occasion with a spirit of rededication to service, of reconsecration to the needs of the people. This spirit of rededication and reconsecration permeates me now as I stand before you.

The National Association for the Advancement of Colored People has for the past twenty-six years accepted the challenge of the times and has ventured forth upon its task, high endeavor for human understanding, and the world has responded to this endeavor. I seem to hear this call, coming from the pioneers of this great movement:

> Come, clear the way; then, clear the way.
> Blind kings and creeds have had their day.
> Break the dead branches from the path.
> Our hope is in the aftermath.
> Our hope is in heroic man,
> Star-led to build the world again.
> To this event all ages ran;
> Make way for brotherhood;
> Make way for man.

This dauntless organization has spent its efforts almost wholly in clearing the way for a race, in breaking dead branches from the paths of liberty and the pursuit of happiness. The success of the early clearers of the way is but an indication of what is yet to be done by those who follow in their train. The dead branches hewn away by those stalwart pioneers left plain and straight the highway which the youths are traveling. That way brought us hope. That is the song which the past has taught us. Now we keep faith with that hope to sing the song which the present challenges.

If I have merited the honor of receiving the Spingarn Medal, it is because my life has been dedicated to the task of breaking the bars to brotherhood. Brotherhood is not an ideal. It is but a state or a condition attendant upon achievement of an ideal. It is one of the components of an ideal. I believe that brotherhood depends upon and follows achievement. In light of this belief, I wish to indicate and develop briefly those fundamental principles and issues involved in bringing about a state of brotherhood.

The law of life is the law of cooperation, and unless we learn thoroughly this fundamental tenet of social organization I fear that the historian of the future, when he attempts to record the history of the black man in America, will write "a people possessed of tremendous possibilities, potentialities and resources, mental and physical, but a people unable to capitalize them because of their racial non-cohesiveness." If we would make way for social and political justice and a larger brotherhood, we must cooperate. Racial cohesion means making a road of all of the achievements of those who have educational advantages until we reach the lowest man, the lowest strata of the masses; that mass that is standing so helplessly waiting for you and for me to administer the human touch.

Unless the people have vision, they perish. What can we see; and, having seen, are we willing to venture? Do we see our large opportunity for the race to produce? Do we see an intellectual interpretation of our religious thought unhampered by superstitious belief, or limited by too great a satisfaction? Do we see the brotherhood of the peoples of the world working out an abundant life in their activities, of duty, of art, of business, of every-day living?

The National Association for the Advancement of Colored People has always sought men of vision to lead the way. Today we pray for the expansion of that vision from a few to an ever-increasing group of prepared men and women and of youths of all races to guide and direct the mass. The veil of ignorance and superstition is not yet lifted. Broad vision, zeal and prepared- ness will do much to lift it. Social group understanding and appreciation are necessary to brotherhood. The dead branches of misunderstanding and lack of appreciation have kept our existence clouded with prejudice. Human understanding is the key to brotherhood. The march of racial advancement is continually hindered by misunderstanding. Misunderstandings clutter up the highways of life which make for true harmonious relations.

But right must triumph and prejudice must be done away with. In this staunch belief, men and women of this organization continue to struggle toward the goal of social justice and to strive for worthy and proper consider- ation for every man in his right to live, to be, to do, to possess, and to pursue happiness. Now is the time for thinking men and women, for thinking youths of every race, to stand up with those who have labored for years and be counted, in their participation in this great forward march of the National Association for the Advancement of Colored People. No greater crime can there be than that one in which a man should be unfair to his neighbor and interferes with his right to develop harmonious relationships and realize the highest attainment of his abilities. The great unrest in the world today, the great doubts which assail men, the enormous amount of mistrust which entangles our lives and makes us look askance at our brothers, all are the products of injustice, wrought by one man upon another.

Equality of opportunity is necessary to brotherhood. We stand in adoration for those who, regardless of the section of the country in which they live, have been big enough, courageous enough, to stand for social justice and equality of opportunity, even at the risk of their lives. The National Association for the Advancement of Colored People has proven the necessity for breaking the bars to brotherhood through their advocacy of the destruction of blind kings and creeds which have been rulers in the lives of humanity. The creeds of selfishness, self-centered ideas, have led to narrow leadership. The creed of over-ambition and self-domination has led to unfair publicity. Let us cease to give allegiance to such unmoral kinship in our lives. Above all, let us cease now to render allegiance to the creed of belief in the inherent superiority of white and the inherent inferiority of black. Let us rest with confidence on the creed of larger development in our narrow selves; greater scope of opportunity to work out our ambitions; sure and certain belief in all convictions which are ours; and towering over all, our belief in becoming free men.

The creed of freedom has not yet been written. Humanity is yet a slave to her desires, her fears, her intelligence, her social standing, her craving for power. Let us as workers under this banner spread truth and make free men—spread truth about economic adjustment; truth about moral obligation; truth about segregation; truth about citizenship; truth about abilities, achievements and accomplishments; truth about home building; yes, truth wherever truth is needed. Then our lives may be lived with freedom and we shall be what ourselves demand us to be.

Who shall disseminate this truth? I would call tonight upon those who are star-led, who have clearly in mind a purpose in life; who do not fear the struggle and the work which must needs be the lot of those who dare to live above the cloud of popular thought and limited desire.

My fellow citizens, in the light of this dream, in the light of this firm hope, in the belief that brotherhood is the desired end in life, in accordance with God's plan, and with a rededication to share in the responsibility of rebuilding and inspiring vision, to keep faith with the ideals and purposes of the National Association for the Advancement of Colored People, I, in the name of the womanhood of America, accept this medal. I accept it with gratitude for the opportunity for God-given service. I accept it as a badge which will mark me before all men as an advocate of respect and justice for all mankind. The brightness which we saw so many years ago has become a light, a star. May we challenge ourselves anew and follow in its radiance, ever thoughtful, ever courageous, ever enduring in molding lives with highest principles. And may those who shall follow after us gain inspiration because we dare to stand at a time like this.

Mr. Chairman, my fellow citizens, I am grateful.

Mary McLeod Bethune Papers, Amistad Research Center, Tulane University; Mary McLeod Bethune Papers, Mary McLeod Bethune Foundation, Bethune-Cookman College, Daytona Beach, Fla.

Letter to Jackson Davis

(1935)

November 14, 1935
(Confidential)
Mr. Jackson Davis
The General Education Board
New York, N.Y.

My dear Mr. Davis:

I have been sitting at my desk, facing my problems squarely, with a picture of thirty-one years of untiring effort—I think with a marked degree of success—in building up an institution in a section of the country where, thirty-one years ago, such an institution was most needed. We have had our successes and our failures—more successes than failures. There has been a steady increase of students, the enrollment for the present year being seven hundred fifty-four, in all departments including our summer school. There has been a steady and most pronounced improvement of the plant. There has been improvement in the calibre and increase in the number of teachers. There has been an increase in the influence and cooperation of the State. The general usefulness of Bethune-Cookman College has grown beyond the state of Florida. There are few significant things in this country in race relations, education and general civic development, where Negroes are concerned, where our institution is not making its contribution. There are few Negro women, if any, who have been privileged to perform for the race and nation such extensive service as has been mine. I have given my best. I am possibly at my peak of usefulness, with a ripened experience and an understanding of the strata of life that I have touched, from the ground-floor up. I feel that this experience may be of great value to my people at this time.

It has been a great struggle, as you know, to maintain this institution and for the past five years I have been backed up against a seeming wall of stone. At this stage of my work, my strength and my accomplishment, I must find some way out.

Two days ago I faced our difficulties squarely across my desk as Mr. L. H. Foster understandingly pointed out our strong points and our weak ones. For the past three years operating problems have been acute. This situation has grown out of a decrease in income to meet normal expenses. The stream that flowed from our donors has almost completely dried up. Many of our friends have passed on and many are involved in the economic situation and unable to give large contributions. For twenty years we had an assured income of twenty-seven hundred dollars from the Thomas H. White Estate, from an investment that Mr. White made for us over twenty years ago. This investment was possibly sixty-five thousand dollars. For the past two years the Estate has been involved in legal difficulties and we have received no income. Labor conditions have been so acute that with the best that parents and students could do, [it] was not sufficient to carry our work through. The church Board has given its best influence, direction and cash, but they are unable to meet our normal needs.

In attempting to find a way out of the situation it occurs to me that there are certain things that can and should be done in the matter of organization and adjustment. I stand willing for any adjustment or reorganization and for the correction of any errors, that we may be placed on the right side of the ledger. Possibly a reorganization of our accounting and a restatement of the accounting set-up, in order that there may be a clearer interpretation of what we are doing, are needed. I want your help and advice. As I have gone over matters with Mr. Foster I can see that there is hardly a way out for us unless something is done. Possibly you and Dr. Holmes, who has given to me most sympathetic help, can plan for something to help us. Dr. Holmes, I believe, would want any reorganization or restatement or replanning possible, for the good of our institution.

I want you to read this letter and meditate upon it. Give it a little extra time when you are not too tired. I am, frankly, bewildered. My bills are unpaid but I am holding on desperately, but I need reinforcement. I am writing you as friend to friend and I want you to give this letter your sympathetic consideration, as friend to friend. Then, I want you to act in your official capacity and do all you can to help save Bethune-Cookman College.

> Sincerely yours,
> Mary McLeod Bethune

General Education Board Archives, Rockefeller Archive Center, Sleepy Hollow, N.Y. Record Group 1.1, Folder 307, Box 304.

Letter to Mrs. Ferris Meigs

(1935)

July 30, 1935
Mrs. Ferris J. Meigs
Bronxville, New York

My dear Mrs. Meigs:

I have just reached home and I am feeling very much better. My operation was a very technical one. I had a fine surgeon and he did splendid work. He did not touch my throat at all—he simply worked on the sinus condition. I had three nurses each day on eight-hour shifts. [In my] room was a bower of flowers and everyone was beautiful to me. I am so grateful to God and my friends for this deliverance. I feel so very much better.

Upon my arrival at the office this morning the check for five hundred ninety-five dollars for my vacation was placed before me. Oh, my dear Mrs. Meigs, how can I show my friends how grateful I am for these sincere thoughts? I shall work with my secretary for one or two days, to check up on things here, and do my best to get things straightened out. There is a very interesting group going to make a tour of Mexico and with the money you have so kindly provided for me, this trip is now a possibility. I have wanted so much to make it, and it will provide educational enlightenment, recreation, rest and change.

May God bless you for your unfailing kindness. I pray that the service that I have endeavored to render, and will continue to render, will compensate you for these thoughts.

I have received the Spingarn Medal, have had marvelous treatment at the University Hospital, and with this vacation, I will surely pull through all right. Thank God, however, my feet are still on the ground.

Gratefully and sincerely,
Mary McLeod Bethune

Mary McLeod Bethune Papers, Mary McLeod Bethune Foundation, Bethune-Cookman College, Daytona Beach, Fla.

Bethune-Cookman's Next Urgent Step

(1938)

Bethune Institute was begun in 1904 as an institution for Negro girls. It grew up as an inspired response to the deep-lying needs of Negro girls in our Southland, and it expressed, in its first purposes, the social and spiritual needs of this expanding womanhood. The circumstances of growth and maintenance within the prevalent pattern of our young Negro institutions dictated union with Cookman Institute. As a single coeducational school these two institutions reached a point of accepted maturity as a junior college. Its properties are now without debt, its buildings sound and adequate, its educational standards regarded as highly creditable. It has developed normally as a coeducational junior college, but it has not been able to carry forward that original and impelling urge which was responsible for its beginning. That purpose of providing a well-rounded and thorough educational experience for Negro girls has become more urgent in recent years.

There are today only two schools in the country in which an educational program can be molded exclusively to the needs and personalities of Negro girls and young women. Over the past ten years the number of young Negro girls in the colleges has been increasing over twice as rapidly as boys. This means, of course, an increasing demand for physical facilities for their accommodation, as well as for a curriculum designed for their special and growing needs. The educational programs in the Negro schools, to avoid the semblance of effeminacy, have, consciously or unconsciously, been shaped to the interests and probable careers of young men. And even though the girls have equaled and even excelled the boys in these academic endeavors, there have been, all too often, in the end artificial and unsatisfactory career objectives for the girls themselves.

It is impossible to get away from the stark fact that the great mass of our young women, from the rural South, from the small towns and cities, are in need of an elementary refashioning of their personalities and life outlook, to overcome the handicaps that are peculiar to these Negro girls. They who are to become the mothers and first teachers of the next generation must themselves be disciplined to habits of poise and understanding self-control, and to wholesome and graceful living. They must become, in greater numbers, the skillful homeworkers and professionals in the domestic arts, the elementary teachers into whose hands will be entrusted the delicate task of nurturing immature and even culturally warped minds into full, sturdy flowering. They must become the civic leaders, the stimulators to heightened standards of living, the creators and conservators of the simple arts of everyday life.

There is the need, that can no longer go unheeded, for the quiet cultivation of those arts and graces that make life, whether humble or grand, a wholesome experience worth sharing with others. We must have women who with unabashed faith and reverence can attune their lives and their deepest emotions to the high sanctions of the Christian religion. If there was anything that gave life and promise to the humble beginnings of Bethune Institute it was this ideal, however crudely stated, and this ideal has continued in the hopes and prayers of its founder.

In a world feverish with the stirrings of social and political unrest, in a country striving to raise its lagging populations to a plane of decent living, in a section held down by poverty, and a race still staggered by the weight of long untutored years, Bethune-Cookman feels its call to return to its first inspiration, an inspiration which it has never abandoned in spirit.

I am impressed that the most important careers of Negro women today are those which they make for themselves, rather than those for which it is usually assumed they can be prepared by set formulas. Their education should therefore be designed intimately with the view to making them socially intelligent and spiritually alive. It should be designed for Negro girls and their peculiar mission in this day.

I therefore propose that, as rapidly as is consistent with the circumstances of transition, Bethune-Cookman reestablish itself as a four-year college for girls. The academic reasons for this proposal lie as deep as the spiritual and social reasons.

1) A two-year tenure in a junior college does not permit sufficient time to develop for the individual student a well-rounded program of experience in learning.

2) There are not enough institutions available for Negro girls in which educational programs can be freely molded to the peculiar social needs and ultimate careers of these girls.

3) A unit program designed exclusively for girls can effect economies impossible in a coeducational institution.

4) There is more urgent need for a full four-year college of standard rank than of a junior college which is, essentially, a preparatory institution for another institution that in the nature of the arrangement can have no control over the important first two years of preparation.

5) There are possible values in the development of such an institution upon the experience and spiritual conviction of a woman whose life began in the unfortunate conditions discussed, and became in itself a living expression of the founding ideals.

6) The value of a private institution is in its ability and will to adjust itself to an urgent present need. As a standard coeducational junior college Bethune-Cookman may be competent, but just another school. As a designed and inspired four-year college for Negro girls it can serve a unique function, one that cannot readily be served by other types of institutions, public or private.

The reorganization of the institution on this basis will make possible the full and free extension of vital home economics courses capable of being utilized as a profession or a domestic skill. It will permit a wholesome living of the educational processes rather than merely teaching. It will permit the assembling of a total faculty dedicated to a program of individualized learning and sympathetically adjusted to the uneven levels of attainment of these girls when they go to college. It will permit the development of a morale and fellow-feeling among these students unconfused by the disturbances of adolescence. It will permit the development of a setting in which work has dignity rather than a specious utility; where cleanliness and hygiene are assumed habits, rather than an occasional social gesture; where the arts, whether homely and domestic or classic, are a part of common life experience, rather than the adornments of the gifted few; where religion is a normal and inspiring spiritual expression, rather than a self-conscious virtue; where problems are not handicaps but challenges to intelligent action.

Letter to Harry Wright McPherson, November 26, 1938. Bethune-Cookman College Papers, Archives Division, General Commission on Archives and History, United Methodist Church, Drew University, Madison, N.J.

Letter to Eleanor Roosevelt

(1941)

April 22, 1941
Mrs. Eleanor Roosevelt
The White House
Washington, D.C.

My dear Mrs. Roosevelt:

May I express to you my sincere gratitude for the opportunity you gave me to talk with you two weeks ago. It seemed that the way was so clear to say to you what I had in my mind and my heart to say. You were so receptive, so generous in your understanding of the things I tried to pour out to you.

First of all, I want to thank you for your acceptance of a place on our Board of Trustees of Bethune-Cookman College. Now you are able to think of our work in an official manner and through this affiliation you may feel free to bring our problems to the attention of friends who may be willing to give us their good-will.

I have such deep appreciation for the fine women who have stood so closely by Martha Berry° and her work and who have helped her meet vital and pressing needs in her marvelous work. For thirty-six years I have been trying to unfold a vision similar to hers, in training Negro boys and girls of the

---

°Berry, a white woman, founded a boys' school in Rome, Georgia, in 1902 that later became a coed junior college.

deep South. We have tried to provide here opportunities for them for opportunities in this section are so few. We have tried to build here a little oasis where they might receive the type of rounded training that will make of them fine American citizens. The masses of our people are exposed to so little in the way of culture and skill. I am not concerned with the idea of "just another school" here. I am concerned about maintaining an Institution that will give unusual opportunity in the things that are needed most by young people in a day like this.

It is my heart's desire to have greater emphasis placed on the Crafts here. Vocational instruction in all of its phases is so very important. If we are to build strong bodies we must begin to put emphasis on physical training. I would like to see here a fine class in Commercial dietetics, for this [is] a field where fine men and women may be developed with splendid cultural background. I am deeply interested in the secretarial courses, particularly those that prepare young women for service in personal care as well as in stenography, typewriting and filing. We need here in Bethune-Cookman a large gymnasium that may be used for recreation and for large gatherings of a musical or literary nature. We would then be in position to have artists like Marian Anderson and be prepared to take care of occasions such as we had when you came to us. There is nothing in this section where we may find participation in the cultural things save what we can provide ourselves.

I am determined to have our vocational work go forward on a parallel with our academic work. We look forward to four years of college work, preparing our young people as strongly in the vocations as in their literary pursuits. You know, of course, our need for a Library building and for more books. Our Library—inadequate though it is—is the only one for Negroes in Volusia County. We want to help our young people in Music—not only in training them in vocal, instrumental and choral music, but in publicizing and preserving their natural talents along this line. This is such a great field for development in so many phases of endeavor.

This is a wonderful spot in the deep South for a fine woman like you to place her active interest and help. It would, through you, challenge the interest of many other fine women who might be willing to help perpetrate the vision of a Negro woman. We need you so much.

I have written you a rather long letter but I felt that I wanted to say these things to you at this time. Please take the time to read this letter calmly and be prayerful, with me, that our work may be preserved and strengthened, and that our service may be revised and expanded to meet the present-day needs of our young people. With you and the friends whom you may touch, with my own untiring effort, and with God as our Guide, I feel that we may go forward.

Always sincerely yours,
Mary McLeod Bethune

Eleanor Roosevelt Papers, Franklin D. Roosevelt Library, Hyde Park, N.Y. File 100.

Letter to Franklin D. Roosevelt

(1941)

November 28, 1941

My dear Mr. President:

It is difficult to write a person in your situation as I am writing you. But, somehow, through the affectionate and understanding relationship I had with your illustrious mother, I have had, possibly a real human strain of approach to you. Therefore, I hope you will permit me to talk to you in terms of Bethune-Cookman College, the child of my creation and toil.

I need not tell you what it has meant in Florida to try to build up a practical and cultural institution for my people. It has taken a wisdom and tact and patience and endurance that I cannot describe in words. However, Mr. President, the college is there as a reservoir of real service in building citizens and a more humane relationship.

We feel this work must go on. It is a community center. A hundred thousand Negroes south of us, to the southeast and southwest of us, are looking to us for guidance, for help in the several fields of life.

Six years ago, at the inception of your great humane program for the youth of the nation, I was called upon to share in the extension of that program to the underprivileged groups of the country, and particularly to the Negroes. Thus, a sacrifice of my time and energy to the college had to be made for this greater service to the nation.

The financial support of the institution depends, oh so largely, upon me. Our endowment reaches only $140,000–$143,000 to be specific. It is supported almost entirely by philanthropic interests. Because of my activities in the country, many friends who did not see as I saw withdrew their financial support.

We are now in desperate need of funds. My nights are sleepless with this load upon my heart and mind. I must have help. I believe there are friends who would want to help.

You told me a year ago that you possibly had two or three young men that you felt you might interest in this work. We now need these young men, or any interest, Mr. President, that you might point our way. You would not blame me, I am sure, if I should say that I need you to help me through whatever channels you might deem wise.

Mrs. Roosevelt is holding a small conference in behalf of the college on the afternoon of the eighth of December, for the purpose of getting a few people together who will actually listen to the story and help. Will you use your influence for this meeting?

With all the responsibilities you have, please know that I realize that this is an unusual course to have you take. But for me, you may be willing to do the unusual thing.

Know always that my prayers are for you daily. My strength and my influence are yours to the end.

Faithfully yours,
Mary McLeod Bethune

Franklin D. Roosevelt Papers, Franklin D. Roosevelt Library, Hyde Park, N.Y. File 100, Letter no. 286.

Minutes of the Special Called Meeting of the Board of Trustees, Bethune-Cookman College

[excerpt] (1942)

MRS. BETHUNE: Thank you, Bishop. I hope you will permit me to remain seated.

First of all, I want you to realize with me that this is a significant moment in my life. This is the moment that I knew, some day, would come, but its coming brings a peculiar spiritual feeling difficult for one who has not had the experience, to realize. Thirty-eight years ago, when we started out here, we realized that there would be a termination some day. As I look back now over the years, as I see the harvest from the seeds that have been sown, as I receive the realization of the dreams of the years in these buildings, grounds and equipments, and above all, in the thousands of young lives that have been touched and inspired—young men and women who are now bearing the torchlight of service here, there and everywhere, I approach this moment with gratitude to the God we all love and serve, for the privilege of spending all of these years—thirty-eight long years—in this one service, and in bringing this school to the place where we now find it.

For the past five or ten days I have been looking into the past, realizing the present and thinking of the future. I want to express my deep appreciation to the Board of Trustees, the Advisory Board and the Alumni Association, and to the great Board of the Church, Foundations and individuals located all over this land, who have given us of their influence, means and service. I do not look back with any regrets. I know that many things have been left undone that should have been done—many things done in a way that might not have been most effective—but though some mistakes have been made our hand has been steadfastly in God's hand during the years, and the light of His countenance has never failed to shine about us.

Today, as I sit in these closing moments of my administrative day in this

Institution that has been the unfolding of my soul, there is a peculiar, strange feeling within me. For the past days I have wanted to be alone—spending time only occasionally with a few friends. I have been questioning my soul, trying to find if there is any selfish motive within me, whether I have given to this Institution of my physical ability to its limit, whether, for the good of the Institution I should, even now, endeavor to make another step. I have been convinced that we have now, as I see it, two important lives to save and perpetuate if we can—the first in importance, because of its wide service and influence, is the life of this Institution. If the life of this school is to be saved I feel that we must work rapidly, in these times, to put vigor and strength and greater vision into the program than I can furnish. I am tired, I am weary; my faith is as strong as it has always been but my physical strength will not answer now to the demands of the things to be done. Therefore, I felt that it was important for the sake of the Institution to ask the Chairman of our Board to call an emergency meeting of the Trustees, in order that important issues of the moment, affecting Institutions of this kind, might not be neglected. Our chairman was in the midst of an important meeting, when I asked him, with trembling voice over the telephone, to call this meeting, but he graciously consented to call the Board at this time.

Then, my trustees, I found myself three or four weeks ago with six doctors around me. Dr. Adams did not undress for two nights but stayed by my bedside. The margin was so narrow that I felt I could no longer fool myself, my trustees and my friends of what needed to be done. My doctors told me that I would have to give up this responsibility and live, or hold it and die. I felt that this life needed to be preserved for a few more days or weeks if only to point the way, to help to guide and exercise influence for the Institution. So I felt that it was necessary for me to make a request for retirement, so that both of these lives might be preserved—the life of the College and my own life. To permit me to retire from the active administrative duties of the College, to find someone younger and more vigorous for the task, someone who could consecrate himself or herself to the needs of the hour, who could shoulder the responsibilities and give to the Institution the leadership that it needs in a day like this—will preserve the life of the Institution. Therefore, with this beautiful plant—thirty-four acres, fourteen buildings, equipments, sixty-six lots, one hundred seventy-eight acres of woodland—a fine faculty and student body, a grand host of alumni and graduates and friends, with the greatest service I have been able to give and the gratitude of my soul—I wish to lay this school upon the hearts and shoulders of this Board. May I say to you that I have done my best and I must now entrust it to you, with the feeling that you will not shrink from the responsibilities that are yours and must be yours as the years go by. You know of the prayers and the hardships, the joys and the sorrows that have gone into the building of this beautiful institution. There is nothing on earth so beautiful to me as this school. I have two children—my son, Albert, and Bethune-Cookman College. I gave birth to both of them and I love them with a devotion that can never die. All that I can give in helpfulness will always be given to them. I am asking you to permit me to retire into general activities that I may be inclined to do. I may be in Australia or London or Africa. I want moments of leisure to think or do whatever my heart or mind may dictate to me.

I have prayed earnestly for a successor—someone to take this work after me. I know that such a person will not do just as I have done, nor do it in the same way I have done it. I do not want that you nor I shall think that someone else will do things in the way Mrs. Bethune did them. Someone must come and in his own way, with the guidance of God and you, according to the needs and demands and developments of the hour, carry on this work.

Several months ago I threw my mantle to the winds. I have traveled, as you know, from Maine to California, from the deep South to the great Northern areas, and have been touching men and women everywhere. I have prayed that my mantle would fall on someone whom it would fit and who could carry on my work. I remember when dear Amanda Smith came to me one day and said, "Mary McLeod Bethune, I have been to Africa three times; I have traveled around the world; I have been looking for someone upon whom to throw my mantle. As I talk with you, Mary Bethune, I believe you are the one to wear my mantle. Get down here, child, and let us pray."° We were in the middle of the grounds, but we dropped to our knees. This consecration that I received as a young woman and the inspiration I received from Dr. Dwight L. Moody have carried me through the years.°° I had hoped that I could find a woman to wear my mantle but it seems that I cannot find one, consequently I have brought to you my recommendation of a young man, thirty-three years of age, consecrated, trained, clean in character, spiritual, with a vision of service. You will not find another president to carry this work as fully as I have had to carry it, because it is my own child. You have a greater responsibility now than you have ever had before. You will be concerned about things now as you have never been concerned before. I am placing this institution on your shoulders and your hearts, and I am recommending as my successor, Mr. James A. Colston, who, with your guidance, help and support will, I believe, carry on this work in a way that will be pleasing to God and to you.

As I retire from the presidency of this beautiful Institution, I retire simply from active service, not from devotion nor helpfulness. May God bless and inspire you and give you faith and understanding to carry on in the days that are to come. My blessings are yours. May my gratitude for the service of thirty-eight years be a rich heritage to those yet to come.

[CHAIRMAN] BISHOP KING: Friends, you have heard Mrs. Bethune's statement, a very moving and remarkable statement. I might have anticipated such a statement as this. I confess that I have no response now to make. I would like to hear from you and ascertain just what your reaction is to this statement.

°Amanda Berry Smith (1837–1915) was a pioneering black evangelist.
°°Moody was an evangelist and the founder of the Moody Bible Institute.

DR. DAVAGE: While we anticipated as you said, Mr. Chairman, that this action would be requested, and anticipated just how Mrs. Bethune would present her request, my own reaction is that, in the first place, we are not prepared to make a fitting response. A fitting response and a formal acceptance should be made at our annual meeting, when we have prepared a program for thirty-eight years of service. This should be done by the trustees, friends and representatives of the annual Conferences. This is not the time. If Bishop King cannot make a response, I am sure I cannot. We can talk out of our hearts, but technically, we cannot let Mrs. Bethune retire from the presidency of Bethune-Cookman College into a little group like this. It seems to me that there are two items requiring the action of the Board. First, to act on Mrs. Bethune's request for retirement. Second, to act on her recommendation of her successor.

I do not like the word "retire"— "release" from the detailed responsibility of administration would be better. We do expect that Mrs. Bethune shall have an active interest in the school even though she is relieved of the responsibility of administration. On behalf of the Board of Education, I can say simply this, that Mrs. Bethune, through the years, has had their confidence and admiration and possibly, because of their confidence, they have placed too great a responsibility upon her. Dr. McPherson, Executive Secretary of the Board, has asked me to express his regret that that he cannot be at this meeting.

December 15, 1942. James C. Colston Papers, Bethune-Cookman College Archives, Daytona Beach, Fla.

Bethune (*third from left*) inspects food preparations at the Daytona Educational and Industrial Training School for Negro Girls. *Florida State Archives, circa 1910.*

Bethune, as a young college president, works at her desk in 1923. That year, her Daytona girls' school became coeducational. *Richard V. Moore Private Collection.*

Facing page:
A Bible-toting Bethune leads her uniformed students at the Daytona Educational and Industrial Training School for Negro Girls. *School Catalogue. Florida State Archives, 1910–11.*

After thirty-eight years of leadership of Bethune-Cookman College, Bethune confers with her successor, James A. Colston. *Library of Congress, January 1943.*

PART IV

Womanist Activism

"We Are Being Heard!" (1917–1949)

Introduction

Elaine M. Smith

IN THE POST-SLAVERY ERA, African American women have been regarded as a cipher by mainstream America. They have been so hampered by the multiple burdens of gender, race, and class that of all groups in the nation, they have been on the farthest fringes of opportunity, economic security, and civic participation. At times the effects of these burdens have intertwined to make it impossible to differentiate the consequences of each. But each has had its circumscribing effect, and combined they have been the bane of this group.

Black women have coped with oppression in part through their own organizations. Typically, these have been womanist associations, whose members address the negative impact of both gender and race without necessarily castigating black men.[1] The more visible of these societies usually have been dominated by educated and self-sacrificing local leaders possessing middle-class incomes and manners and holding Judeo-Christian values, who regard their endeavors as an aspect of race advancement. Frequently they have undertaken the same types of activities as their white counterparts: practicing conservation; subscribing to government bonds; boosting the morale of United States troops; conducting voter registration campaigns; rendering charitable services to individuals, groups, and institutions; establishing welfare and educational facilities; sponsoring youth development programs; engaging in historic preservation; creating recreational and social outlets; cultivating interracial and international relationships; propagandizing career opportunities for women; and lobbying for beneficial government programs. But ebony women have often had to fight for an equal role in a given program. In dealing with white society, often in situations of gender subordination, they have had to struggle for opportunities commensurate with those already available to white women.

In the first half of the twentieth century, the charismatic Mary McLeod Bethune epitomized black women's ability to organize for group goals. She dedicated herself to service, the nearly universal objective of black women's organizations. Moreover, she refused to acquiesce to society's negative stereotyping of her group. Her leadership of women was a common topic for the black media, whose most apt characterization of Bethune appeared, among other places, in *Ebony*'s "Women Leaders." This 1949 review of black women's historic battle for gender and racial equality featured thirteen contemporary luminaries, each described in a one- or two-word caption, including "Servicewoman," "Republican," and "Sorority Head." Pittsburgh's distinguished Daisy E. Lampkin, for example, was designated as "Organizer"; Washington's renowned Mary Church Terrell as "Educator." Bethune garnered the highest accolade: "First Lady."[2] In large measure, this honor could be justified by her power organizing dynamic—her intense motivation, her passion for cohesiveness, and her bold vision and execution. She brought this dynamic to the leadership of four womanist organizations: the Florida Federation of Colored Women's Clubs (1917–1925), the Southeastern Federation of Colored Women's Clubs (1920–1925), the National Association of Colored Women (1924–1928), and the National Council of Negro Women, (1935–1949).

Bethune's intense motivation, the first factor in her organizing dynamic, derived from a soaring assessment of women. "Next to God, we are indebted to women," she declared in the late 1920s, "first for life itself, and then for making it worth having."[3] She never wavered in this conviction. Ever since her days at Scotia Seminary, a North Carolina girls' boarding school, which had grounded her in voluntary gender organizations and earned her middle-class credentials, she had been determined to elevate women. Prior to leading national womanist associations, she implemented a female agenda most visibly through her residential school for girls. From this perspective she mused, "I longed to see women, Negro women, hold in their hands diplomas which bespoke achievement. . . . I longed to see their accomplishments recognized side by side with any women, anywhere."[4] She never doubted such possibilities, provided that black women gained access to greater opportunities. But regardless of experiences, she believed that black women's leadership illuminated the road to racial progress.

In addition to her ability to motivate, Bethune tended to facilitate greater cohesion within an organization. She strove to bring organizational affiliates closer in structure, methods, and goals, and members of differing affiliates closer in their relationships to each other. Since this required business efficiency, she constantly focused on finances, constitutions, parliamentary procedures, dissemination of minutes, and internal networking. She also emphasized public relations through the founding or revitalizing of organizational periodicals: the *Florida Herald*, *Southeastern Herald*, *National Notes*, and *Aframerican Women's Journal* (later called *Women United*).

Bethune's drive for cohesion was showcased most clearly in her leadership of black women's most revered secular organization of the early twentieth century, the National Association of Colored Women, founded in 1896. The NACW endeavored "to furnish evidence of the moral, mental and material progress made by people of color" as well as to elevate the domestic, moral, and civil life of black women.[5] Unhappy with its somewhat amorphous character, Bethune tried to impose a tight discipline to generate a greater "continuity of programs extending from the National through the Regions, States, Counties, Cities, to the Individual Clubs."[6] She believed, for example, that all NACW local units, like Florida's Excelsior Reading Circle in Gainesville, Day Nursery Club in Orlando, and Busy Merry Makers in Tampa, needed to become grassroots cells implementing public policy positions and programs that were common to all ten thousand dues-paying members of the national organization.[7] Effecting such a change, however, was like pouring new wine into old skins, causing much to be spilled. Therefore, Bethune founded a new organization, the National Council of Negro Women.

The third component of Bethune's power organizing dynamic was her bold vision and execution. A contemporary observed, "She sees the end bright and clear and overleaps in the vision of her soul the crosses and the length of the path; thus, the deep convictions of her own mind stamp themselves irresistibly upon the minds of others."[8] Bethune proclaimed to the National Association of Colored Women, "This organization must assume an attitude toward all big questions involving the welfare of the nation, public right and especially the present and future of our race. These questions are both national and international."[9] To implement such objectives, she established the NACW's first fixed headquarters in a large, detached Romanesque building in Washington, D.C., that cost $25,000.

Striking initiatives had been a hallmark of Bethune's presidency of the Florida Federation. The federation was established in 1908. By its second decade, it comprised more than sixty clubs of roughly thirteen members each, in at least twenty cities from Key West to Tallahassee. While working to shore up local communities through self-help, Bethune resolutely led the clubs in facing three macro issues. Two were responses to major national events: the entry of the United States into the First World War and the passage of the Nineteenth Amendment, which enfranchised women. The third was opening a facility for delinquent girls in Ocala, which could accommodate up to fourteen. Given the meagerness of available resources, the "Home for Wayward and Delinquent Girls" could have been initiated only through enterprise of the kind demonstrated by the federation's fourth president.[10]

Bethune exhibited similar enterprise in her leadership of the Southeastern Federation and the National Council of Negro Women, both of which she founded (in 1920 and 1935, respectively). Although Southern leaders had discussed the establishment of a regional structure within the NACW for years, Bethune's initiative transformed talk into reality. While in 1923 the press reported that the Southeastern Federation encompassed two thousand clubs in twelve states, it affected only a small fraction of them, because the organization served essentially as a forum for regional leaders to advance several constructive currents in American life: "get out the vote" activities, interracial programs, and social welfare services. These were enshrined in the group's platform as citizenship, interracial cooperation, and intensive organization.[11]

Bethune's leadership in the Southeastern Federation, however, paled in comparison with her leadership in the National Council of Negro Women. The NCNW was structured to permit "all national bodies of women, young and old, to pool their thinking and all together speak as one voice and mind for the highest good of the race."[12] Like the mostly white National Council of Women of the United States, organized in 1888, the National Council of Negro Women encompassed a spectrum of member organizations. But unlike that model, the NCNW developed local chapters for grassroots power. In 1949 it counted eighty-two of them, plus thousands of other members linked through twenty-two affiliating national women's organizations. These included professional and occupationally oriented groups, academic sororities, women's divisions of fraternal organizations, missionary societies of church denominations, and political associations.

One function of Bethune's womanist organizations was to win recognition in the broader society. Her groups took on white women's organizational hegemony, in particular. In 1901, eleven years before Bethune joined it, the NACW had achieved token integration of the National Council of Women, which subsequently gave it some visibility in the International Council of Women, founded in 1888. In September 1920, as a member of the American Council's ten-woman delegation, the NACW's distinguished former president Mary B. Talbert attended the quinquennial International Council meeting in Christiania (today Oslo), Norway. Summarizing the experience sanguinely, she exclaimed, "THE ORGANIZED COLORED WOMEN OF AMERICA ARE BEING HEARD!"[13] This suggested, however symbolically, the steady breaching of color barriers by African American women, as did events five years later. In 1925, former NACW president Hallie Quinn Brown and NACW president Bethune led their organization in effectively protesting segregated seating at an International Council meeting in Washington, D.C. They later prevailed upon the U.S. National Council of Women to move its biennial conference from Asheville, North Carolina, to Detroit to avoid the racial segregation of members.[14]

While continuing to associate with white women in voluntary organizations, black women leaders increasingly courted the federal government during the Roosevelt administration. As the NCNW president, Bethune believed that her group was projecting itself into the national consciousness. As early as 1941, she reported to the membership, "Our Council activities have brought the Negro woman into the national picture of American life."[15] Eight years later, echoing Mary Talbert's words, she concluded, *We are being heard!* At that time, her organization spoke on a global stage to people requesting "counsel and cooperation and leadership." In concert with other liberal groups, it was being heard, especially at home, in the expansion of wage standards, social security, and government salaries.[16]

While the political and social climate of post–World War II America denied the real fruits of liberty to African Americans, and to a lesser extent women, Bethune's NCNW, more than any other gender-based voluntary society, shortened the fringe on which many women of color stood, along with the fringe on which the body politic perceived them. Certainly Bethune fired the imaginations of black sisters. Inspired by countless newspaper photos of Bethune with First Lady Eleanor Roosevelt and other movers and shakers, New York teenager Shirley Chisholm, for example, pondered the possibility that she too might one day become a national figure. Her day arrived in 1968, when she became the first African American woman to win a seat in the United States Congress. About thirty years earlier, by introducing the idea of running for Congress to a select group of black women in New York, Bethune had anticipated a triumph such as Chisholm's.[17] In effect, NCNW president Bethune redefined black women's status and visibility in civic affairs, particularly on the federal level. While lacking the drama of the then approaching civil rights revolution, this demonstrated the possibilities of organized pressure in effecting democratic change and was foundational to womanist activism in the second half of the century.

DOCUMENTARY SOURCES

Building upon the achievements of her womanist predecessors, Bethune used her power organizing dynamic to further the gender and racial objectives of organized black women. The twenty documents in this chapter, divided into three sections, reveal the circumstances and character of her womanist activities. "Home Ground," the first section, situates Bethune in Florida. "Race Overtures" considers her involvement in the women's interracial movement of the 1920s. "Great Designs" highlights her record in the NACW and the NCNW.

The documents in "Home Ground" illustrate Bethune's early womanist activism in the Sunshine State. She assumed the presidency of the Florida Federation of Colored Women's Clubs when the United States was rushing preparations to defeat the Central Powers in World War I. In a state where more black men than white were drafted into the army (12,904 to 12,769), Bethune energetically endorsed organizational support for the war, as her 1917 open letter to the federation discloses. But the greatest challenge of her presidency was founding and sustaining a home for delinquent girls. As correspondence indicates, erratic and insufficient financial contributions made this a difficult task. After relinquishing the Florida presidency, Bethune used her proven ability and humanitarianism in continued state service. In the wake of a catastrophic hurricane in September 1928 that blasted South Florida, killing as many as two thousand, she toured the devastation, helped to organize relief, and appealed to Black America for assistance in graphic and compelling terms.

As president of the Southeastern Federation in 1920, Bethune, along with other outstanding members of the fledgling regional organization, extended her interracial contacts in response to the increasing interest of white liberals. "Race Overtures" highlights three of Bethune's responses to white initiatives. The first document in this section is a letter to the National Board of the Young Women's Christian Association (1920) regarding a meeting in New York between some board members and notable black women. The second is a plan for interracial interaction, published as "Southern Negro Women and Race Co-operation" (1921), which Atlanta neighborhood activist Lugenia Burns Hope, Bethune, and eight other Southeastern luminaries crafted at the request of representatives from the white Women's Missionary Council of the Methodist Episcopal Church South. The third is an invitation to join the Woman's General Committee of the Commission on Interracial Cooperation, the leading interracial advocacy agency in the South. The minutes of the committee's October 1922 meeting describe black women's entry process.

Having gained this regional organizational experience, Bethune became a national leader of women. The thirteen documents in "Great Designs" mirror her activism at this level. She invested the two national organizations that she successively headed with high hopes, or great designs, the matrix of her life. She articulated them for the NACW most eloquently in her 1926 presidential address in Oakland, California, through which she campaigned successfully for a national headquarters. Bethune's designs were also manifested in her proposal of an NACW European tour. Essentially, this trip turned into a presidential parade through nine European countries in 1927. In that same year, her unbounded aspirations for the NACW lit up her report to the Biennial Convention of the National Council of Women of the United States, a report published the following year. Here she covered headquarters succinctly, despite its being the most arduous and draining endeavor of her presidency—in fact, its signature achievement. When headquarters fell on hard times under successive NACW presidents, as the chair of the Headquarters Trustee Board (a position she held until 1952), Bethune remained committed to its cause, as her letter in 1933 to Julia West Hamilton, an NACW stalwart in Washington, reveals.

Bethune's vision for black women to participate fully in the civic affairs of the country transcended the means the NACW provided and led to the creation of the National Council of Negro Women. Probably only such vision, or great designs, coupled with stellar public achievements, brought the new organization into being, as can be inferred from the minutes of the founding meeting in December 1935.

While Bethune and the NCNW made important strides during the Great Depression, including sponsorship of the 1938 White House Conference on Negro Women and Children, the council operated more propitiously in World War II, when the country mobilized against the anti-democratic Axis while continuing anti-democratic practices at home. In 1940, as the NCNW leader, Bethune publicly sought from President Franklin Roosevelt administrative jobs in national defense for black women. The next year she protested vehemently to Secretary of War Henry Stimson the exclusion of black women from his agency's newly founded national women's advisory council on soldiers' welfare. Combined with other pressures, this brought her onto the advisory council as the NCNW representative. Thereafter she remained closely attuned to military affairs, especially as they involved women. Reflecting this relationship was Bethune's participation in a tour of hospitals in the Northeast (July 16–24, 1945) as a member of the National Civilian Advisory Committee of the Women's Army Corps.

The federal acknowledgment that President Bethune and the NCNW earned during the war carried into peacetime. It facilitated her continued espousal of great designs, especially as they affected the masses. Her advocacy for government-subsidized housing before the Senate Banking and Currency Committee in December 1945 was a case in point. Her interests were wide-ranging and international, however, as her report to the U.S. National Council of Women attested. Moreover, in keeping with the temper of democracy and national self-determination in the postwar world, Bethune became insistent on true democracy at home. For example, in "Americans All: Which Way America???" she contended, "You and I must fight as never before to make our government realize the ideals upon which it was founded. . . . We must help save the soul of our own nation . . . so we can really save the world." In "Don't Miss the Foothold!" she viewed the Truman administration's signature civil rights report, "To Secure These Rights," as a sign that African Americans were making progress toward winning the blessings of liberty through heroic efforts.

In October 1949, Bethune published in the NCNW's periodical her valedictory as the council president. In the address she acknowledged the legions of women through whose arduous labors and sacrifices the National Council had become the organized voice of African American women, heard both at home and abroad. Working together, they had realized a great design.

NOTES

1. The term "womanist" is used in this work as explicated by Elsa Barkley Brown, "Womanist Consciousness: Maggie Lena Walker and the Independent Order of Saint Luke," reprinted in *Black Women in United States History: The Twentieth Century,* vol. I, ed. Darlene Clark Hine (Brooklyn: Carlson Publishing Co., 1990). Following novelist Alice Walker and scholar Chikwenye Okonjo Ogunyemi, womanism is defined here as "a consciousness that incorporates racial, cultural, sexual, national, economic and political considerations."

2. "Women Leaders," *Ebony,* July 1949, pp. 19–33. The other ten leaders cited were Jean Murrell Capers—Public Official; Gertrude E. Anderson—Businesswoman; Arenia C. Mallory—Educator; Elsie Austin—Lawyer; Sue Bailey Thurman—Writer; Jeanetta Welch Brown—Democrat; Eunice Hunton Carter—Republican; Henrine Ward Banks—Lecturer; Harriet West—Servicewoman; and Alice P. Allen—Sorority Head.

3. Bethune quote in Elaine M. Smith, "Mary McLeod Bethune and the National Youth Administration," in *Clio Was a Woman: Studies in the History of American Women,* ed. Mabel E. Deutrich and Virginia C. Purdy (Washington, D.C.: Howard University Press, 1980), p. 149.

4. "A Philosophy of Education for Negro Girls," in Part III of this volume.

5. Quote in Elaine M. Smith, "Mary McLeod Bethune's 'Last Will and Testament': A Legacy for Race Vindication," *Journal of Negro History* 81 (1996): 105; Margaret Murray Washington, "Club Work among Negro Women," in *Progress of a Race,* ed. J. L. Nicholas (Napierville, Ill.: J. L. Nicholas and Co., 1929).

6. "National Association of Colored Women," included in this part.

7. While NACW leaders boasted a membership of 100,000 in the 1920s, at the organization's largest convention of the decade, it could find only 10,000 members in good standing financially. See minutes of the 1928 Convention, NACW Papers, pp. 56–59. Bethune and kindred leaders bandied about inflated membership figures for other womanist organizations as well. As president of the Florida Federation in July 1919, Bethune claimed to represent 3,000 ("Training Colored Children for Citizenship," under "Women's Work," Tuskegee Institute Newspaper Clipping File, Reel 11). Yet a careful reading of documents contemporaneous to Bethune's presidency of the federation suggests that, at best, the Florida organization had fewer than 800 members. With regard to the Southeastern Federation, even with just a few extant records it is obvious that the figure of 50,000 members widely reported in the press in 1923 is skewed, given that there were only 10,000 in the national body. Moreover, in 1940–41, even though reliable numbers are mostly unavailable, the scope of NCNW activities indicated that the council had nowhere near the 800,000 members that Bethune repeatedly claimed. At that time fourteen national groups were affiliated with it. One of them, the Achievement Club, had only 117 members. But regardless of the numbers, including those from local councils which were then being organized, the NCNW national affiliates offered little more than ritual cooperation. Bethune and other womanist leaders probably projected larger organizational memberships than existed in order to give them leverage in dealing with others. Black women, handicapped especially by income, gender, and race, had not traditionally exercised such leverage.

8. Quote from Sadie Stockton, *Chicago Defender,* November 27, 1937, Scrapbook for 1937, BF.

9. President's Address to the Fifteenth Biennial Convention of the National Association of Colored Women, included in this part.

10. Elaine M. Smith, "Facing the Great Issues: The Florida Federation of Colored Women's Clubs during World War I and the Post War Period," presented at the Florida Women's History Symposium, Tallahassee, Florida, May 18, 1995.

11. Elaine M. Smith, "Across and behind Racial Lines: The Southeastern Federation of Colored Women's Clubs, 1920–1925," presented at the Annual Meeting of the Southern Conference on Afro-American Studies, Atlanta, Georgia, February 1993.

12. Bethune quoted in an Associated Negro Press article in *The Weekly Echo,* December 4, 1936, ARC.

13. Talbert, "THE ORGANIZED COLORED WOMEN OF AMERICA ARE BEING HEARD!" *The Competitor,* December 1920, pp. 276–281.

14. See the *Washington Post,* May 6, 1925, pp. 1–2, for the fullest factual account of the event; other *Post* articles are: May 9, 1925, p. 1; May 10, 1925, pp. 1, 7; May 13, 1925, p. 4. The reaction of NACW leaders appears in "Delegates Deplore Segregation 'Bolt' at Women's Meeting," *Pittsburgh Courier,* May 16, 1925, p. 3.

15. Bethune, NCNW Annual Report, October 1941, BF.

16. Bethune, "Stepping Aside . . . at Seventy-four," in this part.

17. Susan Brownmiller, *Shirley Chisholm* (Garden City, N.Y.: Doubleday and Co., 1970), pp. 42–43; *Chicago Defender,* November 27, 1937, 1937 Scrapbook, BF.

Home Ground

Letter to the Florida Federation
of Colored Women's Clubs

(1917)

Dear Co-workers:

As we come to the close of the summer, perhaps the busiest and most exacting in the history of our country, and settle down to our regular winter's work, let each see to it that a place is made on our weekly and monthly schedule for the work that we are pledged to do "not for ourselves, but for others." . . . We need stronger support from our large cities, and the continued support from every little town and hamlet.

We planned great things at our splendid State meeting in June. The education of a worthy girl, the printing of our Minutes, the publishing of the Florida Voice, the forming of Red Cross Chapters and Emergency Circles. Let us not lose a moment's time, dear co-workers. The emergency is here— the need on women's service is greater than ever before in the history of the world. No women in the world, not the women of Russia, nor of England, nor of France can bring to their country's need, truer hearts, deeper devotion, more unselfish service than the tried and true women of the Negro race.

In these strenuous times we dare not think of fatigue or personal gain, but we must go forward in our service for God and humanity.

Many of the clubs have reported good work already. [M]any are keeping up their Red Cross and Emergency work, canning, preserving, knitting, sewing, raising chickens, "doing their bit." Many Clubs are doing most effective work in their Red Cross Chapters and Emergency Circles and are tabulating their reports so that we may get the credit for our service. Please, each Club do this: Keep accurate reports of the number of cans of fruit, vegetables, etc., put up, the number of articles made for the soldiers and their families, the money contributed for War Relief . . . and send in the same to me by November 30th.

Two clubs united into an Emergency Circle have sent $50 for War Relief, prepared fine boxes, bought several Liberty Bonds and are going forward.

Some have sent their dollar toward the Minutes—some have sent their first assessment toward the State work of educating "our girl." All should send this to the Secretary, Mrs. Minnie Berlack, Orlando, Fla., not later than October 1st. You will remember that each Club was taxed $2 per year. It will be easy to send this in two payments.

We feel that most valuable assistance will be rendered this year by the Vice-Presidents who have the supervision of their sections. A monthly letter from them will be appreciated at headquarters.

I shall be pleased to receive any information or to answer questions about our Club work and to render any assistance possible. If you need me on your field, advise me and I shall if possible come to you. Let us conscientiously strive to make this our year of greatest service.

Yours for His service,
Mary McLeod Bethune
Pres. Fla. Federation of Colored Women's Clubs

Palatka Advocate, September 15, 1917. "Women's Work," Tuskegee Institute Newspaper Clippings File, Tuskegee University Special Collections and Archives, Tuskegee, Ala.

Help Establish the Home for Delinquent Girls

(1921)

Dear Friend:

The Negro women of the State of Florida, as you doubtless know, are working to establish a Home for Delinquent Colored Girls at Ocala, [m]oved by the great need of this unfortunate class of girls, many of whom are not criminal, but may become so, by contact with hardened law breakers. Our women are laboring incessantly to prepare a Home where these precious girls may be helped and loved into lives of usefulness and honor.

We were fortunate enough, through the good offices of the people of Ocala, to secure a building there.

By the Father's help, on Sunday, September 25th, at 3:00 p.m., we shall throw open wide the doors and let the neglected girls—our girls—come in. We cannot do the work alone: we need the sympathy and the hearty cooperation of our people. We are calling upon the Churches, the many schools, the Young People's Societies, the Secret Organizations, all over the State, to help us. Send us a contribution for our opening. Send a representative, a letter or a telegram.

All Negroes of Florida must help to save our girls! We believe that if we really start, the great State of Florida will help us.

Come Friends—You help, I help—Everybody help to save the girl that's farthest down!

Yours for Negro Womanhood,
Mary McLeod Bethune
Pres. Fla. Federation of Colored Women's Clubs

September 13, 1921. National Association of Colored Women's Clubs Papers, Bethune File, Headquarters of the NACWC, Washington, D.C.

Letter to Mrs. [F. J.] Payne and [Carrie E.] Jackson

(1923)

My dear Women [Matrons of the Florida Federation Home for Delinquent Girls]:

Your letter brought tears to my eyes. I know what hard times you are having. My hands have been full and I have not had the time to do anything. I am sending you my personal check for $50.00 to pay the grocer bill, Dr [doctor] bill and [any] other expenses you may have. I haven't had the time to see any one. I authorized Mrs. [E. J.] Collier to get your money and pay you. I did not know you were so far behind. Let me know how far behind you are with your expenses. Don't get discouraged [for] as long as I have a penny I am willing to share it with you. Don't give up. I am going to work and raise some money for you.

We are going to try and get this work over to the State this year. I have not been able to get to you myself but I have certainly tried to get others to do so.

With best wishes, I am
Sincerely yours,
Mary McLeod Bethune

March 27, 1923. National Association of Colored Women's Clubs Papers, Bethune File, Headquarters of the NACWC, Washington, D.C.

Mrs. Bethune Tells of Effect of
Intense Hurricane Storm on Florida's Negro People

(1928)

Words are almost inadequate to tell of the conditions as they are. Suffice it to say that the lower East Coast of Florida lies prostrated. Delray, Pleasant City, Palm Beach, West Palm Beach, Canal Point, Bellglade, Pahokee—all have been seriously struck. Never before in my life have I witnessed such suffering, and so many homeless people. The coast has been raked and scraped from Pompano to Stuart. The storm was the most violent ever known in that section. In its rage, it brought all persons down to a common level of mutual help. Negroes and whites alike are sharing in the losses of homes, friends, property, and indeed life. Little has been left of the homes and business places of the Negroes in West Palm Beach. School houses have been destroyed—every church, save one, in the entire city is demolished. All of the public buildings are destroyed. The cries for home and shelter penetrate to one's very soul.

Canteens and dispensaries have been opened up for immediate help in the stricken sections. Whites and Negroes together are receiving aid from the Red Cross, which is rendering every assistance possible.

Our big job has been in the organizing of effective leadership among the Negro group and the securing of executive nurses and social workers to labor hand in hand with the group, in order that the needs of the thousands of suffering might be met.

The suffering among the people is piteous. Mothers separated from their children—women in childbirth being crudely wrapped in mattresses or blankets and carried from place to place for safety.

We were fortunate in that very few lives were lost in Palm Beach proper, and the surrounding cities, but, oh, the distress among the poor people in the Everglades. They were drowned by the hundreds. Great trucks—heaped high with dead bodies—men and women and children, being buried without being identified—many of them having no one left to identify them. Steam shovels were used in the colored and white cemeteries to dig the trenches in which this great mass of stricken humanity was laid to rest.

As we walked through the destitute places, our souls cried out to God for help, because He alone could sustain us under such conditions as these. We are so happy that we were able to help a little and to direct and organize so that efficient service might be rendered those who were suffering so acutely.

Many poor souls swam through the rising waters, or walked twenty-five and thirty miles—seeking shelter. One brave Negro man, J. W. Sanders, saved the lives of eighteen persons at Bellglade—most of them being white women. In the saving of these lives, he became so exhausted that when he took his wife and child and tried to make it with them, his strength left, and his child was lost. But it was only for a season—Our Father does not thus reward valor and unselfishness—the child was rescued by another and when the brave man was receiving aid in the canteen, the little one was brought in with another group. The tears of joy streaming down his cheeks were pitiful to see.

One mother tried to swim across the rushing waters—her baby in one arm and fighting the current with the other. An alligator took off one arm, and she was left thus to save herself and her child. Thank God a rescuer came and they were saved.

The need for assistance in these places is very great. There are more to help than can be reached. The refugees are being sent to nearby points—five hundred Negroes were sent, last evening, to Pompano, where Negro physicians and two nurses were provided to administer to them. Five hundred whites were sent into Miami with a like arrangement. Help is being given to them as rapidly as it is received.

This catastrophe has brought out the fact that there is a brotherhood among men, even though it is sometimes hard to see. Every man and woman who possibly can is working to help his fellowman. We believe that good must and will come out of this disaster.

This is a hard blow for the Negroes of the East Coast. Two years ago we had the great storm of Miami—then the boom bubble burst with fearful results—seven banks in West Palm Beach were forced to close—and then this great storm. We need—WE NEED—WE NEED—your prayers, your financial support, your assistance in every possible way. These homeless people not only need food and clothing, but their little homes, representing years of toil and sacrifice, must be rebuilt. They had no storm insurance—they have no money—nothing is left to them. The people all over the state are rallying nobly to the situation. Physicians, nurses, social workers, and interested, anxious citizens are helping in every possible manner.

An interesting feature of the distressing situation is the safety, through some preternatural warning, of the Indians of the Everglades. Many days before the storm they went through the Everglades saying, "Follow Indian, Indian no fool. Going to dry land, big water coming." The people of the Everglades disregarded the warning—indeed they thought nothing of the prophecy. Had they done so, they would have been saved as were the Indians. They went into Palm Beach and are all safe.

Florida schools will be seriously handicapped this year because of the conditions. There will be no way for boys and girls to be in school. These important issues must be taken care of. We are earnestly soliciting the aid of all American citizens. Please help in some way. Clothing for men, women and children may be sent directly to the Negroes' First Aid Headquarters, Rosemay Street, West Palm Beach, Florida. Attention of Dr. J. H. Terrell, or Mrs. Frederick, and directly to the Negroes' First Aid Headquarters, Delray, Fla., attention of Prof. S. G. Spady. From these two points clothing will be distributed to the other points nearby. Cash contributions may be sent directly to our school office in Daytona Beach, which will be distributed through the local chapter of the Red Cross, to meet the needs of the people. We are continuing to serve here, and we will welcome help from any source. Help must be given to the suffering on the lower East Coast of Florida.

Birmingham Reporter [Birmingham, Ala.], September 29, 1928, p. 1.

Race Overtures

Letter to the National Board of the
Young Women's Christian Association

(1920)

I consider the calling of this conference by the National Board a long step in the right direction. Mutual interests demand mutual understanding. To do team work, we must better understand each other. A new day has come to the Negro woman and for her we are asking the opportunity to rightly interpret her needs and desires. As a factor and a force for the uplift of the womanhood of the world, we desire to bear our part of the responsibility in the furtherance of the work of the Young Women's Christian Association. To this end we ask for representation on the National Board and Field Committee, in order to develop initiative and leadership for our group [and] [f]urther, for a stronger sympathetic cooperation on the part of Negro women and white women everywhere that these great problems may be harmoniously and satisfactorily worked out that peace and justice, and love may reign.

Mary McLeod Bethune

[Bethune presented the preceding statement on behalf of herself and the other eighteen African American women, listed below, attending the conference.]

Mrs. Charlotte Hawkins Brown	Sedalia, North Carolina
Mrs. Lillian Brown	Indianapolis, Indiana
Mrs. S. Joe Brown	Des Moines, Iowa
Miss Nannie Burroughs	Washington, D.C.
Mrs. Addie W. Dickerson	Philadelphia, Pennsylvania
Mrs. Helen Irwin Grossley	Alcorn, Mississippi
Miss Anna Hawley	Brooklyn, New York
Mrs. Elizabeth Ross Haynes	Washington, D.C.
Mrs. John Hope	Atlanta, Georgia
Mrs. Addie W. Hunton	New York, New York
Miss Lucy Laney	Augusta, Georgia
Mrs. M. J. McCrorey	Charlotte, North Carolina
Mrs. Robert R. Moten	Tuskegee, Alabama
Miss Georgia Nugent	Louisville, Kentucky

Mrs. Emma S. Ransom	Oceanport, New Jersey
Mrs. W. H. Valentine	Bordentown, New Jersey
Mrs. R. W. Wilkerson	Orangeburg, South Carolina
Mrs. Frank Williams	St. Louis, Missouri

"National Conference Called by 'Y' Board," *New York Age,* December 18, 1920. "Women's Work," Tuskegee Institute Newspaper Clippings File, Tuskegee University Special Collections and Archives, Tuskegee, Ala.

Southern Negro Women and Race Co-operation

(1921)

We, the members of the Southeastern Federation of Colored Women's Clubs, desire to state our position on some matters relating to the welfare of colored people and to enlist the sympathy and co-operation of Southern white women in the interest of better understandings and better conditions, as these affect the relations between white and colored people.

First of all we wish to express our sincere gratification in the fact that race relations in the South have advanced to the place where the white women of the South are conscious of the part which colored women must play in any successful effort to adjust the unhappy conditions about us which have distressed the hearts of all lovers of right and justice and dangerously threatened the common welfare and the safety of the Nation.

We are also keenly alive to the growing tendency to give a larger place to the influence of womanhood in the affairs of the Nation and to the fact that there is an increasing number of Southern white women whose vision includes the welfare of women of every race and condition; who desire to secure equal opportunities for development to all womanhood and are determined to face the truth without flinching and to give themselves, at whatever cost, to creating an enlightened sentiment among their own people, and establishing a new and better foundation for relations between white and black women in the South.

We have for a long time been painfully conscious of the many unjust and humiliating practices of which colored women in the South have been victims. There is not one of us who has not at various times and places been called upon to face experiences which are common to the women of our race. We, therefore, take this opportunity to call to your attention certain conditions which affect colored women in their relations with white people, and which if corrected will go far toward decreasing friction, removing distrust and suspicion and creating a better atmosphere in which to adjust the difficulties which always accompany human contacts.

1. CONDITIONS IN DOMESTIC SERVICE. The most frequent and intimate contact of white and colored women is in domestic service. Every improvement made in the physical, moral and spiritual life of those so employed must react to increase the efficiency of their service to their employers. We, therefore, direct your attention to —

Long and Irregular Working Hours.
    (a) Lack of provision for wholesome recreation.
    (b) Undesirable housing conditions.

    We Recommend, Therefore,
        (a) Definite regulation for hours and conditions of work.
        (b) Sanitary, attractive and wholesome rooming facilities.
        (c) Closer attention to personal appearance and deportment.
        (d) Provision for and investigation of character of recreation.

2. CHILD WELFARE. The large burden of economic responsibility which falls upon many colored women results in their prolonged absence from home and the consequent neglect of the children of the homes. We direct your attention to —

Child Welfare
    (a) Neglected homes (irregularity in food, clothing, conduct, training.)
    (b) Truancy.
    (c) Juvenile delinquency.

    We therefore recommend —
    Welfare Activities
        (a) Day nurseries, play grounds, recreation centers.
        (b) Home and school visitation.
        (c) Probation officers and reform schools.

3. CONDITIONS OF TRAVEL. Race friction is perhaps more frequent in street cars and railroad trains than in any other public places. To reduce this friction and remove causes for just complaint from colored passengers we call your attention to —

1. *Seating Accommodations on Street Cars.*
2. *Unsanitary Surroundings.*
    (a) At Stations.
    (b) On Trains.
3. *Toilet Facilities.*
    (a) At Stations.
    (b) On Trains.

4. *Difficulty in Securing.*
   (a) Tickets.
   (b) Pullman accommodations.
   (c) Meals.

5. *Abuse of Rights of Colored Passengers* by train crew and white passengers [relative to] occupying seats while passengers stand, smoking, profane language, overcrowding.

Corrective Measures.

   Provision of Equal Accommodations in all public carriers and courteous treatment at the hands of street car and railway officials, for all passengers.

4. EDUCATION. Without education for all the children of all the people we cannot sustain a democracy. Ignorance and crime are the twin children of neglect and poverty. We urge your increasing effort for —

Better Education Facilities.
   (a) Adequate Accommodations for all Negro children of school age.
   (b) Vocational Training in all secondary schools.
   (c) Improved rural schools—longer terms, suitable buildings.
   (d) Training schools for teachers.
   (e) Adequate Salaries for teachers.

5. LYNCHING. We deplore and condemn any act on the part of any men which would tend to excite the mob spirit.

We believe that any man who makes an assault upon any woman should have prompt punishment, meted out to the limit of the law, but not without thorough investigation of the facts and trial by the courts.

The continuance of lynching is the greatest menace to good will between the races, and a constant factor in undermining respect for all law and order. It is our opinion that mob violence incites to crime rather than deters it; and certainly it is less effective in discouraging crime than the watchful, thorough and deliberate processes of a fair and just trial.

Toward the suppression of this evil we appeal to white women to—
   (a) Raise their voices in immediate protest when lynching or mob violence is threatened.
   (b) Encourage every effort to detect and punish the leaders and participants in mobs and riots.
   (c) Encourage the white pulpit and press in creating a sentiment among law-abiding citizens and urge outspoken condemnation of these forms of lawlessness.

6. The Public Press. In the great majority of cases the white press of the South gives undue prominence to crime and the criminal element among Negroes to the neglect of the worthy and constructive efforts of law-abiding Negro citizens. We feel that a large part of friction and misunderstanding between the races is due to unjust, inflammatory and misleading headlines and articles appearing in the daily papers.

We suggest that white women include in their local community program a united effort to correct this evil and to secure greatest attention to worthy efforts of Negro citizens.

7. Suffrage. We regard the ballot as the democratic and orderly method of correcting abuses and protecting the rights of citizens; as the substitute of civilization for violence.

As peace-loving, law-abiding citizens we believe the ultimate and only guarantee of fair dealing and justice for the Negro, as well as the wholesome development of the whole community, lies in the peaceful, orderly exercise of the franchise by every qualified Negro citizen.

We ask therefore, that white women, for the protection of their homes as well as ours indicate their sanction of the ballot for all citizens as representing government by the sober, reasoned and deliberate judgment of all the people.

In these articles offered at your request we are stating frankly and soberly what in our judgment, you as white women may do to correct the ills from which our race has so long suffered and of which we as a race are perhaps more conscious now than ever.

We recall how in the recent day of our nation's peril so many of us worked side by side for the safety of this land and defense of this flag which is ours as it is yours.

In that same spirit of unselfishness and sacrifice we offer ourselves to serve again with you in any and every way that a courageous facing of duty may require as you undertake heroically this self-appointed yet God-given task.

We deeply appreciate the difficulties that lie before you, but as you undertake these things which are destined to bless us all, we pledge you our faith and loyalty in consecration to God, home and country.

Respectfully submitted,
Mrs. John Hope
Mrs. Marion Wilkinson
Miss Lucy Laney
Mrs. Charlotte Hawkins Brown
Mrs. Mary Jackson McCrorey
Mrs. Janie Porter Barrett
Mrs. M. L. Crosthwait

Mrs. Booker T. Washington
Mrs. Mary McLeod Bethune
President, Southeastern Federation of Colored
    Women's Clubs
Atlanta, Ga.   June 30, 1921

June 30, 1921. *The Southeastern Herald*, Florida Number, February 1924, pp. 10–11. Mary McLeod Bethune Papers, Mary McLeod Bethune Foundation, Bethune-Cookman College, Daytona Beach, Fla.

Minutes of Joint Meeting

Woman's General Committee of the Commission on Interracial Cooperation and the Interracial Committee of the Southeastern Federation of Colored Women's Clubs [abridged] (1922)

The Woman's General Committee on Interracial Cooperation through Mrs. Luke Johnson, the Director of Woman's Work of the Commission on Interracial Cooperation called the members of the Interracial Committee of the Southeastern Federation of Colored Women's Clubs to meet them in joint session in Atlanta, Georgia, October 20–21, 1922, for the purpose of forming a plan by which the two groups could work together in greater usefulness.

Those present were:

Mrs. Effie L. Cunningham	St. Louis, Mo.
Mrs. Archibald Davis	Atlanta, Ga.
Mrs. Z. I. Fitzpatrick	Madison, Ga.
Mrs. Luke Johnson	Atlanta, Ga.
Mrs. W. J. Neel	Cartersville, Ga.
(Proxy Mrs. H. M. Wharton)	
Mrs W. D. Weatherford	Nashville, Tenn.
Miss Maude Fambro, Sec'y to Mrs. Johnson	
Mrs. Janie Porter Barrett	Peak's Turnout, Va.
Mrs. Mary McLeod Bethune	Daytona, Fla.
Mrs. Charlotte Hawkins Brown	Sedalia, N.C.
Mrs. M. L. Crosthwait	Nashville, Tenn.
Mrs. John Hope	Atlanta, Ga.
Mrs. Lucy Laney	Augusta, Ga.
Mrs. H. L. McCrory	Charlotte, N.C.
Mrs. Booker T. Washington	Tuskegee, Ala.

Mrs. Johnson called the Committee to order and led a devotional service closing with the song "I Want to be a Christian in My Heart."

Mrs. Johnson called for the election of a Chairman and Secretary for the Joint Committee to serve until plans of procedure could be adopted.

IT WAS VOTED: That Mrs. Johnson serve as Chairman.

IT WAS VOTED: That Mrs. H. L. McCrory serve as Secretary.

The Chair explained that the Woman's General Committee (white) which had been in existence for about two years felt the need of Negro women in the cooperative program, and that action to this effect had been taken by the Committee in a previous meeting.

She further stated that no special program or agenda had been prepared, but that it was hoped that the meeting would be a real conference which would result in definite plans for further work.

Mrs. Archibald Davis was requested by the Chair to make a statement concerning the origin, development and achievements of the white Woman's Committee to date.

She told of the beginnings in the visit of two women from the Methodist Woman's Missionary Council to Tuskegee; of the Conference which followed with the two white women and ten selected colored women leaders in the South; of the Memphis Interracial Conference put on by the Commission on Interracial Cooperation to which one hundred white women leaders of the South were called; of the addresses of four colored women in that Conference which made a deep impression; of the formation of a Continuation Committee to conserve the work of the Conference until such time as an Interdenominational Committee could be officially formed by the Executive Boards of the different groups, naming their own representative on the Continuation Committee; of the official appointments from all these bodies; of the steps taken to date in making plans and policies for recommendations to the Boards through their own representatives, and something of the achievements of these efforts.

The Chair explained the two-fold function of the Committee by blackboard illustrations as follows:

WOMAN'S GENERAL COMMITTEE ON RACE RELATIONS

I. An Interdenominational Committee

Each member officially representing the woman's organization of her church or other Christian agency as follows:

1. Baptist Church—South
2. Disciples (Christian)—National
3. Episcopal—National
4. Methodist—South

5. Presbyterian—South
6. Y.W.C.A.—National
7. Woman's Clubs—Individual

II. Committee on Woman's Work, Commission on Interracial Cooperation
   In this capacity these same women act as the Committee on Women's Work in the Commission in its relation to State, county and local Committees.
   Mrs. Bethune, chairman of the colored Woman's Committee was requested to make a statement concerning the origin and development of the colored Committee. She told of the meeting of the colored women present with two representatives of the Southern Methodist women's organization at Tuskegee in July 1920; of the statement which the colored women issued there as their conviction on the question of race relations, and of the later action of the Southeastern Federation of Colored Woman's Clubs in adopting this statement with slight changes, as their official platform.
   She stated that the attitude of the colored group was one of earnest prayer and desire to cooperate in constructive work for peace and good will, and for a vital working relationship in bringing about better conditions everywhere.
   . . . .

AFTERNOON
   The Committee was called to order. After prayer Dr. T. J. Woofter, Secretary of the Georgia State Committee on Race Relations, presented "Practical Plans of Cooperation," which proved so interesting and helpful that nearly all the afternoon was devoted to it and the discussions which followed.
   He spoke of the three outstanding lines of work which the Committee should consider, viz:

Child Welfare
Education
Lynching
   . . . .

   A further discussion on the lines of work already undertaken by the white Committee in their study of The Negro Home, The Negro School and The Negro Church was held, and copies of the Guides for these three studies were distributed.
   The Chair stated that the day had been used in an effort to present the work of the Committee and the Commission in its past work and future plans. She requested that there should be prayerful and careful consideration of the whole matter before the convening of the Committee on the following day [so] that a definite and constructive program and organization might be adopted.
IT WAS VOTED: To adjourn.

SATURDAY MORNING
    October 21
    The Committee was called to order. The Chair repeated the words, "The Entrance of Thy Word Giveth Light," and asked each woman to repeat some verse hid away in her heart.
    . . . .
    A discussion of methods of organization followed. It was explained that the method for the formation of the Committee is to secure one woman from each denomination or Christian agency to be represented.
    The colored members were requested to name the several colored woman's Christian organizations and indicate the method by which the colored women could be added to the General Committee on Race Cooperation. After full discussion, on motion of Mrs. Weatherford, seconded by Mrs. Bethune,
IT WAS VOTED: That the Chair appoint a Committee of four, two white and two colored members, to retire and work out a plan for the action of the Committee.
    The Chair asked for nominations and the following were appointed:

Mrs. W. D. Weatherford
Mrs. Archibald Davis
Mrs. Mary McLeod Bethune
Mrs. Charlotte Hawkins Brown.

    During the absence of the Committee, Mrs. Janie Porter Barrett, who had just returned from a National Prison Conference in Detroit, was requested to speak on the Conference and its work.
    The Chair stated that Mrs. Barrett had attended the Prison Conference as an official representative from Virginia, . . . having been appointed by the Governor of Virginia.
    The Committee on Organization returned to the room and reported as follows:
    "Your Committee on Organization submits the following:
    I. That the Woman's General Committee of the Commission on Interracial Cooperation as now existing, shall add to its membership seven colored women each representing a different denomination or Christian agency; the organizations and representatives of the same to be chosen by the colored women here present; these appointments to hold good until the meeting of each of these national or general bodies, at which time each representative here chosen shall seek opportunity to present the work, and ask for the appointment of an official representative from the organization.
    II. That the white members and the colored members shall each constitute a sub-committee which shall have the privilege of holding separate meetings, as the needs may demand.
    III. That each of the sub-committees shall be governed by the same rules in elections, etc.

Mrs. W. D. Weatherford, Chairman."

It was stated that the report was unanimously presented by the Committee. It was discussed at length, and, on motion of Mrs. Bethune and seconded by Mrs. [T. W.] Bickett,

IT WAS VOTED: That the report be adopted as read.

IT WAS VOTED: That the colored members meet during lunch hour, select the organizations and nominate the persons to represent each of them, and report at the afternoon session.

IT WAS VOTED: To adjourn for lunch.

AFTERNOON 2 O'CLOCK

After a session of prayer and song the colored Committee on nominations reported as follows:

"We your Committee appointed to nominate the colored women for membership on the woman's General Committee submit the following:

African Methodist Episcopal Church	Mrs. Mary McLeod Bethune
Baptist Church	Mrs. John Hope
Congregational Church	Mrs. M. L. Crosthwait
Episcopal Church	Mrs. Marion Wilkinson
Presbyterian Church	Mrs. H. L. McCrory
Woman's Clubs	Mrs. Booker Washington
Y.W.C.A.	Mrs. Charlotte H. Brown"

IT WAS VOTED: That the report of the Committee be adopted and that those named become members of the Woman's General Committee on Interracial Cooperation.

The Chairman of the nominating Committee announced that as only seven names could be presented that Mrs. Barrett and Miss Laney would not permit their names to be considered for membership.

IT WAS VOTED: That further organization of the Committee be deferred until a future meeting and that the Director of Woman's Work be requested to call the next meeting.

On request, Mrs. T. W. Bickett, Director of Maternity Work in the North Carolina Board of Public Welfare, discussed the Sheppard-Towner Act and explained the methods by which each state could secure this appropriation from the Government.

The Chair spoke on the strategy and wisdom of forming Committees to study and develop the Interracial work as a means of education to them and as a method for creating sentiment and securing the interest and support of many hundreds of women. She called attention to the fact that it might be far easier and perhaps quicker for one or two outstanding persons in a State or community to accomplish some needed thing, but that if we succeed in our task of arresting the attention of large numbers of women and winning them to the work, that patient, persistent effort is necessary in the formation of Committees and the presentation of the principles, needs and methods of the work, and that only a unified and cooperative effort of the women of the several States can bring large permanent results.

Therefore, she urged that we work slowly and constructively, always bearing in mind that it is *all* the women and *all* the homes of both races which must be reached.

It was agreed that the colored members of the Committee should study the Guides for the investigating Committees and other methods now in use by the white group, and [at] a future meeting recommend methods for work with colored women.

The colored group asked if they could aid in financing the work of the Commission.

The Director stated that while personal contributions were made by individuals and organizations, that each State Committee needed funds to finance its meetings, etc., and also that the Woman's Work of the General Commission needed help to do a larger work. The colored members voiced a desire to bear their part in such work if needed.

IT WAS VOTED: That when the minutes are prepared they shall be referred to the local members for acceptance.

. . . .

"I Want to be a Christian in My Heart" was sung and
IT WAS VOTED: To adjourn.

Mrs. Luke Johnson, Acting Chairman
Mrs. H. L. McCrory, Acting Secretary

October 29–31, 1922. Neighborhood Union Collection, Division of Archives and Special Collections, Robert W. Woodruff Library, Atlanta University Center, Atlanta, Ga.

Great Designs

President's Address to the Fifteenth Biennial Convention of the National Association of Colored Women

(1926)

It is an unusual pleasure to be in the Great West, State of California and City of Oakland. All of you share this feeling with me, I know. It is a joy beyond expression to meet you here [and] exchange greetings with all the good people whose generous hospitality was offered us at Chicago. I feel certain of voicing the sentiment of the entire National body when saying that the National Association of Colored Women has been signally honored by the invitation to hold our meeting here.

I thank you one and all for the cordial reception being given me as President of the National. It is a matter of honor and pride which I shall never forget. It gives me special pleasure on behalf of the Association to extend greetings and welcome of the most cordial nature to all those present who have never before attended a session of the National Association of Colored Women.

The Governor of California [and] Mayor of Oakland have honored the Federation by their presence and welcome addresses. Other distinguished and well known citizens have also greeted us and extended their words of welcome. We thank them all and invite them most cordially to attend any of the sessions held during this biennial meeting.

We have had an outpouring of welcome long to be remembered. It is a sign of the generous hospitality for which California's citizens are noted—one of the glories of the Great and Golden West and its people.

The accomplishments for the past two years are the results of the unselfish and energetic co-operation of the members of the body throughout the country. Nothing could have been done without your co-operation. Co-operation is one of the great laws of progressive human society. It is a fixed theory of organization. The real significance of the word "Society" rests upon co-operation, mutual aid in striving for the same common end. Although we do not live in the same neighborhoods and our homes are widely separated one from the other, we have proven that we have some relations and are something more than a crowd, by our co-operation.

A review of the work of the past two years in detail might require time I wish to use in saying other things on this occasion. The details have been printed and distributed among you. I shall deal merely with the main points. It is necessary to emphasize and bring them to the front in our thinking and action. This will enable us to fix our souls, hearts and minds upon the unfinished and newer programs of the National at once.

Briefly, the necessary meetings of the Executive Board have been held for the purposes of the work; departmental chairmen appointed; more than 10,000 pieces of mail and 200 or more telegrams released in pushing the work. I have visited 25 states, addressing men, women and children in connection with the high purposes of the National Association. I have also represented this body in gatherings of [an] inter-racial nature before more than 75,000 people of the white race, attended the National Council of Women of the United States, accompanied by several other representatives of the National Association. In addition, I have represented the N.A.C.W. at Vassar College and several other outstanding institutions of learning through-out the country.

Everything concerning the vital objects of this body has claimed my attention [and] employed my best energies since the Chicago meeting adjourned. No opportunity to assist in overturning the obstacles to our advancement has been shunned. Every one has been accepted gladly and with the courage befitting the high-hearted Negro womanhood I have been proud to represent. I have recollections of experiences in the segregation controversy connected with the recent Quinquennial [of the International Council of Women], and our protest against the meeting place of the National Council [of Women of the U.S.] on account of "hydra-headed caste."

I do not believe that American Christian Civilization will ever be able to speak with authority to the rest of the world if our Nation continues divided upon the main issue of the world's well-being. Therefore I think it the duty of the chosen leader of the National Association of Colored Women to stand firmly, eternally against segregation and discrimination. One God, One People, One Law, and One Destiny for all alike, will make the world kin, and all men brothers. You, my sisters, must consider yourselves lifetime watch-guards of human society's ideal, keep your fires lighted upon the citadels, hilltops and every high eminence and let your watch-cry warn the world of every discord in the human family.

The Douglass Home is an almost completed accomplishment of our Association. Its maintenance must always be considered a highly honorable responsibility. It is a monument to martyrdom for liberty as well as our reverence for the spirit of Frederick Douglass. The home must be preserved as a shrine of liberty for the unborn generations of Negroes. Mary B. Talbert—considerate soul—will ever be cherished in the amber of our memories for her part in leading the National Association of Colored Women to claim and preserve the Douglass Home.

The Scholarship Fund, in process of completion, spells "Opportunity" to the oncoming generations. It also represents a greater awakening of our people to the need and virtue of self-help in education. Education is the solid rock of progress throughout the Universe. I want you to think of yourselves as salesmen of a most necessary commodity to the race—Education. We have been highly successful always as salesmen of Religion; met some success as salesmen of sick and death benefits in life insurance concerns and fraternal bodies. The time has come when we must prove ourselves good salesmen of Education—the most essential foundation of every youth, ambitious to achieve a successful career in the world. We can never forget Hallie Q. Brown for the constructive genius she displayed in proposing the Scholarship Fund to the National Association of Colored Women.

A homeless organization will be constantly drifting without a domestic anchor. Therefore, [we have had] thirty years of shifting from place to place with never a sign of a permanent home headquarters for centralizing the activities and work of the National. Progress has been retarded and the machinery of this organization has been hindered in the efforts made to function properly and efficiently. The efficiency of the organization has been constantly impaired. Countless people of influence and others in need of the services of the National body have found it [a] difficult matter to get in immediate touch with our official machinery. Thus arose the demand for a permanent home and headquarters to be used exclusively for the work of the National Association of Colored Women. The body has always had a head, never a home. Both are essential to progressive and aggressive work. Our association must have a home.

The National Headquarters, home of our National Association will become the center of all its activities. It ought to be made a torchlight, guiding the race throughout the land, a searchlight for discovering facts relating to our hindrances and progress, a lighthouse for those demoralized in the stormy sea of our National existence. It should be a dynamo of propaganda intended to inspire our people to climb higher heights and [to] educate the whole world regarding the true character, better life, needs and advantages and disadvantages of the Negro in America. It ought to be a veritable storehouse of correct and authoritative information regarding the colored people of America and the wide world. The National Headquarters should be, in fact, the powerhouse of our great federation. Thus the work of this association conceived with so much ambition and inspiration to serve the needs of our people, will be perpetuated.

We want unborn generations of Negro youth to make the national home of this federation a shrine to which they will make pilgrimages for inspiration. There will they find their ground for home in the carefully kept records and history of our people. Pictures of women who have wrought well and honorably during their lifetime will adorn the walls of our National home. Young people may thus go away with pictures engraven upon their minds and hearts, of the great souls who are contributing to the advancement of their people and the world by their work in connection with the National Association of Colored Women. This, in a measure, is the ideal to which we are aspiring in the establishment of a permanent home for this Association. And here, I must congratulate you upon the splendid progress being made in the achievement of our object to have a permanent home for our body. It is my earnest desire to see our ambition realized at the dedication of that home in Washington, D.C. on the occasion of our next Biennial Meeting of the National Association of Colored Women.

I come now to a consideration of the three phases of our people in the world. They are:

1. Conditions within the race.
2. Our National environment.
3. The World's condition influencing the present and future of colored people generally.

Your intelligence, I know, will lead you to agree with me in the conclusion that no dependent people can hope to get upon the road to permanent progress without the most careful and considerate and constant study of developments in their immediate environment [and] the situation and progress of the world as a whole. I shall not review history because you are familiar with all that relates to our past and present in America. The present will be emphasized as a foundation of future prophecy.

WITHIN THE RACE

We have conflicting idealisms among our people to be harmonized. Until this is done, we cannot proceed with the full measure of hope which has characterized the history of people who have overcome all obstacles and taken their place among the ranks of the independent, respected races of the earth. The American ideals of citizenship suggests self-support as a primary essential of self-government and service as the "acid test." The conflicting idealism of our race all center around "self-support" and "service" as the mainsprings of our problems and difficulties within the race. Let us acknowledge some truths, face some facts sincerely, honestly, bravely. Stepping out thus we may begin a movement, mark out a path of inspiration. The time has come when we must believe in progress as something more than a creed. We must believe in it in spite of "progressives" among us. When we do, our progress will really begin in America.

We have accomplished little in triumphs in art, science, education and manufacture, as compared with that of the other race; but the very condition should stimulate the thought and energy of our race as never before in the history of a dependent people. It should inspire, lead, drive us to break bonds in achieving our emancipation. The brain and brawn power of our race ought to become a combination for stimulating production. Science, invention, creative achievement will do more than anything else in commanding the respect of other races. Vain boastings of wealth and manifold achievements by a dependent people lead more to humiliation than elevation. Production is the road to wealth, power, influence.

We have developed no middle class to sustain our "social upper crust." Yet we have a minority group of cultured members of the race whose education, native endowments and ambitions fit them well for the enjoyment of any station of life. But the masses must be helped and awakened. We must become greater producers. The one great need of the Negro in America is a great federation, uniting all forces to form one huge engine of production.

Some definite type of action must be named which will challenge the conflicting forces within our race to co-operative effort, and at the same time teach [members of it] the fundamentals of an art in which we have hitherto shown ourselves so woefully inexpert. The trend of Science, Invention, Manufacture and Politics in America have given us a New World constantly changing. We face new and tremendous risks and must turn our attention to the question of pooling our burdens and means to bear them. All the events, circumstances, tendencies of this time should convince us of the great need of one another's help—the starting point of cooperation. We face difficulties in America and difficulties that will tax the resources of the most statesman-like, the knowledge of the expert to the uttermost. But the prospect may well be considered a point to the good, for nothing short of the most difficult task, requiring the full concentration of all our talent will provide our race with sufficient experience and power to ultimately dominate its destiny.

The political mind, the legal mind, the historical mind, the religious mind—each has and will have its own contribution to the solution of the problem of inter-racial relations, diverting the colored and white races in America from the path of strife to the path of cooperation. But in addition to them, we need another and perhaps greater contribution to the solution of the problems of our living in America from trained, scientific, industrial, business, [and] creative minds. Ideal principles must be used but their practical application is a necessity and fundamental to the progress which means prosperity and happiness. To the practical mind falls the task of stabilizing the progress of the race by systematizing business, organizing industry and setting in motion the factors of the race, to guarantee permanent progress and prosperity. We must discover, therefore, a practical mind, [a] workable plan for harmonizing the conflicting orders among our people and bringing them all under the dominance of a common ideal for the good of all.

OUR NATIONAL ENVIRONMENT

Twelve million Negroes are expecting the National Government to re-move all hindrances affecting their liberty, opportunities and protection as American citizens. Those of us who are native to American soil or have adopted this land as our home, dispute the right of any to challenge our enjoyment of the privileges and opportunities afforded in this country of ours. I hold that blood and color does not define an American citizen. We stand upon the law here—written and unwritten. This country belongs to Negroes as much as it does to those of any other race. Our forebears and those of us living in this time have suffered, agonized, bled for this—our land. We have helped to make it what it is today. Denied equal share in the fruits of our sacrificing and suffering, we have protested. We shall protest and protest again. Our patriotism is a conviction, a consuming impulse, [a] devouring flame. We have stood the acid-test. Our patriotism has been proven in time of peace and war.

The country is today arguing over the laws of morality, [and of] racial, social, religious, territorial, national and international relationships in a manner puzzling to the world. And in all this argument, America is disregard-ing its plain duty [and] moral, social economic, political and spiritual obligations to more than 12,000,000 souls of its population because of their heritage of African blood. But one thing America can never disregard is the longing of these millions for something higher that has been rising from the hearts of each generation since the first shipload of slaves was landed on American soil.

America can be changed. It will be changed. Even now the soul of this nation is undergoing a rebirth regarding citizens of Negro blood. Here and there we see bright signs; stars of hope in the distant heavens. To these we must hitch our wagons and keep driving, driving always. We must uphold the status of the Christian religion, resist the implication that we constitute a separate part of this nation, invade every field of activity in America, contribute in every way we can to fostering and perpetuating the honored national ideals, battle should-to-shoulder with the nation's best citizenship for an untarnished service of a free people by public officers of unquestioned character and honor in county, city, state and national governments. This is my conception of the pathway to be followed by our 12,000,000 in facilitating the re-birth of America's soul regarding colored people.

WORLD CONDITION INFLUENCING NEGRO DESTINY

Intolerance, commercial enmities, territorial greed, racial and national hatreds [and] the lust for power and blood are never swept away by war, nor disposed of by a stroke of the diplomatic pen, even when used by the statesmanship of the British Empire, Republic of the United States, French Republic, Germany, Italy or Japan. So today the peace of the world is a matter of concern.

Successful revolution in Russia deepened the roots of world unrest. A wily dictator in Italy has become a dramatic world figure making crowned heads and European governments uneasy. Labor has taken a whirl with the order of things in England. Japan keeps America nervous while Germany and France play checkers with war. Africa, where the seeds of the last World War were rooted, still furnishes friction between greedy nations with bodies and blood to sacrifice. Turkey, India, Morocco, China and Russia keep the world uneasy because of the yokes they wear discontentedly. Spain has her troubles and embers of turmoil are being stirred again in Mexico. Apparently the nations of the earth are again "marking time" with a spirit of restlessness. Let us steady ourselves and aim toward peace and worldwide brotherhood.

I speak to you about the world today because of the various nations, peoples, contentions, for peaceful adjustments and settlement on the recognition of equal rights established and enforced by a common will.

No living thing stands still in this world. It goes forward or backward, grows upward or downward. Standing still brings about stagnation, decomposition, death. The National Association of Colored Women is a live body. I want you to keep it so; make it livelier than it has been in humanitarian interests. Every club has its community significance, state organization [and] a relation to the varied interests of the commonwealth. This great federation has both a national and international mission to perform. A full realization, consciousness of these relations and convictions in the great objects for which this national body stands will keep it living, make it more and more influential and powerful, as we work with determination for success in the local aims of individual clubs, state organizations and the big objectives of the National. Bear in mind, therefore, that the various units of our body are all linked together to form an engine of service far greater than that of any private or individual matter.

This organization must assume an attitude toward all big questions involving the welfare of the nation, public right and especially the present and future of our race. These questions are both national and international. They include the humanitarian, moral, social and economic problems puzzling the world today. Their proper solution will be a test of the Rock of Christianity upon which rests the hope of a stable world order. Efforts to solve them must therefore be dictated by humane regard of all peoples for each other [and] all nations' finest and fairest consideration for others under their dominance. This brings forward the "color question" belting the world; colonial dominions and their attendant evils; political freedom and territorial problems of governments. The future of our people is wrapped up in their proper adjustment. We are especially called upon, therefore, to revise our political program in accord with the national and international trend of things.

Colored people's difficulties are political and economic throughout the world. Through wise politics and statesmanship, they must liberate themselves. Through far-sighted economic leadership, they must master the business of taking care of themselves like other races. Bred, born and living here under the American Flag, we nevertheless bear a relation to others of our blood. Their problems are ours and vice versa. All our wisdom, energy and foresight should be dedicated to the great task of achieving freedom and independence which are the highest goals for human striving.

We must make this national body of colored women not merely a national influence, but also a significant link between the peoples of color throughout the world. I have a firm conviction that the National Association of Colored Women may become a most influential and powerful factor in helping the world to realize the humanitarian ideal for which its better souls are striving in the efforts of nations to achieve a stable order of things. It would surely be a glorious triumph to perform indisputable service helping to win an object so wondrous and sublime in vision. We can, ought and will take up the task!

I have envisioned a world gathering of colored women, a conservative, peace-loving body carrying the torch of freedom, equal rights, human love [and] holding it high and brightening the world with rays of justice, tolerance and faithful service in God's name. It is my judgment that this great Association is the lever with which to overturn racial intolerance and artificial prejudices. They hinder human unity in America and throughout the world where a deadline has been drawn between the white races and people of colored blood. This knowledge suggests a great work about which I want you to think soberly, sincerely and seriously. It constitutes the international mission of the National Association of Colored Women.

Finally, what shall constitute our means for undertaking a mission of such great proportions, and what the method?

We must first establish, dedicate and operate our National Headquarters in Washington. We must make it a clearing house of cooperative effort among American colored women in the fine objects at the very foundation of this body. We must make it a conservative dynamo, directed against the evils in our nation, a lighthouse, beckoning all other colored women on the stormy world-sea to America for cooperation in their struggles for existence, peace, prosperity and independence. It can be done by thinking, planning, working and the kind of fighting which fits all human beings for both life and death.

We must create a literature propaganda for the education of our people and all people in America, about the purposes and any international program of this Association. This should be spread over the world wherever colored people abide. We must create a literature directed against the evils that obstruct our path, expressing our thought and feeling about them in no uncertain terms. We must create a literature to fire the souls of unborn generations of Negroes with love of liberty and the determination to fight for the very highest goal of human life. We must in truth create a literature that will make all races of the world know that we are their human equals and determined to have just consideration in all the affairs of world society. And I insist that we must have this literature because of my firm conviction that the greatest possible instrument to be used against the tyranny of racial intolerance in all its forms is the trained human mind, set free from the idols of ignorance and prejudice.

Negro women of America: Rise to the challenge. This is your opportunity and mine. Be your best! Give your best!

If you can't be a pine on top of the hill,
    Be a scrub in the valley;
But be the best little scrub
    That grows by the rill.
Be a bush, if you can't be a tree.
    If you can't be a tree, be a bit of the grass,
And some highway the happier make.
    If you can't be a muskie, just be a bass,
But be the liveliest bass in the lake.

We can't all be captains, we've got to be crew,
    There's plenty of work for us here.
There's a big work to do, and a lesser;

But our task is the one that is near.
If you can't be a highway, just be a trail,
If you can't be a sun, be a star.
It's not in your size that you win or lose,
Be the best, of whatever you are!

August 2, 1926. Mary McLeod Bethune Papers, Amistad Research Center, Tulane University, New Orleans, La.

President's Monthly Message

Good Will and Investigation Tour Abroad during the Summer of 1927

I, Mary McLeod Bethune, do hereby propose to the women of the N. A. C. W. a "Good Will and Inspection Tour," abroad, under the auspices of the National Association of Colored Women, every woman defraying her own expenses and becoming a member of the party. EVERY WOMAN IS INVITED.

If Ethiopia is to stretch forth her hands, then, those hands must belt the seas, and to belt the seas, it is fitting that the women of the N. A. C. W. should know from actual observation and touch, just how to go about their work. How woefully ignorant we are of true conditions! So few of us have seen and actually know. The time has come when, instead of [going] as individuals, we must go as an organized unit. The more informed people we have, the easier our work.

TEAM WORK is my theme in the finer things of life, as well as in the lowliest.

We shall have experts, who have been abroad, to plan our trip. Advice is ours for the asking

How nice it would be for us to visit Helen Curtis in Liberia, Africa! What an inspiration it will be to the Art Department of Fannie Givens' to have our women visit Florence and Rome, Italy. We shall study the educational systems of Europe and caste problems also. Charlotte Hawkins Brown will then find it an easier matter to get over an educational program. The wonderful hospitals and health conditions will be seen and Dr. Mary Waring can push her Department as never before.

We shall not forget Flanders Field, where the poppies grow, and where our boys sleep.

The American Home Department under Estelle Davis can be compared with foreign homes and we shall get a better understanding concerning ourselves and how we measure up or down with the poor of other countries. The wonderful *Libraries* and *Theatres* shall be visited and our Department of Program and Literature under Maria Lawton will take on new life. We shall note the Youth of the East and better plan our Junior Federation, Beatrice Child's Department.

The Industrial Centers shall not be left unseen nor unstudied, and Mazie Griffin and Nannie Burroughs will be able to interest more of our women in "Women in Industries and Business."

Every phase of life will be religiously observed and studied[. A]nd lastly but more far-reaching than any of these I have mentioned, the Churches will be studied, yea, the different Religious and Forms of Worship will receive our careful attention. Christine Smith, Chairman of Church Relations and Religious Education, will have fertile soil for cultivation, because we shall have seen and known.

Governments will be studied, and our National Committeewomen, Mamie George Williams, and Mollie Booze, together with our veteran politicians, Mary Church Terrell and Hallie Q. Brown, will be made happy, in that our women will no longer close their eyes to the value of the ballot and true citizenship.

Our membership in the International Council of Women of the World will stand us well.

THIS IS NO DREAM, WOMEN. This is the first chance for our group. It is perfectly possible and will cost very little more than our recent trip to California.

I must know, by the last of February, just who will go, so as to perfect arrangements. Most likely we shall leave in June and return whenever we plan.

LET ME HAVE YOUR REACTION ON THIS MATTER.

> Yours in "Lifting as We Climb,"
> Mary McLeod Bethune, President

National Notes [periodical of the National Association of Colored Women], January 1927, p. 3. Tuskegee University Special Collections and Archives, Tuskegee, Ala.

National Association of Colored Women

(1928)

National Association of Colored Women
12th and O Streets
Washington, D.C.

MRS. MARY McLEOD BETHUNE, President
REBECCA STILES TAYLOR, Secretary

Founded in 1896 to obtain for colored women the opportunity of reaching the highest standards in all fields of human endeavor and to promote interracial understanding so that justice and goodwill may prevail among all people.

Since our last Biennial [of the National Council of Women] in Detroit, the National Association of Colored Women has recorded many creditable achievements in the various fields of its broad program through its several avenues, namely:

The National itself; its five Regional Federations; its forty-two State Federations; its hundreds of County, City and District Federations; its Young Women's Department; Junior Federation; Cradle Roll and Miscellaneous Clubs.

The National Association (in its own right) met in its thirtieth year or fifteenth Biennial in Oakland, California in August, 1926, and was attended by more than 1,000 women. It was one of the most inspiring and beneficial gatherings held in the history of the Association. The women of the West were electrified and the Eastern women caught a vision of the breadth of their country and its countless possibilities.

At this meeting our Constitution was revised to meet the needs of today. An official Directory was authorized—the same has been compiled and broadcast throughout the country and contributes wonderfully to the solidarity and influence of our Association. Ample provisions were made for the completion of our $50,000 National Scholarship Fund, which will begin to operate in 1928. The building of a Keeper's house at the Frederick Douglass Home in Anacostia, as well as a maintenance fund for the Home, were authorized and provided.

Authority was given for the purchase of National Headquarters in Washington, D.C. Our Headquarters there, at 12th and O Streets, have been secured and we are very proud to report that we shall throw wide our doors for a grand opening in August, 1928, when we shall meet in our sixteenth Biennial Convention.

Our National Organizer is now in the field and the work moves steadily on.

The official organ of the National Association of Colored Women is *National Notes,* and is twenty-nine years old. It is published monthly. Through this medium we reach the women of the country.

Through our twenty major and twenty minor departments, with their Regional and State Chairmen, we propagate and develop our program.

Our major departments are: Headquarters, Business, Publication, Young Women, Junior Federation, Health and Hygiene, Educational Standards and Achievements, Social Work, American Home, Big Sister, Fine Arts, Program and Literature, Music, Citizenship, Legislation, Peace and Foreign Relations, Fraternal Relations, Women in Industry, Church Relations and Religious Education.

Our minor departments are: Cradle Roll, Sanitation, Tuberculosis, Hospitals, Illiteracy, Vocational Education, Physical Education, Rural Education, Home Economics, Kindergarten, Race History, Conservation of Natural Resources, Housing, Temperance, Recreation, Community Centers, Maternity and Child Welfare, Delinquency, Child and Adult, Arts and Crafts.

There is a continuity of programs extending from the National through the Regions, States, Counties and Cities to the Individual Clubs. In this way we have been able to develop similar State Programs, covering State Training Schools for delinquent girls and boys. Each State in the entire Southeastern Region is working out this particular program—there being very limited, if any adequate provision made by the States themselves for Negro girls and boys. Many State Federations are furnishing State Scholarship Funds for deserving students, while many are cooperating with the Rosenwald and Anna T. Jeannes Funds, in providing adequate schoolhouses and longer terms for the great uneducated mass so long neglected and so anxious to become, in truth, law-abiding American citizens.

Hospitals are being built in the Southland in the Northern, Central and Western sections in which Negro physicians, male and female, may function. Smaller plants are being standardized and Negro nurses are becoming registered.

Many State Federations and City Federations are raising funds, etc., for Negro colleges, in order that they may become accredited. Many are agitating and assisting in securing High Schools, State Club Houses and City Community Centers. All of these are being bought and operated by our women. From these centers, health and recreational programs of city-wide proportion are radiated. Many public clinics are provided for in the Centers by Club Women.

The activities of the members and units of our Association are too numerous to mention here. With them everything is needed and calmly, but persistently, they are striving to do whatever lies in their power to carry out their motto, "Lifting As We Climb."

All of our activities are covered by our seven-plank platform: Education,

Industry, Thrift, Citizenship, Social Service, Racial Solidarity, and Interracial Relations.

The work of the City Federation is a replica of the State, as the State is of the National, with the exception of one or two outstanding State or National projects. The Regions promote regional programs controlled by the existing conditions therein.

To better understand national or international conditions, and people in general, the President of the National Association of Colored Women visited nine countries of Europe this past summer. Many other outstanding Negro women toured Europe during the past summer, studying conditions and widening their visions by contacts made in these foreign countries. To these women, America presents wonderful possibilities not found elsewhere, while at the same time they plainly see the great need of the united efforts of the women of America, white and colored, for purifying the channels of our national life whereby we may strengthen our forces for a practical, Christian country—a real "Land of the Free and Home of the Brave."

The National Association of Colored Women is proud of its membership in the National Council. It extends cordial fellowship to its sister organizations and pledges its loyalty and support to the Council in helping to provide greater opportunities for service, and in working out, together, the culmination of all of our desires for peace and justice and fair play to all.

Year Book and Directory of the National Council of Women of the United States, Inc. (New York, 1928), pp. 146–148.

Letter to Julia West Hamilton

(1933)

My dear, dear Julia:

The great National has had its Convention and I guess now that the National Officers are settling down to their various duties. I earnestly hope that our good President will hold solidly in check the work we have all struggled so hard to establish. I think that the greatest concern is our National Headquarters because our Douglass Home is secured and in action. What we need to do now is to actually get those who are in authority to see the importance of the functioning of National Headquarters. We have put too much money, time and thought in it to see it fail. When we see what the White Women are doing with their National Headquarters right there in Washington, a few blocks from our Home, there should be no reason why a single doubt should come about our work.

Please, Julia, my dear, for the sake of all of us who hold the National

Headquarters as a sacred trust, don't give up the work as Custodian of National Headquarters. Hold on to it. Do not think of packing our things away. Make the Headquarters function. Get hold of the Club Women—make it their headquarters—get the young girls interested in it—organize clubs among them. Get in touch with the civic groups. Develop the outdoor recreation. Make a bid for the Club Women who are passing through the city. Send out National Releases to the Club Women—send out the *National Notes.* Put on a campaign for subscribers. Who has been elected editor of *National Notes?* I do hope that Dr. [Mary] Waring [President of the NACW] will appoint Nannie Burroughs. Call a meeting of Nannie Burroughs, Mary Church Terrell, the Club Women of Washington and vicinity. Put the fire works under the whole thing and make things buzz there—I know you can do it.

It is my plan to be in Washington on the second of October enroute north and I will spend a full day with you at Headquarters. I don't want you to think that I am not interested or asleep—my hands have just been tied and I have been awfully busy for many months. I am willing to work, fight and pray through till the end—I am not a quitter and I am not going to become discouraged. We are going to get together and put our heads together and fight this thing through. Don't let yourself become discouraged. Hold on to things.

The death of Emily Williams has brought a great loss to our club work. She was a good worker.

Now, Julia dear, get things to humming and I am behind you one hundred percent. I haven't heard from our National President as yet, although I have written her. I guess she is busy getting her office set up. I will write her again in the near future.

Sincerely yours,
Mary McLeod Bethune

September 5, 1933. Mary McLeod Bethune Papers, Mary McLeod Bethune Foundation, Bethune-Cookman College, Daytona Beach, Fla.

Minutes of the Organizational Meeting of the National Council of Negro Women

(1935)

A luncheon meeting of outstanding women to form a National Council of Negro Women was held at the 137th Street Branch of the Y.W.C.A. in New York City, Thursday, December 5, 1935.

Mrs. Mary McLeod Bethune called the meeting to order at 1:10 p.m. After the blessing was said the ladies enjoyed a delicious luncheon especially prepared for the occasion.

Mrs. Carita V. Roane, Honorary President of Theta Chapter of the Iota Phi Lambda Sorority presented Mrs. Bethune with a beautiful bouquet of flowers from Theta Chapter. She also placed upon Mrs. Bethune the Spingarn Medal which was awarded to her on June 28, 1935, by the NAACP for merit. The ladies present felt highly honored because this was the first time the medal had been worn by the recipient. Mrs. Bethune stated very sweetly her appreciation for the beautiful flowers.

At 2:15 p.m. the business end of the meeting was begun. Mrs. Bethune was asked to act as temporary chairman and Florence K. Williamson, as temporary secretary. The next order of business was presentation of guests and each person was asked to tell of her affiliation with any National Organization. They are as follows:

Mrs. Mary McLeod Bethune—Here in the interest of Negro Woman of America. President of Bethune-Cookman College, Daytona Beach, Fla.

Mrs. Charlotte Hawkins Brown—National Association of Colored Women. Principal of Palmer Memorial Institute of Sedalia, N.C.

Miss Bell Davis—National Health Circle for Colored People, Rockefeller Center, New York City

Mrs. Caroline Thomas—Mite Missionary Ass'n of A.M.E. Church, Orange, New Jersey

Mrs. Florence Reddick Tyler—Jamaica, N.Y.

Mrs. Lillian Alexander—National Association of College Women, New York City

Mrs. Mattie F. Powell—National Baptist Women's Organization, New York City

Mrs. Addie W. Hunton—National A.K.A. [Alpha Kappa Alpha] Sorority, New York City

Mrs. Ruth Roberts—New York City

Miss Olyve L. Jeter—National Women's Council of the Department of Racial Relations connected with the Federated Council of Churches

Mrs. Charlotte Riley—Young Womanhood, A.K.A. Sorority, New York City

Mrs. Mamie L. Anderson Pratt—National Business Women of America, N.Y.C.

Mrs. Clara Burrell Bruce —National Association for Housing, New York City

Mrs. Bernia L. Austin—President, Eutopia Neighborhood Club, New York City

Mrs. Violet L. Watson—New York City

Mrs. Mabel Hopkins—Omicron Chapter of the National Iota Phi Lambda Sorority, N.Y.C.

Mrs. Irene E. Maxwell—Women's Auxiliary of National Baptist Convention, N.Y.C.

Mrs. Sari Price Patton—Theta Chapter of the National Iota Phi Lambda Sorority, N.Y.C.

Mrs. Mary Church Terrell—National Association of Colored Women, Washington, D.C.

Mrs. Mabel Keaton Staupers—National Association of Graduate Nurses, New York City

Mrs. Carita V. Roane—National Iota Phi Lambda Sorority; President of Social Workers of Greater New York, N.Y.C.

Mrs. Junior Hawkins—National Delta Sigma Theta Sorority, New York City

Mrs. Edna Holland—New York City

Mrs. Cecelia Cabiness Saunders—Executive Secretary of Y.W.C.A., New York City

Mrs. Julia Coleman Robinson—National Business & Professional Women's Club, N.Y.C.

Mrs. C. A. Wynn—National Staff of the National Board of Y.W.C.A. of America, N.Y.C.

Mrs. Daisy Lampkin—N.A.A.C.P., Pittsburgh, Pa.

Miss Eva D. Bowles—New York City

Mrs. Addie W. Dickerson—National Business & Professional Women's Club, Phila., Pa.

Mrs. F. K. Williamson—Regional Directress of National Iota Phi Lambda Sorority, N.Y.C.

TELEGRAMS RECEIVED STATING HEARTY APPROVAL OF SUCH AN ORGANIZATION:

Dean Lucy D. Slowe—Howard University, National Ass'n of College Women, Wash., D.C.

Mrs. John Hope—Atlanta, Ga.

Mrs. Bertha M. Black—Grand Basileus of Sigma Gamma Rho, St. Louis, Mo.

Mrs. Ruby Peek—St. Louis, Mo.

Mrs. Catherine White Williams—St. Louis, Mo.

Mrs. Abbie M. Johnson—Grand Daughter Ruler of the Elks, New York City

Miss Mae Belcher—Indianapolis, Ind.

Atty. Eunice Carter—New York City

Mrs. W. Gertrude Brown—Minneapolis, Minn.

Mrs. Georgia Douglass Johnson—Washington, D.C.

A brief but interesting talk was made by Mrs. Bethune. She stated that:

Most people think that I am a dreamer. Through dreams many things have come true. I am interested in women and believe in their possibilities. The world has not been willing to accept the contributions that women have made. Their influence has been felt more definitely in the past ten years than ever before. We need vision for larger things, for the unfolding and reviewing of worth while things.

Through necessity we have been forced into organizations. The fraternal organizations through their groups have made things better for communities and this has been wonderful. They have created better leadership and have been able to give better service.

Six years ago I visited a National Baptist Convention[. T]here was a large group of reports from crude places, but it showed that they were blazing away for better things. No organization has done a greater job for womanhood than the National Association of Colored Women. The Business and Professional Women have made an enviable record, also the Sororities with the high ideals. But for the past seven years I have thought seriously of all National Organizations as well as individuals forming a Council of Colored Women so that we can make a stronger appeal for putting over big projects.

The National Council of Women has 43 organizations with only one Negro organization and we have no specific place on their program. We need an organization to open new doors for our young women and when the council speaks its power will be felt. For seven years I have been dreaming; I have given no publicity to my ideas; I feel that we who are present should make the hub and have the National Organizations as the spokes. It will take work and representation on our part. My appeal to you is to begin to think of the big things done by past leadership who dared to stand for right and let us fight today with Negro womanhood in mind. If we are on the right track let us know.

Endorsements and expressions of approval were made by the following:

Mrs. Lucy Slowe: Wired her approval and hearty cooperation and desire to push it to the top.

Mrs. Bertha M. Black: Dates changed, regret attendance impossible. As Grand Basileus I request that you include Sigma Gamma Rho Sorority as a charter member of proposed council. Inform us of detail deliberations and we will cooperate. Best wishes and sincere regards.

Mrs. Carita V. Roane: I am very much interested and I think it a wonderful thing. I am interested in seeing young women placed in the many avenues of the government and feel that if a Council is organized it could bring pressure to bear and Negro women would be able to secure better positions.

Mrs. Mabel Hopkins: I endorse the movement and feel that we are on the right track.

MISS OLYVE JETER: I am willing to face all the obstacles that go along with the organization of a Council and I shall cooperate wholeheartedly.

MRS. MAXWELL: I give my personal approval for the organization, but will have to carry the object[ive] to the board meeting for their approval.

MISS TYLER: I am from the Episcopal Church and I think it a splendid idea.

MRS. BOWLES: Best movement started in years. Best person to head the organization, Mrs. Bethune.

MRS. CHARLOTTE HAWKINS BROWN: Air castle building and dreaming are wonderful if only the dreamer works very diligently to make them come true. I have been in on it from the beginning and feel that there are too many organizations. There is a need for a Council or Conference but none for an organization. Such a Council could be used as a clearing house for all organizations. Intelligent leadership is what we need because no ladder is stronger than its weakest rung.

MRS. SAUNDERS: I endorse the idea. I feel that most organizations are hurt because of political squabbles. If each pays her own way, it is better—no price, better membership. We should be represented in federal and state organizations. I am in so many and I do realize how powerful we are. We can do something in this kind of thing and we should have all women organized. We have talked so we are ready to work.

MRS. HUNTON: We have got enough organizations. The rest of the Negro world looks to the American Negro for culture. During the last three years I spent in Europe, I visited many conferences. At one there were 30 nationalities present. Many embarrassing questions were asked me about how our group organized in the United States. Our problem is a world problem; no problem is settled until our problem is settled. We must solidify. [T]he Herald-Tribune Council stresses solidarity. This council will give our Negro women a status. There is not a great group behind our women to push them. We need push in representation in Congress and we can do what we elect to do.

MRS. BELL DAVIS: Mrs. Bethune has always been on the right track, she has circled the world. I heartily endorse the movement. I spent three years as a teacher at Bethune College and I know her well. I do feel that we have failed to stress the health situation of Negroes.

MRS. BRUCE: I am in hearty sympathy and feel the time is ripe for such a movement. We have been thinking too long on individual problems instead of national ones. The League of Women Voters are well informed on International problems and National affairs. We need to corral the forces of our group.

MRS. MARY CHURCH TERRELL: Reluctantly, I did not believe in the idea. Theoretically, I believe everything that has been said. But I can't see how this organization can help. I do not see how the mistakes made by other groups will not be made by this one. Back in 1896, I organized a National Association of Colored Women. I may not be so hopeful and I don't think this Council will be any more successful than other organizations have been. I cannot see any reason how this group can do any more than others, but I think it worthwhile.

MRS. SAUNDERS: I feel that the majority should rule in everything. I am willing to help but don't feel that the organization is needed. God Bless You.

MRS. STAUPERS: I think that we should have a permanent organization. It was not an easy task to have women come here from many cities just to listen to a discussion.

A motion was made by Mrs. Hunton and second by Mrs. Staupers that the group become a permanent organization known as the National Council of Negro Women. Voting was unanimous.

Mrs. Terrell moved that the secretary be instructed to cast a unanimous ballot that Mrs. Bethune be president.

Mrs. Florence K. Williamson, acting secretary, was instructed by the chair to cast the vote and she did so, making Mrs. Bethune the first president of the National Council of Negro Women.

It was moved and seconded that a committee be appointed by Mrs. Bethune to prepare plans for this Organization. Voting [was] unanimous.

There being no further business the meeting adjourned at 4:45 p.m.

> Mary McLeod Bethune, President
> Florence K. Williamson, Acting Secretary

December 5, 1935. National Council of Negro Women Papers, Mary McLeod Bethune Council House National Historic Site, National Park Service, Washington, D.C.

Letter to President Franklin D. Roosevelt

(1940)

My dear Mr. President:

At a time like this, when the basic principles of democracy are being challenged at home and abroad, when racial and religious hatreds are being engendered, it is vitally important that the Negro, as a minority group in this nation, express anew his faith in your leadership and his unswerving adherence to a program of national defense adequate to insure the perpetuation of the principles of democracy. I approach you as one of a vast army of Negro women who recognize that we must face the dangers that confront us with a united patriotism.

We, as a race, have been fighting for a more equitable share of those opportunities which are fundamental to every American citizen who would enjoy the economic and family security which a true democracy guarantees. Now we come as a group of loyal, self-sacrificing women who feel they have a right and a solemn duty to serve their nation.

In the ranks of Negro womanhood in America are to be found ability and capacity for leadership, for administrative as well as routine tasks, for the types of service so necessary in a program of national defense. These are citizens whose past records at home and in war service abroad, whose unquestioned loyalty to their country and its ideals, and whose sincere and enthusiastic desire to serve you and the nation indicate how deeply they are concerned that a more realistic American democracy, as visioned by those not blinded by racial prejudices, shall be maintained and perpetuated.

I offer my own services without reservation, and urge you, in the planning and work which lies ahead, to make such use of the services of qualified Negro women as will assure the thirteen and a half million Negroes in America that they, too, have earned the right to be numbered among the active forces who are working towards the protection of our democratic stronghold.

> Faithfully yours,
> Mary McLeod Bethune
> President

Letter dated June 4, 1940, in "Extension of Remarks of Honorable Louis Ludlow of Indiana in the House of Representatives, Saturday, June 22, 1940," *Congressional Record,* Appendix, vol. 86, pt. 16, p. 4191.

Letter to Secretary of War Henry Stimson

[abridged] (1942)

[When the War Department failed to invite either a representative of the National Council of Negro Women or any other black women's group to join representatives of thirty-one other organizations in planning for an advisory council on soldiers' welfare, Mary Bethune chided the Secretary of War. The black press carried the essence of her letter.]

We are anxious for you to know that we want to be and insist upon being considered a part of our American democracy, not something apart from it. We know from experience that our interests are too often neglected, ignored, or scuttled unless we have effective representation in the formative stages of these projects and proposals.

We are not blind to what is happening. We are not humiliated. We are incensed! We believe what we have asked is what we all desire. . . . a unity of action, thought and spirit. We still seek this end and urge upon you that Negro representation be included in this advisory council and in all future plans sponsored for the purpose of promoting our morale and strengthening our defense.

We militantly and respectfully speak through this voice for the Negro womanhood of America.

"Mrs. Bethune Protests to Secretary Stimson," *Atlanta Daily World*, October 19, 1942. Atlanta University Center, Division of Archives and Special Collections, Mary McLeod Bethune Vertical File.

Report of a Hospital Tour in the East

[abridged] (1945)

I would like to express appreciation to the War Department through Secretary Marshall for the privilege I had as a member of the Advisory Committee of the Women's Army Corps [WACs] to observe the work done in certain designated General Hospitals of the First, Second and Third Service Commands. There were five groups of women designated for this kind of observation and our group was assigned our portion of the Hospitals to be visited. We were assigned to Cushing Hospital at Framingham, Massachusetts; Rhoads at Utica, New York; Halloran at Willowbrook, Staten Island, New York; Mason at Brentwood, Long Island, New York; England in Atlantic City, New Jersey; and Phoenixville, in Valley Forge, Pennsylvania. We had the privilege of observing the housing of the WACS, the adequacy of the training given them, the ways in which the WACS assist as technicians in implementing the medical services to patients, nurses and doctors.

It was a most informing, inspiring and satisfactory tour. It brought to our visual and mental attention the unparalleled work that the war department is doing for the physical and mental rehabilitation of our returned soldiers.

My companions on the tour were [the following:] Mrs. Kathryn Land Sharp of Alexandria, Virginia, Consultant for Prisoner of War Service in the Eastern Area for the American Red Cross, [who] is the wife of Major General William Fletcher Sharp; Mrs. Mary Pillsbury Lord of New York City, Chairman of the Women's Activities of the National War Fund; Miss Mary Ward of Boston, Massachusetts, Assistant to the Chief of Education Service of the National Citizenship Education Program; Dr. Marion Kenworthy of New York City, Professor of Psychiatry at New York School of Social Work; and Captain Juanita Stryker, who has just returned from service in the Southwest Pacific Area.

All of us got a realization of the most efficient organizational work possible as we met the Commanding Generals of the Several Service Commands. We were face to face with men of great soul, of mind and of real understanding of human dealings. From the Generals down to the Commanding Officers of every Hospital we attended [on] through to the Service Staff and to the patients, we got a feeling of a united team work; of a sympathetic understanding, and of an efficiency that enveloped the entire set-up. The morale was beautiful under the most technical conditions. Technicians were patient and efficient. Patients were demonstrating a spirit of confidence and courage that awed us more frequently than we could express. The democratic spirit of integration and service to all patients and to nurses and WAC Technicians spelled out for me democracy in action.

At the Halloran General Hospital there were 75 Negro WACS distributed here and there in the different Departments, working enthusiastically at their tasks [and] expressing a great satisfaction in having a chance to do the thing they came to do, and in broader terms, to adjust themselves to whatever tasks may be assigned to them. This made me very happy. I found Negro Nurses integrated into the general program of nurses. There were officer's club rooms, Dining room Service, and recreational activities—all without the least sign of demarcation. I found one of our fine young women, Lieutenant Ruth Wallace, working there on the Dietitian's staff. My black soldier boys with just one hand, or with just one leg, or with both hands or both legs gone, or with only one eye—greeted me with a smile and with these words, "It does me good to see you here!"

At England General Hospital we found 100 Negro WACS with the hundreds of other WACS under the leadership of Lieutenant Hall, doing a very efficient job—occupying important posts of service and training in a way that fully integrates them into the complete program of the hospital. All of them were enthusiastically giving their best for the restoration of the noble sons of America who had given themselves so freely that the four freedoms may envelope the world.

It was more stirring than I can tell you as we walked into Dennis Hotel [in Atlantic City] where returned soldiers are sojourning for a time—where they meet their wives and mothers—all together. [T]hey were white, black, officers and mere soldiers. Some brought their wives up from Mississippi, some from Florida, Georgia, or from New York or Illinois [or] from the various ends of America to sojourn with them in this palatial cultural setting for a while, to restore the spirit and morale, which they had so fully spent on the other side. I remember well how Channing Tobias, Walter White and I sat for thirty minutes at the desk of President Roosevelt when plans were being made for [a segregated] Theresa Hotel in New York, a similarly large one in Chicago, and a place for white soldiers at Dennis Hotel. [H]ow we plead[ed] with the President to see that the idea of New York and Chicago be dismissed and that the great Dennis Hotel be set up for ALL soldiers. We told him that it could be done without friction with the proper staff to promote it. As I conferred with Colonel Cooper on this tour of [the] Dennis Hotel, he said, "Mrs. Bethune, there is not a single sign of friction; all moves smoothly here.

These are soldiers of the United States of America—everyone of them; they are so regarded in this Institution." It was a real joy to see efficient Albert F. Washington, Person[nel] Affairs Officer, gliding through without compromise, integrating his men in this vast cosmopolitan project in a way that America herself felt that it could not be done. But it is being done at Dennis Hotel. The two nights that I spent in the Hotel with my comrades—five wonderful white women—there was the realization of a dream, and as I write, I realize that it will not only happen in Atlantic City, but it will spread throughout America if men at the top will only have courage to see it through.

At Valley Forge General Hospital in Phoenixville, Pennsylvania, we had the privilege of viewing the experiments being carried forward in the Plastic Surgical Service. There were WACS assisting in making plaster masks for soldiers for use in planning future operative work. Valley Forge is designated as a center for Physical Therapy.

At Cushing, Rhoads and Mason, there are no Negro Nurses or WACS. Mason Hospital has a large number of Negro patients and Negro technicians serve on the staff. Rhoads Hospital also has a number of Negro patients.

Our Contacts in meeting the Governors of the several states were most satisfactory. Their interest in the whole program, their testimony to the worthwhileness of the program of the WACS in services of the General Hospitals, and their desire to have this program sifted on down to local communities and counties in the several states was indeed gratifying. If every governor had this same interest in the program as is evidenced in the General Hospitals of the First, Second and Third Commands, the G.I. Bill [which provides veterans' benefits] would be efficiently and effectively administered throughout the United States.

My one desire as we completed the tour was to see in the hospitals where we have now no Negro Nurses or WACS that they be speedily integrated into the work. We found no Negro Physicians on these efficient staffs that have been set up throughout this area. I came away with a great question mark in my mind as to why. I have every hope that very speedily from among the eminent technicians in the Negro World, may be selected men to serve the soldiers of America whether they be white or black. We want to help others as others are helping us. We are more and more wanting to work *with* others than to have others work *for* us.

Those who are serving these important hospitals have a great challenge. Those who are entering these hospitals have a great safety zone for rounded restoration. Mine was a grand experience. May God bless our Government, and help the peoples of America to know the great good that is being done behind the great doors through which the weary soldiers enter to find renewed life, and determination to live their lives fully again.

[July 1945.] Mary McLeod Bethune Papers, Mary McLeod Bethune Foundation, Bethune-Cookman College, Daytona Beach, Fla.

Statement before the Senate Banking
and Currency Committee on S. 1592

(1945)

As President of the National Council of Negro Women, I welcome the opportunity of testifying in support of the Wagner-Ellender-Taft general housing bill now being considered by this Committee.

The National Council of Negro Women is an overall coordinating organization, comprised of 19 affiliated national organizations and 20 metropolitan councils. . . . The aggregate membership of the affiliated groups is in excess of 800,000 women located in every State in the Union. The Council, in turn, is affiliated with the National Council of Women of the United States and the International Council of Women. Our programs have been concentrated in such vital areas as employment, housing, veterans' rights, consumer education, general education, family welfare, and health. Among these, we have consistently recognized the importance of housing, which has been the subject of discussion and study in our annual Workshop.

Certainly the Senators Wagner, Ellender, and Taft, who have made such long, diligent, and thorough study of this problem in their respective Committees and have brought forth this comprehensive bill, merit the highest commendation of the American people. The evolution of this bill is representative of democracy at its best.

The National Council is happy to note that this bill carries the names and is sponsored by leaders of both the great political parties. We interpret this bi-partisan approach and the long study and preparation that went into it as the typical American attack upon a recognized, well-defined social need. In this same spirit, the National Council would like to pledge to the sponsors full support of the principles of this bill as well as those contained in this statement.

The subject of this proposed legislation has long commanded the interest and study of the National Council of Negro Women. In 1943, our Post-War Planning Committee prepared a pamphlet entitled "Disease, Death, and Delinquency are Bred in Slums." This pamphlet outlined an action program with a slogan "Don't Rest Until Every Home Unfit for Human Habitation is Stamped out of Your City!" This slogan is indeed a complement of the worthy goal proposed under S. 1592—"a decent home and suitable living environment for every American family." To say that the National Council of Negro Women endorses this goal would actually be an understatement, for we have long and earnestly plead for freedom of all people from the slums.

Members of my Council staff have studied carefully the provisions of this bill and have advised me that, in general, the testimony offered by such organizations as the American Council on Race Relations, the National Association for the Advancement of Colored People, and the National Urban League, have covered adequately the technical provisions, and I heartily concur with their endorsements as well as with their constructive criticisms of the bill. But as the matter was discussed with me, I thought it to be of such paramount importance to Negroes and similar low-income groups that I am impelled to make a statement in behalf of the Council.

This is a crucial period in the life of the Negro in the United States. We Negro women—mothers of families—have deep anxiety for the future of these families. Thousands of our people have migrated from farms to cities, and from the South into the North and far West. They have crowded into these cities to help in the war effort at the call of their National Government. Now that the war is over, thousands more are following them. As a group, they are crowded into severely restricted, veritable slum ghettos of cities from coast to coast. Negroes are losing their war jobs, and Congress has not yet seen fit to continue the President's Fair Employment Practices Committee, nor to act on Full Employment Legislation to assure remunerative job opportunity for all workers. Our employment picture for the future is dark. We are confused and restless. I can recall that after the first World War similar conditions led to open conflict and violence. In each instance, the terrible housing conditions contributed largely to these upheavals. I see in this piece of legislation a ray of hope that may help relieve these conditions. I see a ray of hope because this bill does have a number of provisions which aim to help families of low and medium income, and through the use of public funds, to provide for the beginnings of large-scale slum clearance.

But the provision for urban redevelopment and public housing is almost like a candle flame in a sea of darkness. These slums are the most cancerous sore in the American life. Many of us had hoped, therefore, that American ingenuity would strike America's slums with the same resourcefulness, vigor and sweeping attack that was used in marshaling our industries and national resources to over-power the Axis. The bill is good, but in terms of the magnitude and importance of the job it is too timid for the courageous and pioneering spirit of America. I understand that twenty-two million dollars per annum for four years is provided in this bill to subsidize public housing and only four million dollars per annum for five years is provided to subsidize the slum clearance–land assembly plan. This totals twenty-six million dollars a year. We spent almost that much on a heavy cruiser during the war. The amount would not even buy a battleship or an airplane carrier. I should urge that we turn loose a whole task force in our attack upon this stronghold of crime, ill-health, delinquency, and racial tension.

I also note that the larger part of the job is to be done by private enterprise with the Federal Government's help through the Federal Housing Administration. We hope that this aid will be extended to Negroes in accordance with their need and economic qualifications, but our experience so far with the FHA has been that even the upper middle income level of Negroes had undue difficulty getting housing assistance through these channels. The provisions of Title IV of the bill, directed toward assisting private enterprise to develop decent housing for lower income groups, strikes at the heart of the housing need so widespread among the families of racial minority groups. I would especially commend the sponsors for proposing the long neglected protections for consumers. The warranty provision requiring the builders' guarantee is especially essential for housing aimed at the low-cost levels. And the lapse payment provisions will give the struggling home-buyer a chance he has long needed to protect his home. Lack of responsibility for the interest of the consumer has long been a deficiency in the administration of federal aids under the National Housing Act. I think this has been due to failure of administration to recognize that the primary purpose of housing legislation is, as Senator Murdock has so well stated, "That we supply the American citizen who is interested in a good home with a good home." We should no more permit the dealers in housing to sell bad structures under a Federal stamp of approval then we would permit a merchant to sell tainted meat; certainly not with Federal aid.

I cannot help but feel that while this bill has great potentialities in it for good, it has certain possible dangers, particularly for Negroes and other racial minorities. This bill puts considerable Federal power and funds, belonging to all the people, in the hands of a few agencies which will affect profoundly the housing policy of the Nation. I further observe the tremendous power vested in local communities under the provisions of this legislation. While I respect the unassailable concept of local responsibility, I must ask you to recognize the potential abuses of this approach in the absence of legislative safeguards for those groups isolated from the mainstream of community life and influence. We must recognize the fact that democracy has not been achieved equally with respect to certain of our citizens in thousands of communities in the United States. The powers governing a place to live are powers governing life itself. And the authority of life and death cannot be casually assigned, with Federal aids and sponsorship to those who have not proved worthy of so sacred a trust. If these Federal funds and power are utilized in behalf of democratic living, it can make a great contribution to our way of life. On the other hand, if they are misused, especially when it comes to the participation of Negroes and other races, it may set up divisions which may imperil national life. This was dramatically recognized by Mr. Justice Keiler Mackay of the Ontario Supreme Court in his recent ruling against restrictive covenants in Canada. Said he:

> In my opinion, nothing could be more calculated to create or deepen divisions between existing religious and ethnic groups in the province or in

this country, than the sanction of a method of land transfer which would permit the segregation and confinement of particular groups to particular business or residential areas. It appears to be a moral duty at least to lend aid to all forces of cohesion and similarly to repel all tendencies which would imperil national unity.

It should be noted that Mr. Justice Mackay, in arriving at his decision, rested the case upon the principles of the Atlantic Charter and the United Nations Organization.

Here is an opportunity to strike a blow for the democracy we all profess. The President of the United States, himself, has given us a lead. He has stated and restated his belief in support of non-discriminatory policy in employment. He has urged that this policy be implemented by specific clause and by administrative machinery. Following that lead, I would urge that this bill contain a sweeping clause which would require that wherever Federal funds, powers, or instruments are utilized to guarantee, aid, or subsidize slum clearance or housing development, the benefits of the bill be extended in accordance with need and economic qualifications and without regard to race, creed, color, religious or political affiliation.

The provisions of this bill for protection of families to be displaced from redevelopment areas are to be highly commended. I believe that the highest responsibility of true statesmen is the protection of those who stand most defenseless because of economic, social, and political impotence. Certainly, highest statesmanship was achieved in the drafting of these protective sections of the bill. Indeed, the land assembly and urban redevelopment title of the bill would be unalterably opposed by racial minority groups if these provisions had not been included. I, therefore, want to go on record as urging that Section 604 of Title VI be accepted precisely as stated in the bill and that all proposals to modify it by eliminating such conditions as the requirement of facilities prior to displacement be rejected by this Committee.

In commenting on the amendments to the United States Housing Act of 1937, with exception of the one establishing a 20 percent "gap" which I do not favor, I would like to say that the public housing administration has been a bright light in the whole dreary picture of housing available to Negroes during the past ten years. It stands in startling contrast with the irresponsible and vicious practices of the Federal Housing Administration which has not only failed to contribute toward the solution of the housing problems that face Negroes but has actually intensified these problems.

It is my earnest hope that this Congress, in passing this General Housing Bill, effect every possible measure to establish clearly in the administrative agencies, responsibility for extending their programs to meet the fundamental needs to which the legislation is directed. Titles IV and V cannot possibly reach the needs of racial minority groups if obstructed by the prevailing practices, so ably described by the NAACP, of the Federal Housing Administration.

The reason I do not favor the 20 percent gap between public and private housing is simple. I do not see how the objective of the bill can ever be fully achieved when such a broad income sector, embracing millions of families, is not provided for. Furthermore, if this gap is retained, how are we to have standard housing available for "graduates" of public housing at prices they can pay?

I cannot too highly praise the recognition of the housing needs of rural areas of this nation. Today, with our declining birth rates in urban centers, the nation's future generations and, thus, the nation's future lies in the vast manpower reserves of rural life. Decent homes for the tenants, the share-croppers, the migrant farm laborers, and the poorer farmer will truly be a profitable investment in America's future.

Before I close my comments, I would like to quote from that great and beloved champion of decent housing, the late Dr. Edith Elmer Wood:

> It will help if we remember not to put the cart before the horse. The consumer really does not exist by Divine Providence to provide profits for business and industry. On the contrary, business and industry, mechanisms of wholly human origin, exist to maintain the multitude of homes, big and little, which contain men, women, and especially children who are to carry on the human race.
>
> The equality of opportunity in which we all believe (however far we have fallen short of achieving it) involves a fair chance to every individual for bodily and spiritual health and for a normal family life.
>
> It has been well said that there is no better test of the civilization of a nation than the kind of homes the masses of its people live in.
>
> Either democracy will destroy the slums, or the slums will destroy democracy.

December 12, 1945. Mary McLeod Bethune Papers, Mary McLeod Bethune Foundation, Bethune-Cookman College, Daytona Beach, Fla.

Memorandum to Mrs. Harold V. Milligan, President of the National Council of Women of the United States

(1946)

SUBJECT:
REPORT OF THE NATIONAL COUNCIL OF NEGRO WOMEN
FOR 1943 TO 1946

During the past three years the NCNW has continued to press forward in several fields of endeavor in fulfilling the purpose of building better race relations, of developing leadership among Negro women, of disseminating pertinent information concerning the activities of women and increasing our knowledge of the activities with other women throughout the world. All the work that the Council has endeavored to do has been carried out on an interracial basis so that there is no sharp cleavage between the interracial aspects of our work and the program as a whole. However, special emphasis is placed upon cementing friendship with other women, enlarging our contacts and thinking, [and] planning and working together in all activities concerned with human welfare.

CONFERENCES

Building Better Race Relations: The NCNW initiated in 1944 a national planning conference on Building Better Race Relations at which time many organizations were represented. Out of this was formed a Coordinating Committee. This Committee meets at regular intervals to hear and exchange information from other members on current situations which involve minorities and to appraise the work of the various organizations in this area. This group has achieved a deep sense of fellowship while working together during the past two years. The various reports which have been exchanged have helped to widen the thinking of all of the participants as well as to form a basis for further program planning.

Participation in World Security Conference [United Nations Conference in San Francisco]: Through the president of the NCNW in her capacity as associate consultant to the American delegation and through other members of the Council who were with her, the NCNW participated in one of the most important meetings on international affairs. In addition, the Council was also represented at the Bretton Woods Conference in New Hampshire.

Compulsory Military Training: The NCNW participated in the conference on Compulsory Military Training sponsored by the Secretaries of War and Navy.

World Security: The NCNW was represented at the conference on World Security under the sponsorship of the Americans United Organization and the State Department. An important development of this conference was the meetings and discussion groups which were held throughout the country on the Dumbarton Oaks Agreement.

Work Shops: During the war the Council conducted yearly work shops in place of conferences to consider the most pressing problems facing the nation. Special emphas[e]s for the program of the Council were explored and directives and guidance given to the participants. A resume of work shop findings w[as] sent to all Metropolitan Councils and others.

Others: The Council has been represented at other conferences on housing, consumer problems, employment, child welfare, education and others.

War Activities

The NCNW joined with other organizations in seeking a Fair Employment Practice Commission [FEPC], held a "Hold Your Job Week," maintained a great interest in the Women's Army Corps, intervened in the case of four WACS who were severely punished without a fair opportunity to state their case. The court martial decision in this case was rescinded. The Council also worked with other organizations to secure the permission of Negro women in the WAVES [an abbreviation for Women Appointed for Voluntary Emergency Service, the popular designation for women in the navy] and Marine Corp[s]. Just before the cessation of hostilities, Negro women were taken in the WAVES.

War Bonds: Negro women through the Metropolitan Councils bought and sold millions of dollars in War Bonds.

Volunteer Service: The NCNW participated in voluntary services in local communities through the American Red Cross, American Volunteer Service, Civilian Defense, USO [United Service Organizations] and others.

Legislation

The NCNW distributed thousands of flyers and other literature on various phases of legislation including material on a permanent FEPC, the Wagner-Murray-Dingell Health Bill, full employment, minimum wage bills, price control, Federal aid to education, and anti-poll tax.

Publications

The Council continued to publish *The Aframerican Woman's Journal,* a quarterly magazine, and Telefact, a current news bulletin issued monthly. Booklets on the purpose and make-up of the Council and pamphlets on the cost of living and job security projects were issued.

Recognition of Outstanding Women

The Council initiated a roll of honor for the outstanding women in American life who are a symbol of the mind, the heart and soul of the womenhood of the world [and] who unitedly work for a world of peace, freedom and justice for all. Those honored in 1944 included among others Mrs. Eleanor Roosevelt, Mrs. Mabel L. Staupers, Miss Ann Hedgeman and Miss Katherine Shryver.

The second roll of honor for the women in 1945 was announced at a public presentation held at Council House and included Mrs. Agnes Myers, Mrs. Paul Robeson, Mrs. Helen Gahagan Douglas and Mrs. Daisy Harriman.

Liberty Ship

The NCNW requested that a Liberty Ship be named after the great patriot and lover of freedom Harriet Tubman. The ship was christened at Portland, Oregon, in June 1945.

International Activities

The Council is a member of the Pan-American Union and has received many visitors at Council House from foreign countries. Each year at the work shop an international program is given at which time representatives from all Embassies in Washington are invited to participate. Madame [Vijaya Lakshmi] Pandit of India was one of the speakers at one of the most recent work shops. Correspondence between women of several foreign countries is maintained.

The Council sponsored two delegates at the Congress of Women held in Paris in 1945.

National Headquarters

One of the most important accomplishments of the Council has been the purchase and furnishing of its national headquarters in Washington, D.C., entirely free of debt. The Council House is dedicated to the use of all women everywhere and the reception rooms, library and bed rooms have been used freely by women of all races, religions, belief, political philosophy and creeds. It is a place where the people of all the world can find beauty, comradeship and inspiration to continue the struggle for the cause of human welfare and human rights.

National Council of Negro Women Papers, Mary McLeod Bethune Council House National Historic Site, National Park Service, Washington, D.C.

Americans All: Which Way, America???

(1947)

We are approaching a critical juncture in the history of the World, and the destiny of our Nation. One road can take us from suspicion of other nations, to disagreement, conflict and war of unimagined fervors that would blast civilization, as we know it, from the face of the Earth. That road is easy and all down hill. The other road is up-hill, tortuous and rocky and only for strong men to tread. It is the road of national and international understanding, resolving of differences, compromise, agreement and peace, which can lead to fields brighter in promise than the Sun of the Renaissance opened to man.

Which way, America? All of us are proud to see our nation assume its rightful place of world leadership. Proud to see our way of life held up before the men of all races and creeds and colors as a way of life that holds promise for the little men of Earth everywhere. We are glad to follow our leaders on the path of bringing Democracy to war-torn Europe and Asia—to Greece and Turkey—to China, Korea, Japan, Italy and Germany. We are proud to be part of a nation that stretches out the hand of Christian fellowship to raise up the brother who has fallen into the dust, and help him to help himself.

We are proud, yet we are moved and confused. As Negro citizens and members of a disadvantaged minority group everywhere we are very much concerned as to what kind of Democracy, what way of life we are to take to the nations of the world. Is it to be the way of the Spirit, or the way of the Sword? Are we to show our strength in guns and tanks—in atom bombs? Or, in food for the hungry, plows to till the field, and in bringing peace to men of good will? Are we to win our way by virtue and persuasion and peace, or are we to shove it down unwilling throats with money and bayonets and war?

Is it to be the Democracy of the lynching mob and flaunted law? Of intimidation and threat and fear? Or, is it to be the Democracy of law and order, of the 14th Amendment really enforced, of the sanctity of the individual, of the protection of person and home against brute strength and fear?

The shame of Monroe or Greenville is no more the business of Georgia or South Carolina only. Riot in the streets is no longer the concern of Detroit only. These blots on our escutcheon are now not only the concern of the entire nation, but they are now the business of Russia and of China and of India—of the United Nations and the world. It is the concern of all of us, black and white alike, that America goes before the world with clean hands. We cannot find and bring to down-trodden nations the Holy Grail of peace and international accord while our hands are soiled with the lyncher's rope and the bull whip. We must all strive to hold high the integrity and sanctity of every individual like a flaming torch to a darkened world.

Will we take the up-hill road that leads to the Democracy of equal opportunity for all men—regardless of his station or the color of his eyes or of his skin or the nation of his origin? Or, is it to be the down-hill road, where there is a way of life only for him that hath, for the chosen few, for those of high birth, for the select, for those of the "right" religion or the "right" race? Our strength has arisen out of our way of keeping the door of opportunity wide open to all—so that the rail-splitter may rise to be President. That the unlettered may learn. That a man can go as far as his energy and skill and determination can take him. That the strength of each may be the strength of all. That the meek may inherit the kingdom. The chance for work, for jobs, for employment must be wide open so that each may enter and go forward in accordance with his abilities and without regard to race, creed, color or national origin. We must strive to hold wide open the door of equal opportunity so that all men may see the glory of America.

Is it to be the down road which leads to the Democracy of the slum and the blasted hearthstone, of the crowded ghetto, with its trail of congestion, ill health, delinquency and crime? Or, the up-hill road which leads to a way of life that gives every American a chance to have a decent home in which to raise his children and his family? Is it to be the life of open streets and playgrounds, of schools and hospitals, of smiling women and laughing children? Or, is it to be a Democracy that turns its back upon the filth and blight of our cities, that says people make the slums, that good homes are only for the few and the wealthy, that the rest are of no consequence? We must strive together to show the world that American strength lies in happy homes and clean streets and healthy families. We must strive manfully to take this kind of Democracy before the world—the way of security, of equality of opportunities, of equal chance for job and home; for health and education and recreation well within the reach of all. You and I must fight as never before to make our government realize the ideals upon which it was founded. We do this, not for Negroes or other minority races, we do this not only for the good of our city and our state and our nation. It is our obligation now to do it for the world. We must help save the soul of our own nation and its way of life so we can really save the world.

As Negroes, this is our great opportunity and our great obligation. We see all about us our boys home from the wars who fought to save Democracy, confused and frustrated because the Democracy they won is denied them. It is our job to rally them again to the ramparts to fight on to save that democracy at home. It means pressing on to get a chance for learning and training; it means hammering at the doors of opportunity until they open, as they must; it means preparing well and fighting for jobs.

It means saving and struggling to secure decent homes for our families; it means climbing farther up the way over which our fathers trod. Above all, it means hammering on the portals of government, it means qualifying, registering and voting so we can have the kind of government that we want and the kind of Democracy we want and the kind the world needs. We must do this for ourselves, but more important, for the strength and glory of the nation we want to see in the forefront of the world.

This is a call to battle, not of guns and blood, but of courage and of spirit and of peace. The world today needs audacity[. I]t needs audacious men and women in the high and noble sense. We must be audacious in fighting for Christian principles and dominating moral and spiritual enemies. The instrument used in the fight is faith. This will lift us to the far goal and carry us to goals that seem in[ac]cessible. We call upon the people of the nation to assist in bringing leadership and strong public sentiment to lead us on to the high road where peace, security and justice will be found for all minority groups here in America. And, again, as we have always done, it must be the women of our race and our nation that must supply the driving force and the inspiration needed as we take the up-hill road to peace. The united effort of women is paramount. For women have always been concerned with putting a floor on the necessities of life—namely, food, clothing, shelter. We can help provide the spiritual strength that buoyed up our fathers and grandfathers before us. We must help our boys and our men to know the way and find the light; bind up their wounds and wipe away their tears of defeat and frustration. We must rally them on no matter how dark the way. Today we will not only help a race to secure the fruits of full Democracy, but we will be cleansing the soul of a nation that would lead the world to peace. Let us then rededicate ourselves anew to the principles of true Democracy for all the people of the world.

June 22, 1947. Mary McLeod Bethune Papers, Mary McLeod Bethune Foundation, Bethune-Cookman College, Daytona Beach, Fla.

Don't Miss the Foot-hold!
Women and the Civil Rights Report

(1947)

It has been a month, now, since the report of the President's Committee on Civil Rights stirred American thought as it has not been stirred in our time.

Thank God for the report and for the Committee that produced it. Thank God that He has made for us this solid foot-hold for the tough, grinding climb up the face of opposition and indifference and lack of understanding, to the heights of full citizenship in a true democracy!

God, in His wisdom, has given us this means to scale the heights—He has not given us the heights. They are for us to win, day by day, year by year—in the local community, in the state community, in the national community. We have been given a foot-hold to a fuller life. We dare not slip. We dare not pause in the ascent.

One of our great Negro newspapers, through which we speak to the world, has said, "It will be a long, hard journey, but true democracy is worth every step of the way."

The reaction of the Negro press from all parts of the country, to this most significant report, is impressive and important. There has been no empty jubilation. There has been searching analysis. There has been Thankfulness for this Government-initiated challenge. There has been acceptance of responsibility. Our press has said, in a nutshell, "Hallelujah! The gauntlet is down. Let us get to work!"

One editor says that "it is up to Congress, the state governments and the President, to give reality to the report's recommendations." Another says, "This new blueprint for freedom is in essence a restatement of the basic principles which . . . distinguish our form of government from totalitarianism, whether of the right or of the left." Still another reminds us of that ancient adage that he who would be free must help free himself—and points to the ballot box.

I, also, would point to the ballot box, women, for who is the Congress? Who are the state governments? Who is the President? All are men and women selected by the ballot. Their achievements, their failures, are also ours.

The Civil Rights Report has set the whole nation to thinking. And, as has been aptly pointed out, it has put these problems "in the laps of ALL Americans . . . and focused on them the pitiless light of publicity." With the eyes of the whole world now centered on America, America must not fail. We, the electorate—even now the disfranchised electorate—must not let her fail!

We have just finished a great fight to remove the legal fences of residential covenants from around the ghettos that confine us to outmoded, inadequate homes in the most inconvenient and undesirable locations in our towns and cities. In every locality we must intensify this fight for decent housing, for breathing space. And we must keep up the fight for the right to clean waiting rooms and washrooms in railroad and bus stations and boat terminals. We must keep up the fight for the right to absolutely equal school facilities— impossible under a segregated system; for the right to worship our God freely and without embarrassing restrictions, wherever Christians gather. We must keep up the fight for the right to use whatever facilities are established for the edifications and uplift of America's citizens—libraries, museums, theaters, forums—all those institutions which bring our minds together and help us to know and understand one another.

We liberals, of all races, must carry on the fight—insistently, persistently—but we must carry it on without bitterness and without rancor. These can only defeat us, whoever we may be, and by whatever means we carry on.

I am reminded of a story which has recently been included in a national weekly—a very touching story of a young minister in a college town, intent on living the religion he preached. This young man, paying a pastoral call on his church's Negro handyman, one day, discovered that the unsightly, dilapidated alley shacks which housed the Negroes of the town, were owned by his leading parishioner. He came to grips with the situation, manfully, and the author, Nelia Gardner White, makes the owner—rebuked publicly when she would not listen privately—admit her responsibilities to the community and to the people whose homes she owned, and prepare to make good these obligations. I think it is healthfully significant that publishers are now accepting stories with such themes.

Now, we may not always hope for so propitious an ending as the result of our efforts, but we dare not fail to try, as the young pastor tried—honestly, earnestly but without bitterness, even though bitterness may be expected in return.

All reaction to the Civil Rights Report has not been favorable. All *will not* be favorable. But every unfavorable, unfriendly response is a challenge—to our knowledge of situations, to our methods of approach, to our ability to win these pre-judging people over to the side of democracy, by our own poise and understanding. I do not mean yielding principle—I never mean that! I do not mean fawning on those with favors to dispense. I just mean assuming that, like the owner of the alley shacks, our fellow men and women, by and large, are people of good conscience, who can be shown, and can be convinced. *Some* of our fellow Americans will fail us. *Most* will not.

Not long ago, our papers carried a story of a young white woman reported to have been evicted from a private home, in Madison, Wisconsin, because she had been escorted to an entertainment by a Negro. I wrote to the Dean of Women at the University of Wisconsin, asking for full information on the case. Was the home one approved by the University? Was the young man respectable? What was the University's policy? I received a full and cordial answer. The home was not on the University's approved list. The University's policy against racial discrimination was unchanged. The girl had refused to provide the school with the name of the young Negro.

I was so glad I had taken the time to ask, instead of attributing to that great University—by protest—a fault of which it was not guilty. That dean was made just as aware of my concern, and of the concern of Negro women, as she would have been by premature protest. Very often we *must* protest. Often, there is no alternative. Knowing this, let us, each time, be sure of our facts. *Let us learn to raise questions,* so that our protests, when they are made, may be more effective.

And, women, let us reinforce our questions and our protests by putting our own houses in order—literally and figuratively. Are we teaching democracy in our homes, at our own hearthstones? While we insist—as we must insist—on full democracy for ourselves, are we teaching our children not to dislike the *color,* or the *nationality* or the *religion* of a person who has done wrong, but to dislike the wrong? Are we teaching them not to dislike Jews, but to regard the Jewish merchant with the same spirit of brotherhood that we feel for the great Jewish philanthropist?

How many unsightly alley properties do *we* own? When our lovely Lena Horne said that some of us were sitting satisfied in plush-lined ghettos, while the problems of our fellow-creatures passed us by without touching us, how close was she to fact? Too close for comfort, I fear.

But women, today we are pulling up to that new foot-hold which the Civil Rights Report has hewed for us on the steep slopes of discrimination. Those of us who may, unwittingly, have sought the false security of "plush-lined ghettos" will open the doors of our minds, and make common cause with our sisters whose makeshift, unfit homes have no plush linings—no comforts and luxuries—to lull them into forgetfulness of the unseen barriers that separate them, physically and mentally, from their fellows.

This is a day in which we look farther out into a world in which we have achieved a new significance with relation to our fellow men. Today, we are the yardstick by which American democracy is being measured. Let it never be said of us that we are so full of imperfections that democracy cannot be accurately measured by what happens to America's minorities.

We must conquer these heights of prejudice, of discrimination, of segregation, of disfranchisement, of economic proscription and religious sham. As we move upward we must test ourselves and the ropes of our leadership and the footholds of our programs. Nothing is unimportant. We do not know which friend who is given to us today, we shall need tomorrow. Make friends! Keep abreast of every issue—local, national, yes, and international—which affects our lives as citizens of America and of the world. We must press for the ballot as never before and we must use it. We must get ready to renew our fight to remove the poll-tax and all other devious and varied community stumbling blocks in our path to full citizenship.

The day is here! The hour has struck! The Civil Rights Committee has given us the foot-hold. The climb up through the bruising rocks is ours! Let us move forward with stout hearts. The ropes of leadership will hold if we choose them well. The Committee's report has shortened the path. We shall yet look out on the horizons of the world, from the summit of full American citizenship!

December 5, 1947. Mary McLeod Bethune Papers, Mary McLeod Bethune Foundation, Bethune-Cookman College, Daytona Beach, Fla.

Stepping Aside . . . at Seventy-four

(1949)

Women United goes to press as I make ready to turn over the president's desk at our national headquarters in Washington, to younger, stronger, surer hands, and I find, constantly passing through my mind, the faces of the women who have helped to make the foundation-laying of the National Council of Negro Women, during the past fifteen years, a work of joy.

I want to pay tribute to them! There are so many of these women, old and young. Fine, strong, alert women, clear-headed, far-seeing leaders in many fields. How much they have meant to me! There was no idea so big they could not grasp and develop it. No task so humble that they scorned it.

How they came around me and worked early and late, on problems which affected their individual lives [and] the lives of all women. They sought and found ways to integrate women into jobs; they joined forces to help push through legislation designed to lighten the burden of women and children; and in the far-flung areas, trained and encouraged women to use the franchise to their advantage. These women worked at makeshift desks in the living room of my little apartment on Ninth Street, where my tired secretary would fall asleep, after the last volunteer had left with the dawn. And all this at the end of a hard day's work on important full-time jobs! I can never forget the friends of those early days, in the life of our beloved organization.

Yes, this has been a work of joy—joy in the struggle and responsibilities which we sought and accepted. A means to the realization of a dream for the Negro women of America, united with their sisters of all races, throughout the world.

It was a dream of being able to say, "We will be heard!" It was a dream of hearing the voices of women united for progress, without regard for race, creed, color or political affiliation. Voices ringing out in places of authority to support the interests of the masses of our people, and of all forward-looking programs.

And, as I look down at my desk, piled high each day, with correspondence from all manner of people from all over the world—people in government; executives and administrators; leaders in the civic, economic and spiritual life of this nation, and of many nations from the plain people, relating their difficulties—all asking for the counsel and cooperation and leadership of the National Council of Negro Women, I know that one part of this dream at least, has been realized. This is the evidence, wage standards have been raised, social security broadened, government salaries increased. *We are being heard!*

The soft velvet rug that carpets the staircase that leads to the office of the president, has felt the tread of many feet—famous feet and humble feet; the feet of eager workers and the feet of those in need; and tired feet, like my own, these days. I walk through our headquarters, beautifully furnished by friends who caught our vision, free from debt! I walk through the lovely reception room where the great crystal chandelier reflects the colors of the international flags massed behind it—the flags of the world! I go into the paneled library with its conference table, around which so many great minds have met to work at the problems of the past years. I feel a sense of peace.

Women united around The National Council of Negro Women, have made purposeful strides in the march toward democratic living. They have moved mountains. Our headquarters is symbolic of the direction of their going, and of the quality of their leadership in the world of today and tomorrow.

I have no fear for the future of women. I was sixty years old when this dream first took shape, on December 5, 1935. Now, at seventy-four, with the minds and hearts of thousands of women united to the task, I step aside. The cane of Franklin Delano Roosevelt, which supported me physically and served as a spiritual inspiration since his passing, now stands in the corner by the big chair in my room . . . and I can rest awhile!

May God bless all the women who have united with me in this effort, wherever they may be. They have the brains! May they have the moral power, and grant that He give them the spirit to carry on, to bulwark gains already made, to blaze new trails.

In Washington or wherever I am, my door and my heart will be open to all, to serve in the work of the world, in whatever way I can, within the limits of my strength. God bless them all!

Mary McLeod Bethune

Women United [periodical of the National Council of Negro Women], October 1949, pp. 14–15. National Council of Negro Women Papers, Mary McLeod Bethune Council House National Historic Site, National Park Service, Washington, D.C.

Participants in a June 1918 patriotic parade in Daytona Beach, Florida, include children and delegates to the annual meeting of the Florida Federation of Colored Women's Clubs, hosted by Bethune at the Daytona Educational and Industrial Training Institute. Bethune was president of the Florida Federation, an affiliate of the National Association of Colored Women. *The Competitor, 1920.*

Bethune, president and founder of the National Council of Negro Women, speaking at the annual meeting in Washington, D.C. Attendees include Charlotte Hawkins Brown, founder and principal of Palmer Memorial Institute (*front row, right*). *Bethune Council House, National Park Service, 1946.*

In 1945, as a member of the Women's Army Corps' National Civilian Advisory Committee, Bethune attends a luncheon during an inspection tour of the first WAC Training Center at Fort Des Moines, Iowa. She is seated with Captain Dovey M. Johnson, a personnel officer at the center. Bethune promoted successful efforts to integrate the Corps with black women officers. *Schomburg Center for Research in Black Culture, New York.*

Bethune at Miami International Airport upon her return from Haiti, where she was presented with the Order of Merit and Honor (worn on her dress), Haiti's highest decoration, in recognition of her "Service to Humanity." She is holding a cane that belonged to FDR, given to her by Eleanor Roosevelt after the president's death in 1945. *Bethune Council House, National Park Service, July 2, 1949.*

PART V

Politics and Public Issues

Stateswoman in Washington (1936–1945)

Introduction

Elaine M. Smith

MARY McLEOD BETHUNE took Washington by storm. During the era of rigid legal segregation and discrimination against people of African descent—eighteen years before the United States Supreme Court's repudiation of "separate but equal"—she "gathered everything and everybody under her very ample wing. . . . She occupies undoubtedly the most strategic position in the administration," columnist Edward Lawson reported, "simply because she has managed to bring together for unified thought and action all the Negroes high in government authority. Only one who has been in Washington for some time can understand what a big order that was." Two years later, in 1939, Howard University philosopher Alain Locke told Bethune that her unfolding accomplishment in Washington was "the most constructive single piece of work that has been done in the Negro field with respect to the New Deal, because in addition to upholding the New Deal you have helped to improve its shortcomings, and in a way that has strengthened its hold upon the public mind."[1]

Lawson and Locke both intimated that Bethune was a stateswoman in Washington. Gunnar Myrdal clearly acknowledged her status as such in *An American Dilemma,* his authoritative and panoramic survey of race in America near the mid-twentieth century. Recognizing that superior leadership in elevating the status of African Americans required political skills of the highest caliber, he named as statesmen ten individuals who had exhibited such skills. Bethune stood out as the lone woman among a group that included Frederick Douglass, Booker T. Washington, W. E. B. Du Bois, and James Weldon Johnson. Myrdal believed that had they been white, and thus free to direct their stellar political talents toward issues other than race, they undoubtedly would have been "national leaders" as opposed to "race leaders." He characterized these first-rate politicians as having "a set of practical ideals, a training in strategy, and a respect for courage, patience, and loyalty" derived from working on race advancement.[2]

While Bethune was a celebrated personage before moving to America's capital city in 1936, it was there that she made an indelible impression on the national consciousness. She became a redefining force in government by elevating public opinion about the level of administrative responsibility that African American women could handle, as well as about other legitimate aspirations of her race, from the right to share equitably in federal programs to the right to vote freely. She began her Washington sojourn during the

Great Depression, after President Franklin D. Roosevelt's New Deal, veering left, created Social Security, labor union legislation, and lesser-known liberal programs. One was the National Youth Administration, established, in part, to inculcate young people with a democratic ideology, as well as to enable them to cope with the Depression economy. It spent more than $685 million over eight years to assist almost 5 million people, including about 500,000 blacks. Through intense public relations for the NYA, Bethune parlayed her status as one of thirty-five members of the agency's National Advisory Committee into a full-time staff job. In this position, she could more effectively champion the NYA's mandates to assist youth with vocational training, work-relief programs, and job placement, and to help them remain in high school and college.[3]

Bethune's zeal, her age (she was then in her sixties), her influential connections, and her political know-how made her government tenure unique. Even though seven years of mostly state-controlled programs militated against equitable benefits to the dusky young, blacks perceived the agency as more evenhanded than any other New Deal establishment, thanks in good measure to the leadership of Bethune. Its status was such that in 1941 one commentator stated, "The National Youth Administration is the model from which all other government agencies should pattern their policies with respect to giving equal opportunities for advancement to capable and efficient Negroes." The capable and efficient ranking black at the NYA viewed her job as essentially an interpretive one: first interpreting the NYA to African Americans, and then interpreting the needs of African American youth for white Americans, particularly NYA administrators in Washington and state capitals. She excelled at it. NYA administrator Aubrey Williams exclaimed, "No one can do what Mrs. Bethune can do." Most state directors agreed. For example, after Bethune swept through Oklahoma in 1938, Hornton A. Wright exulted, "Her visit was an inspiration to me personally, to all of my people who came in contact with her, and needless to say she showed great leadership and great ability to stimulate, to lead her own people. . . . I hope she can return soon." Like all NYA state directors, Wright was white and almost certainly had never before had to receive an African American, male or female, much less pay homage to one.[4]

Bethune broke new ground in other ways. When the NYA was given nominal jurisdiction of the Civilian Pilot Training Program, she put black college students in the skies, thus preparing the way for black pilots in the military. West Virginia State College, the first black school to develop an aviation program, received a War Department airplane in 1939 "through the assistance of Mary McLeod Bethune and other officials of the N. Y. A." Tuskegee Institute and the other black colleges that began civilian pilot programs most likely benefited from her services as well.[5] Also in 1939, when the Civil Service elevated Bethune's NYA unit to the Division of Negro Affairs, Bethune, as director, became the highest-ranking black woman in government up to that time, and among the twenty or so top female admin-istrators in the New Deal. Unlike any other black bureaucrat in Washington at this time, she administered a budget totaling $609,930 over seven years. It extended blacks' opportunities for higher education and in the process pioneered affirmative action. She also developed a network of black assistants in states with large black populations, a key aspect of her division's responsi-bility to extend NYA benefits to its constituency. This "black power" approach raised both the quantity and the quality of assistance given. By the summer of 1939, NYA funds had helped push the number of students in black colleges back up to the 1930–31 level; and in 1943, NYA training and job placement were the most prominent means for young black women to enter the war industry as skilled workers.[6]

Bethune's status in Washington was also unique in that she became the administration's lead race representative, and her office developed into the federal headquarters for Afro-America. Operating "across all agencies—in Washington and across the country," she confronted issue layered upon issue.[7] But whether she was dealing with education, job placement, housing, health care, the military, or civilian defense, the quest for civil rights, and the respect and recognition concomitant with them, dominated her civic agenda. To heighten the consciousness of the government and the country, Bethune organized two national conferences on the "Problems of the Negro and Negro Youth." They were the first federally initiated assemblies to solicit the counsel of notable African Americans regarding the responsibility of govern-ment to combat the racism that pervaded American life. Even though the government generally ignored the counsel, the meetings established a re-form agenda, reinvigorated black leaders' strides toward integration, and gave some bureaucrats "a more sympathetic understanding of the problems of Negroes and other minority groups." Bethune's informal Federal Council on Negro Affairs, the "Black Cabinet," created in her residence in August 1936, ensured the conferences of a high standard of organization and expertise. They were the most visible manifestation of Bethune-initiated pressures to focus the government and the country on civil rights. Robert Weaver, vice-chair of the council, explained, "In those days we had no political strengths—it was like building brick without straw. We had to create our own pressures to get things done." Learning much about politics from Bethune, he unabashedly promoted the political party that provided blacks the greater recognition, however imperfect it may have been. Accordingly, Bethune, Weaver, and their white-collar council bureaucrats accelerated the flow of African Americans into the Democratic Party. In 1966, under Demo-crat Lyndon B. Johnson, Weaver became the first African American in a presidential cabinet.[8]

During World War II, while continuing to lobby the White House to end discriminatory practices against African Americans, Bethune necessarily focused on war-related issues. In September 1939, when Hitler's blitzkrieg in

Poland ignited the global conflagration, she sensed that the United States could not remain on the sidelines even though most Americans were shrouding themselves in isolationist sentiment. As a member of the Committee to Defend America by Aiding the Allies, she spoke on national radio early in 1941 along with other celebrities to generate support for Lend-Lease. After Congress declared war, Bethune exhorted African Americans to rise to the defense of country in ringing, unequivocal terms: "THIS IS AMERICA'S WAR. AND WE, TOO, ARE AMERICANS," she proclaimed. In September 1942 in Wilmington, California, this high-profile patriot presided over the launching of the U.S. Maritime Commission's *Booker T. Washington* Liberty Ship, the first ocean-going cargo vessel in military service to be named for an African American.[9]

In tandem with buoying patriotism, Bethune and the National Council of Negro Women, of which she was president, took on the well-being of blacks in the military. Like other NCNW members, Bethune visited various army camps to address the unfair conditions under which blacks trained and served.[10] She focused especially on servicewomen. It was primarily because of Bethune that blacks constituted about 10 percent of the first officer class of the Women's Army Auxiliary Corps (later Women's Army Corps) in the summer of 1942. As the special assistant to the secretary of war who selected the prospective black officers, she greeted them at Fort Des Moines, Iowa, on their first day of training. She also did her best to promote equal opportunity for them and their successors. Later, when the army chose to mete out undue discipline to some blacks in the WAC, she and her National Council rose to their defense. Their struggle embraced not only blacks in the WAC, but all branches of the female military. With widespread support from blacks but virtually none from white women's organizations, Bethune and the council achieved token victories near the war's end, when President Roosevelt required the Navy, the Coast Guard, and the Navy Nurse Corps to accept a small number of African American women. The female Marines held out against blacks until 1949.[11]

Bethune's closest relationships were with Colonel Oveta Culp Hobby and other ranking personnel in the WAC. Working with them behind closed doors, she wangled for Daytona Beach, her adopted hometown, the second WAC Training Center. Although this facility was restricted to whites, Bethune must have reasoned that it did no injury to her black sisters, because they received identical training at Fort Des Moines, and that the welfare of the country eclipsed all other considerations. Nonetheless, this was a risky move for a renowned black leader.[12]

Bethune's statesmanship in Washington stemmed from her wealth of earlier experience as a leader in the explosive racial climate of the South. Like other blacks who donned the mantle of unselfish leadership in the region, she was a courageous soul. On the one hand, she had to maintain the confidence of a mostly impoverished, disfranchised, and defenseless people. On the other, she had to cross the racial divide to influence white movers and shakers to permit blacks greater opportunities without arousing animosity. To be productive and acceptable to both racial blocs simultaneously was an art. And even as she mastered it, she could only chip away at racism rather than launch a sweeping demolition.[13]

Like other Southern black leaders of the early twentieth century, Bethune, a Republican, blended militancy with accommodation. The oppressiveness of racial subjugation was so stark at that time that militancy sometimes meant "you walked down the street with your head up."[14] This Bethune did and more. She flouted the prevailing racial etiquette and law, most notably by maintaining desegregated seating at her educational institution in Daytona Beach, Florida. At the same time, she sometimes went out of her way to accommodate racism. On November 13, 1915, for example—just a day before the death of Booker T. Washington, the era's most acclaimed African American leader—even as segregation and discrimination weighed heavily upon blacks in her adopted hometown, this schoolmarm, writing in Washington's style, declared that Daytona extended "a fair measure of justice to the Negro."[15] While the imperative to cultivate relationships with influential whites remained constant, Bethune never again appeared so acquiescent to the racial status quo. Nevertheless, in 1939, at the Waldorf-Astoria Hotel in New York, she told a meeting of the NYA National Advisory Committee that "a few more darkies" should be privileged to participate, and "I'd like to see a few more Negroes dotting around here."[16] Despite these assertions, in keeping with the loosening parameters of African American life and her own maturation, she moved from camouflaging racism to branding it a cancer to be exorcised. In 1944 she described the Harlem Riot of the previous year "as a part of a world people's movement" for freedom in the tradition of the Boston Tea Party. Writing perceptively at the end of her Washington sojourn, Morehouse College president Benjamin Mays observed, "Most leaders grow conservative with age. Mary McLeod Bethune has grown more militant with the years."[17]

Documentary Sources

Part V, "Politics and Public Issues: Stateswoman in Washington," contains nineteen documents coving the zenith of Mary Bethune's career in Washington, which paralleled the presidency of Franklin D. Roosevelt. The section "Separate but Equal" presents two speeches on the broad sweep of race as it affects African Americans. The section "National Youth Administration" samples Bethune's thinking and actions as the agency's ranking "Negro specialist." Finally, "Leadership at Large" considers the broader stage on which she promoted democracy at home and abroad.

In the nation's capital, Bethune tended to be more candid about race than she had been earlier. In "Closed Doors," the first speech in "Separate but Equal," she unmasked the strictures that galled her personally, along with millions of others. Later, in "Clarifying Our Vision with the Facts," she addressed the extensive psychological damage that slavery and "separate but equal" citizenship had inflicted upon the race. She challenged members of Carter G. Woodson's Association for the Study of Negro Life and History, of which she was president, to repair that damage by unearthing and disseminating the salient facts of black history.

The section "National Youth Administration" presents four documents on Bethune's bureaucratic modus operandi. The excerpt from the proceedings of the second National Advisory Committee meeting reveals her positive, upbeat approach in serving youth. This is probably the most authentic indication of her presentation to President Roosevelt when the Advisory Committee met with him later. The second document, a transcript of a telephone conservation with the Indiana state director of the NYA in 1938, reveals that Bethune's determination to have black assistants to state directors was a multifaceted political process worked out on a state-by-state basis. In Indiana, it culminated the next year in the employment of William Vernon Shields. In a letter to First Lady Eleanor Roosevelt during the summer of 1940, Bethune responded to a charge of discrimination in the administration of the California NYA. Aware of the divisiveness among African Americans over this state program, she chose to refute the accusation. In the final document in this section, an excerpt from the NYA Conference on the College Work Program in Atlanta, Bethune urges black college administrators to creatively marshal all resources to meet young people's needs in training and education. This document attests to Bethune's advocacy of higher education as much as vocationalism.

While the NYA was the means by which Bethune assisted several hundred thousand, it was also a base, giving her official status, personnel, and funds that permitted at-large leadership and a claim on statesmanship. During the New Deal, it was desirable to have an across-the-board leader, or "generalisimo of Negro welfare," to keep track of mushrooming federal programs, to aggressively implement them, and to create strategies for maximizing their benefits to blacks. Bethune took on these responsibilities because of her access to administration officials at all levels through the good offices of Eleanor Roosevelt and her brain trust in the form of the "Black Cabinet."

The documents in the final section, "Leader at Large," reveal Bethune's extensive reach in behalf of Black America during the New Deal and World War II. Six of these documents originated within the context of the Depression-induced New Deal. The first relates the circumstances leading to the formation of the "Black Cabinet." The next, a letter to President Roosevelt, conveys the findings of a three-day National Conference on the Problems of the Negro in 1937. Whereas the conference examined a broad range of issues, Bethune demonstrates expertise on very specific matters in a letter to the executive secretary of the president's Special Committee on Farm Tenancy, of which she was a member. Two years later, general issues nega- tively affecting African Americans were her focus once more, as is clear in her opening statement to the Second National Conference on the Problems of the Negro. Later that year, within sight of the 1940 presidential campaign, she wisely recanted an earlier recommendation for a similar conference in a memo to NYA administrator Aubrey Williams. Shortly thereafter, she drafted a letter to President Roosevelt suggesting how the administration might accommodate some aspirations of African Americans and also capture their vote in anticipated close elections in the North.

World War II was an even more opportune time than the New Deal to press for rights long denied. In this total war, the country could ill afford to ignore a vocal minority thirteen million strong and constituting 10 percent of the population in light of the national imperative for democratic propaganda. The first document from this period considers the consequences of the threatened March on Washington under the leadership of labor leader A. Philip Randolph. While failing to clarify her certain role in the negotiations relative to the march, Bethune expresses to Eleanor Roosevelt her satisfac- tion with the end results: the momentous Executive Order 8802 banning discrimination in defense employment and government and mandating the establishment of a Fair Employment Practices Committee. Bethune pro- moted Chicago alderman Earl Dickerson as a committee member, a choice President Roosevelt accepted. About a month later, in a speech delivered to twenty thousand gathered for a patriotic fest in Detroit, Bethune enumer- ated reasons for African Americans to give their utmost to the defense effort. Once the United States officially entered the war, she seized the moment to host a conference of twelve other black leaders, resulting in recommenda- tions to the government for morale-building in Black America. A few months later in Nashville, she addressed the Southern Conference for Human Welfare, then the foremost liberal organization of white Southerners and friends, on the topic "What Are We Fighting For?" The next year, in a letter to the vice chairman at large of the American Red Cross, Bethune sought to alleviate segregation and discrimination in that agency through a familiar process: formulating recommendations based on a black consensus, submit- ting them to appropriate officials, and then urging implementation.

Several months before the war ended, the at-large leadership of states- woman Bethune diminished with the death of President Roosevelt. On the eve of his White House funeral, she delivered in reverent cadences a eulogy over national radio to a dazed and mournful country. Her connection to the White House, symbolized by this eulogy and attendance at the small White House funeral, facilitated her most cherished wartime and career honor: she wangled from a reluctant State Department an appointment as associate consultant with the National Association for the Advancement of Colored People to the United Nations Conference on International Organization in

San Francisco. She was the only African American woman there in an official capacity. Bethune discussed this momentous meeting, which drafted the U.N. Charter, in "San Francisco Conference."

NOTES

1. Lawson, "Straight from the Capitol" [column], *The Charleston Messenger,* January 23, 1937, BF; Locke to Bethune, July 6, 1939, BF.

2. Gunnar Myrdal, *An American Dilemma: The Negro Problem and Modern Democracy* (New York: Harper, 1944), p. 987. Mydral ranked Bethune on a level below the four men named in the text. She was classed with Elmer Carter, Lester Granger, Charles Johnson, A. Philip Randolph, and Walter White. However, scholarly investigations, historical perspective, and increased respect for the work of career women have spawned an academic reassessment of Bethune that places her in the highest tier of African American leaders.

3. For a relatively recent interpretation of the NYA, see Richard A. Reiman, *The New Deal and American Youth: Ideas and Ideals in a Depression Decade* (Athens: University of Georgia Press, 1992). For interpretations of Bethune within the NYA, see Elaine M. Smith, "Mary McLeod Bethune and the National Youth Administration," in *Clio Was a Woman: Studies in the History of American Women,* ed. Mabel E. Deutrich and Virginia C. Purdy (Washington, D.C.: Howard University Press, 1980), pp. 149–177; B. Joyce Ross, "Mary McLeod Bethune and the National Youth Administration: A Case Study of Power Relationships in the Black Cabinet of Franklin D. Roosevelt," *Journal of Negro History* 50 (January 1975): 1–28.

4. "Equality in the NYA," *Chicago Bee,* February 2, 1941, BF; Williams to W. S. Snead, June 28, 1939, Aubrey Williams Papers, FDRL; Wright to Richard R. Brown, May 14, 1938, National Council of Negro Women Papers, Series 4, Box 1, BM-A. Stetson Kennedy to the Author, May 20, 1991, describes relations between blacks and whites within the NYA at the state level in the South.

5. Quote from "Education," *The Brown American,* October 1939, p. 8; Smith, "Bethune," in *Clio Was a Woman,* p. 165.

6. The comment on black college enrollment is found in "Education," *The Brown American,* p. 8. References to NYA-trained black women workers are "Education and Training," *Monthly Labor Review* 57 (November 1943): 951–953; and Mary Anderson, "Negro Women on the Production Front," *Opportunity* 21 (April 1943): 37–39.

7. Quote from William J. Trent, "Her 'Boys' Remember," *Time* [special publication of the National Council of Negro Women], July 10, 1974.

8. Quote from William H. Shell to Bethune, January 28, 1939, BF; Weaver quoted in "Honoring Mary Bethune: A Proud, Principled Woman," *Washington Post* [July 1974], pp. B1, B7.

9. *Pittsburgh Courier,* September 23, 1939, p. 8; *Pittsburgh Courier,* February 15, 1941, p. 1; Bethune, "We Too, Are Americans," *Pittsburgh Courier,* January 17, 1941, p. 8; "Notables and Workmen Participate in Impressive Ceremonies at Booker T. Washington Launching," *Pittsburgh Courier,* October 10, 1942, pp. 2–3.

10. Bethune to Florence K. Norman, September 3, 1941, NCNW Papers, Series 4, BM-A; "Outstanding Women to Visit Army, Navy and Make Complaints," *Pittsburgh Courier,* October 25, 1941, p. 9; "Suit Actions to War Needs," *Pittsburgh Courier,* May 9, 1942, p. 10.

11. Elaine M. Smith, "Mary McLeod Bethune," in *Notable Black American Women,* ed. Jessie Carney Smith (Detroit: Gale Research, 1992), pp. 6–92; "Des Moines Scene Unparalleled in History," *Pittsburgh Courier,* August 1, 1942, p. 10;

"National Council of Negro Women Outlines Aims," *Pittsburgh Courier*, November 10, 1945, p. 8; NCNW Findings [October 1944], p. 10, NCNW Papers, Series 2, BM-A; Jesse J. Johnson, ed., *Black Women in the Armed Forces, 1942–1974* (Hampton, Va.: By the Author, 1977), pp. 33, 41, 63.

12. Elaine M. Smith, "Mary McLeod Bethune," in *Black Women in America: An Historical Encyclopedia*, ed. Darlene Clark Hine (New York: Carlson Publishing Co., 1993), p. 124.

13. An inkling of the severity of racism during Bethune's zenith may be gleaned from the initial strategy of the celebrated Montgomery Bus Boycott in 1955, the year Bethune died. Martin Luther King Jr. and his associates carefully avoided demanding an integrated public transit but aimed instead for changes in the segregated system. They requested, in part, that whites be seated from the front to the rear, and blacks from the rear to the front. They did not authorize attorneys to file suit to desegregate the buses until January 31, 1956. Jo Ann Gibson Robinson, *The Montgomery Bus Boycott and the Women Who Started It* (Knoxville: University of Tennessee Press, 1987), pp. 135–136.

14. Louis E. Martin, "Dope 'n' Data" [column], *Tri-State Defender* [Memphis], June 4, 1995, p. 5.

15. Bethune, "City Officials Visit the Training School," in Part III of this volume.

16. Proceedings, National Advisory Committee, NYA, September 6–7, 1939, p. 215. B. Joyce Ross ("Bethune and the National Youth Administration," pp. 4–5) uses remarks made by Bethune at this meeting to draw the conclusion that Bethune was "a Janus-faced figure who presented a public position to bi-racial and white groups which often differed appreciably from her privately expressed attitudes." With virtually no other evidence presented, Ross's sweeping indictment of Bethune as something of an Uncle Tom lacks credibility.

17. Bethune, "Certain Unalienable Rights," in Part I of this volume; Mays, "Mrs. Bethune's Successor," November 12, 1949, BF.

Separate but Equal

Closed Doors

(1936)

Frequently from some fair minded speaker who wishes his platform utterances to fall on pleased ears, comes this expression—"Do not continually emphasize the fact that you are a Negro, forget that," and quite as frequently there is always the desire to hurl back this challenge, "You be a Negro for just one short twenty-four hours and see what your reaction will be." A thousand times during that twenty-four hours, without a single word being said he would be reminded and would realize unmistakably that he is a Negro.

These are some of the experiences he would have that would be exactly as mine often are:

One morning I started to catch a train. There was plenty of time to make the train with ease. Although several taxicabs passed as I stood on the corner trying to hail one, several minutes passed before one would stop to serve me, and so caused me to be three minutes late in catching that train.

On another occasion with time to spare, with sufficient money in my pocket to have every comfort that was necessary, I found that I was compelled to take a "jim crow" car in order to reach my destination in Mississippi. As a passenger on that "jim crow" car there was no service that I could receive in securing a meal, although from every other coach accommodations could be had.

When last winter, a number of Negro women were discussing where their respective children should attend school they were *forced* to the limitations of Negro schools exclusively, since they were all members of a southern community. Then as they thought of further education for their children they were again limited to those institutions which will accept a limited number of Negro students.

Some little while ago one of the best lecturers in this country was giving a lecture at the close of the Mid-week religious service, and there again, although the services and the lecturer appealed to me, there was no way that I could, with any sense of self-respect, enter when I realized the segregation and separation that awaited me on that occasion.

Not only the cultural avenues, but the economic fields are closed also. My boy belonged to a labor union, but when there came the chance for the distribution of jobs, it was not until all white applicants had been supplied, and then even though he is a skilled laborer, nothing was offered him in his own field, but he was forced to accept a job as a common laborer.

The white collar jobs are largely closed to the majority of Negroes, although they have given themselves to the making of this country. The very forests that the Negroes have turned into fertile fields are often not open to them.

As I walked down the street, passing restaurants, cafes, hotels, not necessarily with brazing, glaring signs, but with a subtle determination there is the expression "no admittance."

Whether it be my religion, my aesthetic taste, my economic opportunity, my educational desire, whatever the craving is, I find a limitation because I suffer the greatest known handicap, a Negro—a Negro woman.

As the director—mother of the next generation guiding the Negro youth of this land, the citizenry who must share the responsibility of this country, whatever it is, I find that the Negro youth cannot have, and enjoy, the highest places of citizenship, but must measure up to that standard, nevertheless. As a part of the citizenry of this country, the greatest country in all the world, he is expected to be a superior being despite the ever increasing limitations. The outstanding Negro has proportionably more than met this requirement in the fields of letters, music, economics and research education, in fact, in every line of endeavor.

The doors in almost every field, political, educational, economical and social are closed, barred against him, but they must be opened. Shall it be a question whether or not the Negro, himself, will batter down the doors; whether or not the government will open some of them for him; whether or not the fair-mindedness of the country shall force them to open is a question. But they must be opened if the Negro is to live up to, and attain, unto his best.

Theoretically, to be an American citizen implies that every American citizen shall have life, liberty and pursuit of happiness without anyone else's let [permission] or hindrance. Yet, this rule does not apply equally to the Negro as it does to the white man. There are very many doors that are shut against the Negro, but all of these are not barred. They may be opened with tact, skill and persistence.

The first privilege of a citizen is to be well-born. The day of the midwife is largely passed, and the expectant mother should have the best care of physician and hospital. Many children are handicapped for life by not having had the proper medical attention preceding birth, at birth and immediately following birth. Even when there is general medical assistance along these lines for white people, the door is generally shut to the Negro. In many places, if he be taken into the hospital at all, he is taken into the cellar or some isolated corner and given scarce attention by unwilling hands. The necessary food for mother and child is often beyond the reach of such persons, not only because of poverty, but because of color only. These handicaps follow child and adult in the Southland and are often present in the Northland, where equality, on the surface, is pretended.

Next to birth and life itself come housing and sanitary conditions. The Negro sections of most southern towns are just across the railroad where there are neither paved streets, under drainage nor sufficient lighting. Nor are there rules of health that compel those who occupy these sections to observe the most common rules of sanitation. The Federal Housing and Community Bills have not gone far enough to penetrate across the railroad where the people who most need them may be accommodated. And even in the north and more liberal communities the Negro often finds himself in the old, and often abandoned part of the community, where the better class of white people have left to move into up-to-date, better ventilated, better heated and better constructed homes.

The child handicapped at birth for want of proper medical and home surroundings most often finds that his school facilities are both very limited and very poor. The school houses, if such they may be called, are poorly constructed and lighted, and have straight-back benches with seats often too high for small children, or too small for older pupils, neither properly lighted nor properly heated. When the parents are too poor to buy suitable books, no provisions are made for buying them. In many places there is an attempt to segregate colored taxation to colored schools, which means the white child gets ten months of schooling under favorable conditions while the colored child gets four or five months with very poor facilities, and poorly educated and equally poorly paid teachers. These conditions make it very easy for the Negro in after years to "knock and not be heard." The Negro is expected to be a citizen and obey all laws which he often has no facilities for knowing and certainly no opportunity for making.

It is notorious that the Negro is deprived of his civil rights in public places. He has no opportunity to contact the white community in those things which make for right living, worthwhile accomplishments and high citizenship.

The cultural advantages of the concert, lectures and public discussions are closed to him. He is further handicapped by not being able to work at the ordinary trades controlled by labor unions. It matters not what a Negro's qualifications are, it is difficult for him to become a member of a united labor organization, and to function as a member of the AFL [American Federation of Labor]. These labor organizations control most of the worthwhile employment and scrupulously exclude the Negro from membership and even where the Negro is permitted to join he is given the most menial work, and the least paying jobs.

In railroad travel the Negro is segregated in the South and made to ride in filthy, dingy, unsanitary cars. At the railroad station there is some kind of a toilet facility marked "colored." But even these facilities are denied those who by virtue of their economic conditions are forced to ride in buses. These bus lines often have only one set of toilet accommodations for men and for women which means white men and women. The colored passenger who often has to shift for himself, has to go to a nearby house or go to the woods and bushes in order to get an opportunity for the proper evacuations. Then too, when he enters the buses he is assigned to the seats over the wheels where he is both cramped and jolted.

A colored man may be a fireman on a southern train, and may know all about how to run the engine, but if the engineer gets sick or dies a white man must be sent for to move the train off the tracks into the barn. The labor union forbids him to join the union or place his hand on the throttle.

In states in which the State Board controls the sale of liquor, such as Pennsylvania, a colored man is not permitted to be a salesman, but [permitted to be] a janitor or truck driver. And although the government will furnish him money by way of relief to buy the liquor, the government will not see that he has a chance to earn a living for his wife and family through dispensing the liquor.

In the armed branch of the government the Negro can be little more than common fodder. In the Navy it matters not what his qualifications may be, he can rise no higher than a mess boy, and the same thing is generally true of the Army. The once vaulted 9th and 10th Cavalries and the 24th and 25th Infantries have virtually been abolished to the colored man and he can only be a cleaner in that branch of the government. But in case of actual war, he is conscripted and sent to the front as shock troops. This prejudiced viewpoint on behalf of the government not only deprives colored men of the privilege of playing soldier, but also prevents them and their families from getting what could come to them through wages.

Beginning as the Negro did with the founding of the colonies, contributing as he has to every phase of American life, he should have the same rights, privileges, immunities and emoluments that have been and are accorded to any American citizen, and the government standing in loco parentis should neither make nor allow any discriminations or differences in any of her citizens, and should go a step further and see that no citizen, group of citizens, municipal or State government treat the Negro differently from all other citizens. That means that in the positions of responsibility, honor and trust, without . . . the right to earn a living at any trade or occupation for which he is qualified, the government should see to it that the Negro is not barred therefrom.

The Negro wants a fair chance to work out his own destiny and to continue to contribute to the honor and glory of the nation. But, this is impossible if he is to be handicapped, circumscribed, separated and segregated.

The Negro wants equality of opportunity. He asks the privilege of entering every door and avenue that he may be able to prove his value. The Negro asks: "Can America, the land of the free, continue to refuse to answer his knock at these now closed doors; to refuse to grant him these requested opportunities of equality whereby he will make a finer, higher and more acceptable citizen?"

The Negro must go to a separate church even though he claims to be of the same denomination [as some whites]. He is not allowed to sing, in unison with the white man, the grand old hymns of Calvin, the Wesleys—the triumphant songs of Christ and eternal glory.

When at last he is called to his final resting place on earth even his ashes are not allowed to mingle with those of his white brother, but are borne away to some remote place where the white man is not even reminded that this Negro ever lived.

Judging from all that has preceded the Negro in death, it looks as if he has been prepared for a heaven, separate from the one to which the white man feels he alone is fit to inhabit.

Thus in death and for eternity, as in life, the white man would see the Negro segregated.

The rankest injustice is meted out to the Negro when he has helped in every way the development of the country, and yet finds that he is not permitted to share fully and freely in that development.

The principle of justice is fundamental and must be exercised if the peoples of this country are to rise to the highest and best, for there can be neither freedom, peace, true democracy or real development without justice. The closed door of economic inequalities, of educational limitation, of social restrictions comprise the greatest injustice possible. None need fear the change for which we plead. The door of opportunity with all its ramifications, leading into every avenue can be opened without this evolution causing revolution. This is a high challenge to America—to the church—and to the State. Just now there seems to be an effort on the part of our great leader, the President of the United States, to open for the Negro some of the doors that have been closed. Too, there is a determination on the part of the Negro to open, or batter down some of these closed doors. But *more,* there must be an equal plan or cooperation on the part of the American public to join in the effort. How will this challenge be met?

It seems to me that here is his challenge to America. Can it—will it? If it further closes the door of opportunity to a part of its own citizenry, it will be guilty of the very outrage that led to its own founding.

Awake America! Accept the challenge! Give the Negro a chance!

Mary McLeod Bethune Papers, Amistad Research Center, Tulane University, New Orleans, La.

Clarifying Our Vision with the Facts

(1938)

John Vandercook's *Black Majesty* tells the dramatic story of Jean Christophe, the black emperor of Haiti, and how he moulded his empire with his bare hands out of the rugged cliffs and the unchained slaves of his native land. One night, in the midst of his Herculean struggles, Sir Home, his English Adviser, accused him of building too fast and working his subjects like slaves until they were discontent. . . . "For a long moment Christophe was silent. . . . When he spoke, his full rich voice seemed suddenly old.

"You do not understand. . . ."

He stopped again, seemed to be struggling for words. Then he went on:

"My race is as old as yours. In Africa, they tell me, there are as many blacks as there are white men in Europe. In Saint Domingue, before we drove the French out, there were a hundred Negroes to every master. But we were your slaves. Except in Haiti, nowhere in the world have we resisted you. We have suffered, we have grown dull, and, like cattle under a whip, we have obeyed. Why? Because we have no pride! And we have no pride because we have nothing to remember. Listen!"

He lifted his hand. From somewhere behind them was coming a faint sound of drumming, a monotonous, weird melody that seemed to be born of the heart of the dark, rearing hills, that rose and fell and ran in pallid echoes under the moon. The King went on.

"It is a drum, Sir Home. Somewhere my people are dancing. It is almost all we have. The drum, laughter, love for one another, and our share of courage. But we have nothing white men can understand. You despise our dreams and kill the snakes and break the little sticks you think are our gods. Perhaps if we had something we could show you, if we had something we could show ourselves, you would respect us and we might respect ourselves.

"If we had even the names of our great men! If we could lay our hands"—he thrust his out—"on things we've made, monuments and towers and palaces, we might find our strength, gentlemen. While I live I shall try to build that pride we need, and build in terms white men as well as black can understand! I am thinking of the future, not of now. I will teach pride if teaching breaks every back in my kingdom."

Today I would salute in homage that wise old emperor. I bring you again his vibrant message. Our people cry out all around us like children lost in the wilderness. Hemmed in by a careless world, we are losing our homes and our farms and our jobs. We see vast numbers of us on the land sunk into the degradation of peonage and virtual slavery. In the cities, our workers are barred from the unions, forced to "scab" and often to fight with their very lives for work. About us cling the ever-tightening tentacles of poor wages, economic insecurity, sordid homes, labor by women and children, broken homes, ill health, delinquency and crime. Our children are choked by denied opportunity for health, for education, for work, for recreation, and thwarted with their ideals and ambitions still a-borning. We are scorned of men; they spit in our faces and laugh. We cry out in this awesome darkness. Like a clarion call, I invoke today again the booming voice of Jean Christophe—

"If we had something we could show you, if we had something we could show ourselves, you would respect us and we might respect ourselves. If we had even the names of our great men! If we could lay our hands on things we've made, monuments and towers and palaces, we might find our strength, gentlemen. . . ."

If our people are to fight their way up out of bondage we must arm them with the sword and the shield and the buckler of pride—belief in themselves and their possibilities, based upon a sure knowledge of the achievements of the past. That knowledge and that pride we must give them "if it breaks every back in the kingdom."

Through the scientific investigation and objective presentation of the facts of our history and our achievement to ourselves and to all men, our Association for the Study of Negro Life and History serves to tear the veil from our eyes and allow us to see clearly and in true perspective our rightful place among all men. Through accurate research and investigation, we serve so to supplement, correct, re-orient and annotate the story of world progress as to enhance the standing of our group in the eyes of all men. In the one hand, we bring pride to our own; in the other, we bear respect from the others.

We must tell the story with continually accruing detail from the cradle to the grave. From the mother's knee and the fireside of the home, through the nursery, the kindergarten and the grade school, high school, college and university,—through the technical journals, studies and bulletins of the Association,—through newspaper, storybook and pictures, we must tell the thrilling story. When they learn the fairy tales of mythical king and queen and princess, we must let them hear, too, of the Pharaohs and African kings and the brilliant pageantry of the Valley of the Nile; when they learn of Caesar and his legions, we must teach them of Hannibal and his Africans; when they learn of Shakespeare and Goethe, we must teach them of Pushkin and Dumas. When they read of Columbus, we must introduce the Africans who touched the shores of America before Europeans emerged from savagery; when they are thrilled by Nathan Hale, baring his breast and crying: "I have but one life to give for my country," we must make their hearts leap to see Crispus Attucks stand and fall for liberty on Boston Common with the red blood of freedom streaming down his breast. With the *Tragic Era* we give them *Black Reconstruction*; with Edison, we give them Jan Matzeliger; with John Dewey, we place Booker T. Washington; above the folk-music of the cowboy and the hill-billy, we place the spiritual and the "blues"; when they boast of Maxfield Parrish, we show them E. Simms Campbell. Whatever man has done, we have done—and often, better. As we tell this story, as we present to the world the facts, our pride in racial achievement grows, and our respect in the eyes of all men heightens.

Certainly, too, it is our task to make plain to ourselves the great story of our rise in America from "less than the dust" to the heights of sound achievement. We must recount in accurate detail the story of how the Negro population has grown from a million in 1800 to almost 12 million in 1930. The Negro worker is today an indispensable part of American agriculture and industry. His labor has built the economic empires of cotton, sugar cane and tobacco; he furnishes nearly 12 per cent of all American bread-winners, one-third of all servants, one-fifth of all farmers. In 1930, we operated one million farms and owned 750,000 homes. Negroes operate today over 22,000 business establishments with over 27 million dollars in yearly receipts and payrolls of more than five million dollars. Negroes manufacture more than 60 different commodities. They spend annually for groceries over two billion dollars, a billion more for clothes, with total purchasing power in excess of $4^{1}/_{2}$ billion dollars. Negro churches have more than five million members in 42,500 organizations, owning 206 million dollars' worth of property and spending 43 million dollars a year. Some 360,000 Negroes served in the World War, with 150,000 of them going to France. Negroes are members of legislatures in 12 states; three or more states have black judges on the bench and a federal judge has recently been appointed to the Virgin Islands. Twenty-three Negroes have sat in Congress, and there is one member of the House at present. Under the "New Deal," a number of well qualified Negroes hold administrative posts.

Illiteracy has decreased from about 95 per cent in 1865 to only 16.3 per cent in 1930. In the very states that during the dark days of Reconstruction prohibited the education of Negroes by law, there are today over 2 million pupils in 25,000 elementary schools, 150,000 high school pupils in 2,000 high schools and 25,000 students in the more than 100 Negro colleges and universities. Some 116 Negroes have been elected to Phi Beta Kappa in white Northern colleges; over 60 have received the degree of Doctor of Philosophy from leading American universities and 97 Negroes are mentioned in *Who's Who in America.* It is the duty of our Association to tell the glorious story of our past and of our marvelous achievement in American life over almost insuperable obstacles.

From this history, our youth will gain confidence, self-reliance and courage. We shall thereby raise their mental horizon and give them a base from which to reach out higher and higher into the realm of achievement. And as we look about us today, we know that they must have this courage and self-reliance. We are beset on every side with heart-rending and fearsome difficulties.

Recently, in outlining to the President of the United States the position of the Negro in America, I saw fit to put it this way: "The great masses of Negro workers are depressed and unprotected in the lowest levels of agriculture and domestic service while black workers in industry are generally barred from the unions and grossly discriminated against. The housing and living conditions of the Negro masses are sordid and unhealthy; they live in constant terror of the mob, generally shorn of their constitutionally guaranteed right of suffrage, and humiliated by the denial of civil liberties. The great masses of Negro youth are offered only one fifteenth the educational opportunity of the average American child."

These things also we must tell them, accurately, realistically and factually. The situation we face must be defined, reflected and evaluated. Then, armed with the pride and courage of his glorious tradition, conscious of his positive contribution to American life, and enabled to face clear-eyed and unabashed the actual situation before him, the Negro may gird his loins and go forth to battle to return "with their shields or on them." And so today I charge our Association for the Study of Negro Life and History to carry forward its great mission to arm us with the facts so that we may face the future with clear eyes and a sure vision. Our Association may say again with Emperor Jean Christophe: "While I live I shall try to build that pride we need, and build in terms white men as well as black can understand! I am thinking of the future, not of now. I will teach pride if my teaching breaks every back in my Kingdom."

Journal of Negro History 23 (January 1938): 10–15.

National Youth Administration

Proceedings of the Second National Youth Administration Advisory Committee Meeting

[excerpt] (1936)

[In the absence of Dr. Mordecai Johnson, the Chairman of the Subcommittee on Negro Youth, NYA, the Advisory Committee Chairman Charles W. Taussig asked Bethune to "say a few words" regarding the effectiveness of NYA among African Americans.]

Mrs. Bethune: I thank you, Mr. Chairman. I regret exceedingly that Dr. Johnson is not here, because I think that this is a very vital and important part of the program and needs to have the very special attention of this committee because of its uniqueness in the country.

I want first of all to express on the part of the Negro people, our appreciation for the vision of our illustrious President, and his committee, in extending to the nation this NYA program. In my opinion, and I think I am thinking in terms of thinking Negro people, I believe it to be one of the most stabilizing projects for the benefit of the American of tomorrow, than possibly any one thing that we have done.

It seems to me that the giving of opportunity to the youths of today to round out in training and in vision for the citizen[s] of tomorrow is vitally important.

The Negro views with deep interest the national program for all youth and approves most highly its objectives. More particularly is the Negro interested in those phases of the program, which for the first time in the history of the nation, affords to Negro youth through Federal benefits, larger opportunities for education, productive work and cultural and wholesome recreation. Among the most invaluable outcomes of the National Youth program as related to the Negro youth have been:

1. His optimistic awakening to the responsibility of citizenship made possible through the channels of training provided through the program of the National Youth Administration.

2. The fine spirit of cooperation of the general Negro public in fostering the objectives of the program of the NYA.

3. The fine spirit of cooperation and healthy participation on the part of Negro educators and leaders, and state and local NYA Administrators.

I think, Mr. Chairman, and members of this committee, this NYA program has afforded the finest opportunity for interracial cooperation and understanding in these local communities, than any one thing that we have had come among us, particularly in our own southern section.

Through the program of the National Youth movement touching the humblest black boy of the South has come a realization on the part of thousands of untutored Negro parents that the government does care,—for "even the least of these."

In places where there is no need for a separate program, for Negro and white groups, we most heartily recommend the one program. And in fields where it is necessary for us to have a separate program, we most heartily recommend a separate program, taking, of course, under advisement, the necessity of the proper leadership and guidance that we might be able to do the most effective work.

It is recommended that this committee accept as a matter of policy the following: Continuing the policy adopted by the committee at its previous meeting regarding the appointment of qualified Negroes as members of staffs of state and local organizations; and the recognition of the value of Negro Supervision for strictly Negro work projects.

May I advise the committee that it does not matter how equipped your white supervision might be, or your white leadership, it is impossible for you to enter as sympathetically and understandingly, into the program of the Negro, as the Negro can do. Then it will give, also, the thing that we very much need nowadays, that opportunity for the development of leadership among the Negro people themselves, and it is becoming more important that the right type of leadership be produced. They can only become efficient by having the opportunity to develop and grow in participation in these programs.

We recognize that great care and diplomacy are necessary in certain places to bring this idea to pass. I want you to keep that in mind, for all of these years I have been reared and working in a community where it takes the type of understanding leadership, to take steps slowly but surely. Sometimes we are standing still rather than breaking up and organizing; but if you will stand by the policy of opening the doors as rapidly as possible, with sane qualified leadership, you are going to find that it will build more substantially for permanency and for the type of citizenship that we want to mold.

Notwithstanding this difficulty the committee must not permit itself to be turned aside from the prosecution and realization of the major objectives of the National Youth program, chief of which is the development of an appreciation of citizenship values in the minds of American youth regardless of race, creed or color.

Since in some states, particularly in the South where Negroes have not had the opportunities for preparation for college life, it is recommended that funds be earmarked to be used specifically for Negro youth in equalizing educational opportunities in certain states where the Negro has not been able to obtain equal educational opportunities.

I beg this Committee, whose position is so sacred in administering this program as handed down by our illustrious President, to keep eternal vigilance to safeguard the interest and welfare of all the youth of America. I speak particularly in behalf of the Negro youth. (Applause.)

CHAIRMAN TAUSSIG: I not only want to thank Mrs. Bethune for her able report, but again to call the attention of the committee to the fact that Mrs. Bethune has been one of our most active members and has traveled over great areas of the country, and has given a great deal of fine sympathetic attention to this problem.

MRS. BETHUNE: Mr. Chairman, may I just state to you that we have organized very recently, what we term the National Council of Negro Women. This council brings into one group all of the national organizations of women, educational, fraternal, religious, civic and otherwise. We are putting straight before this group the importance of this NYA program, and it has been most gratifying how the club women, and the fraternal women and the church women, through their conferences and through their sub-meetings throughout the country, have put into action their cooperation and helpfulness in carrying forward this program.

I believe that the Negro women behind this program [are] going to be in the future a very great and influential power.

April 28–29, 1936, pp. 135–139. NYA Publications File, National Youth Administration Papers, Record Group 119, National Archives, Washington, D.C.

Telephone Conversation with Robert S. Richey

[transcript] (1938)

Mary McLeod Bethune to Robert S. Richey, State Director for Indiana, September 29, 1938——10:30 A.M.—After preliminary "How are you's":

MRS. BETHUNE: Now, Mr. Richey, I had a very full conference with Mr. [Orren H.] Lull [NYA Deputy Administrator] yesterday.

. . . .

MR. RICHEY: Fine, I am glad to hear that.

MRS. BETHUNE: I told him of our situation there locally and he agrees with the idea that you and I concluded upon—that it will be wiser for you to select someone that can give to you the service that you need there and who can get the cooperation of the people.

I have tried to get hold of Porter, but it has come to my attention that Porter has resigned his position and has accepted a professorship in one of the Junior High Schools here in the city—therefore, we are free from that. I will talk with him today so that he will understand that we are not depending upon any future arrangements so far as he is concerned.

You are at liberty to go forward and get your set-up there. A very strong recommendation has come in here from Congressman Louis Ludlow, recommending Paul Hill. I do not know who Paul Hill is.

MR. RICHEY: I will check on him. What about Administrative Funds, Mrs. Bethune?

MRS. BETHUNE: I am sure that what you lack, Mr. Lull will take up with you.

MR. RICHEY: I will have to have that. I cannot make the appointment on our administrative staff until I can get administrative funds for this person. Of course, I could put him on the project payroll—you can tell Mr. Lull that—but he could not get leave privileges, etc.

MRS. BETHUNE: We do not want that. We want these people on the administrative staff. We do not want them on the project payroll. I will talk to Mr. Lull when I am through with this conversation with you.

MR. RICHEY: Well, you tell Mr. Lull that I can put him on the project payroll but he will not be entitled to annual leave.

MRS. BETHUNE: But, we don't want him on the project payroll. We want a strong administrative person. We have been playing with this thing for three years.

I am going to [meet] Mr. [Aubrey] Williams [NYA Administrator] at noon today. If I can't get the kind of help I need to give you men the kind of cooperation you need and intelligent cooperation—there is no use putting them on. There is no use putting anybody on unless you pay them well.

MR. RICHEY: I can put on a strong person, but would rather that you get— you understand—additional administrative funds.

MRS. BETHUNE: I will talk with Mr. Lull as soon as I get through talking to you. I am simply asking for administrative leadership of Negroes in the states. Have you the man that you want for Indiana?

MR. RICHEY: Yes, we have three applications of well-qualified young men. I will send them to you to look over before I make any selection.

MRS. BETHUNE: I am doing some work today on this matter for all the states that need Negro leadership.

. . . .

Well, good-bye and you will hear from me.

MR. RICHEY: Thank you Mrs. Bethune. Good-bye.

September 29, 1938. NYA Division of Negro Affairs, National Youth Administration Papers, Record Group 119, National Archives, Washington, D.C.

Letter to Eleanor Roosevelt

(1940)

My dear Mrs. Roosevelt:

Miss Thompson [your secretary] has asked me to write you what I know about the situation which exists in California with regard to the abolishing of the NYA Division of Negro Affairs.

The situation is briefly this: there was opposition on the part of some of the Negro leaders to a Division of Negro Affairs, as such, because they felt that it would bring about a form of segregation in the State. Others were agreeable to the set-up as it was. In order to attempt to bring about a satisfactory adjustment, the office of the Division of Negro Affairs was abolished and the plan is to appoint Negro administrative workers on the State staff and a reasonable number of Negro clerical workers in the State office.

In abolishing the Division of Negro Affairs, Mrs. [Vivian Osborne] Marsh has the privilege of applying for one of the administrative positions on the staff. The selection of the Negro personnel is entirely in the hands of Mr. Burns, our State Administrator. From observation and reports, we feel that Mrs. Marsh has done excellent work in the State.

The many differences of opinion have made it difficult for us to bring about an adjustment that would be satisfactory to all the people of the State. Our Administrator is doing all he can to adjust matters, and we feel sure that everything will work out all right.

I would tell President George R. Vaughns of the Dumas League that the policies of the NYA are determined by the Administrator here in Washington. The policies, activities, and records of the NYA show definitely that discrimination because of race will not be, and has not been, tolerated.

To carry out the NYA program the work has been set up on a state basis, and the State Administrator is charged with the function and responsibility of selecting his staff personnel. There would be evidence of discrimination if the State Administrator refused to employ Negroes in any capacity, but my understanding is that he is willing to use them in clerical and supervisory positions. I am sure that the State Administrator is in a better position than I to determine whether the Negro youth population is so scattered in the various sections of his state as to justify a Division of Negro Affairs.

If I can furnish you with any further information with regard to this matter, kindly let me know.

> Sincerely yours,
> Mary McLeod Bethune
> Director, Division of Negro Affairs

August 1, 1940. File 70, Eleanor Roosevelt Papers, Franklin D. Roosevelt Library, Hyde Park, N.Y.

NYA Regional Conference on the College Work Program for Negroes

[excerpt] (1940)

[Toward the beginning of the conference, Presiding Officer Dr. Rufus Clement, President of Atlanta University, introduced Bethune as the NYA Director of the Negro Division, noting that she "is one of us."]

Mrs. Bethune's speech:

May I thank Professor Clement for the privilege of being with you. I want first to congratulate myself for being privileged again to meet with you and to think with you. These are very interesting days in which we are living—days calling for profound thinking. Everywhere there is a tense feeling. We are seeking first of all the guidance of an Unseen Eye that we may not stumble.

I thank God for sufficient restoration of strength to just be present with these leaders and these promoters in the great field of education, if only to help point the way by past records and present emphasis, and to help inspire youths to greater heights of service. I want to express my appreciation for the great founder and promoter of the spirit and atmosphere reflective of the National Youth Administration.

I wonder if we take the time to try to think what has happened in the past five years as the program of the National Youth Administration has tunneled its way into the rural and urban conditions of our country, awakening and inspiring thousands and thousands of youths, opening doors of opportunity through your institutions and through your guidance which lead these youth to higher heights. I wonder if we take the time to try to think how privileged we are today—when bombs are falling over Europe and millions of lives are at stake—to sit here in pleasant and cultural surroundings and think in terms of how we can stimulate and better use the facilities that are ours and put them into action for greater work for the boys and girls who are to make their living in the years to come.

I am expressing my gratitude for the opportunity we have had serving thousands. Whatever has happened to the Negro in the forty-eight states, we are responsible. We together have worked. I want us to bring the appreciation of my office in Washington to the college constituents, state administrators and their staffs for the fine cooperation they have given us in helping to steer the way and broaden the road for others as they have for thousands of youths who have participated in the program. I have another interest in the National Youth Administration. I would like to come to you as a member of the National Advisory Committee for the National Youth Administration. When the President set up the Committee, he placed on it two Negroes—Dr. Mordecai Johnson and myself.

I am especially interested here today from the viewpoint of the administrator of the program of the National Youth Administration as it affects Negroes, particularly youth, even to the islands of the sea. I want to say to you that my whole body, my mind, my soul—all that I am has become impregnated with the idea of giving my best to the people, in strengthening youth today into fine citizens, into the spirit of brotherhood. I feel that the National Youth Administration has done more to stimulate brotherhood in the youth of the country, particularly the youth of the Southland, than any one thing that I know.

I have had the opportunity of sitting close to the State Administrators and interpreting to them the needs of black boys and black girls who have not had, prior to this, as full an opportunity for development as they have today, whose school facilities were poor. [T]housands [were] unable to go to school because they could not pay tuition, had no car fare, had no books, had no shoes, could not do this and could not do that. They could not get training of the hands because of the few shops. They could not all go to Hampton [Institute]. So many needed just little things—thousands [were] just waiting for somebody to expose them to something.

I have stood with administrators whose visions had not been broadened in that direction and have seen them open up and have seen how the Negro youth has been integrated into the entire program as have been other youth. I have said to them, "When you have a swimming pool over here for whites, why not have one over there where some of us can go in order that all of us might have our chance?" How the Southern white man has broadened in his viewpoint! How concerned the administrators are now! They come to see me and discuss their problems and go away with their hearts and souls lifted up. New channels are looming up before them for a larger opportunity for these boys and girls who have been neglected so long and who, through the opportunities of the National Youth Administration, have forced their way into a more fertile field. The administrators of the North have become conscious of the fact that there is something to be done for Negroes in Boston just as there is something to be done for Negroes in Atlanta. I have found it just as necessary to call the attention of the State Administrator of Massachusetts to the needs of Negroes living in Boston as I have to call the attention of the State Administrator of Alabama to the needs of Negroes there.

It has been a marvelous opportunity for me and I have grown in respect for Mississippi, Alabama, Texas, Florida, Georgia, and Louisiana. I can sit with my State Administrator and hear him discuss on a basis of open-mindedness the needs and possibilities of all the youth.

I want to congratulate the presidents of our colleges on your alertness and on your willingness to look around you and to see what the possibilities are for your institutions and to take advantage of them as definitely as you have been able to. One thing I want to ask of you this morning is this: As leaders you must not only think in terms of the National Youth Administration as it concerns the students that come to your school, but you must look out beyond your college to help Negroes—assist to bring into operation everything that we possibly can bring to the Negro youth and to the Negro adult. What you have not gotten during the past five years has not been the fault of my office. I have worked and fought with my sleeves rolled up night and day.

When I went into my office in Washington, we had very few students in our graduate schools. Atlanta University had none. Howard did not have many; Fisk did not have a large number. All of them needed money. It was hard to get money for graduate schools. We tried to get the authorities to see the importance of giving special opportunities to Negroes in the upper tiers of training in order that we might get the masters' degrees and the doctors' degrees necessary for persons to head up our schools, to give the leadership that we needed. And so I begged for a $100,000 extra. Mr. Aubrey Williams wondered what we were going to do with it. I said "We need more leaders with masters' degrees and doctoral degrees. We need more social workers. We need men in the ministry; we need them in all the upper tiers of training." I said, "Negroes haven't the money to get it. I wish you would give me $200,000, but if you cannot, just give me $100,000, and I will be happy. Give it to me on my desk; let me say where it will go. Let me be boss of that. Let us see what we can do to help steer the way for a larger opportunity for men in the upper tiers—lawyers, doctors, social workers, ministers. Let me work in just that field." They pretty much felt up there that whatever I wanted I wanted. They had the idea that if she knows what she wants, let her have what she wants.

The very first year we turned over to Howard University for the graduate school twenty thousand dollars. The tears trickled down my cheeks and my hands trembled as I signed the check to go to Howard University for graduate students so that black boys and black girls could go in and get a chance. If we could begin by giving them $40.00 per month as a maximum and $30.00 per month as a minimum, we could figure on increasing it. I turned over to Atlanta University $16,000 or $18,000 for graduate work and sent something to Fisk for graduate work. How stocks went up!

From that year until this [one,] we have been helping through the National Youth Administration to stimulate people in the upper tiers to get training in graduate work. Even in other fields of service into which we have gone during the last two or three years, we have been doing something with that $100,000, not only for graduate work but for undergraduate work. We have been helping to put [resources] into specific projects for training, giving stimulation to the chef and cook training program at Tuskegee. We gave a start to that and they showed that it was possible. Because we did that, Dr. [Frederick] Patterson has been able to get money from other sources to help in this field. Prepare men [for jobs] that are in demand today. There is much for you to do; there is much more for you to get if you will get up and go after it. There is a great deal more for you to get from your state if you will stay close to your State Administrator and give courage to the Assistant on Negro Affairs. Have the Advisory Committee to keep in contact with you. Find out what the needs of your state are; then insist as far as the budget will go that these needs be supplied. Whenever you find you are not getting the kind of help in your state that you should, just send a note up to my office, and Mrs. Bethune gets right with the State Administrator and we get our heads and our hearts pretty close together and get that thing done.

The masses of Negroes do not know what to expect. They do not know what the New Deal is. You have to tell them about the swimming pools and the beauty culture classes. They think all they can get is cooking, sweeping, and agriculture. They do not know that there are cultural things as well as fundamental things. They do not know that this rounded program for the training of the youth over the country is here. One hundred million dollars has been appropriated by Congress for the use of the administrators. It is up to men like you—administrators, leaders, promoters—to see to it that they are informed as to your needs and to help devise plans, ways and means by which as many of these dollars as possible can get through to our black boys and our black girls. They are the ones that need it most. Our big-hearted President made this order for the people who need it, and certainly the Negroes need it.

. . . .

[The question of whether to give NYA assistance to a promising athletic student was raised.]

MRS. BETHUNE: . . . If he can make a definite contribution, I am not a president who feels that it is a crime to say that we should make a contribution to a student because he is a good athlete. It does have some appeal to the program. I do not know whether to say to the presidents that we would not interpret a contribution that a good student may make in athletics in the same light as we might in music or in cooking. It is a contribution in my thinking constituting growth of the school, and I do not know whether the National Youth Administration would be out of line in helping a student in that field. Of course, we are taking into consideration his ability in the academic line. I think there are more fields of education than just what we are able to do with French, or geography, or things of that kind.

The program of the National Youth Administration should so stimulate itself and broaden itself as to build up those things. I do not know whether I was an A or B student or what. I know I had a vision. I know I wanted a stepping stone on which I could rise. It would have been very discouraging to

Mary McLeod Bethune if someone had not helped because I was not a B student. My vision has not failed me up to this point.

I would rather bend backward trying to help a child that does not need it than to take a chance on not giving one a sandwich if he does need it. I would rather see your emphasis in the selection of your students based on needs, aspirations, and desires. Be honestly careful that you do not get too far from the child who needs advantages and needs help based upon kind philosophy and the kind of things that I have just tried to say here.

I never see a child upon a street without thinking, "That might have been Mary McLeod Bethune." Sometimes you say you will not give a preacher's child help. You cannot always tell by outside appearances. Let us continue to dig deeply. I want this Committee to think. Whatever we do, let us be sure that the money that is appropriated to our schools is carefully and thoughtfully distributed to these boys and girls. All of them might not be starring. I never starred. I know my field. I want you to have creative minds. Sit down to your desks and create things. Make up jobs and put them into motion. Get as many students as you can give jobs or make jobs for . . . jobs that will be helpful and stimulating and inspiring. Yes, I would think very seriously of the old boy who is a good athlete.

. . . .

[Later, the vocational training program and its accessibility to African Americans became the conference focus.]

MRS. BETHUNE: I am hoping that more and more we are going to get into the closest possible cooperation with the Vocational Department of the Board of Education as Mr. [Joseph H. B.] Evans has said, and have them to join their facilities with whatever facilities we have. If we have no facilities, have them build shops that will take care of both boys and girls. Ninety-nine per cent of the work that was done by men is being done by women today in Europe. It is vitally important that we get these shops and facilities where not only boys are prepared but girls also. We must do all we can to tie these shops up with schools under the Smith Hughes Fund, Vocational Agricultural Department, and so forth.

Some of the private schools are doing this. In order to participate they are turning over certain parcels of land to the county or state boards. They are joining with the Smith-Hughes Fund, NYA, and WPA [Works Progress Administration]—everybody coming in to make possible these funds for the defense program that we must have.

We are calling on land grant colleges to extend their borders as we have never called on them before, not only to help the immediate students that go to their schools but to reach out in the community miles around for students to come in. Give students an opportunity. Build tents for these boys to study so they can come in. Whatever is done now, get these young people prepared with their hands to learn these technical things that they must have to carry on now. I would advise that you bestir yourselves and do everything you possibly can to bring that into action. The masses are depending upon the colleges and leaders.

This defense program is the program we must think about in everything we are doing. I wish we had more of the types of projects that Dr. Patterson was wise enough to start up about three years ago—more chef cook courses. They will be in demand more and more as time goes on. There will be a need for young men who are going to be prepared in all fields—in the field of cookery and technical work. We will do all we can to apply for all the aid we can get from the Smith-Hughes Fund and all the other places we can.

. . . .

DR. PATTERSON: I wish there was some way that the various institutions could know what the requirements and opportunities are. If the information is given out from the state office or the Washington office, I know that some schools could make some preparation.

MRS. BETHUNE: I thank you for that suggestion. I shall make it one of the efforts of our office to see to it that as these new suggestions come up, we will send them through to the heads of colleges over the country so that you in turn can get in touch with the state administrators and cooperate with them in putting these things into action. Many of the things coming up we do not know anything about at all. The Negro is left out because there is no place for Negro work. Our office will take the responsibility in doing more than we have done in that respect. Any request that you write to me, not only in regard to NYA, I shall be happy to give you the finest cooperation that I can and we shall do our best to keep you abreast on happenings.

. . . .

September 6, 1940, pp. 3–7, 11–12, 14–15. Richard V. Moore Papers, Bethune-Cookman College Archives, Daytona Beach, Fla.

Leadership at Large

Minutes of the Federal Council on Negro Affairs

(1936)

A meeting was held Friday, August 7, 1936 at the home of Mrs. Mary McLeod Bethune, 316 Tea Street, Northwest, for the purpose of discussing plans for the full integration and participation of Negroes in the different fields of national endeavor. The following persons were present: Mrs. Mary McLeod Bethune, Director, Division of Negro Affairs, National Youth Administration; Dr. Frank S. Horne, Assistant Director, Division of Negro Affairs, National Youth Administration; Mr. Alfred E. Smith, Administrative Assistant, Labor Relations Division, W.P.A. [Works Progress Administration] . . . ; Lieutenant L. A. Oxley, Chief, Division [of] Negro Labor; Dr. Robert S. Weaver, Advisor on Negro Affairs, Department of Interior; Mr. Dewey Jones, Associate Advisor on Negro Affairs, Department of Interior; Dr. J. A. Atkins, Specialist, Education Relief for Negroes [W.P.A.;] and Mr. H. L. Trigg [Office of Education, Department of Interior].

Mrs. Bethune opened the meeting stating in part: "We have a greater opportunity than the representatives in the individual states. We have had a chance to look down the stream of the forty-eight states and evaluate the type of work and positions secured by Negroes. The responsibility rests upon us. We can get better results by thinking together and planning together. We must think about each other's problems. Let us band together and work together as one big brotherhood and give momentum to the great ball that is starting to roll for Negroes. The exceptional things have been done for the white people. Let us get some of the exceptional things done for the Negroes. The people of the white race are ignorant as to what is being done by and for Negroes. They must be enlightened. I feel helpless without the fellowship, interest and cooperation of all of you."

Mrs. Bethune stressed the point that it is necessary to get personally acquainted with each other in order to get a thorough understanding of the work of the several departments. There must be combined interest in finding out what is most needed for the Negro people. The program must be extended in the most effective manner. She stated: "We must think in terms of strategic attacks at this time. Let us forget the particular office each one of us holds and think how we might, in a cooperative way, get over to the masses the things that are being done and the things that need to be done. We must think in terms as a 'whole' for the greatest service to our people."

Mr. Oxley stated that many things are being done for Negroes. As an example, he mentioned the building project at Newport News which is being manned entirely by Negroes—Negro contractors, Negro plumbers, Negro electricians etc. He stated that Negroes can do the job and can do it well. An opportunity is all they ask.

Mr. Smith, complimenting Mrs. Bethune on her recent [NYA] appointment, stated that he knew of no one better fitted for that particular position. He said that on the project at Newport News, they encountered difficulty in securing skilled labor for the job and it had been suggested that white skilled labor be employed. This idea, however, did not materialize and the Negroes were kept on. He heartily approved the plan of working together.

Mrs. Bethune stated: "I have been meeting large numbers of interracial groups such as the Bethesda Mission, where more than 2,000 people were gathered; Lakeside with probably 2,000 or more and Lancaster, with an equal number. I dramatized the work of the adult education program and explained the work of the NYA. The thing to do, is to keep the issue alive. The people must be informed. I have been asked what the Negroes are doing in Washington. I would suggest a piece of literature in booklet form on what is being done for Negroes in all departments."

Dr. Weaver stated in part: "Three years ago I attempted to organize the Negro heads of the various departments for the same purpose and I found out that better and more effective results can be obtained by not publicizing certain facts. Our problem is an important one and a difficult one. Many things can be done by various agencies working closely together, but we must be careful as to the facts released and the manner in which they are released."

Mr. Oxley stated that the idea was a good one but it would have to be conducted in a diplomatic way. He stated: "What we want to show is what is actually being done for Negroes, giving expression to the talents of Negroes. Stress the point that 26,000 Negroes are maintained in colleges, even in Mississippi where educational facilities for Negroes are limited. Stress the housing projects manned by Negroes. We should get our facts together and present them in such a manner that they would be clearly understood, with no political issue involved, but just tell the story."

Dr. Weaver stated: "Those statistics are available in my office. There has never been any effective publicizing or factual presentation of what is being done. We come across a series of individual discrimination but the finer things are overlooked. I think it is possible for each one of us to compile a statement of what is going on in our particular fields and get together and boil it down to the point we want it. There is great danger in facts being exaggerated to the extent that they are not recognized in print."

Mr. Jones stated: "If we are agreed to work more collectively and not individually, let us take the matter seriously and work out a program in approval with the various offices. The idea is to forget where we are and work for the greatest interest and greatest good of the Negro . . . to determine whether or not Negroes have been benefitted during the administration. Facts in related order are powerful and cannot be destroyed. We are here as promoters and leaders and let us work together as such."

The discussion ran generally as to the best way to get authorization to release these facts. The following persons were selected to get together and draft a letter to be submitted to the President, outlining the purpose of the release, in order to obtain authorization to publish . . . Dr. Horne, Mr. Smith, Dr. Weaver. Because of Mrs. Bethune's ability to interview the President unofficially, Mr. Oxley was selected to go with her to the President and present the facts and the letter.

It was agreed that Dr. Horne, Mr. Smith and Dr. Weaver meet at [a] luncheon on Tuesday afternoon at 12:30, August 11th, to draft the letter to be presented to the President.

Mr. Oxley suggested that no discussion be held with the superior heads of the divisions [regarding] what is being planned until the plan is completed and can be presented in an intelligent and complete manner.

The meeting adjourned to meet again at the home of Mrs. Bethune on Thursday, August 13th for further discussion of plans.

August 7, 1936. Mary McLeod Bethune Papers, Mary McLeod Bethune Foundation, Bethune-Cookman College, Daytona Beach, Fla.

Letter to Franklin D. Roosevelt

(1937)

My dear Mr. President:

I submit to you herewith the recommendations of the National Conference on the Problems of the Negro and Negro youth held in Washington at the Department of Labor January 6th, 7th, and 8th, 1937.

These recommendations are the result of the serious deliberations of 100 representative Negro citizens from all parts of the nation as they considered the fundamental problems facing the Negro and Negro youth of America today.

Our Country opens wide the door of opportunity to the youth of the world but slams it shut in the faces of its Negro citizenry. The great masses of Negro youth are offered only one-fifteenth the educational opportunity of the average American child. The great masses of Negro workers are depressed and unprotected in the lowest levels of agriculture and domestic service while the black workers in industry are generally barred from the unions and grossly discriminated against. Their housing and living conditions are sordid and unhealthy; they live in constant terror of the lynch mob, shorn of their constitutionally guaranteed right of suffrage, and humiliated by the denial of civil liberties.

The conference is mindful of the fact that during the past four years many benefits have come to the Negro that before that time he did not have and we are deeply grateful. However, it is also their opinion that, until now, opportunity has not been offered for Negroes themselves to suggest a comprehensive program for their full integration into the benefits and the responsibilities of the American Democracy.

The conference, speaking with one voice for the twelve million American Negroes, offers these recommendations as the basic outline for a program as a challenge to the social consciousness of the present national administration. We feel now that this is the one time in the history of our race that the Negroes of America have felt free to reduce to writing their problems and their plans for meeting them with the knowledge of sympathetic understanding and interpretation.

We petition that these recommendations be brought to the attention of the Cabinet officers, the heads of administrative departments and members of the 75th Congress in the interest of the entire American people.

It is the will of the Conference that I confer with you personally relative to the attached recommendations and to further express their loyalty to you and the leaders of our nation.

> Respectfully submitted,
> Mary McLeod Bethune, General Chairman
> National Conference on the Problems of the
> Negro and Negro Youth

[Conference recommendations were in four areas: "Increased Opportunity for Employment and Economic Security"; "Adequate Educational and Recreational Opportunities"; "Improved Health and Housing Conditions"; and "Security of Life and Equal Protection under the Law."]

Report of the National Conference on the Problems of the Negro and Negro Youth, January 18, 1937. Mary McLeod Bethune Papers, Mary McLeod Bethune Foundation, Bethune-Cookman College, Daytona Beach, Fla.

Letter to L. C. Gray

(1937)

My dear Mr. Gray:

In regard to the present draft of the chapter on "Conclusions and Recommendations" for the Tenancy Report, I generally concur with the basic findings and recommendations as to Federal direction of the new homestead policy, and the employment of education, regulation and subsidy in improving landlord and tenant contractual relations.

Thinking of the masses of Negro farm workers to be affected, I appreciate that our objectives of creating a land tenure system affording opportunity for security, freedom of "absentee" control, a decent standard of living and preservation of soil resources will not automatically be attained by farm ownership. The recommendations supply the precautions of soil fertility, economical size, available markets, commensurate prices and terms, careful selection of tenants, aid and guidance in management and the supplying of operating credit at reasonable cost.

Specifically, in the interest of some 700,000 Negro tenant farmers in the south, I would call your attention to the following items:

1. *Selection of farm operators*—The need for federal supervision of the selection of tenants to be afforded opportunity for land ownership or rehabilitation loans to prevent the operation of racial discrimination. The recent National Conference on the Problems of the Negro and Negro Youth definitely went on record as favoring federal over state control of all projects.

2. *Participation*—It might be advisable to write in clauses that would guarantee the full participation of the unprotected Negro masses on the lowest rung of the agricultural ladder in the homestead and rehabilitation loan program. The PWA [Public Works Administration] housing division technique of clauses in construction contracts calling for a certain percentage of employment of skilled Negro labor and the requirement of the NYA school aid program that "the number of young men and women of any racial group given aid shall not represent a smaller proportion of the total number aided than the proportion this racial group represents of the population" might be noted as examples. While need should be the only gauge, traditional local attitudes may obscure the judgment.

3. *Local Boards of Arbitration*—I see little hope for justice to the masses of Negro farmers in the settlement of tenant-landlord contractual differences before *local* boards in areas where the franchise and civic liberties are denied Negroes to the extent that they fear and shun the courts. Here, certainly, the strong arm of the federal government is needed as his bulwark and protection. Without this, the entire machinery of written leases, compensation for improvements, termination after notice, protection from emergencies and housing requirements are impotent and without control.

4. *Peonage*—Participation in the federal homestead program or rehabilitation loans should be denied those states in which it is a misdemeanor to quit a contract while in debt, since this serves to abrogate federal anti-peonage laws, just as they are to be denied to states that do not enact legislation providing at least certain minimum requirements for regulating landlord-tenant relationship[s].

5. *Education*—Since the very back-bone of the projected system of land tenure must rest upon an integrated educational program, and since the very states where the masses of Negro farm operators reside are unable to supply such programs, and since the rural educational resources are at the bottom of even these inadequate state programs, it is absolutely necessary that extensive federal support, equitably allocated, must be afforded to supply adequate schools, farm and home extension agents, vocational teachers of agriculture and home economics, boys and girls club work, rehabilitation programs, cooperative organizations, libraries and health clinics. The Division of Negro Affairs has offered to the National Youth Administration such a project for the interlocking development of school and community through the operation of what we have termed "Family Schools" to lay the educational background for the operation of the "family" farm and the integration of rural Negro family life.

The Technical Drafting Committee is to be complimented on the comprehensive scope of its job and the direct attack made upon the realistic problems at the root of the farm tenancy evil. I appreciate the privilege of sharing in this report and offering the few brief comments above. I sincerely hope my statement will arrive in time and will be of some value.

Very sincerely yours,
Mary McLeod Bethune
Director, Division of Negro Affairs

January 23, 1937. Farm Tenancy Committee Papers, Bureau of Agriculture Economics, Record Group 83, National Archives, Washington, D.C.

Opening Statement to the Second National Conference on the Problems of the Negro and Negro Youth

[transcript] (1939)

Ladies and gentlemen, two years ago on January 6, 7, and 8, 1937, there met in this building [Department of Labor Auditorium] under the auspices of the National Youth Administration, the first National Conference on the Problems of the Negro and Negro Youth. More than 100 representative Negro citizens from all parts of the nation considered the fundamental problems facing the Negro and Negro Youth in America. After careful deliberation a set of recommendations was drawn up and presented to the President of the United States, members of his cabinet, the heads of various administrative departments of the Federal Government and to the members of the 75th Congress. Several thousand copies of these recommendations were released to representative organizations and individuals throughout the nation.

We are again calling you together specifically to do two things: First, to note our progress since the last conference; and second, to consider new developments and devise new approaches to the solution of our basic problems.

The President of the United States in the past six years has invited and called various groups of consultants to Washington—such as the Advisory Committee on Education and the National Emergency Council which most recently submitted their epoch-making report on Economic Conditions of the South. In like manner, you have been called here to bring to the Federal Government the benefit of your special counsel.

At a time like this when the basic principles of democracy are being challenged at home and abroad, when racial and religious prejudices are being engendered, it is vitally important that minority groups in this nation express anew their adherence to the fundamental principles of democracy. We feel sure that this conference will feel disposed to wholeheartedly approve this doctrine of democracy enunciated by the President in his opening message to the 76th Congress.

"Democracy, the practice of self-government," he declared, "is a covenant among free men to respect the rights and liberties of their fellows. . . . In meeting the troubles of the world we must meet them as one people—with a unity born of the fact that for generations those who have come to our shores, representing many kindreds and tongues, have been welded by common opportunity into a united patriotism. If another form of government can present a united front in its attack on a democracy, the attack must be met by a united democracy. Such a democracy can and must exist in the United States."

With these precepts of democracy's leading exponent, we are in complete accord. But we recognize that no such "united democracy" can possibly exist unless this "common opportunity" is available to all Americans regardless of creed, class, or color. A "united patriotism" is the fruit of political equality, economic opportunity and the universal enjoyment of basic civil rights. Only when these objectives are fully achieved will our country be able to stand before the world as the unsullied champion of true democracy.

In this spirit, ladies and gentlemen, we are met here today. Through the channel of this conference we, as a group of loyal American citizens, are offered the unusual opportunity, not only to contribute to the development of our own racial group, but also to insure a united democracy. (Applause.)

Before presenting to you our chief in this conference [NYA Administrator Aubrey Williams], I have the honor of presenting to you a small group of people who have gathered themselves together here in Washington, because of the strategic positions they hold in working in the several departments of Government, into what is termed the Federal Council on Negro Affairs. This is the group that is responsible for the working out of the program that you will have during these three days. I have been privileged to express a dream or to give a suggestion. These fine people have produced the program that you will execute, I hope, during these three days.

Now I will present the Council. This is the Vice-Chairman, Dr. [Robert] Weaver[, Special Assistant to the Administrator, U.S. Housing Authority]. If you will all come this way our Vice-Chairman might call you by name and the posts you hold. Will all you members please come forward?

[The conference transcript states, "Dr. Weaver introduced the members of the council." It fails, however, to provide their names. Correlating the list of conference consultants (since most consultants were in the council) with council members listed on September 29, 1939, in Bethune's letter to Miss

C. M. Edmunds of the U.S. Information Service, Weaver most likely presented the individuals below:

Works Progress Administration: James A. Atkins, Specialist in Negro Education; Sterling Brown, Editor on Negro Affairs, Federal Writers Project; Dutton Ferguson, Special Assistant Information Service; Alfred Edgar Smith, Administrative Assistant; John W. Whitten, Junior Race Relations Officer.

U.S. Housing Authority: Charles S. Duke, Associate Architect; Dr. Frank Horne, Assistant Consultant on Racial Relations; Henry Lee Moon, Special Assistant, Information Service; J. Parker Prescott, Associate Management Supervisor.

Farm Security Administration: Constance Daniel, Special Assistant, Information Service; Joseph H. B. Evans, Race Relations Specialist; Cornelius King, Assistant to the Governor.

Department of Justice: William L. Houston, Assistant to the Attorney General; Capt. Louis Mehlinger, Attorney; Louis Lautier, Assistant to Mr. Mehlinger.

Department of Labor: Vinita Lewis, Special Consultant, Child Welfare Services, Children's Bureau; Lieut. Lawrence Oxley, Field Representative; J. Arthur Weiseger, Research Assistant, U.S. Employment Service.

Department of Interior: Dr. Ambrose Caliver, Senior Specialist in Negro Education; William J. Trent, Adviser on Negro Affairs.

Agricultural Adjustment Administration: James P. Davis, Head Field Officer, Little Rock, Ark.

Civilian Conservation Corps: Edgar G. Brown, Adviser on Negro Affairs.

Department of Commerce: Joseph R. Houchins, Assistant Specialist on Negro Statistics.

District of Columbia Employment Service: Harper Fortune, Junior Counselor.

District of Columbia Recorder of Deeds: Dr. William J. Thompkins.

National Youth Administration: R. O'Hara Lanier.

Post Office Department: Ralph E. Mizelle, Attorney, Solicitor's Office.

Department of Treasury: Howard D. Woodson, Civil Engineer, Procurement Division.]

January 12, 1939, pp. 1–3. Mary McLeod Bethune Papers, Mary McLeod Bethune Foundation, Bethune-Cookman College, Daytona Beach, Fla.

Memorandum to Aubrey Williams

(1939)

Subject: Third National Conference on the Problems of the Negro and Negro Youth

Because of the lack of opportunity for a serious talk with you on important issues, I am writing this memorandum. I hope you will take the time to consider every sentence carefully.

I have carefully gone over the advisability of having a Third National Conference on the Problems of the Negro and Negro Youth. Before we conclusively decide upon calling such a conference, it would be well to direct your attention to the following facts:

1. Prior to the Second National Conference, there were four Evaluation Committees set up to determine the progress or lack of progress which had been made since the first conference in the fields of Health and Housing, Employment and Economic Security, Education and Recreation, and Civil Liberties.

2. In the main, these evaluation reports indicate that some progress has been made. At the same time, they point to the following glaring deficiencies which continue to exist:

(a) Insufficient Negro personnel in policy-making positions in the Civil Service Commission, the Federal Loan Agency, the Federal Works Agency, the Federal Security Agency, the Department of Justice, the Department of Labor, the Department of Commerce, the Home Owners Loan Corporation and the Women's Bureau of the Department of Labor.

(b) Failure to appoint Negro representatives on important Emergency Committees such as the National Emergency Council, the Federal Committee on Apprenticeship Training and the Committee now making a study of the National Labor Supply.

(c) Lack of attention to the integration of the Negro in active combat units of the United States Army and the United States Navy.

The Negro has limited opportunities in the Army, no opportunities in the United States Marine Corps and his status in the Navy is confined to positions as stewards and messmen.

(d) A marked decrease in the appointment of Negro messengers and clerical help in the State Department, United States Treasury, the Department of Justice, the War Department, the Navy Department and other old line government agencies.

While there have been increases in the numbers of Negroes employed in the New Deal Emergency Agencies and on relief rolls, there has been a steady decline in employment figures among Negroes in the government agencies regarded as permanent.

3. As early as September 8, the office of the Republican National Committee in Charge of the Negro Press has focused national attention upon the deficiencies set forth above.

I believe immediate action should be taken upon recommendations of the two preceding conferences before the call for a third conference is issued. This immediate action will prevent our having to answer many embarrassing questions which are already being posed by persons who look to us for guidance and leadership.

The attached article from the September 8 issue of the *Northwest Enterprise,* Seattle, Washington, also appeared in newspapers throughout the country. This news story is an indication of the attack which a third conference would precipitate.

I have given you the above facts in order to make known to you the actual situation with a hope that you, in some way, will convey to the President these facts for his perusal and consideration. I hope you will be able to find out if there is anything outstanding that can be done now regarding these situations. If not, it is my serious advice that we do not attempt a third conference on the eve of election. We do not have sufficient ground to stand upon to ward off the bombardment from the opposition. They see clearly the inadequacies in the numerous federal departments. If we can get something outstanding done for the Negro, it will furnish us with ammunition which we do not now have.

. . . .

Mary McLeod Bethune

October 17, 1939, BF. Mary McLeod Bethune Papers, Mary McLeod Bethune Foundation, Bethune-Cookman College, Daytona Beach, Fla.

Letter to Franklin D. Roosevelt

[draft] (1939)

My dear Mr. President:

For several weeks I have made it my business to talk with thoughtful and informed Negroes in various parts of the country. Those conferences and reports which have come to me cause me to place before you these observations on what appears to be a situation serious enough to merit careful study by yourself and others concerned with the continuation of the ideals of your administration.

I have found deep affection for you and Mrs. Roosevelt among colored Americans in all walks of life. They share the feeling of many other Americans that at least so far as the heart is concerned you are genuinely concerned with the well being of and improvement of opportunities for all Americans, and particularly those who are disadvantaged. But over and above this personal regard for yourselves is a widespread and growing feeling of despair, distrust, and even bitterness because of the apparently increasing control of party policy, so far as Negroes are concerned, by southern congressmen, senators and others who are bitterly anti-Negro. I refer to such figures as Senators Connally, Byrnes, Glass, Smith, George, Harrison and Bilbo whose Negro-phobia reached its climax in the vicious attacks on the Negro during the filibuster against the Anti-Lynching Bill. There is puzzlement and bitterness among Negroes because even northern Democratic senators did not raise their voices against the ofttimes ridiculous attacks on the Negro. However, they are not unaware of the fact that Republican senators were equally mute.

It is my conviction that it would be a serious mistake to believe that the Negro vote is irrevocably fixed in the Democratic ranks. It would be equally a mistake to believe that not only the leaders of Negro opinion but the rank and file are satisfied with the deal the Negro has received even under your administration.

I have also found that very extensive plans are being made by the Re-publicans who are determined to win back the Negro vote in the 1940 elec-tion. Intelligent Republicans know that the seventeen states where the Negro vote potentially holds the balance of power may and probably will determine the outcome of the next election, particularly in such pivotal states as Illinois, Indiana, Ohio, Pennsylvania, New Jersey, New York, Maryland, Kentucky and Missouri.

I have encountered evidence of liberal spending by Republicans already. The Party will doubtless spend much more not only in attempting to pur-chase purchasable Negro (and white) votes but in legitimate propaganda. For example, the Republican National Committee about a year ago employed Prof. Ralph J. Bunche of Howard University to make a study of the reasons why Negroes left the Republican Party. This report has been kept secret but we shall see during the next twelve months how many of its recommendations will be followed. Senator Taft has employed Perry W. Howard, Republican National Committeeman from Mississippi, to line up southern delegates, white and Negro, in his behalf. Thomas E. Dewey has appointed three high type Negro assistants in his office—which is in marked contrast to the fact that there are no Negroes in the United States Attorney's office in New York City. And he sent a very strong letter of greeting to the recent Richmond convention of the National Association for the Advancement of Colored People, [a] copy of which is enclosed.

In addition, more Republican members of the House of Representatives signed the Discharge Petition on the Gavagan Anti-Lynching Bill than Democrats and this fact has been widely publicized in the Negro press. Emmett J. Scott, former secretary to Booker T. Washington, and also former Secretary-Treasurer of Howard University, has been employed by the Republican National Committee to handle publicity among Negroes.

The results [are] already being seen in recent elections in Pennsylvania, Ohio, New York and other states. In the *New York Times* of November 26 Arthur Krock features the efforts of the Republicans to win the support of farmers, white collar workers, possible labor, and particularly Negroes in order to win in 1940. These are but straws in the wind which I think it is imperative we pay attention to.

As I have already said, Negroes generally are grateful to you and Mrs. Roosevelt for the attitude which you have shown, but the status of the Negro is so desperate that they are naturally disturbed about the many things which could have been done but which have not been done by the present administration. For example, your silence during the filibuster against the Anti-Lynching Bill has been widely commented upon among Negroes. The appointment of a Negro as District Judge in the Virgin Islands has been heralded, but Negroes know that it is not a District judgeship of a constitutional court, with the indefinite tenure of office of Federal judges.

Discrimination against Negroes by such agencies as the Federal Housing Administration, the Tennessee Valley Authority in the office personnel, and on other federal-financed project[s], have added to this unrest.

Permit me to summarize some of the shortcomings which I have found Negroes to feel exist and which should be remedied if we are to continue to have the support of Negro voters:

1. Some tangible means of securing enactment of federal legislation against lynching and particularly limiting filibuster with its vicious attacks upon Negroes by southern senators.
2. Support of federal legislation against discrimination in federal-financed projects similar to that provided in contracts of the WPA [Works Progress Administration] under Mr. [Harold] Ickes and of the United States Housing Authority under Mr. [Nathan] Straus.
3. Active administration support for safeguards in proposed legislation for federal aid to education and health which would insure equitable distribution of federal moneys for these purposes in states where there are separate schools, hospitals, clinics, etc., for Negroes.
4. The issuance of an executive order abolishing the use of photographs with civil service applications and the substitution therefore of fingerprints or some other suitable method; and (b) ordering appointment from competitive registers strictly according to rank instead of giving the appointing officer, as at present, the right to select any one of the

three certified by the Civil Service Commission. There are undoubted advantages to honest appointing officers in this latitude but it has been used in both the North and the South to pass over Negroes and select white persons who made lower marks.

5. At least one qualified Negro lawyer of ability and character should be appointed to one of the present vacancies on the federal bench in continental United States, either in the District Court or the Circuit Court of Appeals. It is interesting to note that the press generally and Negro newspapers in particular are featuring the recent suggestion that Charles H. Houston of Washington be appointed to the United States Supreme Court bench.

6. There should be three or four outstanding appointments in Washington of qualified Negroes to posts where they can render services directly affecting pressing needs of Negro citizens. By this I do not mean Negro advisory jobs but posts of real authority where their mere presence will help to establish the fact that the Negro is an integral and important part of the American government. I have in mind such posts as a member of the Civil Service Commission, an assistant secretaryship of labor and important posts of that sort.

7. Appointment of a Negro assistant in the division of personnel supervision and management in every department and independent establishment, one of whose main duties shall be that of assisting the director of the division in integrating qualified Negroes more widely into the department or establishment.

8. Next to the matter of jobs, the Negro is more concerned than ever before over the right to vote. He is not naive enough to believe that this is a panacea but he does recognize fully the value of the ballot. He knows that if he had the same access to the ballot box as other citizens he could help elect officials ranging from the occupant of the White House down to local school boards who would thereby be sensitive to protests against racial discrimination from which the Negro suffers. Any movement, therefore, by the administration which will accelerate the removal or the easement of the restrictions now affecting the exercise of the ballot will earn the gratitude of the Negro and will deprive the Republicans of one of their chief arguments.

In addition to the preceding specific items there may be mentioned the following:

More that six and a half million of the twelve million American Negroes are engaged in agriculture either as farm owners, tenants, or sharecroppers. Anything which can be done towards relief of the distress of Negro agricultural workers would be welcomed.

The administration's record so far as housing is concerned is, on the whole, excellent. Mr. Straus, as administrator of the United States Housing Authority, appears to have done all he could to keep down discrimination both in employment in construction of housing projects and also in occupancy. But more can be done to back up Mr. Straus' efforts and particularly in extending the benefits of housing as far as Congress will appropriate funds for such furtherance of decent housing.

One of the sorest points among Negroes which I have encountered is the flagrant discrimination against Negroes in all the armed forces of the United States. Forthright action on your part to lessen discrimination and segregation and particularly in affording opportunities for the training of Negro pilots for the air corps would gain tremendous good will, perhaps even out of proportion to the significance of such action.

In conclusion, we are dealing with an increasingly independent and thinking group. The Negro has done a good deal of housecleaning during recent years in getting rid of venal politicians of his own race. At the same time he is looking with an increasingly skeptical eye upon the lip service of white politicians of all parties. I have found him increasingly aware of how he and other members of his race have been used and are being used. Deeds rather than empty promises are increasingly important to perpetuate the support of this important group. I trust, therefore, that serious consideration may be given to the urgent necessity of specific action on the above issues and any others which may occur to you. Unless this is done I seriously doubt that we shall have the support of any considerable percentage of this group in 1940.

November 27, 1939, BF. Mary McLeod Bethune Papers, Mary McLeod Bethune Foundation, Bethune-Cookman College, Daytona Beach, Fla.

Letter to Eleanor Roosevelt

(1941)

My dear Mrs. Roosevelt:

I am sending this note to let you know how happy I am over the many things that are taking place in such a quiet way yet so far reaching. I was most happy that we were able to ward off the march on Washington. We can never express our appreciation to you for your interest in the whole affair and the signing of the Executive Order by our President on June 25. Not since Abraham Lincoln spoke on that memorable day of the emancipation of the slaves has such a far-reaching Executive Order come forth for the benefit of my people. God bless our President, and you, dear Mrs. Roosevelt, who has stood so closely by him in these days of great crisis. In my own weak way I am standing on the sidelines trying to help to direct the emphasis of thought and action in the right direction. I want you to feel that you can always depend upon me and if there is any suggestion or consultation I can give please let me know.

I am now greatly concerned about the appointment of the five-man Board which will investigate discrimination among Negroes in the defense industries. I am sincerely hoping that Earl Dickerson of Chicago will be one of them. I think, Mrs. Roosevelt, from many angles, he is the safest man for Negro representation that we can have placed on that Board. I hope you will use your influence in that direction if it can be done.

You will receive a letter from the Cook County Physicians Association of Chicago that I hope you will give careful attention. If it is possible for you to see them, please inform me so that I may let them know when and where. I am sorry to bring all these things to your attention but many things confront us now that we must work out.

When it is possible for you to see me, please permit me to do so.

Sincerely yours,
Mary McLeod Bethune, Director
Division of Negro Affairs

July 10, 1941. File 100, Eleanor Roosevelt Papers, Franklin D. Roosevelt Library, Hyde Park, N.Y.

The Negro and National Defense

(1941)

Here in this hot bed of feverish defense preparations, where the clang of steel rings day and night, where defense armaments and equipment roll off the assembly lines in continuous streams, here in Detroit—I am more than happy to see this demonstration of interest, this demonstration of concern, this demonstration of loyalty on the part of America's Negroes.

It is no empty boast when we say a Negro has never betrayed this country. It is a record we must keep. Yes, we must keep that record despite the denial of opportunity to us to render our full and wanted share of help in the defense program of our nation; we must keep it despite the attitude of some employers in refusing to hire Negroes to perform needed skilled services; we must keep the record clear despite the denial of the same opportunities and courtesies to our youth in the armed forces of our country. We must not only keep our record clear, we must blazon it with deeds of valor and loyalty and sacrifice. For a new day is dawning and we must not be found wanting.

The first bright ray in the dawn of that new day broke through the clouds of denied opportunity and despair when our grand President issued an Executive Order outlawing discrimination in defense industries and defense training and creating a committee to enforce his decree. For the first time since Lincoln issued the Emancipation Proclamation freeing us from the bonds of slavery, an executive order, word in the form of law, has issued from the White House to open the doors a little wider for Negroes.

Of course, that Order did not solve our problems over night. No order, no law, no regulation could work such a miracle. There is yet before us a tremendous task. We ourselves must be ever alert, we must know the provisions and benefits of the various government programs available to us. We must guide and teach our brothers and fellow-men how to take advantage of what we do have. We must steel-ring our courage to demand what we should have.

Do you know the facts so you can tell them to others? You must make yourselves aware of the programs of the Department of Agriculture. Learn about its Extension Service which is set up to assist farm people in understanding the practical issues involved in defense activities. Teach them about the impact of changing world conditions on our situation, and why they must exercise to the fullest their opportunities and obligations of citizenship in the present situation. Show them how its extension workers are conducting educational programs in rural areas relating to nutrition, housing and agricultural production and adjustments in the general building of defense morale.

You should know of the work of the Farm Credit Administration, which provides a source of credit enabling farmers not only to maintain but to strengthen their economic position. You should know the work of the Farm Security Administration. Its rehabilitation program for the rural needy, for tenant farmers, embraces a medical program, a housing program, a nutrition program. The Farm Security Administration also has the task of relocating farm families forced to move by expanding military activity in rural areas. You should certainly know of the program of the Agricultural Bureau of Home Economics.

You should be well-versed in the programs of the Social Security Board, understanding clearly its provisions for aid to the aged, to the blind, and to dependent children, and its employment service activities. The masses of our people can only receive these benefits through your intelligent leadership.

You must know the functions of the Public Health Service in the prevention and control of disease, and its reports on matters pertaining to child life and child welfare, infant mortality, etc. You must know of the Women's Bureau of the Department of Labor which promotes the welfare of wage-earning women, increasing their efficiency, improving working conditions, and advancing their opportunities for profitable employment.

You must acquaint yourselves with the purposes and functions of the United States Housing Authority, set up to assist the several states and cities to remedy the unsafe and unsanitary housing conditions, and the acute shortage of decent, safe, and sanitary dwellings for families of low income. When we think of the many improvements that have been made in the living facilities of thousands and thousands of our people we truly have reason for great rejoicing.

You should know that the Electric Home and Farm Authority will give aid in the distribution, sale and installation of electrical and gas apparatus, equipment and appliance, by financing the purchase of domestic electric and gas appliances and electrical wiring for homes and farms.

You should be aware of the facilities of the Home Owners Loan Corporation, and of the Federal Housing Administration for aiding persons in becoming home owners.

You should keep informed of the work of the Office of Education; of the appropriations of millions of dollars made to that agency annually for the assistance and expansion of educational facilities in the several states. You should be informed of the program of the Civilian Conservation Corps, where thousands of our boys are being trained to be good citizens and strong men. You should know more about the Work Projects Administration in their aid and training programs.

If you have need for further information to strengthen your position concerning the defense program, make inquiries of Dr. Robert C. Weaver, in the Office of Production Management, or Mr. William Pickens in the Defense Savings Division of the Treasury Department, or Mr. Robert Taylor in Defense Housing. If you need information about the Army, make contact with Judge William Hastie; about Selective Service, Major Campbell Johnson. They are all our representatives in these various departments and agencies and are ready and willing to aid you, as is Crystal Byrd Faucett, our woman and race representative in the Office of Civilian Defense.

I wonder how many of you know of the work of the National Youth · Administration, which I represent as its Director of Negro Affairs. Do you know of the training opportunities we are providing through actual work experience to our boys and girls, of the assistance we are giving to keep over 60,000 of them in school in order that they may properly continue their education? They are learning to use their hands as well as their heads, to run machines, and to construct buildings, to mold and shape metal, to cook and to sew, and to become proficient in business courses, music and art. Since the beginning of the National Youth Administration in 1935, over 400,000 Negro youth have received work experience. A staff of over 700 Negroes assists in the administration of this program. The training that these young people receive is preparing them for work, and thousands of them are leaving our program regularly for jobs in private industry.

Whereas we realize our program in NYA is not yet perfect, we believe we are on the right track. When the President issued his Order to abolish discrimination in the defense program, Aubrey Williams, the able and understanding Administrator of the NYA, issued a reaffirmation of the policy of the

National Youth Administration to provide equal opportunity to every eligible youth citizen regardless of his race, his creed, his color, or his national origin. In Washington, we are sincere about that policy—and should it not be adhered to, we want to know about it.

The NYA is playing a major role in our defense efforts. Today in workshops throughout the country we are preparing skilled mechanics, machinists and welders for the shops tomorrow. Every three months a new army for behind-the-lines will be sent out from NYA defense projects better equipped for today's defense efforts and better prepared for tomorrow's living.

All these things and many more the government of the United States is doing under the present administration, which has demonstrated its interest in the social improvement of the masses, regardless of race, creed or color. These things you must know. Such knowledge is necessary if we are to play our part in building the morale and the spirit of patriotic loyalty that is imperative today. The loyalty of the Negro of America has never been questioned, even though they have not received all the courtesies and opportunities extended to the soldiers of the other race. Negro women give their sons to their country with as much enthusiasm and loyalty as other women. It must ever be so! And we must offer ourselves in whatever capacities we can for service. We must do all we can to preserve the spirit and morale, in spite of discrimination and handicaps that confront us in both industry and the general defense programs. We must not fail America and as Americans we must insist that America shall not fail us.

A new day is dawning! We are being called upon to perform. We are facing tomorrow. This is the opportune time for us to pool our interests.

We must not be content to sit and wait for someone to bring the opportunities of today to us. If you are not called in on the ground floor of these various programs in your communities, organize into groups and ask to be heard and insist that you be considered.

And above all, as we fortify ourselves with information on what is happening today, as we project ourselves into these various programs for the benefit of our less fortunate brothers and sisters, let us stress the spirit of *unity* in our actions and thoughts. There is no time for us to stop and ask "What are we fighting for?" Our job is to join hands, join minds, join resources and pull together in one direction. We must fight with our best. As far as others are concerned, Americans are one and we are Americans. Time has never passed so swiftly as it is passing today. The Negro is facing tomorrow. He has been challenged—he must be strong, united, ready to defend America with the best he has, and to defend his race.

August 3, 1941, BF. Mary McLeod Bethune Papers, Mary McLeod Bethune Foundation, Bethune-Cookman College, Daytona Beach, Fla.

Statement of Conference on
Negroes in National Defense

(1942)

In as much as the nation is now engaged in a total war, world wide in scope, and which threatens the subversion of our cherished democratic principles and the blotting out of the American way of life; and in as much as our defensive measures, both in arms and production, are dangerously weakened by the persistent, contemptuous rejection of the earnestly proffered services of the colored American, RESOLVED

That it is the sense of this conference that to end this condition so hurtful to the morale of millions of the best of Americans, and to appreciably bolster our all-out efforts to defend our heritage, we earnestly recommend:

(1) That immediate measures by taken to secure the appointment of a colored American as a member of the proposed National Labor Supply Committee.

(2) That immediate measures be taken to secure the appointment of a colored American as a member of the War Labor Board.

(3) That the President be urged to order the acceptance of a larger number of colored Americans in the Officers' Training Schools.

(4) That a colored American be appointed as an Administrative Assistant to the President of the United States.

In addition, we desire to go on record as stating with emphasis that the colored people of the United States and their friends are strongly opposed to any measures looking to the abridgment of the activities of the National Youth Administration, the Civilian Conservation Corps, the Work Projects Administration, the Farm Security Administration, the Farm Tenant Aid, and all other programs of socio-economic significance, representing the gains of the last eight years, as destructive to that high morale which is absolutely necessary to render arms, guns, tanks, munitions, ships, and planes effective to vindicate democracy and to save America.

[Those attending this meeting, over which Mary McLeod Bethune presided, were: George Murphy, Marshall Shepherd, R. O'Hara Lanier, Alexander Martin, F. D. Patterson, Gordon Hancock, Walter White, Bishop R. R. Wright, Horace Mann Bond, William J. Thompkins, T. Arnold Hill and Harry S. McAlpin.]

January 7, 1942. Mary McLeod Bethune Papers, Mary McLeod Bethune Foundation, Bethune-Cookman College, Daytona Beach, Fla.

What Are We Fighting For?

(1942)

What are we fighting for?

America is the richest land in the world. Beautiful automobiles roam the streets like swarms of bees. Houses of everyday living compare with palaces in other countries. Banks are bulging with the money of depositors. Corporations make huge profits and pay staggering dividends. Wages paid workers top the average of any other nation. The overall standard of living is highest right here in America.

Is this what we are fighting for? It represents a brilliant national achievement! Though, I believe, we all realize that these things have not yet reached down and touched each and every American. Not all of us own automobiles—some of us do not have shoes in which to walk comfortably. Not all of us live in palaces—some of us cannot truthfully say we have a shelter over our heads. Not all of us have money on deposit in the banks—some of us do not have money for the next meal. Not all of us draw dividends from the huge profits of corporations. Not all of us are paid the high wages common to America—some of us, though loyal Americans, are denied the right to work for victory for no better reason than the color of our skins. Not all of us enjoy the high standard of living by which America is identified—some of us yet live in poverty and squalor and disease.

Then, what are we fighting for?

First—who are "we"? We are Americans—all of us. True, loyal, courageous, unyielding Americans. We are Americans who cherish the liberty and the pursuit of happiness that have been achieved by the founders and pioneers of this country. We are Americans who reverence the blood that flowed in 1776, in 1865 and in 1918, for the independence and the permanency of our country.

We are Americans who cherish in our hearts a desire for one practical democracy for all; who seek freedom from poverty, from ignorance, from discrimination, from religious and racial hatreds, from mob violence and brutality.

The waters of the past have gone under the bridge. We are standing tonight on the threshold of a new era, of a new vision, of a new world. Our men have their backs to the wall in Manila Bay. Our cities are in danger from enemy bombs. And yet there are those who value the ghosts of old prejudices, more highly than they do the freedom of our country.

We are fighting for a baptism in that spiritual understanding that all mankind has been created in the image of God—that all mankind is endowed with certain inalienable rights which we as individuals, North, East, South and West, must respect and protect under the democratic ideals of this new day.

As the Negro people march into battle they know that there are many hindrances to full participation in the country's battle for freedom; but march they must, and march they will, because they do understand that every hope they have for full democracy hinges upon the outcome of this war. They understand that the fate of America is the fate of the Negro people; we go up or down together.

I would not be true to my duty as an American if I did not say to my fellow White Americans in the South that the task of removing obstacles to the full participation of every Negro American in this great struggle for freedom, is not the task for the Negro alone but of every American, North, East, South and West, who loves democracy and cherishes our country's democratic tradition.

All of us have but one task, one duty, one sacred obligation—to give the best that we have and all that we have for national unity and for victory.

And these are not the days for word battles. These are not the days for prolonged indecision. These are the days for action!

These are not the days to consider from whence one came, nor the traditional customs of social standing, caste and privilege. These are the days for a united front with a united purpose to fight for that victory which we must have, or, regardless of caste, creed or position, we will all sink together.

What are we fighting for? We are fighting for the perfection of the democracy of our own beloved America, and the extension of that perfected democracy to the ends of the world.

May God, the father of all of us, grant that we shall not fight in vain!

Program, Southern Conference on Human Welfare. Mary McLeod Bethune Papers, Amistad Research Center, Tulane University, New Orleans, La.

Letter to James L. Feiser

(1943)

My dear Mr. Feiser:

About a year ago a special committee, of which I was a member, that represented a large committee of colored citizens drew up a number of recommendations which we submitted to the Red Cross officials through you. It was the hope of that committee that these recommendations would have been so acted upon that a program of building goodwill among colored people might have resulted.

The reaction of the Negro to the discussion that has gone on in the public press and by word of mouth with regard to the blood plasma differential has not given the Red Cross the reputation it deserves among our people. We were hoping that by increasing the participation of colored people on local, state and national levels in the official program of the American Red Cross would, in a large measure, compensate for the loss of goodwill which the Red Cross has sustained on account of the condition above referred to.

Since we submitted our recommendations, the Red Cross has employed Jesse O. Thomas on its national staff. While he has the confidence and respect of Negro and white people of America, we have long since advanced beyond the point where the employment of one colored person is accepted as totally representing all that we have a right to expect from a great organization like the American Red Cross. We are more interested in programs and policies calculated to extend the benefits to and receive the benefits from the entire Negro population than we are in the "token" employment of one individual.

In view of the above, I am writing to suggest that we have another meeting of the committee that met with the Red Cross in September 1942 so that we might be brought up to date on the extent to which the recommendations submitted at that time have been given favorable consideration and what, if anything, this committee of representative Negro citizens might do toward enhancing the appeal of the American Red Cross and its 1944 financial campaign.

> Sincerely yours,
> Mary McLeod Bethune
> Director of Negro Affairs

October 16, 1943. Mary McLeod Bethune Papers, Mary McLeod Bethune Foundation, Bethune-Cookman College, Daytona Beach, Fla.

Tribute to Franklin D. Roosevelt

(1945)

Others before me have spoken—others after me will speak—of the greatness of our late beloved President of this nation of ours and the world.

Let me tell you simply and sincerely what the passing of this benefactor and champion has meant to Negro people.

He came into high office when our hearts were dragging the depths of despair. We were economically destitute—politically confused—and socially bereft of the things that make for a full American life.

He came into high office at a critical time in the lives of all men and gave strength—and now his life—that all men, irrespective of their creation, should live better. It was no accident then that my people along with all other suffering minorities, should have been taken up into the arms of this humane Administrator of our government.

It was not single acts of his for which we felt so grateful as they were being unfolded. It was the largeness of his heart—the breadth of his philosophy—and the intensity of his determination.

I shall never forget that evening of the early days of his administration when he sat alone in his private office and I was privileged to talk with him. I can see him now as he stretched forth his gracious hand in greeting. I can hear the pathos of his voice as he said: "Hello, Mrs. Bethune. Come in and sit down and tell me how your people are doing."

I poured out of my heart and mind and into his ears the needs—the desires and the aspiration of my people. Since that visit, we have seen the path of our opportunities broadened into a wide thoroughfare. He believed truly that all men should have equality of opportunity regardless of race, creed or color.

Today we breathe a sigh—we wipe a tear—we are filled with remorse. Negroes shall confront their tomorrows with the stern resolution and conviction that he gave us in his time.

We shall not worship the past.

We shall not fear the future.

We shall carry on in the manner and in the spirit that he would have us do.

May God take into His household this servant. May He protect those dearest to him who have been left behind.

And may this nation and its people—this world—prosper in the vision that Franklin Delano Roosevelt saw.

Mary McLeod Bethune

April 13, 1945. Mary McLeod Bethune Papers, Mary McLeod Bethune Foundation, Bethune-Cookman College, Daytona Beach, Fla.

San Francisco Conference

(1945)

The United Nations Conference on International Organization was a great historic occasion. It was with a deep sense of humility, pride and responsibility that I received my appointment by the State Department as an official associate consultant to the American delegation to the Conference. Humility, because even though I had some little experience in the broad field of human relations, I knew so little about the technical, international problems that would necessarily be a major part of a world conference. Pride, because I had been selected to be one of so important a group as that of official–associate consultant. Responsibility, because I, too, had the conviction expressed by Britain's Foreign Secretary, Anthony Eden, in his eloquent speech the second day of the Conference, when he said: "Here humanity has its last chance to build a world of peace."

San Francisco was appropriately selected as the locale of the Conference. A great cosmopolitan city—actively mobilized for the business of aiding the Nation and her Allies in winning the War—with a spirit of group tolerance and cooperation that one sensed everywhere. In this democratic climate, in this city nestled in the most magnificent harbor in the world, the conference was held.

The Opera House in San Francisco's beautiful civic center, was the scene of the plenary sessions. The setting in the Opera House was magnificent. Four ornamental pillars, gilded and festooned with olive green garlands, stood on the stage—claimed by many as symbols of the "Four Freedoms." Set between these pillars were fifty flag poles, with the flags of the participating nations arranged in alphabetical order. It was an impressive sight. Over three thousand serious minded men and women, delegates, official consultants, experts, observers—just plain folk—assembled "to create the structure, provide the machinery which will make future peace not only possible—but certain." It was a colorful, international, interracial assembly.

Among the nations in prominent roles were the original Big Three—the United States, Russia and Great Britain—increased to five with China and France. Present also were the "middle" countries such as Canada and a third significant group composing a majority of the delegations, representing countries small in size and population, but pivotal in the world drama. Conspicuously absent were the large populations of Indonesia (the 70,000,000 inhabitants of the Netherlands East Indies), the vast area of Burma, and the 200,000,000 indigenous peoples of Africa. These are the colonials whose future status is vitally tied up with that of all racial minorities the world over.

The delegates came from fifty nations, and attracted endless attention. All races of mankind except the American Indian were represented. Anglo-Saxon whites, Orientals, swarthy men from the Near East, dark-skinned South Americans and Negroes from Ethiopia and Liberia—all mingled together. For once in a lifetime, such superficial things as robes, beards, turbans and the color of the skin had no bearing on one's status. There were many dramatic moments when these delegates gave testimony in formal and informal speech to the cause of world peace.

There were many interesting personalities at the conference, who had no official status, but who made a definite contribution. Such a person was Madame Vijaya Lakshmi Pandit, sister of Jawaharlal Nehru, the Indian leader and co-laborer with Gandhi. She held numerous press conferences and informal gatherings in her living quarters and gave vivid testimony of the millions of distressed peoples of India who long for independence.

The work of the Consultants and associate consultants' groups of which I was privileged to be a part, was an important and significant part of the conference. Representatives of 42 national organizations of labor, industrial, agricultural, educational, church and other responsible bodies made up this group. The personnel was an interesting cross-section of American life, each equally important because of his influence as a molder of public opinion. The consultants and associate consultants held regularly scheduled meetings with delegates and technical experts on pivotal questions. Our job was to advise through discussion with and later in recommendations to the American delegation, ideas and principles of the Charter. It was here that Dr. W. E. B. DuBois and I as associate Consultants and Walter White, Consultant, representing the National Association for the Advancement of Colored People, played a distinctive role as members of the greatest racial minority in America. It was here that I never failed to voice the hopes and aspirations of the Negro people. I interviewed and conferred with many important persons, delegates, experts, and consultants, winning them to sympathy and support for a liberal position with regard to the abolition of colonialism, the international bill of rights, and the inclusion of an adequate educational and cultural program into the Charter of the United Nations.

May I here and now give expression to my deep appreciation of the statesmanlike leadership which the American delegation, through the chairman, Former Secretary of State Edward R. Stettinius, and its other four members, gave to the Conference. Likewise, I would voice appreciation for the liberal recognition given by the State Department to the part which organizations play in crystallizing public opinion on international affairs, as evidenced by the interest and importance given to the entire groups of consultants and their [opinions]. It marked a new day in international diplomacy.

It was heartening to me to see the Negro manifest so much interest in the San Francisco Conference. There were assembled at the opening of the Conference, representatives from almost every national Negro organization, [including] church, fraternal, [and] political [ones]. They were there as observers with no official connection but making a plea for the masses of Negroes who could not speak for themselves. There was a conspicuous getting together at the Conference by the darker races that was interesting and stimulating. Thank God, the Negro is not asleep—he is doing some serious thinking as was evidenced in San Francisco. He had an unprecedented opportunity in this World Conference to lift his vision to encompass a world view of the problems of peace. This was not only a challenge to the Negro to broaden his vision but to establish on a firmer basis his own fight for a better status in America and the world.

Not all that many of us hoped for was accomplished at San Francisco, but no one can deny that the Conference was certainly a definite start in the right direction. It is up to us here and now to put our best efforts into this framework of world peace. The preamble to the Charter sets forth the democratic aims of the United Nations and is the soul of the document. I hope sincerely that every one of you here as well as every man, woman and child will read the Charter. It is an historic document, written in five languages, setting forth with direct and firm speech, the fervent hopes and aspirations of the two billions of peoples of the world. I quote a few phrases from the preamble:

> We the people of the United Nations . . . determined to save succeeding generations from the scourge of war, which twice in our lifetime has brought untold sorrow to mankind . . . reaffirm our faith in the fundamental human rights of men and women of nations large and small. . . .
> promote social progress and better standards of life, and larger freedom, and for these ends. . . .
> to practice tolerance and live together in peace with one another as good neighbors. . . .
> For these reasons do hereby establish an international organization. . . .

To put life and meaning into these words, this is the job for all of us today. As you read the Charter, you will find that the gateway to future peace has been clearly opened in the inclusion of the program for the world in the Economic and Security Council. For we all know how JOBS, FOOD, SHELTER, CLOTHING, HEALTH and HAPPINESS of all the millions of common peoples are tied up with the economic and social structure of the world. The provision for the inclusion of a broad educational and cultural program in the Charter is another progressive forward step in this world document. One half of the world knows so little about the other half of the world. We all need to know one another so much better than we do. For it is only through knowing people better, that we come to understand them; and understanding, we come to appreciate the qualities they possess—and finally we come to realize that fundamentally the human spirit is the same the world over.

The conference is a great challenge to America. She must do a great deal of house cleaning in her treatment of minority groups here at home, and especially her treatment of the Negro, if she can ever hope to hold her rightful place among the leadership of the Nations of the world. She must set to work seriously to build a bridge to span the chasms of misunderstanding— the tensions of racial inequalities and the devastating currents of economic differentials that lurk in the hearts of so many Brown American citizens. AMERICA MUST SET HER HOUSE IN ORDER BY MAINTAINING CONSISTENTLY, HERE AND NOW, A FIRM PROGRAM OF ACTION WHICH WILL BE TO GIVE THE NEGRO HIS FULL RIGHTS AND PROTECTION, FULL SECURITY AND THE PURSUIT OF HAPPINESS that he so richly deserves at the hands of the country he has so loyally supported in every hour of need. Let us hope that we have learned sufficiently well by hard experience that we live in an interdependent world.

Those of us who attended the Conference in San Francisco were impressed more than ever by the increasing emphasis upon the importance of unity of action in the solution of the problems of our people, our nation and our "ONE WORLD."

The masses of the peoples of the world are demanding a major role in the shaping of the new civilization which began to dawn in San Francisco. The world tomorrow must be a "people's world"—if our civilization is to survive. The hardships and losses of this war have developed a passion for freedom in the hearts of men and women the world over. Thirteen millions of Negroes here in America and their counterparts elsewhere in the world are dreaming, suffering, struggling, fighting, dying for freedom, justice, liberty, security and peace. It is my fervent hope, it is my earnest prayer, that America will not fail in her role as a major world power to give now, in this new day of world brotherhood, equal economic, social, political, freedom to all her citizens regardless of race, color or religion. For only then shall we have real peace, permanent peace here in America, and a claim to the righteousness that exalteth a Nation.

June 1945. Mary McLeod Bethune Papers, Mary McLeod Bethune Foundation, Bethune-Cookman College, Daytona Beach, Fla.

At the Second National Conference on the Problems of the Negro and Negro Youth, Bethune is flanked by National Youth Administration director Aubrey Williams and First Lady Eleanor Roosevelt. *Schomburg Center for Research in Black Culture, January 12, 1939.*

Bethune joins the New Negro Alliance's long-standing picket line around a Washington, D.C., drug store chain. With her is Mrs. Hastie, mother of Judge William Hastie, dean of Howard University Law School. *Spingarn Research Center, August 1939.*

Bethune watches a game of Chinese checkers at the USO Club for black soldiers at the Phillis Wheatley Young Women's Christian Association in Washington, D.C. She is surrounded by several of the junior hostesses to whom she had just awarded certificates for completing their USO training.   *Library of Congress, July 1943.*

Bethune with fellow NAACP consultants Dr. W. E. B. Du Bois (*left*) and executive secretary Walter White. They were part of the advisory team to the U.S. delegation at the United Nations Conference on International Organization in San Francisco. Bethune was the only African American woman attending in an official capacity. *Bethune Council House, National Park Service, 1945.*

PART VI

The Last Years

"Building a Better World" (1951–1955)

Introduction

Elaine M. Smith

O UR CHILDREN must never lose their zeal for building a better
world," a reflective Mary McLeod Bethune observed late in life.[1] While
the building process is most frequently associated with the young and the
vigorous, this woman of more than seventy years continued to constructively
reshape her world between 1950 and 1955, despite having retired from her
leadership of Bethune-Cookman College, the Negro Division of the National
Youth Administration, and the National Council of Negro Women. She used
the resources available to the masses: acquiring information, becoming
aware of trends, sharing material substance, and encouraging and praying for
others. Obviously, building a better world for her meant advancing sociological and spiritual frontiers rather than those of a technical and materialistic
nature.[2] In January 1954, for example, three of her four most vital issues were
"ending segregation and discrimination for ever," "strengthening and sustaining the United Nations," and "the spiritual undergirding of all our
efforts." Bethune's sense of world citizenship justified her first two issues:
eliminating racism was mandatory because it constituted "the first step to
world peace"; supporting the UN because it "promoted the unity essential to
peace."[3]

Bethune's world view was of long duration. In her late seventies she
declared, "All my life I have been stirred by the idea of one God creating one
world."[4] She became increasingly emphatic about this as she met people from
all over the world. Of special importance was her friendship with Madame
Vijaya Lakshmi Pandit, an Indian nationalist and world-class politician. At
the beginning of the 1950s, Pandit headed the Indian Delegation to the
United Nations. In 1953–54, she served as president of the UN General
Assembly. When she visited Bethune-Cookman College in April 1951, she
was the Indian ambassador to the United States, the first woman ambassador
to this country. Bethune affirmed from her personal dealings with Pandit and
other international residents that "the yearnings of our hearts are about the
same."[5]

During the last ten months of Bethune's life, her internationalism soared.
At a two-week World Assembly for Moral Re-Armament in Caux, Switzerland, she experienced a profound transformation, which was manifested in
the filtering of all her thoughts and actions through this philosophical
movement's four absolute principles: honesty, purity, unselfishness, and love.
While skeptics viewed MRA as an opulently financed, high-rolling move-

ment which deceived as well as enlightened, Bethune embraced it whole-heartedly. As a human relations specialist, she believed it had the potential to restructure the world by changing hearts, one at a time.[6]

Although internationalism played an important part for Bethune in "build-ing a better world," the process began at home and centered on home. She desired a better America for all, but as a woman, she worked of necessity with women's groups, black and white, to overcome gender prejudices and to contribute a female perspective to public discourse and action. She operated especially through the National Council of Negro Women, the National Association of Colored Women, and the United Beauty School Owners and Teachers Association.[7] In the 1950s, her pride and joy on the gender front was the precedent-setting Women's Leadership Conference for "Strengthening the Forces of Freedom," held April 4–6, 1952, at Bethune-Cookman Col-lege. Even before the United States Supreme Court's repudiation of racial segregation, representatives from the country's most notable black and white women's organizations and delegates from Turkey and Germany responded to the call of this African American woman to meet at a Southern black college. Both the convener and the delegates understood that "American women have a significant role to play in the unifying of world ideas and practices."[8]

While working to overcome gender limitations, Bethune also labored to surmount the pervasive effects of racism. She participated in an array of activities to promote this and other interests through Americans for Demo-cratic Action, the National Democratic Party, the National Civil Defense Advisory Council, the National Conference on Aging, and the re-election campaign of United States senator Herbert Lehman, a New York Democrat. In a more race-specific vein, she championed the United Negro College Fund, the National Association for the Advancement of Colored People, the Association for the Study of Negro Life and History, and the Southern Conference Educational Fund. She also continued to work for her beloved Bethune-Cookman College, in consultation with its third president, Dr. Richard V. Moore.

Another of Bethune's racial priorities was developing Bethune-Volusia Beach. This project was of marked significance in "separate but equal America" because African Americans had extremely limited access to either public or private beaches. Located about twenty-four miles south of Bethune-Cookman College, Bethune-Volusia Beach covered two and a half miles of sand along the Atlantic Ocean and stretched back to the nearby northern arm of the Indian River. In the 1940s, Bethune, G. D. Rogers, and some partners had purchased it for $125,000. In late 1952, Bethune and her associates opened the $100,000 two-story cinderblock Welricha Motel on the property. While welcoming all, the beach and motel were black-owned and thus a proud emblem of race entrepreneurship.[9]

Bethune's greatest contribution to a better world in the 1950s both embraced race and transcended it. She established the Mary McLeod Bethune Foundation for all races, creeds, classes, and colors. Dedicated on March 17, 1953, it was a charitable and educational corporation created to perpetuate her ideals. Bethune launched it for a variety of reasons. While some of those reasons were self-serving—establishing the foundation satisfied the need of her take-charge personality to control an institution, gratified her large ego, and provided a stimulus for her to organize her files for a contemplated autobiography—she had more idealistic intentions as well. She wanted the foundation to preserve her papers, to support Bethune-Cookman through scholarships, to foster interracial goodwill, and to inspire youth.[10] Before her death in 1955, she deeded her modest two-story white frame home, appraised at $40,000, to the foundation.

As the nature of her foundation illustrates, Bethune's better world embraced all of humanity. But given the stultifying limitations on African Americans during the first half of the twentieth century, most of her work can be described as race leadership. In "My Last Will and Testament," a literary legacy addressed specifically to African Americans, Bethune acknowledged this fact. There she identified nine maxims that had guided her long career and accounted for much of her success in the midst of American apartheid. These maxims can be categorized into three frames of reference. The first covers attributes of character central to society's spiritual ideals: namely, faith, hope, and love. The second comprises society's crucial cultural responsibilities, consisting of "a thirst for education"; "a respect for the uses of power," or collective political action to promote democracy; and "a responsibility to young people," meaning the nurture of youth. The third category incorporates principles of holistic living essential for the maturity of the black race as America's most challenged minority. These are "racial dignity," the core of which is facing whites as equals; "a desire to live harmoniously with your fellow men," that is, attempting to cultivate positive relations with whites; and "the challenge of developing confidence in one another," or supporting self-help businesses.[11] These three frames of reference—spirituality, cultural responsibilities, and holistic living—informed Bethune's endeavors in the 1950s, which then benefited from her new opportunities, more insightful knowledge, and increased flexibility.

DOCUMENTARY SOURCES

The eight documents in this part reflect the building process through the vicissitudes of life as Bethune viewed or achieved it. Because her spiritual ideals are reflected in all her documents, this sampling focuses on the two other frames of reference—"Cultural Responsibilities" and "Holistic Living"—evident in "My Last Will and Testament."[12] Of the four documents in the first section, two relate to political issues. "Statement to President Truman at the White House Conference," crafted when the United States was rapidly mobilizing in the war against Communism in South Korea, represented a black leadership consensus forged by labor leader A. Philip Randolph. Of the twelve signatories, Bethune was the only emeritus-titled person, the only woman, and one of four spokespersons. The emotionally charged "The Lesson of Tolerance," delivered in Englewood, New Jersey, during the McCarthy hysteria, was written after the city, having branded Bethune a Communist subversive, permitted her to speak at an Englewood public school because of widespread public pressure. "My Foundation" illustrates Bethune's sense of responsibility to young people. It also shows her penchant for telling an interesting story at the expense of facts. Her home never consisted of just "two little rooms"; both James Gamble and Thomas White had been dead for decades; her idea for the foundation had crystallized two years earlier, rather than one; Bethune had toured Switzerland in 1927, not "about a year ago"; and she beheld her storied rose garden in Marseilles, France, not Bern, Switzerland.[13] The last of the documents in "Cultural Responsibility," "U.S. Will Make 'the Grade' in Integrating All Its Schools," was Bethune's final newspaper column, published posthumously. It addresses education in relation to the desegregation of schools in the face of the massive and mushrooming resistance to the Supreme Court's 1954 *Brown v. Board of Education* decision.

In contrast to the cultural mandates of political participation, the nurture of youth, and the pursuit of education, the section "Holistic Living" consists of four documents involving principles that many African Americans might have been inclined to ignore, given the three hundred years of enforced subservience to whites in America. Yet Bethune was convinced that adherence to these principles was critical for the maturation of blacks as a minority. The first document, "Yes, I Went to Liberia," speaks of racial dignity, the sine qua non maxim in Bethune's "Last Will." She wrote it after the second inaugural of Liberian president William Tubman, a gala she attended as one of four official U.S. representatives. "S.O.S. Call—To the Negro Citizens of America" addresses the issue of self-help businesses. In this case, Bethune-Volusia Beach, having been given discriminatory treatment by financial institutions and the government, appeared desperate for funds to satisfy a mortgage payment. The next two documents point to African Americans' contribution to positive race relations. In "Probe of Southern Conference Educational Fund Shocks Writer," Bethune supported two white friends against unfounded charges of Communism when most white Southerners shunned them for their interracial activity, and most black leaders, fearing a Communist taint, avoided them as well.[14] In "Address to the National Council of Negro Women Brotherhood Luncheon," Bethune spoke to about eight hundred diners at Washington's Willard Hotel in what appears to be an extemporaneous, vintage-style response to the program that kicked off a year-long celebration of the NCNW's twentieth anniversary.

NOTES

1. See "My Last Will and Testament," in Part II of this volume.

2. Bethune, "Mary McLeod Bethune," *Chicago Defender*, August 12, 1950.

3. Bethune, "Most Vital Issues," typescript, January 14, 1954, BF, Reel 2. The fourth of Bethune's priorities was "scientific advance toward the elimination of physical and mental diseases."

4. Bethune, early draft of "My Last Will and Testament," BF, Reel 2.

5. Bethune, draft *Chicago Defender* column, no date, Florence Roane Papers, used by courtesy of Dr. Joseph E. Taylor.

6. The comprehensive critique of MRA is Tom Driberg, *The Mystery of Moral Re-Armament* (New York: Alfred A. Knopf, 1965); Bethune's attitude toward it is revealed, for example, in "A Letter from Switzerland," "Telefact" [newsletter of the National Council of Negro Women], July–August 1954, BF, Reel 19. For further information on Bethune and the MRA, see "Address to a World Assembly for Moral Re-Armament in Caux, Switzerland," in Part II of this volume.

7. General assessments of Bethune's retirement years are based to a large extent on her diary entries from January 1950 through May 1955. BF, Reels 5 and 6.

8. Bethune, "Significant Events of My Life since 1950," typescript for *Our World* [1955], Florence Roane Papers.

9. Elaine M. Smith, "Mary McLeod Bethune's Last Will and Testament: A Legacy for Race Vindication," *Journal of Negro History* (1996): 113–115.

10. Elaine M. Smith, "Introduction: The Mary McLeod Bethune Foundation—Origins, Vicissitudes, and Prospects," in *Guide to the Microfilm Edition, Mary McLeod Bethune Papers: The Foundation Collection, Part I* (Bethesda, Md.: University Publications of America, 1997), pp. v–xi.

11. Smith, "Bethune's Last Will and Testament." Here Bethune's nine principles are divided into three reference benchmarks, stated as ideological positions to vindicate the race. The author acknowledges Dr. V. P. Franklin and Dr. Bettye Collier-Thomas, special editors of the 80th Anniversary Issue of the *Journal of Negro History*, for the challenge to analyze Bethune's principles in a way resulting in such a categorization.

12. The multidimensional character of some documents may make their categorization seem arbitrary to some readers.

13. Built in 1914, Bethune's home at 641 Pearl Street was her private residence, although it was advertised as part of her girls' school. She initially called it the "Model Home." It was a place where students received practical training in a home. See "Mary McLeod Bethune, An Appreciation," *National Notes*, May 1923, pp. 6–7; and Sheila Y. Flemming, *The Answered Prayer to a Dream: Bethune-Cookman College, 1904–1994* (Virginia Beach: Donning Co., 1955), p. 31. Bethune's friends Gamble and White died in 1932 and 1914 respectively; Bethune first mentioned the foundation in her diary on May 6, 1952; other than in July 1927, she did not write in her diaries of a trip in Switzerland until she went in July 1954. During her European tour, June 3–July 28, 1927, Bethune recorded in one diary that on July 25, 1927, in Marseilles, France, she saw a wonderful rose garden containing every specimen of rose, including the black rose. See Bethune Papers, ARC.

14. In late March 1954, Aubrey Williams and James Dombrowski had appeared
before the United States Senate Subcommittee on Internal Security in New Orleans,
over which Senator James Eastland of Mississippi presided, in the absence of the
chair, William E. Jenner of Indiana. Ostensibly the purpose of the hearing was to
uncover a Communist conspiracy, but in reality it was designed to destroy the
pro-integration white leaders. Williams's biographer wrote that after Eastland
smeared SCEF leaders, both Williams and the organization declined. See John
Salmond, *A Southern Rebel: The Life and Times of Aubrey Willis Williams, 1890–
1965* (Chapel Hill: University of North Carolina Press, 1983), pp. 219–269.

Cultural Responsibilities

Statement to President Truman at
the White House Conference

(1951)

We are keenly aware of the increasing responsibility that rests upon the
President of the United States as a result of the perilous world situation. So,
we have not come to add to your cares, which are equally ours, but rather to
make some suggestions which we believe will contribute something worthwhile to our moral health and to our national well being. We are solidly
behind you and our government in the fight to stop the spread of communism
and to maintain and improve our democratic way of life. We support the
President of the United States in his declaring a state of national emergency
and we accept in full the point of view expressed in his state of the union
message.

Although we are not unmindful of the defects in our democracy, we
believe that the United States of America is actually and potentially the
greatest country on earth. Believing this, we want to play, in this crisis, our
full role as American citizens, unhampered and unfettered by those forces
which weaken our democracy in the eyes of the world and which all too
frequently give our enemies a justifiable reason to spread dangerous propaganda against us.

In this hour of global crisis, we should demonstrate to the world that we
are a united people and that we are not only talking democracy and fighting
for it across the earth, but that we are actually and sincerely demonstrating it
in practice here at home. We are convinced that in order to defeat communism we must be militarily strong. But we are equally convinced that
communism cannot be overcome by military might alone, however powerful
that may be—not even by the superior possession and use of atom and
hydrogen bomb; nor by the use of the bacteriological implements of war.

In addition to military power, we believe that in order to overcome communism and to make the United States an impregnable citadel of freedom and democracy, our country must stand above reproach in the treatment it accords all of its peoples.

We believe that it would increase our national unity, weaken communist propaganda, strengthen our cause among the colored peoples of Asia, Africa, the Isles of the Sea, the West Indies, the United States and freedom-loving peoples everywhere, if you, Mr. President, would exercise the powers inherent in your office to extending the domain of democracy and to make possible the fullest use of the services of the Negro citizens in this hour of national emergency.

In the light of these convictions, we, a group of representative Negro Americans, have come today to request you to do six things:

1. To use your power and influence to abolish, immediately, racial segregation in the nation's capital. Washington is the capital of the greatest democratic country in the world and yet we are incessantly embarrassed by virtue of the fact that it is the most segregated national capital on the earth.
2. To appoint qualified Negroes on the administrative and policy making level of our government. We have had consultants and advisors, but we have had hardly any Negroes in government who actually shared in making and determining policies in the various branches of the government.
3. To integrate Negroes in all new agencies that are being established and will be established as a result of this emergency. New agencies and new positions are being created all the time—Negroes are usually the forgotten people. Especially do we urge that Washington tell regional and state offices which the Federal Government has and will set up with federal money that Negroes are to be utilized and integrated on the same basis as other peoples without regard to color, race or national origin.
4. To appoint Negroes more widely in the foreign and diplomatic service of our country. The contribution of Ralph Bunche to world peace is one of the many contributions that Negroes would make if given a chance.
5. To issue an Executive Order guaranteeing the maximum use of all manpower in all production efforts irrespective of color, race or national origin in the defense emergency and provide an adequate machinery for its enforcement.
6. To abolish once and for all racial segregation of Negro soldiers in the United States Army.

We cannot make it too clear, Mr. President, that we come to you today not as Negroes defending Negroes. We come as American Citizens pleading for our country and concerned chiefly with advancing the cause of democracy and freedom in the United States and in the world. We believe, Sir, that the time is ripe for such actions as we have requested.

Respectfully submitted, we are:

. . . .

1. William Y. Bell, Bishop, Colored Methodist Episcopal Church
   North Main Street, South Boston, Virginia

2. Mary McLeod Bethune, President Emeritus, National Council of Negro Women
   1318 Vermont Avenue, N.W., Washington, D.C.

3. J. Robert Booker, President, National Negro Bar Association
   Century Building, Little Rock, Arkansas

4. Dowdal Davis, President, Negro Newspaper Publishers' Association
   Kansas City, Missouri

5. Lester Granger, Executive Secretary, National Urban League
   1133 Broadway, New York City

6. Elmer Henderson, Director, American Council on Human Rights
   1130 Sixth Street, N.W., Washington, D.C.

7. Charles S. Johnson, President, Fisk University
   Nashville, Tennessee

8. Benjamin E. Mays, President, Morehouse College
   Atlanta, Georgia

9. A. Philip Randolph, International President of the Brotherhood of Sleeping Car Porters, A.F. of L. [American Federation of Labor]
   217 West 125th Street, New York City

10. Channing H. Tobias, Director, Phelp-Stokes Foundation
    101 Park Avenue, New York City

11. Willard S. Townsend, President, United Transport Service Employees of America, CIO [Congress of Industrial Organizations]
    3452 South State Street, Chicago, Illinois

12. Walter White, Executive Secretary, National Association for the Advancement of Colored People
    20 West 40 Street, New York City

Theodore E. Brown, Secretary
To Group of Negro Leaders

February 28, 1951. Mary McLeod Bethune Papers, Mary McLeod Bethune Foundation, Bethune-Cookman College, Daytona Beach, Fla.

The Lesson of Tolerance

(1952)

My dear friends, had I not been reared in the tradition of tolerance I would not be here with you, tonight.

A year ago, I addressed the words that follow, to my readers throughout the country, and I want the citizens of Englewood, whatever their color or creed or nationality, or organizational affiliation, to listen to them, now, for they were never more true, than now. Listen!

"In spite of the evident dangers to this or any nation, from the activities of persons opposed to its basic principles, there is, to my mind, an even greater danger, from the noisome odor of suspicion that seems to attach itself to decent and forthright disagreement, even within the framework of those principles."

And continuing, "I have repeatedly expressed my deep conviction of the need for a 'Loyal opposition' in the conduct of group affairs—public or private. Some of the thoughts which I have passed on to you before, I repeat—because today's alarms and today's pressures seem to be heading us, very rapidly, into the unfruitful 'Panic' against which I cautioned at that time—*and to be building up toward a sterile conformity, in the mistaken belief that conformity constitutes loyalty—or begets it.*

"The essence of Democracy is the concept that no one group or individual is all-wise or has a monopoly of all the virtues.

"Training ourselves and our children to have both tolerance and respect for opinions diverging from our own, is one of the best possible ways to promote brotherhood—among the peoples of the world, and among our neighbors in our block! They who admit righteousness, sincerity, good intentions, understanding—*and loyalty*—in no one but themselves[, and] who can brook no opposition to their personal or group opinions, are unprepared for Democratic living.

"Tyranny of opinion must never be our goal, for it is not the goal of Democracy or of Christianity. We must learn to *differ without denouncing; to listen without distrust; to reserve judgement.* 'Judge not that ye be not judged. For with what judgement ye judge ye shall be judged. And with what measure ye mete, it shall be measured unto you again.' You know the words, my friends.

"But listening to the 'other side' is a lesson in which we need training. Too often, in crisis, we 'Panic.' We lose our sense of values—of fairness. We scoff at each other; we make sarcastic remarks and 'go righteous' as an alternative to thinking through our situations, calmly, with those who agree and those who do not agree.

"A little poise—a little tranquility of spirit—a little meditation and *matur-ing of the mind,* and we shall be able *to listen,* to learn, and *to go forward with those of other views,* of other races, and nations, and of other faiths, knowing that in every group that is worthwhile we shall find, and should encourage, a robust opposition—to whet our minds, strengthen our souls, and keep us on our toes."

Today, all of us are living in even graver days than were those when the words that I just read were written. I said then, and I say now, we need to strengthen our democratic principles—and to apply them more forthrightly and effectively. *For this task we need the aid and loyalty of all citizens devoted to their country and the good for which it stands.*

"*We cannot instill loyalty into the hearts of men by coercion and fear. Loyalty is a child of the spirit—and not a child of fear.* No one should know better than we Americans who are also Negroes, *how sterile and stultifying are the fruits of fear,* and, conversely, how loyalty grows joyfully and brings forth solid fruit, under the warming sunshine of confidence and opportunity for full development. In the late years of a life devoted to strengthening our faith in democracy as a way of life, the sight of a generation of fearful conformists, in this, *my country,* would make me heartsick, indeed. The true practice of Brotherhood can save us from such a spectacle. Belief in and respect for others will produce, without panic, or repression, or injustice to any man, the loyalty we seek."

I had no way of knowing, when I wrote those words, how soon they might apply to *me*—to Mary McLeod Bethune! But what was evident to all who were concerned about the freedoms of our country, and who were taking time to think, calmly, was [that] the hue and cry of "subversive" hysteria was sweeping the country, twisting, rending, demolishing and engulfing every-thing in its path, like some savage tornado. Some gave it one name, and some another. I do not call names nor use cliches. Since I do not like them applied to me, I do not use them in relation to others. *I merely describe what I see.*

Fifty-two weeks a year for more than three years—for 170 weeks—without interruption, my opinions have been on record in the press. My column, published each week on the editorial page of one of our largest weeklies, has addressed itself, repeatedly, to the sickness of communism *and of totalitarianism in all its forms*—and to the need for an articulate, loyal leadership that will stand, unafraid, as I am standing here, tonight, and dispute any point of view—any action—that gives evidence of being detri-mental to the best interests of our common country, or to any part of its body politic.

In whole or in part, my story has been told in literally dozens of books and periodicals. Nothing could be more open than my thoughts on all phases of human relations. Yet the great question was raised with regard to me, as heedlessly as a smoldering match or cigarette is dropped from careless hands among the dry leaves of the woodland—starting a great conflagration whose scars may remain for generations in a wasted forest.

The world, today, is ablaze with the fires of hate and suspicion. The hands of too many men today are raised against their brothers. In these trying days the reputation of no man—no woman—is safe from suspicion and attack. The enemy has come among us! What then, my friends, must we do to be saved? We must cast out the devils of suspicion when they lay hold upon us, so that they may no longer make mockery of decent human relationships.

I wonder if people, inherently decent and honest—*people who think that they are being good citizens*—know what they are doing *to their country* when they permit themselves to take part in or be influenced, not only by outright, deliberate smears, but by such uninformed challenges of the actions and philosophy of an individual as those which were directed toward me in this City of Englewood?

I wonder if people in little cities and towns all over America realize that the enemy technique of "divide and conquer" is fast being replaced with the technique of "confuse and control?"

From time to time, in recent months, the Department of State has been issuing some most interesting pamphlets on Soviet techniques used to control East Germany. The first pamphlet of this series, called "confuse and control," State Department publication No. 4107, is well worth reading by those who cherish their freedoms, because it shows so clearly how the Soviets work to divide a house against itself; how they work to divide a nation against itself; how it teaches the peoples it would control, to kill their leaders. Freedom loving Americans should be ashamed to use these very tactics against their own fellow citizens.

We should be fully aware, by now, that what the enemies of Democracy cannot gain by a frontal attack on Democratic institutions, they will attempt to gain by the more subtle techniques of question and innuendo, directed toward responsible leadership. Once a leader is subjected to suspicion, all the thousands who look to that leadership for direction become affected. If they stand fast with the leader, they become a part of the environment of suspicion which has been created—they are marked with the same question mark. If they desert, through fear, the effect is the same. The enemy has done his work.

Let us not work for the enemy. Let us not destroy with the virus of hysteria, the work which through the years the enemy has not himself been able to destroy. Let us rather, even in these days of hysteria, strive to preserve the basic principles of freedom of speech, freedom of the press, and freedom of assembly.

Think it over, my friends, when next you ask a fellow citizen to appear before you. If it is worth your time to listen to a speaker, you have a right to know who he is and what he stands for. But for the sake of your community and your country, decide for yourselves whether you want to hear him. Do not let others decide this for you. Do not let ignorance of the facts lead you into the position of joining hands with the enemy who seeks to divide and conquer—*to confuse and control.*

I am glad that I have been able to return to Englewood and that those who were responsible for questioning my loyalty have not only learned how mistaken they were, but have publicly acknowledged it. It is always a pleasing experience to be cleared of any suspicion—no matter how baseless was the origin of the suspicion. However, I was first cleared by my own conscience. I have always been cleared by the American people who know where I have always stood and where I now stand—as one who loves her country dearly— but who likewise will not bow down before those whose actions tend to destroy the basic freedoms of our people by the process of fear and confusion.

The immortal words of our great leader Franklin D. Roosevelt are as true today as they were when he uttered them, "We have nothing to fear but fear itself."

June 16, 1952. Mary McLeod Bethune Papers, Mary McLeod Bethune Foundation, Bethune-Cookman College, Daytona Beach, Fla.

My Foundation

(1954)

I have lived in this house for forty years or more. It had two little rooms when I came, and I had a very, very small amount of furniture. I had my little son and myself, and we just grew step by step. We just built room by room, until we had set up here what we think is a very comfortable little home. Mr. James N. Gamble of Cincinnati, Ohio (Procter & Gamble—you know them I am sure) and Mr. Thomas H. White of Cleveland, Ohio (The White Sewing Machine man—I am sure you know him) are very good friends of mine. They used to come and see me at my task here, trying to build my little School and trying to have a little home in which to live; and they put much money into this house that you see to make it comfortable for me during the years. I have always felt that I would like to have a home, a lovely home, not one of these expensive homes, but a beautiful, comfortable one where people might come and might chat and exchange ideas and give out thoughts that might be helpful to others. So we grew into this home that you see.

It is strange that you came in today. You know at 12 noon today I was seventy-nine years old; I have entered now into my eightieth year. God has been so kind to me. So many friends are praying for me here and there, all over the country. As I look around this home and think of the years I have spent here, it seems very sacred to me. So about a year ago I decided I would not leave this for my children. I have a place where they can live, where they can be sheltered. I felt that this was too sacred a place.

I wanted it to act as a kind of inspiring spot for young men and young women, boys and girls, and older people, too. . . . We have gathered things from all over America; you will find things from all the world. I have solved some very good little problems here, and I have had to shed a good many tears here, too. It is marvelous how God has provided.

So a year ago we decided that when I should go away, not to come back, that we would have this house as a shrine. We would call it the Mary McLeod Bethune Foundation. . . . Do you know when I was a little girl, I walked ten miles a day—five miles each morning and five miles every evening? I lived in a little log cabin down by the branch. We didn't have glass windows; we had windows made out of boards; my father used to make them. Then I saw houses like you white people live in. You had beautiful houses, beautiful glass windows; I said, "Oh, how I wish I could live in a house with glass windows." [A]nd now you know, gentlemen, when I wake up in the morning and look around, see my glass windows, I see my Bible on my table, see the rug on my floor, my bathroom, my bath tub, I have a thanksgiving in my heart for what God has done for me.

So I want this to always be kind of a sacred place—a place to awaken people and to have them realize that there is something in the world they can do; and if they try hard enough, they will do that thing. I thought that the money that would come in from others would be used for scholarships for leaders. I think we need leaders now so much. I thought that we would hold conferences, interracial conferences with women of all classes and creeds that we might sit together, think together, and plan together how we might make a better world to live in. Then I thought that we would have a Finding Place here. [A]ll the material on my life that we could get our hands on would be placed so that those who want to write about me in the years to come could find the material here that would give them the information. I just want this to be a place for people. You know, I love people. Long, long ago, I made up my mind that nothing belonged to any particular race; I belong to the great Human Family, the family of mankind.

You know, it was about a year ago I was in Switzerland—by the way, I am leaving for Switzerland on Monday afternoon of this coming week to be the guest of the Roosevelts. People there are trying to build a better nation and bring people together. I am going as their guest and will remain there just as long as they say. When I was in Switzerland before, I went to Bern. I saw their beautiful Rose Garden; I never saw such a beautiful garden before. You know I live right here in Florida where we have all kinds of roses; then I have been to California many times. You know the types of flowers and roses we have in California. I never saw a garden so beautiful, roses of all colors. A great man, who knew just how to grow roses, did the growing or the planting of them. He would mix the soil so they would be properly fertilized; he would make the rows so the drainage would go in the right direction and he would have it so that they received the sunshine that they needed.

Roses of every color! And in the midst of the garden I saw a great big Black

Velvet Rose. I never saw a Black Velvet Rose before, and I said to myself, "Oh! This is the great interracial garden; this is the garden where we have people of all colors, all classes, all creeds. People, every single one of them, getting their full chance to become the best they can become." I realized that the Red rose did not want to be the Black rose; the Black rose did not want to be the Yellow rose. Every Rose just wanted to be itself, [to] have an opportunity to make that self the best self it's capable of becoming. . . . So I said to myself, "This shall always be before me as a great Interracial Garden where men and women of all tongues, all nations, all creeds, all classes blend together helping to send out sunshine and love and peace and brotherhood that makes a better world in which to live."

July 1954. Mary McLeod Bethune Papers, Mary McLeod Bethune Foundation, Bethune-Cookman College, Daytona Beach, Fla.

U.S. Will Make "the Grade" in Integrating All Its Schools

(1955)

Implementation of the famous decision made by the Supreme Court last May abolishing racial segregation in our public schools is soon to be ordered by the Court.

There will be those who will still wish to delay putting this tremendous decision into effect. There will be those who will continue to intimidate, who will claim it will not be good for the country, or that the Negro himself does not want it.

I wish to say that every major stride made by democracy was spoken of similarly by the doubting Thomases who contributed nothing but a retarding influence on progress.

Train That Made the Grade

It reminds me of the story of the long freight train which was approaching a very steep mountain grade when the engineer commented to the fireman that this was the heaviest load he had ever attempted to pull over this particular hill.

As the train was ascending the grade, the engine slowed more and more and the throbbing puffs from the boiler became more violent and further apart. Finally they reached the summit, then one car after the other followed over the top until the mid-point of the freight train was over the crest.

As the train began to gain momentum, finding new energy in its descent, the engine's load becoming lighter and lighter, the engineer said, "Well, we made it, but it was quite a struggle."

"Yes," replied his co-worker. "I had the brakes on all the time so we would not slide back."

Now the attitude of many people toward segregation is just like this. They have so much doubt and fear of progress [that] they are applying brakes instead of steam. But the American people will "make the grade" on this issue. And this is why:

INTEGRATION IS THE ONLY DEMOCRATIC WAY. The Supreme Court wisely saw this. The Justices knew when they rendered their decision that we stand at the crossroads in this issue.

SEPARATE BUT EQUAL THEORY

They considered the fact that the "separate but equal" theory was not real in practice: Negro schools have been separate but they have not been equal.

The Justices did not make their decision on this basis alone, however, for on this basis they could have declared educational facilities for Negroes inadequate and simply ordered better ones.

The basis on which the Court made its declaration was a great principle which is deep in the heart of democracy: SEGREGATION IS NOT DEMO-CRATIC.

When the Court said that separate schools are IN PRINCIPLE unequal, they were not speaking merely of physical facilities. They were speaking of human principles.

SPLIT PERSONALITY

Social psychologists have spoken of the "split personality of our nation." Segregation is a sort of national Schizophrenia or split personality of the mind and the soul of America.

For the good of our own souls, segregation must go—from every quarter of our national life.

In a democracy, all men have equal rights. At the least that is the theory. All citizens pay taxes, all share in the national welfare. They are subject to national conscription during war, and now, even during peace.

Neither nature nor the government makes any racial distinctions in these matters. Yet, when it comes to the privileges of citizenship in a democracy, we find all sorts of distinctions have been drawn.

NOT DEMOCRATIC

. In practicing racial discrimination we are not being democratic. And we cannot exist half-democratic. Integration of the races in public education is the only democratic way.

We live, as a nation, before the eyes of the world. America has become great as a leader among the nations of the world. Yet, those we would lead excel us in the matter of racial equalities as they practice them in their countries.

All enlightened Christian people who have a sense of human values, who believe in world brotherhood and who have heard the conscience of America speak through the Supreme Court will work with zeal for the full implementation of the Court's decision.

[Column], *Chicago Defender,* June 4, 1955, p. 10.

Holistic Living

Yes, I Went to Liberia

(1952)

The New Year brought to me the fulfillment of a life-long dream—to tread the soil of Africa from which my forebears came, and to stand erect, *in Africa,* on the soil of Liberia, the only republic in that great expanse of nearly twelve million square miles.

Liberia is a staunch little toe-hold of freedom, on the lower side of the great bulge where West Africa faces Brazil across the waters of the Atlantic Ocean. The only other independent area on the Great Continent is Ethiopia, the mountain empire of Haile Selassie, which lies across the continent, five thousand miles to the east. All other political divisions of Africa, whatever their size, are under the control of one of the great powers.

The especial significance of Liberia is its origin, its friendship, and its strategic position as a self-determining nation in the midst of colonies. While a few of the Negro Americans who settled the country and later established it as a republic were free men, like the churchman, Lott Carey, many others, in spite of their talent, training and high purpose, were slaves who were granted their freedom that they might go to Africa and help to develop there a free Negro settlement. Harrison Ellis, the theologian, whose freedom and that of his family was bought by the Presbyterians to permit him to serve as a missionary in Liberia, was such a freed pioneer.

I went to Africa to attend the second inaugural of President William V. S. Tubman, as a representative of the United States Government, and as I flew across the Atlantic I was thinking of those who had crossed in the early years of the last century, under conditions so different, to live as free men and women in a land to which they were strangers in all but sentiment, and among a people to whom, for long years, they were aliens from across the seas.

I thought of the pestilence that wiped out many of the first settlers, and of the crowding in of the great powers, from the establishment of the Republic, in 1847, to our own day and generation—whittling away at her frontiers until evidence of the friendly interest of the United States checked further encroachments. It was marvelous to realize how Liberia had survived all these challenges to her existence and had reached the broad highway of real development and progress.

So what is Liberia like, today? It is a land of great contrasts—the front door a stretch of coastal plain on which one finds most of the towns, including Monrovia, the capital city, and behind that rising land leading into the interior.

On our arrival we drove, with Ambassador Dudley, from Roberts' Field, at Marshall, where we landed to the capital at Monrovia, and all along that fifty-mile route were evidences of progress.

The American Embassy, with its compound, is located on a promontory high up over the Atlantic. Great ships have always passed on that horizon, but in the eight years of President Tubman's leadership they have begun to come into the harbor of Monrovia, which is now a great port where the big ships can dock, discharge their goods, and take on the commodities which Liberia is now producing for export.

And for the information of you business girls, Monrovia is one of fewer than fifty "free ports" in the world, including New York—ports where the ships of any friendly country are free to enter and leave without being liable for port duties or inspections. Before the opening of the freeport, in 1948, the big ships had to anchor way out, and discharge their cargoes and passengers by small boats called lighters. So many ships did not stop at Monrovia. Since the opening of the freeport the big ships of many countries dock regularly at Monrovia, greatly stimulating Liberia's commerce. Watch it, girls! Over there lies opportunity!

My eyes opened wide as I entered Liberia's executive mansion, where the President met us. The home of Liberia's chief executive is impressive and dignified and provides a fitting background for the unaffected dignity which is so much a part of President Tubman. The beautiful buildings that house the Liberian Government gave me a feeling of great pride.

And what a man President Tubman is! The foreign diplomats respect him and the people love him. He is constantly thinking of his people—not just of the few thousand who populate Monrovia and the other towns along the coast, but the million unmixed Africans back in the Hinterland—the tribal people with their chiefs, their palavers, or tribal councils—all making their wants known, all counting on him to establish justice and make opportunity.

President Tubman possesses a great feeling of service and unashamed reliance and faith in God. In the midst of the inaugural ceremonies he fell upon his knees in the presence of thousands, calling on God for wisdom and guidance.

One of the experiences that I shall never forget was the reception for the native chiefs, when all of the foreign delegates to the inauguration stood with President Tubman to shake the hands of 126 tribal chieftains, clad in their gorgeous native robes. They came to renew their allegiance to the leader who had counseled with them and worked ceaselessly to advance the welfare of the back country people throughout his first administration.

Later I was privileged to visit the nearby interior to see the iron mines and rubber and banana and cocoa plantations that are bringing Liberia into an era of prosperity, after the long, lean years of struggle to maintain an independent existence.

I went into the thatched huts of native villages and into the palaver houses where justice is dispensed and the business of the tribes carried on through interpreters. I spoke and prayed with the people, and with great feeling they would reply, "Amen." Ever since my student days at Moody Bible Institute in Chicago, in the "Nineties," when I so much wanted to find happiness as a missionary to Africa, I had seen myself doing just this—counseling and praying with the native people in the far-away land of my ancestors—and here I was. It was wonderful!

Remarkable missionary work has been going on in Africa, and especially in Liberia. In the brief time that I was there I was able to visit schools and missions conducted by Baptist, Methodist, African Methodist Episcopal and Catholic churches. A much greater and more rapid expansion of this work is needed.

But the hungry cannot listen well to any teaching but that which relieves their hunger. Jesus knew this when he fed the multitude. The Liberian masses, for many reasons, are undernourished. They need meat proteins. They need the technical assistance that will teach them how to meet their needs.

Much of this information and instruction has been reaching them, now, for several years, first through the programs of the Foreign Economic Administration and now through the State Department's "Point Four" program of self-help. Outstanding in the administration of that program in Liberia is Frank E. Pinder, one of "my boys" who heads its agricultural mission there, and has been there from the beginning of the original FEA program. They call him "superman," out there, because he shows them how to do so much with so little.

A wonderful health program is being conducted by the coordinated efforts of the Liberian Government and the Firestone Plantations, Inc., which is producing vitally needed rubber on the soil of this friendly country and is encouraging native planters to do the same.

It is very interesting to see that most Liberian rubber planters were making provision or the housing and health of their workers similar to that supplied by the Firestone Company, which has constructed neat housing units on which it pays the "hut tax" required of each native, and has set up modern facilities for medical research, medical care and education. Most of the rubber workers have their own farms, back in the "bush," to which they return for planting and harvesting at the appropriate seasons.

Business men and women are finding that Liberia offers many attractive opportunities for people with imagination, who are willing to put forth the effort to get the necessary facts and make the adjustments that are a part of all pioneer effort. I found Col. John West, of Washington, over there, with a radio station, a furniture manufacturing business and other interests.

As I once heard my friend, Mrs. Pearl Buck, tell a graduating class—there are those who help to make progress and those content to just ride along after someone else has made it.

Liberian women, themselves, are making progress and making history. They are in the Liberian cabinet, where one is assistant Secretary of War, and another Under Secretary of Education. They are active in the churches and welfare. Back in the Hinterland, some of the top chiefs of the tribes are women.

I should like nothing better than to see more of our alert, stable women looking across the great Atlantic . . . to join hands with other men and women of spirit, native and American, in the advancement of our sister Republic.

Responsibility [Periodical of the National Association of Negro Business and Professional Women's Clubs], 1952, pp. 7–8. Mary McLeod Bethune Papers, Mary McLeod Bethune Foundation, Bethune-Cookman College, Daytona Beach, Fla.

S.O.S. Call—To the Negro Citizens of America

(1952)

May I make one long, strong, definite appeal to you for assistance in saving, for the possession and control of Negroes of Florida and America, the finest Atlantic Beach site on the East Coast of Florida—2 ½ miles on the great Atlantic, 2 ½ miles on the Northern arm of the Indian River. We hold, for your possession and control, this beautiful stretch of land that cannot be duplicated, but it must be made secure by your immediate help.

For 34 years we have worked and sacrificed to acquire and hold this property. Since its purchase, after years of trying to secure it, it has been burdened by a large mortgage, which we have reduced as much as possible from income accruing from property and stock sales. The mortgage on the unsold portion of the property is now $89,000. It is held by a White financier of Coral Gables, Florida. It became due on May 15, 1952 and is being sought on all sides by interested people of the other race. If the property is to be saved for Negroes of our own and future generations, we must immediately satisfy this mortgage obligation.

May I earnestly call upon you, the Negro citizens of America—individuals and groups—to invest in this project, in order that it may be held by and for Negroes? We have sent out a call to 10 outstanding Negro business men to invest $10,000 each in the project, take over the mortgage and approve further development of the project, to enhance the sales program. We are soliciting and inviting your participation, through the purchase of Capital Stock at $50 a share. We are earnestly requesting the consideration of any Negro group or groups to take over the full mortgage on this valuable property, or to invest $5,000 or $10,000 on a mortgage basis. 860 lots have been sold and there are 1600 left for sale, with a conservative sales value of $325,000.

Because of the natural recreational facilities and splendid year-round climate, Florida has become a very popular State. People are coming here in great numbers, buying every foot of land they can possibly secure. We have struggled valiantly to hold to this property, because of the difficulty that Negroes have in purchasing Beach sites. The late G. D. Rogers, Sr., of Tampa, shared with me the dream that there would be, some day, a beautiful Beach subdivision on Florida's East Coast—owned and controlled by the Negroes of America. Since the passing of Mr. Rogers, I have served as President of our Corporation, for I am the founder of Bethune Beach. A few of us have pooled our resources, at great personal sacrifice, to cut roads through much of the area, bring in electric power and build a simple bathing pavilion. One of our property owners has built a beautiful Beach home and garage apartment, another, a General Store, and a group is now building a modern Motel. The latter is one-half completed, with 14 units finished and furnished. They are in great demand by the constant stream of visitors to the Beach.

Our Corporation for handling this property is organized under the laws of the State of Florida. Prof. J. N. Crooms, veteran Educator of Sanford, Florida, is first Vice-President; Mr. George W. Engram, progressive Business man of Daytona Beach, is executive Vice-President and General Manager; Mrs. Minnie L. Rogers, wife of the late G. D. Rogers, Sr., Tampa's most outstanding Negro Business Executive, is treasurer; Mrs. Bertha L. Mitchell, with twenty-five years' experience in institutional business, is Secretary and Accountant. Our office is maintained in Daytona Beach. Our 32 stockholders and 300 property Purchasers are located all over America.

We need cooperation and reinforcement from Negroes who have faith in the working and investing strength of our own people. We want Negroes to own and control this Beach subdivision. It has national as well as State prominence. On July 4, 1952, there were between 8,000 and 10,000 people on this Beach—a glorious sight. Bethune Beach is about forty minutes' drive from Bethune-Cookman College. During the years [that] we have been struggling to hold it, we have received the finest cooperation from the White residents of this area.

May I call upon the Churches, Business and Professional men and women, groups of all types—fraternal, business, social, civic—ordinary men and women of all walks of life, to pool their strength and help make this long, strong pull to keep the property in the possession of Negroes.

I am writing this letter just after my 77th Birthday. This is my last, long, earnest call for this type of endeavor. It is not a call for charity, but for an investment that will be of benefit to our own generation and our posterity. We are trying to build a resort that may be open to all people—not a segregated resort—one that is owned and controlled by Negro people.

Will *you* answer my *Call*?

> Mary McLeod Bethune
> Founder-President
> BETHUNE-VOLUSIA BEACH, INC.

July 18, 1952. Mary McLeod Bethune Papers, Mary McLeod Bethune Foundation, Bethune-Cookman College, Daytona Beach, Fla.

Probe of Southern Conference Educational Fund Shocks Writer

(1954)

I do not recall any event that has shocked me as much in recent years as the Jenner Committee's purported investigation of the Southern Conference Educational Fund.

It seems incredible that this organization together with two such staunch humanitarians as Aubrey Williams and James A. Dombrowski should be questioned concerning their democratic ideals by a man like James Eastland.

James Eastland was elected to the United States Senate from the State of Mississippi. He belongs to that peculiar political class known as Dixiecrats.

The brand of Democracy practiced by this "class" is well-known—as a matter of fact, too well-known in this country and by friends and enemies alike throughout the world. Their brand of "democracy" is a fundamental perversion of democratic princip[le]s and Christian ethics.

It is a much more insidious enemy of real democracy than communism, because it masquerades completely under the guise of democracy. Its representatives are allowed to sit in the halls of Congress where they may function more effectively to defeat legislation designed to make democracy real and effective in this country. Its representatives perform their act of character-smear behind the all t[oo] protective cloak of "congressional immunity."

The Southern Conference Educational Fund, on the other hand, is an organization engaged in the fight to rid our democracy of discrimination and segregation. I am proud to be a Board Member of the SCEF, and I am convinced that the organization is as American as the Bill of Rights.

The membership is made up of outstanding persons of both [*sic*] races.

These people seek only to achieve the blessings of democracy for all persons, without regard to race.

In this objective they are attempting to do our country a service which is in keeping with its founding princip[le]s and upon which premise it pretends to stand before the world as a living example of the way in which free men and women should abide under a democratic form of government.

I grant that the Conference Educational Fund has been righteously bold in its efforts to achieve the ends of democracy. Perhaps some of you may remember the interracial youth conference the fund sponsored in Columbia, South Carolina, about a year ago.

This interracial youth conference was held in the home state of another member of that peculiar political spawn known as Dixiecrats. In connection with the Fund I would also recommend that those of you who are not familiar with its philosophy read at least one of its publications called "The Untouch-ables."

It brings out into the light one of the shames of the south. Such violations of human decency in the name of "democracy" should no longer dwell in the convenient darkness of perverted conscience. They should be exposed where all may see.

It is for activities such as these that a SENATOR from the State of Mississippi (of all places) called the Southern Conference Educational Fund officials "Communistic."

When I examine the record of men of the Dixiecrat ilk I become rightfully suspicious of their intent to conduct investigations into Communistic activi-ties. Communistic activities should be investigated. And such activities when discovered should be run to earth and stamped out. But the investigators MUST have clean hands—not to mention clear records.

The unperverted record will show that Aubrey Williams has clean hands, as well as a clear record of living the type of democracy for which the United States is supposed to stand.

It is time the voters of this country rid our congressional halls of men of the Eastland type. I urge everyone of my readers to contact their representatives in the Senate and make them aware of the fact that these Southern investiga-tions are a veiled attack upon the Negro communities of this country.

Further, I would urge all to write Senator Jenner directly and tell him that the SCEF's cause is the cause of all who believe in democracy.

The long suffering people of the South are too near the realization of a type of democracy of which we need no longer be ashamed—too near to be thwarted by hypocritical cries of "communism."

[Column], *Chicago Defender,* April 17, 1954, p. 11.

Address to the National Council of
Negro Women Brotherhood Luncheon
(1955)

This is a very moving moment for me. This is not the time for me to speak. This is the time for me to sit in great humility with my head bowed, my soul looking upward with a gratitude to God who has made it possible for one like me to stand before an audience like this who came to pay homage to a simple and ordinary human being who came from the depths of ignorance and poverty to a platform of service—service to mankind. It is moving; there is a spiritual undergirding I feel now that is saying to me, "Be quiet, let the tears of gratitude flow because you have been humble enough to permit a great God to take a life, reshape it and mold it and send it out to give off sunshine and love, peace, [and] brotherhood among all men regardless of their creed, their caste, their color."

I do want to thank you for all that you are contributing by your presence here and your endorsement of the efforts that we have been putting forth during all the years to let mankind nearby and to bring them closer together to rid them of hate and to fill them with love, to take away the spirit of segregation [and] discrimination and bind us together as one in a great democracy made by a great God.

I am very grateful to you, my daughters. I have been the dreamer. But, oh, how wonderfully you have interpreted my dreams. You are the interpreters and now as I stand on the sidelines, as I watch the great throng go by, I want to ask you to take the torch that was placed in our hands, possibly twenty years ago, and carry that torch higher and higher and higher until the spirit of brotherhood shall have enveloped the world, and mankind everywhere will understand the change of heart and mind, the doing away with walls, the doing away with the things that are intended to keep us apart and building more solidly the bridge that we can walk over all types of difficulties and bring into action that brotherhood, that fellowship that the world needs today.

I heard a great leader say one day [that] if he could only get the peoples of the world to realize the necessity of a change in their attitude and in their spirits, in their ideals, in their traditions and the taking on of the challenge of the great spirit of love and peace, there would be no need for war—none whatever. If we could imbibe every single one of us today that spirit of absolute purity. Oh, God, can we imbibe it? Absolute honesty? Absolute unselfishness? Absolute love? There would be no need for guns and cannons. [M]ankind living each for the other will have imbibed that spirit of humility and fair play and all the differences will fly away.

If I have any last words, my daughters, to leave with you, I want you to keep your hand in God's hand. I want you to keep your feet on the ground. I want you to see men going up and with all the power you have—help to push them up. And I want, if you should see men down, in whatever area of life it may be, I want you, my daughters, to be big enough to reach down and pull them up and give to them that something that I cannot express in words, that spiritual something that will allow them to stand and be counted among the peoples of the world that are doing something. I am very grateful to you for this tribute today.

God bless you. God inspire you. God dedicate every single one of you [to] a new today, to go out and shine! shine! so that your light may be seen in distant places and men and women everywhere will know the spirit of brotherhood, the spirit of the great Christ who gave Himself that we might have life and have it more abundantly.

February 26, 1955.Mary McLeod Bethune Papers, Mary McLeod Bethune Foundation, Bethune-Cookman College, Daytona Beach, Fla.

Bethune was the lone woman among twelve black leaders who met with President Harry Truman at the White House on February 28, 1951. *Standing, left to right:* E. Anderson, Benjamin E. Mays, Willard S. Townsend, A. Philip Randolph, Bishop William Y. Bell, Dowdal Davis, Charles S. Johnson, Channing H. Tobias (*hidden*), J. Robert Booker, and Lester Granger (*rear*). *Seated, left to right:* Mary McLeod Bethune, President Harry Truman, and Walter White. *Fred Harris, Bethune Council House, National Park Service.*

Bethune watches the third president of Bethune-Cookman College, Dr. Richard V. Moore, greet her friend Madame Vijaya Lakshmi Pandit, the Indian ambassador to the United States. As president emeritus, Bethune continued to attract outstanding personalities to the campus. *Richard V. Moore Private Collection, April 1951.*

Bethune (*at head of table*) hosts a dinner for visiting friends and dignitaries attending the Fiftieth Anniversary Celebration of Bethune-Cookman College. *From left to right:* Arrabella Dennison, Bethune's alter ego; unidentified, partially hidden person; Majorie Joyner, president of the United Beauty School Owners and Teachers Association; Dr. Ralph Bunche, United Nations Secretary and 1950 Nobel Peace Prize winner; Bethune; and renowned poet Langston Hughes. The others are unidentified. *Florida State Archives, March 17, 1954.*

Between a chain of outstretched hands, honored guests walk from the funeral of Mary McLeod Bethune to her burial site (*under white canopy, right center*) on the campus of her beloved Bethune-Cookman College on May 23, 1955.   *Dr. Marion M. Speight's scrapbook, Dr. Joseph E. Taylor's Private Collection.*

Milestones: A Selected Chronology

July 10, 1875   Born the fifteenth child of Sam and Patsy McLeod at their home on Raccoon Road near Mayesville, South Carolina.

October 1885   Began her formal education at the Trinity Presbyterian Mission School near Mayesville.

June 13, 1894   Graduated from the Normal and Scientific Course of Scotia Seminary in Concord, North Carolina.

July 1894   Enrolled in the Bible School for Home and Foreign Missions in Chicago, later named the Moody Bible Institute.

October 1896   Began teaching at Haines Normal and Industrial School in Augusta, Georgia.

May 6, 1898   Married Albertus Bethune at the parsonage of the Second Presbyterian Church in Sumter, South Carolina.[1]

February 3, 1899   Gave birth to Albertus (Albert) McLeod Bethune at home, 529 Roberts Street, in Savannah, Georgia.

October 3, 1904   Opened the Daytona Educational and Industrial Training School for Negro Girls in a rented house on Oak Street in Daytona, Florida.

September 1907   Relocated the Daytona School to a permanent campus on Second Avenue (now Dr. Mary McLeod Bethune Boulevard) in Daytona.

1912   Established the McLeod Hospital and Training School for Nurses at the Daytona School.[2]

June 21, 1917   Elected fourth president of the Florida Federation of Colored Women's Clubs at its annual meeting in Orlando.

March 7, 1918   Presided over the dedication of White Hall, a $44,000 edifice of offices, classrooms, and auditorium at the Daytona School. U.S. vice president Thomas Marshall gave the principal address.

September 25, 1921   Presided over the dedication of the Florida Federation of Colored Women's Clubs' home for delinquent girls in Ocala.

March 6, 1923   Presided over the dedication of Curtis Hall, a $62,000 dormitory at her school, then called the Daytona Normal and Industrial Institute.

April 17, 1923   Signed the contract merging the Daytona Institute with Cookman Institute in Jacksonville, Florida, through sponsorship of the Board of Education for Negroes of the Methodist Episcopal Church. Bethune-Cookman College developed from the merger.

July 27, 1923   Elected thirteenth president of the National Association of Teachers in Colored Schools at its annual meeting at Tuskegee Institute.

August 8, 1924   Elected eighth president of the National Association of Colored Women at its biennial convention in Chicago.

May 5, 1925   With Hallie Quinn Brown, former president of the National Association of Colored Women, led the protest against segregated seating at the "U.S.A. Musical Evening," sponsored by the International Council of Women at its quinquennial meeting in Washington, D.C.

June 3–July 28, 1927   Toured nine European countries: England, Scotland, France, Belgium, the Netherlands, Germany, Switzerland, Italy, and Monaco.

July 31, 1928   Presided over the dedication of the National Association of Colored Women's headquarters building at Twelfth and O Streets, Washington, D.C. Mary Church Terrell, first NACW president, gave the principal address.

November 19–22, 1930   Participated in her first White House Conference. The subject was Child Health and Protection.[3]

December 1930   Listed eighth on journalist Ida M. Tarbell's list of "Fifty Great Ones," published in the *Woman's Journal*.

December 1931   Bethune-Cookman College achieved a "B" Rating from the Southern Association of Colleges and Secondary Schools.[4]

March 10, 1935   Presided over the dedication of Science Hall and a new Faith Hall at Bethune-Cookman College. The buildings cost $88,000.

June 28, 1935   Received the annual Spingarn Award for meritorious service to the race from the National Association for the Advancement of Colored People at its annual meeting in St. Louis.

December 5, 1935   Organized the National Council of Negro Women and was elected its president in New York City.

June 24, 1936   Assumed full-time government employment in Washington, D.C., as the ranking specialist on Negro affairs in the National Youth Administration.

August 7, 1936   Convened a meeting of a few government employees in Washington, D.C., which led to the organization of the Federal Council on Negro Affairs, commonly called the Black Cabinet.

October 27, 1936   Elected president of the Association for the Study of Negro Life and History during its annual meeting at Virginia State College in Petersburg.

January 6–8, 1937   Presided over the National Conference on the Problems of the Negro and Negro Youth at the Department of Labor in Washington, D.C., sponsored by the National Youth Administration.

April 4, 1938   Presided over the National Council of Negro Women White House Conference on Governmental Cooperation in the Approach to the Problems of Negro Women and Children.

January 12–14, 1939   Presided over the second National Conference on the Problems of the Negro and Negro Youth at the Department of Labor in Washington, D.C., sponsored by the National Youth Administration.

April 26–May 10, 1939   Delegate at large to the historic conference that united the Methodist Episcopal Church, the Methodist Episcopal Church South, and the Methodist Protestant Church in Kansas City, Missouri.

February 18, 1940   Presided over the Thirty-fifth Anniversary Celebration of Bethune-Cookman College. Director of the National Youth Administration Aubrey Williams and First Lady Eleanor Roosevelt gave the principal addresses.

March 1, 1942   Presided over the dedication of the $21,500 Harrison Rhodes Memorial Library at Bethune-Cookman College.

April 20, 1942   Received the Thomas Jefferson Award for outstanding service to the South from the interracial Southern Conference for Human Welfare at its meeting in Nashville.

June 27, 1942   Assisted in the initial selection of officer candidates for the

Women's Army Auxiliary Corps through a five-day detail from the National Youth Administration to the War Department in Washington, D.C.

September 29, 1942   With singer Marian Anderson officiated at the launching in Los Angeles of the *Booker T. Washington*, the first Liberty Ship to be named for an African American.

December 15, 1942   Resigned the presidency of Bethune-Cookman College.

October 15, 1944   Presided over the dedication of the National Council of Negro Women headquarters building at 1318 Vermont Avenue NW, Washington, D.C. Publisher–social worker Agnes E. Meyer, educator Charlotte Hawkins Brown, and First Lady Eleanor Roosevelt gave addresses.

April 24, 1945   As an associate consultant to the United States delegation, began a five-week stint at the United Nations Conference on International Organization which drafted the United Nations Charter in San Francisco.

July 1, 1946   Resumed the presidency of Bethune-Cookman College for one year.

February 21, 1949   Received from Rollins College, in Winter Park, Florida, a Doctor of Humanities Degree, the first honorary degree awarded by a Southern white college to an African American.

July 12–22, 1949   Visited the Republic of Haiti as a guest of its government and received the Order of Honor and Merit, the country's highest award.

November 15–18, 1949   Lauded by President Harry Truman and other luminaries at her last National Council of Negro Women Convention as president, in Washington, D.C.

January 5–14, 1952   Attended the second inauguration of President W. V. S. Tubman in Monrovia, Liberia, as a representative of the United States government and received from the Liberian government the Order of the Star of Africa.

April 4–6, 1952   Convened a Women's Leadership Conference at Bethune-Cookman College, which brought together representatives from the country's most notable women's organizations, black and white.

April 24, 1952   Denied the right to speak from a public school platform in

Englewood, New Jersey, because some alleged her to be a communist. A storm of protest led to the rescinding of this ban.

July 4, 1952   Witnessed thousands crowd onto Bethune-Volusia Beach, an ocean resort about twenty miles south of Daytona Beach, which she and other blacks owned.

March 17, 1953   Honored during a dinner at Bethune-Cookman College at which the Mary McLeod Bethune Foundation, 631 Pearl Street, was dedicated. Former First Lady Eleanor Roosevelt gave the principal address.[5]

March 17, 1954   With Bethune-Cookman College president Richard V. Moore presiding, honored during the Fiftieth Anniversary Celebration of Bethune-Cookman College. Ralph Bunche, the 1950 Nobel Peace Prize winner and the director of the United Nations Department of Trusteeship, gave the principal address.

July 14–28, 1954   Attended the World Assembly for Moral Re-Armament in Caux, Switzerland.

May 18, 1955   Died of a heart attack at her home, the Bethune Foundation, which was then adjacent to the Bethune-Cookman College campus.

Compiled by Elaine M. Smith

NOTES

1. The first published marriage date appeared in Frank Lincoln Mather, *Who's Who of the Colored Race* (Chicago, 1915), p. 25. Later publications provide a different wedding day but all agree that the marriage occurred in May 1898. The state of South Carolina has no 1898 records of marriage certificates for Sumter County.

2. Some sources give 1911 as the year in which the hospital was established. Yet the preponderance of evidence favors 1912. See *Eleventh Annual Catalogue, Daytona Educational and Industrial School for Negro Girls and Its Extension Work, 1915–1916*, p. 12; and "A Normal School's Notable Progress," *Pittsburgh Courier*, July 26, 1912, which noted that Bethune was "spending the summer in the north where she is soliciting funds with which to erect a girls' trades building and an infirmary." Moreover, Helen W. Ludlow, "The Bethune School," *Southern Workman* 41 (March 1912): 149, failed to mention a hospital but observed that a new staffer (Portia Smiley) had come to teach handicrafts and for "the nursing of sick students."

3. Rackham Holt, in *Mary McLeod Bethune* (New York: Doubleday, 1964), pp. 186–187, wrote that President Calvin Coolidge called a Child Welfare Conference and asked Bethune to attend. Holt then related Bethune's impression of the president at the meeting. Based on this secondary source, some historians have linked Bethune to Coolidge. The economy-minded Coolidge, however, never convened a Conference on Child Welfare. According to *Time* magazine, the presidents who

convened White House Conferences on the Child were Theodore Roosevelt (1909), Woodrow Wilson (1919), and Herbert Hoover (1930); "Child Welfare," December 1, 1930, pp. 38–40.

Bethune probably met President Coolidge on May 7, 1925, when he entertained the United States contingent to the Sixth Quinquennial Convention of the International Council of Women. A photograph of conference participants on the White House lawn appeared in the National Association of Colored Women's *National Notes,* June 1925, p. 2.

4. The Southern Association of Colleges and Secondary Schools, the regional accrediting agency, did not accredit black colleges during this era because that would have implied membership in the association, an idea abhorrent to the white South. Instead, beginning in 1930, it provided a courtesy rating of black colleges to indicate quality programs. A Class "B" rating meant that an institution had failed to meet in full one or more of the association standards. Nevertheless, when stamped on a junior college, it signified that the general level of its work warranted the admission of its graduates into the junior year of any standard four-year college. A Class "A" rating meant that a black college had met the same standards as member colleges of the association. For a discussion of the rating issue see "Why a Class 'B' Negro College," *Journal of Negro Education* 2 (October 1933): 427–431.

5. A more conventional dedication of the foundation occurred on the site Sunday, May 10, 1953.

Sources

The documents presented in this volume are located in manuscript collections, specialized library holdings, books, and periodicals as indicated below.

MANUSCRIPT COLLECTIONS

Mary McLeod Bethune Papers, Amistad Research Center, Tulane University
"A Philosophy of Education for Negro Girls" [1920?]
President's Address to the Fifteenth Biennial Convention of the National Association of Colored Women, Oakland, California, August 2, 1926
"Response, Twenty-first Spingarn Medalist," June 28, 1935
"Closed Doors" [1936]
"What Are We Fighting For?" Program, Southern Conference on Human Welfare, 1942

Mary McLeod Bethune Papers, Mary McLeod Bethune Foundation, Bethune-Cookman College
"Southern Negro Women and Race Co-operation," June 30, 1921, *The Southeastern Herald,* Florida Number, February 1924, pp. 10–11
Letter to P. J. Maveety, December 15, 1926
Letter to Ada Lee, June 29, 1932
Letter to Julia West Hamilton, September 5, 1933
"The Educational Values of the College-Bred," May 29, 1934
Letter to Mrs. Ferris Meigs, May 18, 1935
Minutes of the Federal Council on Negro Affairs, August 7, 1936
Letter to Franklin D. Roosevelt, Report of the National Conference on the Problems of the Negro and Negro Youth, January 18, 1937
Opening Statement to the Second National Conference on the Problems of the Negro and Negro Youth [transcript], January 12, 1939
Memorandum to Aubrey Williams, October 17, 1939
Letter to Franklin D. Roosevelt [draft], November 27, 1939
Charles S. Johnson, Interview with Mary McLeod Bethune [1940]
"The Negro and National Defense," August 3, 1941
Statement of Conference on Negroes in National Defense, January 7, 1942
Letter to James L. Feiser, October 16, 1943
Tribute to Franklin D. Roosevelt, April 13, 1945
"San Francisco Conference" [June 1945]
Report of Hospital Tour in the East [July 1945]
Statement before the Senate Banking and Currency Committee on S. 1592, December 12, 1945
"Spiritual Autobiography" [abridged], 1946

"Americans All: Which Way America???" June 22, 1947
"'Don't Miss the Foothold!' Women and the Civil Rights Report," December 5, 1947
Statement to President Truman at the White House Conference, February 28, 1951
"Yes, I Went to Liberia," *Responsibility* [Periodical of the National Association of Negro Business and Professional Women's Clubs], 1952, pp. 7–8
"The Lesson of Tolerance," June 16, 1952
S.O.S. Call—To the Negro Citizens of America, July 18, 1952
"My Foundation" [July 1954]
Address to a World Assembly for Moral Re-Armament in Caux, Switzerland, July 27, 1954
Address to the National Council of Negro Women Brotherhood Luncheon, February 26, 1955

Mary McLeod Bethune Papers, Florida State Archives, Tallahassee, Florida
    Sixth Annual Catalogue of the Daytona Educational and Industrial Training School for Negro Girls, 1910–11 [abridged]

Bethune-Cookman College Papers, Archives Division, General Commission on Archives and History, United Methodist Church, Drew University, Madison, N.J.
    "Bethune-Cookman's Next Urgent Step," Letter to Harry Wright McPherson, November 26, 1938

Charlotte Hawkins Brown Papers, Schlesinger Library, Radcliffe College
    Letter to Charlotte Hawkins Brown, October 29, 1927

James C. Colston Papers, Bethune-Cookman College Archives
    Minutes of the Special Call Meeting of the Board of Trustees, Bethune-Cookman College [excerpt], December 15, 1942

Farm Tenancy Committee Papers, Bureau of Agriculture Economics, Record Group 83, National Archives, Washington, D.C.
    Letter to L. C. Gray, January 23, 1937

General Education Board Archives, Record Group 1.1., Rockefeller Archive Center, Sleepy Hollow, New York
    Letter to Robert Ogden, Folder 303, Box 33, September 11, 1905
    Letter to Jackson Davis, Folder 307, Box 34, November 14, 1935

Richard V. Moore Papers, Bethune-Cookman College Archives
    National Youth Administration Regional Conference on the College Work Program for Negroes [excerpts], September 6, 1940

National Association of Colored Women's Clubs Papers, Bethune File, Headquarters of the NACWC, Washington, D.C.
    "Help Establish the Home for Delinquent Girls," September 13, 1921
    Letter to Mrs. [F. J.] Payne and [Carrie E.] Jackson, March 27, 1923

National Council of Negro Women Papers, Mary McLeod Bethune Council House National Historic Site, National Park Service (formerly Bethune Museum-Archives), Washington, D.C.
> Minutes of the Organizational Meeting of the National Council of Negro Women, December 5, 1935
> Memorandum to Mrs. Harold V. Milligan, President of the National Council of Women [1946]
> "Stepping Aside . . . at Seventy-four," *Women United,* October 1949, pp. 14–15
> "My Last Will and Testament" [1955]

National Youth Administration Papers, Record Group 119, National Archives, Washington, D.C.
> Proceedings of the Second National Youth Administration Advisory Committee Meeting [excerpt], April 28–29, 1936, NYA Publications File
> Telephone Conversation with Robert S. Richey [transcript], September 29, 1938, Division of Negro Affairs

Neighborhood Union Collection, Division of Archives and Special Collections, Robert W. Woodruff Library, Atlanta University Center, Atlanta, Georgia
> Minutes of Joint Meeting: Woman's General Committee of the Commission on Interracial Cooperation and the Interracial Committee of the Southeastern Federation of Colored Women's Clubs [abridged], October 29–31, 1922

Eleanor Roosevelt Papers, Franklin D. Roosevelt Library, Hyde Park, New York
> Letter to Eleanor Roosevelt, File 70, August 1, 1940
> Letter to Eleanor Roosevelt, File 100, April 22, 1941
> Letter to Eleanor Roosevelt, File 100, July 10, 1941

Franklin D. Roosevelt Papers, Franklin D. Roosevelt Library, Hyde Park, New York
> Letter to Franklin D. Roosevelt, File 100, November 28, 1941

Julius Rosenwald Papers, Department of Special Collections, The Joseph Regenstein Library, University of Chicago
> Letter to Julius Rosenwald, December 1, 1915

Mary Church Terrell Papers, Library of Congress
> Letter to Mrs. Booker T. Washington, March 20, 1923

Booker T. Washington Papers, Library of Congress
> Letter to Booker T. Washington, November 3, 1902

Specialized Institutional Holdings

Atlanta University Center, Division of Archives and Special Collections, Mary McLeod Bethune Vertical File
> Letter to Secretary of War Henry Stimson, in "Mrs. Bethune Protests to Secretary Stimson," *Atlanta Daily World,* October 19, 1941

Florida A & M University Archives
   "A Common Cause," *Florida State Teachers' Association Bulletin,* March 31–
      April 2, 1932, pp. 3–4

Hampton University Special Collections, Peabody Newspaper Clippings Collection
   Letter to the *New York Times,* "To Help Negro Girls," April 18, 1920, in "Negro
      Schools"

P. K. Yonge Library of Florida History, University of Florida
   Twenty-fifth Annual Report of the President, 1929, published as an issue of *The
      Advocate* [periodical of Bethune-Cookman College] 25, no. 9
   "A Tribute to My Friend and Co-Worker, Frances Reynolds Keyser," *The
      Advocate* 28 (September 1932): 3–4

Tuskegee University Special Collections and Archives
   Letter to the Florida Federation of Colored Women's Clubs, *Palatka Advocate,*
      September 15, 1917, in "Women's Work," Tuskegee Institute Newspaper
      Clippings File
   Letter to the National Board of the Young Women's Christian Association,
      "National Conference Called by 'Y' Board," *New York Age,* December 18,
      1920, in "Women's Work," Tuskegee Institute Newspaper Clippings File
   President's Annual Address to the National Association of Teachers in Colored
      Schools [abridged], *The Bulletin* [Periodical of the National Association of
      Teachers in Colored Schools], 1924
   "President's Monthly Message: Good Will and Investigation Tour Abroad dur-
      ing the Summer of 1927," *National Notes* [Periodical of the National Associa-
      tion of Colored Women], January 1927, p. 3

BOOKS

Logan, Rayford, ed. *What the Negro Wants.* Chapel Hill: University of North
   Carolina Press, 1944.
   "Certain Inalienable Rights," pp. 248–258

*Year Book and Directory of the National Council of Women of the United States,
   Inc.,* New York, 1928.
   "National Association of Colored Women," pp. 146–148

PERIODICALS

Daytona Morning Journal
   Letter to the Editor, "City Officials Visit the Training School: Daytona Educa-
      tional and Industrial Training School Honored with a Visit from Mayor Titus
      and the City Council," November 13, 1915, p. 1

Birmingham Reporter [Alabama]
   "Mrs. Bethune Tells of Effect of Intense Hurricane Storm on Florida's Negro
      People," September 29, 1928, p. 1

Journal of Negro History
   "Clarifying Our Vision with the Facts," 23 (January 1938): 10–15

Congressional Record
   Letter to President Franklin D. Roosevelt, June 4, 1940, in "Extension of
      Remarks of Honorable Louis Ludlow of Indiana in the House of Represen-
      tatives, Saturday, June 22, 1940," 76th Congress, Third Session, Appendix,
      vol. 86, pt. 16, p. 4191

Chicago Defender
   "Probe of Southern Conference Educational Fund Shocks Writer" [Column],
      April 17, 1954, p. 11
   "U.S. Will Make 'the Grade' in Integrating All Its Schools" [Column], June 4,
      1955, p. 10

Bibliography

BOOKS

Anderson, James D. *The Education of Blacks in the South, 1860–1935.* Chapel Hill: University of North Carolina Press, 1988.

Birmingham, Stephen. *Certain People: America's Black Elite.* Boston: Little, Brown, and Co., 1977.

Bowie, Walter. *Women of Light.* New York: Harper and Row, 1963.

Brawley, James P. *Two Centuries of Methodist Concerns: Bondage, Freedom and the Education of Black People.* New York: Vantage Press, 1974.

Brownmiller, Susan. *Shirley Chisholm.* Garden City, N.Y.: Doubleday, 1970.

Collier-Thomas, Bettye. *The National Council of Negro Women, 1935–1980.* Washington, D.C.: *National Council of Negro Women,* 1981.

Curruth, Ella Kaiser. *She Wanted to Read: The Story of Mary McLeod Bethune.* Washington, D.C., Associated Publishers, 1931. Rpt. New York: Abingdon Press, 1966.

Daniel, Sadie. *Women Builders.* Revised by C. H. Wesley and T. Perry. Washington, D.C., 1970.

Davis, Elizabeth. *Lifting As They Climb.* Chicago: National Association of Colored Women, 1937.

Daytona Educational and Industrial Training School for Negro Girls and Its Extension Work: Eleventh Annual Catalogue, 1915–1916.

Deutrich, Mabel, and Virginia Purdy, eds. *Clio Was a Woman.* Washington, D.C.: Howard University Press, 1980.

Driberg, Tom. *The Mystery of Moral Re-Armament.* New York: Alfred A. Knopf, 1965.

Dunn, Marvin. *Black Miami in the Twentieth Century.* Gainesville: University Press of Florida, 1997.

Durr, Virginia. *Outside the Magic Circle.* New York: Simon and Schuster, 1985.

Dykeman, Wilma, and James Stokely. *Seeds of Southern Change: The Life of Will Alexander.* New York: W. W. Norton, 1962.

Egerton, John. *Speak Now against the Day: The Generation before the Civil Rights Movement in the South.* New York: Knopf, 1994.

Embree, Edwin. *Thirteen against the Odds.* Viking Press, 1944. Reprint, Port Washington, N.Y.: Kennikat Press, 1968.

Evans, Sara. *Born for Liberty: A History of Women in America.* New York: The Free Press, 1989.

Farnham, Christie, ed. *Women of the American South: A Multicultural Reader.* New York: New York University Press, 1997.

Fields, Mamie Garvin, with Karen Fields. *Lemon Swamp and Other Places: A Carolina Memoir.* New York: Free Press, 1983.

Fitzgerald, T. E. *Volusia County: Past and Present.* Daytona Beach, Fla., 1937.

Flemming, Sheila. *The Answered Prayer to a Dream: Bethune-Cookman College, 1904–1994.* Daytona Beach: Donning Publishers, 1995.

Giddings, Paula. *When and Where I Enter: The Impact of Black Women on Race and Sex in America.* New York: William Morrow, 1984.

Green, Carol. *Mary McLeod Bethune: Champion of Education.* Chicago: Children's Press, 1993.

Greenfield, Eloise. *Mary McLeod Bethune.* New York: Cromwell, 1977.

Halasa, Malu. *Mary McLeod Bethune: Educator.* New York: Chelsea House, 1989.

Hall, Jacquelyn Dowd. *Revolt against Chivalry: Jessie Daniel Ames and the Women's Campaign against Lynching.* New York: Columbia University Press, 1979.

Harlan, Louis R., and Raymond W. Smock, eds. *The Booker T. Washington Papers.* Vol. 6: *1914–15.* Urbana: University of Illinois Press, 1977.

Harley, Sharon, and Rosalyn Terborg-Penn, eds. *The Afro-American Woman: Struggles and Images.* Port Washington, N.Y.: Kennikat Press, 1978.

Harlow, Leroy F. *Without Fear or Favor: Odyssey of a City Manager.* Salt Lake City: Brigham Young University Press, 1977.

Hicks, Florence Johnson, ed. *Mary McLeod Bethune: Her Own Words of Inspiration.* Washington, D.C.: NU Classics and Science Publishing Co., 1975.

Higginbotham, Elizabeth Brooks. *Righteous Discontent: The Black Women's Movement in the Baptist Church.* Cambridge, Mass.: Harvard University Press, 1993.

Hine, Darlene Clark, ed. *The State of Afro-American History: Past, Present, and Future.* Baton Rouge: Louisiana State University Press, 1986.

Hine, Darlene Clark, and Kathleen Thompson. *A Shining Thread of Hope: The History of Black Women in America.* New York: Broadway Books, 1998.

Hine, Darlene Clark, et al., eds. *Black Women in America: An Historical Encyclopedia.* New York: Carlson, 1993.

Holt, Rackham. *Mary McLeod Bethune: A Biography.* New York: Doubleday, 1964.

hooks, bell. *Ain't I a Woman: Black Women and Feminism.* Boston: South End, 1981.

Hughes, Langston. *I Wonder As I Wander.* New York: Hill and Wang, 1956.

Hunter, Tera W. *To 'Joy My Freedom: Southern Black Women's Lives and Labors after the Civil War.* Cambridge, Mass.: Harvard University Press, 1997.

Johnson, Jessie J., ed. *Black Women in the Armed Forces, 1942–1974.* Hampton, Va.: By the author, 1977.

Kelso, Richard. *Building a Dream: Mary McLeod Bethune's School.* Austin, Tex.: Raintree-Vaughan, 1993.

Kirby, Jack B. *Black Americans in the Roosevelt Administration: Liberalism and Race.* Knoxville: University of Tennessee Press, 1980.

Klibaner, Irwin. *Conscience of a Troubled South: The Southern Conference Educational Fund, 1946–1966.* Brooklyn, N.Y.: Carlson, 1989.

Lerner, Gerda. *Black Women in White America: A Documentary History.* New York: Pantheon, 1972.

Logan, Rayford. *What the Negro Wants.* Chapel Hill: University of North Carolina Press, 1944.

Malson, Micheline, et al., eds. *Black Women in America: Social Science Perspectives.* Chicago: University of Chicago Press, 1988.

Mather, Frank Lincoln. *Who's Who of the Colored Race.* Vol. 1. Detroit: Gale Research, 1976 [1915].

McKissack, Patricia, and Fred McKissack. *Mary McLeod Bethune: A Great American Educator.* Chicago: Children's Press, 1992.

Metzer, Milton. *Mary McLeod Bethune: Voice of Black Hope.* New York: Alfred Knopf, 1979.

Morton, Patricia. *Disfigured Images: The Historical Assault on Afro-American Women.* New York: Praeger, 1991.

Mueller, Ruth, ed. *Women United: Souvenir Year Book.* Washington, D.C.: National Council of Negro Women, 1951.

Myrdal, Gunnar. *An American Dilemma: The Negro Problem and Modern Democracy.* New York: Harper, 1944.

Neverdon-Morton, Cynthia. *Afro-American Women of the South and the Advancement of the Race.* Knoxville: University of Tennessee Press, 1989.

Noble, Jeanne. *Beautiful, Also Are the Souls of My Sisters: A History of Black Women in America.* Englewood Cliffs, N.J.: Prentice Hall, 1978.

Painter, Nell Irvin. *Sojourner Truth: A Life, a Symbol.* New York: Norton, 1996.

Peare, Catherine Owens. *Mary McLeod Bethune.* New York: Vanguard Press, 1951.

Perkins, Linda. *Fanny Jackson Coppin and the Institute for Colored Youth.* New York: Garland Press, 1987.

Reed, Linda. *Simple Decency and Common Sense: The Southern Conference Movement, 1938–1963.* Bloomington: Indiana University Press, 1991.

Reiman, Richard A. *The New Deal and American Youth: Ideas and Ideals in a Depression Decade.* Athens: University of Georgia Press, 1992.

Robinson, Jo Ann Gibson. *The Montgomery Bus Boycott and the Women Who Started It.* Knoxville: University of Tennessee Press, 1987.

Salem, Dorothy. *To Better Our World: Black Women in Organized Reform, 1890–1920.* Brooklyn: Carlson, 1990.

Salmond, John. *A Southern Rebel: The Life and Times of Aubrey Willis Williams, 1890–1965.* Chapel Hill: University of North Carolina Press, 1983.

Shaw, Stephanie J. *What a Woman Ought to Be and to Do: Black Professional Women Workers during the Jim Crow Era.* Chicago: University of Chicago Press, 1996.

Sicherman, Barbara, and Carol Hurd Green, eds. *Notable American Women: The Modern Period.* Canbridge, Mass.: Belknap Press of Harvard University Press, 1980.

Sitkoff, Harvard. *A New Deal for Blacks: The Emergence of Civil Rights as a National Issue.* New York: Oxford University Press, 1978.

Sklar, Katherine. *Catherine Beecher: A Study in American Domesticity.* New York: William Morrow, 1976.

Smith, Jessie Carney, ed. *Notable Black American Women,* Book 2. Detroit: Gale Research, 1996.

Smith, Jessie Carney, ed. *Notable Black American Men.* Detroit: Gale Research, 1998.

Sternsher, Bernard, ed. *The Negro in Depression and War: Prelude to Revolution, 1930–1945.* Chicago: Quadrangle Books, 1969.

Sullivan, Patricia. *Days of Hope: Race and Democracy in the New Deal Era.* Chapel Hill: University of North Carolina Press, 1996.

Thurman, Howard. *With Head and Heart: The Autobiography of Howard Thurman.* New York: Harcourt Brace Jovanovich, 1979.

Walker, Margaret. *This Is My Century: New and Collected Poems.* Athens: University of Georgia Press, 1989.

Weiss, Nancy J. *Farewell to the Party of Lincoln: Black Politics in the Age of FDR.* Princeton: Princeton University Press, 1983.

Wesley, Charles. *The History of the National Association of Colored Women's Clubs: A Legacy of Service.* Washington, D.C.: By the Association, 1984.

White, Deborah. *Arn't I A Woman? Female Slaves in the Plantation South.* New York: Norton, 1988.

Year Book and Directory of the National Council of Women of the United States, Inc. New York: By the Council, 1928.

ARTICLES

Anderson, Mary. "Negro Women on the Production Front." *Opportunity* 21 (April 1943): 37–39.

"The Battle of Washington." *Crisis,* July 1925, pp. 114–115.

"Bethune." *New Jersey Herald News,* October 14, 1939.

"Bethune Files Suit in Florida." *Pittsburgh Courier,* April 16, 1955.

"Bethune High on Pay List." *Amsterdam News,* November 2, 1938.

"Bethune Sends Protest in Florida Killing." *Washington Afro-American,* June 17, 1939.

Brown, Elsa Barkley. "Womanist Consciousness: Maggie Lena Walker and the Independent Order of Saint Luke." Reprinted in *Black Women in the United States History: The Twentieth Century,* vol. 1, ed. Darlene Clark Hine. Brooklyn: Carlson, 1990.

"Child Welfare." *Time,* December 1, 1930, pp. 38–40.

Cohen-Jones, Camille. "An Interview with President Mary McLeod Bethune." *California Eagle* [Los Angeles], August 6, 1926, p. 1.

Collier-Thomas, Bettye. "Mary McLeod Bethune and the Black History Movement, 1920–1955." *Journal of African-American Speeches* 3, no. 1 and 2 (1993): 8–11.

"Delegates Deplore Segregation 'Bolt' at Women's Meeting." *Pittsburgh Courier,* May 16, 1925, p. 3.

"Des Moines Scene Unparalleled in History." *Pittsburgh Courier,* August 1, 1942, p. 10.

"Education." *The Brown American,* October 1939, p. 8.

"Education and Training." *Monthly Labor Review* 57 (November 1943): 951–953.

"The 50 Most Important Figures in U.S. Black History." *Ebony,* February 1989.

"Her 'Boys' Remember." *Time* (special publication of the National Council of Negro Women), July 10, 1974.

"Honoring Mary McLeod Bethune: A Proud and Principled Woman." *Washington Post,* July 8, 1974, pp. B1, B7.

Knapp, Elizabeth. "Volusia County Recalls: The Day WACS Arrived." *Pelican,* May 16, 1982.

Lawson, Edward. "Straight from the Capital" [Column]. *The Charleston Messenger,* January 23, 1937.

Leffall, Delores C., and Janet L. Sims. "Mary McLeod Bethune—The Educator." *Journal of Negro Education,* Summer 1976, pp. 342–359.

Linsin, Christopher E. "Something More Than a Creed: Mary McLeod Bethune's Aim of Integrated Autonomy as Director of Negro Affairs." *Florida Historical Quarterly* 76 (Summer 1997): 20–41.

Ludlow, Helen. "The Bethune School." *Southern Workman* 41 (March 1912): 144–154.

Martin, Louis, E. "Dope 'n' Data." *Memphis Tri-State Defender,* June 4, 1955.

"Mary McLeod Bethune: An Appreciation." *National Notes,* May 1923, pp. 6–7.

McCluskey, Audrey Thomas. "Mary McLeod Bethune and the Education of Black Girls." *Sex Roles: A Journal of Research* 21, no. 1/2 (1989): 113–125.

———. "Multiple Consciousness in the Leadership of Mary McLeod Bethune." *NWSA Journal* 6, no. 1 (Spring 1994): 69–81.

———."Ringing Up a School: Mary McLeod Bethune's Impact On Daytona." *Florida Historical Quarterly* 73, no. 3 (October 1994): 200–218.

———. "Self-Sacrificing Service: The Educational Leadership of Lucy Craft Laney and Mary McLeod Bethune." In *Women of the American South: A Multicultural Reader,* ed. Christie Farnham, pp. 189–203. New York: New York University Press, 1997.

———. "We Specialize in the Wholly Impossible: Black Women School Founders and Their Mission." *Signs* 22, no. 2 (1997): 403–426.

"National Council of Negro Women Outlines Aims." *Pittsburgh Courier,* November 10, 1945, p. 8.

"Negro Angel: Mary McLeod Bethune, College Founder Sees Bright Future for Her Race." *The Literary Digest,* March 1938, p. 39.

Newsome, Clarence G. "Mary McLeod Bethune and the Methodist Episcopal Church North: In but Out." *Journal of Religious Thought* 49, no. 1 (1992): 7–20.

"A Normal School's Notable Progress." *Pittsburgh Courier,* July 26, 1912.

"Notables and Workman Participate in Impressive Ceremonies at *Booker T. Washington* Launching." *Pittsburgh Courier,* October 25, 1942, pp. 2–3.

"Outstanding Women to Visit Army, Navy and Make Complaints." *Pittsburgh Courier,* October 25, 1941, p. 9.

Perkins, Carol O. "The Pragmatic Idealism of Mary McLeod Bethune." *Sage* 1, no. 1 (1988): 30–36.

Perkins, Linda. "The Impact of the 'Cult of True Womanhood' on the Education of Black Women." *Journal of Social Sciences* 39, no. 3 (1983): 17–28.

Roosevelt, Eleanor. "My Day." New York *World Telegraph,* August 9, 1940.

Ross, B. Joyce. "Mary McLeod Bethune and the Administration of the National Youth Administration." *Journal of Negro History* 40, no 1 (January 1975): 1–28.

Schmich, Mary T. "They Had a Dream: Bethune Beach." *Florida* (magazine), *Orlando Sentinel,* March 31, 1985.

"School That Began with $1.50." *New York Evening Post,* May 22, 1912.

Scott, Anne Firor. "Most Invisible of All: Black Women's Voluntary Associations. *Journal of Southern History* 56 (February 1990): 3–22.

Smith, Elaine M. "Federal Archives as a Source for Determining the Role of Mary McLeod Bethune in the National Youth Administration." In *Afro-American History: Sources for Research,* ed. Robert L. Clarke, pp. 47–52. Washington, D.C.: Howard University Press, 1981.

———. "Introduction." In *Guide to the Mary McLeod Bethune Papers: Bethune-Cookman College Collection,* pp. v–xvii. Bethesda, Md.: University Publications of America, 1995.

———. "Introduction—The Mary McLeod Bethune Foundation: Origins, Vicissitudes, and Prospects." In *Guide to the Mary McLeod Bethune Papers: Mary*

McLeod Bethune Foundation, pt. 1, pp. v–xi. Bethesda, Md.: University Publications of America, 1997.

———. "Mary McLeod Bethune." In *Black Women in America: An Historical Encyclopedia,* ed. Darlene Clark Hine et al., pp. 113–127. Brooklyn: Carlson, 1993.

———. "Mary McLeod Bethune." In *Encyclopedia of African-American Education,* ed. Faustine C. Jones-Wilson et al., pp. 50–52. Westport, Conn.: Greenwood Press, 1996.

———. "Mary McLeod Bethune." In *Notable American Women: The Modern Period,* ed. Barbara Sicherman and Carol Hurd Green, pp. 76–80. Cambridge, Mass.: Belknap Press of Harvard University Press, 1980.

———. "Mary McLeod Bethune." In *Notable Black American Women,* ed. Jessie Carney Smith, pp. 86–92. Detroit: Gale Research, 1991.

"Mary McLeod Bethune and the National Youth Administration." In *Clio Was a Woman: Studies in the History of American Women,* ed. Mabel E. Deutrich and Virginia C. Purdy, pp. 149–177. Washington, D.C.: Howard University Press, 1980.

———. "Mary McLeod Bethune's 'Last Will and Testament': A Legacy for Race Vindication." *Journal of Negro History* 81 (1996): 105–122.

———. "Scotia Seminary." In *Black Women in America: An Historical Encyclopedia,* ed. Darlene Clark Hine et al., pp. 1016–1018. Brooklyn: Carlson, 1993.

"Southeastern Federation of Negro Women's Clubs Meets." *New York Age,* July 23, 1921.

"Suit Actions to War Needs." *Pittsburgh Courier,* May 9, 1942, p. 10.

Talbert, Mary B. "The Organized Colored Women of America Are Being Heard!" *The Competitor* 2 (December 1920): 276–281.

"That Sweetheart Again." *Amsterdam News,* January 15, 1938.

"200 Negro Singers Refuse to Appear at Music Festival." *Washington Post,* May 6, 1925, p. 1.

Washington, Margaret M. "Club Work among Negro Women." In *Progress of a Race,* ed. J. L. Nicholas. Naperville, Ill.: J. L. Nicholas and Co., 1929.

"Why a Class 'B' Negro College." *Journal of Negro Education* 2 (October 1933): 427–431.

"Women Leaders." *Ebony,* July 1949, pp. 19–23.

SELECTED PUBLISHED ARTICLES AND LETTERS BY MARY MCLEOD BETHUNE

"The Adaptation of the History of the Negro to the Capacity of the Child." *Journal of Negro History* 24 (January 1939): 9–13.

Address to the National Council of Negro Women Brotherhood Luncheon. February 26, 1955. In *Mary McLeod Bethune: Her Own Words of Inspiration,* ed. Florence Johnson Hicks, pp. 46–47. Washington, D.C.: NU Classics and Science Publishing Co., 1975.

Address to World Assembly for Moral Re-Armament in Caux, Switzerland. July 27, 1954. In *Mary McLeod Bethune: Her Own Words of Inspiration,* ed. Florence Johnson Hicks, pp. 42–44. Washington, D.C., 1975.

"The Association for the Study of Negro Life and History: Its Contribution to Our Modern Life." *Journal of Negro History* 20 (October 1935): 406–410.

"A Century of Progress of Negro Women." In *Black Women in White America: A Documentary History*, pp. 579–584. New York: Pantheon, 1972.

"Certain Unalienable Rights." In *What the Negro Wants*, ed. Rayford Logan, pp. 248–258. Chapel Hill: University of North Carolina Press, 1944.

"Clarifying Our Vision with the Facts." *Journal of Negro History* 23 (January 1938): 10–15.

"A Common Cause." *Florida State Teachers' Association Bulletin*, March 31–April 2, 1932.

"Educational Values of the College-Bred." *Southern Workman*, July 1934, pp. 200–204.

"Faith That Moved a Dump Heap." *Who, the Magazine about People*, June 1941, pp. 32–35, 54.

"God Leads the Way, Mary." *Christian Century*, July 23, 1952, pp. 851–852.

"I Work with Youth." *The Brown American*, October 11, 1939.

"I'll Never Turn Back No More." *Opportunity*, November 1938, pp. 324–326.

Letter to George R. Arthur, November 1, 1930. In *Black Women in White America: A Documentary History*, ed. Gerda Lerner. New York: Pantheon, 1972, pp. 143–146.

Letter to the Editor, "City Officials Visit the Training School: Daytona Educational and Industrial Training School Honored with a Visit from Mayor Titus and the City Council." *Daytona Morning Journal*, November 13, 1915, p.1.

Letter to the Editor, "To Help Negro Girls." *New York Times*, April 18, 1920.

Letter to the Florida Federation of Colored Women's Clubs. *Palatka Advocate*, September 15, 1917.

Letter to the National Board of the Young Women's Christian Association. "National Conference Called by 'Y' Board," *New York Age*, December 18, 1920.

Letter to Franklin D. Roosevelt, June 4, 1940. "Extension of Remarks of Honorable Louis Ludlow of Indiana, 22 June 1940." *Congressional Record*, vol. 86, pt. 16.

Letter to Secretary of War Henry Stimson. "Mrs. Bethune Protests to Secretary Stimson," *Atlanta Daily World*, October 19, 1941.

Letter to Booker T. Washington, November 3, 1902. In *The Booker T. Washington Papers*, Vol. 6, pp. 573–574.

"Mrs. Bethune Tells of Effect of Intense Hurricane Storm on Florida's Negro People." *Birmingham Reporter* [Alabama], September 29, 1928, p. 1.

"My Foundation" [July 1954]. In *Mary McLeod Bethune: Her Own Words of Inspiration*, ed. Florence Johnson Hicks, pp. 39–41. Washington, D.C., 1975.

"My Last Will and Testament." *Ebony*, August 1955, pp. 105–110.

"My Last Will and Testament." In *I Hear a Symphony: African Americans Celebrate Love*, ed. Paula L. Woods and Felix H. Liddell, pp. 304–309. New York: Anchor Books/Doubleday, 1994.

"My Secret Talks with FDR." *Ebony*, April 1949, pp. 42–51.

"National Association of Colored Women." In *Year Book and Directory of the National Council of Women of the United States, Inc.*, pp. 146–148. New York, 1928.

"The Negro in Retrospect and Prospect." *Journal of Negro History* 36 (January 1951): 9–19.

"Notes for the Address before the Women's Club." In *Black Women in White America: A Documentary History,* ed. Gerda Lerner, pp. xxxv–xxxvi. New York: Pantheon, 1972.

"Pledge of Faith." *Quarterly Review of Higher Education among Negroes* 11 (July 1943): 50–51.

President's Annual Address to the National Association of Teachers in Colored Schools. *The Bulletin* [periodical of the National Association of Teachers in Colored Schools] 4, no. 4 (1924): 13–19.

"President's Monthly Message: Good Will and Investigation Tour Abroad during the Summer of 1927." *National Notes* [periodical of the National Association of Colored Women], January 1927, p. 3.

"Probe of Southern Conference Educational Fund Shocks Writer" [Column]. *Chicago Defender,* April 17, 1954, p. 11.

"The Problems of the City Dweller." *Opportunity,* February 1925, pp. 54–55.

"Spiritual Autobiography." In *American Spiritual Autobiographies: Fifteen Self-Portraits,* ed. Louis Finkelstein, pp. 182–190. New York: Harper, 1948.

"Stepping Aside . . . at Seventy-four." *Women United* [periodical of the National Council of Negro Women], October 1949, pp. 14–15.

"The Torch Is Ours." *Journal of Negro History* 36 (January 1951): 9–11.

Tribute to Franklin D. Roosevelt. April 14, 1945. *Aframerican Woman's Journal,* June 1945, pp. 8, 23.

"A Tribute to My Friend and Co-Worker, Frances Reynolds Keyser." *The Advocate* [periodical of Bethune-Cookman College] 28 (September 1932): 3–4.

Twenty-fifth Annual Report of the President, 1929. *The Advocate* 25, no. 9.

"U.S. Will Make 'the Grade' in Integrating All Its Schools" [Column]. *Chicago Defender,* June 4, 1955, p. 10.

"We, Too, Are Americans!" *Pittsburgh Courier,* January 17, 1941, p. 8.

"Yes, I Went to Liberia." *Responsibility* [periodical of the National Association of Negro Business and Professional Women's Clubs], 1952, pp. 7–8.

The largest concentration of Mary McLeod Bethune's published writings consists of her columns in the following periodicals:

Aframerican Women's Journal (renamed *Women United*), 1940–1949.
Chicago Defender, October 16, 1948–June 4, 1955.
National Notes, 1924–1928.
Pittsburgh Courier, January 23, 1937–June 18, 1938.

UNPUBLISHED MATERIALS

Blackwell, Barbara Grant. "The Advocacies and Ideological Commitments of a Black Educator: Mary McLeod Bethune, 1875–1955." Ph.D. dissertation, University of Connecticut, 1979.

Kifer, Allen Francis. "The Negro under the New Deal, 1933–1941." Ph.D. dissertation, University of Wisconsin, 1961.

"Letter from Dora Maley." Mary McLeod Bethune vertical file, n.d., Volusia County Historical Society, Daytona Beach, Fla.

Martin, Earl Devine. "Mary McLeod Bethune: A Prototype of the Rising Consciousness of the American Negro." M.A. thesis, Northwestern University, 1956.

McCluskey, Audrey Thomas. "Mary McLeod Bethune: An Historical Assessment." Association for the Study of Afro-American Life and History, Charleston, S.C., October 5, 1996.

———."Mary McLeod Bethune and the Education of Black Girls, 1904–23." Ph.D. dissertation, Indiana University, 1991.

———. "Representing Her People: Mary McLeod Bethune and the Press." American Studies Association Annual Conference, Washington, D.C., October 31, 1997.

"Personal Remembrances of a Great Woman by One of Her Students." Bethune Foundation, n.d.

Rawick, George. "The New and Youth: The Civilian Conservation Corps, the National Youth Administration and the American Youth Congress." Ph.D. dissertation, University of Wisconsin, 1957.

Rodriguez, Edward. "Bethune-Cookman College Anniversary Address." N.d. Copy of speech given to A. T. McCluskey by author in 1990.

Smith, Elaine M. "Across and behind Racial Lines: The Southeastern Federation of Colored Women's Clubs, 1920–1925." Southern Conference on Afro-American Studies, Atlanta, Georgia, February 1993.

———. "A Chip Off Two Blocks: Mary McLeod Bethune and Mentors Emma Wilson and Lucy Laney." Association for the Study of Afro-American History, Los Angeles, 1997.

———. "A Defining Force: Mary McLeod Bethune in the National Association of Colored Women." Centennial Conference of the National Association of Colored Women's Clubs, Howard University, July 1996.

———. "Facing the Great Issues: The Florida Federation of Colored Women's Clubs during World War I and the Post War Period." Florida Women's History Symposium, Tallahassee, Florida, May 18, 1995.

———. "The Most Severe Test: Mary McLeod Bethune as College President, 1924–1936." Southern Historical Association, New Orleans, 1995.

"Step Up the Pace." Mary McLeod Bethune Papers, Bethune Foundation, Daytona Beach, Fla.

Taylor, Joseph Earl. "Two National Conferences on the Problems of the Negro and Negro Youth 1937 and 1939: A Comprehensive Program for the Full Integration into the Benefits and Responsibilities of the American Democracy." Ph.D. dissertation, Catholic University, 1985.

Thirteenth Census of the United States, 1910. Daytona, Fla., Precinct no. 8. Washington, D.C., 1910.

Index

Audrey Thomas McCluskey is Associate Professor of Afro-American Studies at Indiana University. Her publications on black women educators and activists have appeared in several journals, including *Signs, The Florida Historical Quarterly, The Western Journal of Black Studies,* and *The Black Scholar.*

Elaine M. Smith, on the history faculty at Alabama State University, is an authority on Bethune and has published articles in the *Journal of Negro History* and *Black Women in America: An Historical Encyclopedia.* She also wrote the introduction to the *Guide to the Mary McLeod Bethune Papers* for two different collections.